T0360829

Reconceptualizing Organizational Control

Organizational control addresses the fundamental yet vexing managerial problem of aligning workers' capabilities, activities, and performance with organizational goals and aspirations. In recent years, the onset of COVID-19, combined with new developments in information and communication technologies, has brought about profound changes in organizations, and even in the nature of work itself. We have seen surges in virtual and remote work, progression of alternative work arrangements (especially in the gig economy), and an increasingly widespread reliance on algorithmic monitoring and control. These changes have exacerbated the tension between the pursuit of individual and organizational interests, exposing the limits of traditional approaches to organizational control and questioning whether they still reflect contemporary organizational realities. Providing a comprehensive discussion of the multi-disciplinary approaches to organizational control, this book integrates the new and evolving trends in technology, organizations, and society into a reconceptualization of organizational control for twenty-first-century organizations.

MARKUS KREUTZER is Professor of Strategic and International Management at EBS Business School, EBS University of Business and Law, in Germany. He received his doctorate and postdoctoral lecturing qualification in strategic management from the University of St. Gallen, Switzerland. Prior to joining EBS, he worked as Assistant Professor of Strategic Management at the Institute of Management at the University of St. Gallen and as Visiting Professor at the Entrepreneurship Department at IESE Business School. His research interests, along with organizational control, include interorganizational strategy-making, strategic renewal and adaptation, and business model innovation. He has published his research in peer-reviewed journals, such as *Academy of Management Annals*, *Academy of Management Review*, *Journal of Management Studies*, *Strategic Management Journal*, and *Strategy Science*.

JORGE WALTER is Professor of Strategic Management and Public Policy at the George Washington University School of Business. He received his doctorate in strategic management from the University of St. Gallen, Switzerland, was a visiting researcher at the Wharton School at the University of Pennsylvania, and a postdoctoral researcher at the Stern School of Business at New York University. His research interests include strategy formulation and implementation processes, knowledge/technology transfer, social networks, and social capital. He has published more than twenty articles in peer-reviewed journals, such as *Academy of Management Journal*, *Journal of Management*, *Journal of Management Studies*, *Organization Science*, *Personnel Psychology*, and *Strategic Management Journal*.

Reconceptualizing Organizational Control

Managing in the Age of Hybrid Workplaces, Artificial Intelligence, and the Gig Economy

Markus Kreutzer

EBS University of Business and Law

Jorge Walter

George Washington University

CAMBRIDGE
UNIVERSITY PRESS

Shaftesbury Road, Cambridge CB2 8EA, United Kingdom

One Liberty Plaza, 20th Floor, New York, NY 10006, USA

477 Williamstown Road, Port Melbourne, VIC 3207, Australia

314–321, 3rd Floor, Plot 3, Splendor Forum, Jasola District Centre, New Delhi – 110025, India

103 Penang Road, #05–06/07, Visioncrest Commercial, Singapore 238467

Cambridge University Press is part of Cambridge University Press & Assessment, a department of the University of Cambridge.

We share the University's mission to contribute to society through the pursuit of education, learning and research at the highest international levels of excellence.

www.cambridge.org
Information on this title: www.cambridge.org/9781009282758

DOI: 10.1017/9781009282765

First published 2025

A catalogue record for this publication is available from the British Library

Library of Congress Cataloging-in-Publication Data
Names: Kreutzer, Markus, author. | Walter, Jorge, author.
Title: Reconceptualizing organizational control : managing in the age of hybrid workplaces, artificial intelligence, and the gig economy / Markus Kreutzer, EBS Business School (Germany), Jorge Walter, George Washington University, Washington DC.
Description: New York, NY : Cambridge University Press, 2025. | Includes bibliographical references and index.
Identifiers: LCCN 2024011983 | ISBN 9781009282758 (hardback) | ISBN 9781009282765 (ebook)
Subjects: LCSH: Organizational behavior – History – 21st century. | Management – History – 21st century.
Classification: LCC HD58.7 .K757 2025 | DDC 658–dc23/eng/20240524
LC record available at https://lccn.loc.gov/2024011983

ISBN 978-1-009-28275-8 Hardback

Contents

Figures

Tables

Acknowledgments

We would like to thank Valerie Appleby, our Senior Commissioning Editor at Cambridge University Press, for her enthusiasm and support for our book project, as well as Senior Editorial Assistant Carrie Parkinson for helping us get our manuscript ready for print. We also benefitted from two anonymous reviewers' feedback on our initial submission and Wilhelm Retief's skilled copy-editing.

We are grateful to our mentors, who have influenced our thinking on organizational control since our dissertation days: Christoph Lechner (University of St. Gallen), who introduced both of us to academic research and served as our formal (Markus) and informal (Jorge) dissertation advisor; Günter Müller-Stewens (University of St. Gallen), who served as a role model for both of our academic careers; Laura B. Cardinal (University of South Carolina) and C. Chet Miller (University of Houston) for their inspiration and the countless organizational control-related discussions during prior collaborations; Sim Sitkin (Duke University) for suggesting that we write an academic monograph on organizational control; and last, but not least, Steven Floyd (University of Massachusetts Amherst), who passed away during our work on this book, and whose boundless curiosity, intellect, and kindness have left a lasting influence not just on us but on scores of well-known scholars across the strategic management field.

We would also like to acknowledge the support and advice we have received from a number of colleagues – Herman Aguinis (George Washington University), Chaomei Chen (Drexel University), Stefan Haefliger (Bayes Business School), Fabrice Lumineau (University of Hong Kong), Kirsten Martin (University of Notre Dame), Jorge Rivera (George Washington University), Alexander Souza (Algomia), and Piers Steel (University of Calgary) – and we owe thanks to a number of current and former PhD students for their help with proofreading the manuscript and serving as sparring partners for bouncing around ideas – David An, Hala ElShawa, Pascal Engelmann, Pia Kerstin Neudert, Valentin Pfeffer, Maximilian Rinn, and Marius Weber. Jorge also promised to acknowledge the support he received from his son Maximilian and his daughter Sophia, who helped proofread the data coding and the results tables. All remaining errors are our own.

Markus would like to thank EBS University of Business and Law. Jorge is grateful to the George Washington School of Business, especially Dean Anuj Mehrotra, Vice Dean Jiawen Yang, and his department chair Ernie Englander, for their generous support during the writing of this book.

A project like this would not be possible without the unwavering support from our families – Karin with Moritz, Marlene, and Philipp, and Erin with Sophia and Maximilian – who provided us with support and encouragement during the almost two years of work on this manuscript. This book is dedicated to them.

Part I

(Re-)introducing Organizational Control

The fundamental problem of organization – or, more properly, the management of organizations – is the control of the labor process. (Van Maanen & Barley 1984: 290)

The new world of work is on our doorstep, and organizational studies seems woefully unprepared. Our research, historically steeped in what Barley and Kunda (2001: 82) label, 'petrified images of work' tied to jobs in hierarchical organizations, will lose its relevance unless we can better capture where and how work is done today. (Ashford et al. 2018: 24)

As our two opening quotes suggest, organizational control remains fundamental to all forms of organizing and, at the same time, a vexing challenge for both theorists and practitioners. Recent developments in organizational environments, such as advances in digital surveillance, the proliferation of remote work, the progression of alternative work arrangements, including in the gig economy, and the increasingly wide-spread reliance on algorithmic surveillance and control, have not resolved organizational control's fundamental problem: the tension between the pursuit of individual interests and organizational interests. On the contrary, many recent developments have made managing this tension even more challenging. Despite organizations having access to unprecedented amounts of information about their workers and business partners and being capable of almost limitless surveillance of their members and affiliates, organizational control in contemporary organizations is plagued by implementation challenges, unintended consequences, and worker resistance, which makes organizational control as challenging as ever. These trends and shifts in organizational environments have further exposed the limitations of our theories and managerial approaches to organizational control. As researchers interested in this phenomenon, we need to have a conversation about bridging the gap between today's organizational challenges and our theoretical understanding of organizational control. This book is intended as our contribution to the quest of reconceptualizing organizational control for the twenty-first century.

1

1 Introduction

1.1 Organizational Control as a Fundamental Organizational Challenge

The fundamental challenge of organizations is to obtain cooperation among a collection of individuals or units who have, at best, only partially overlapping objectives (Barnard 1938; Weber 1947). Left to their own devices, individuals would pursue partially congruent or incongruent goals, and their efforts would remain uncoordinated. Any pursuit of organizational objectives therefore requires finding the means to obtain cooperation among individuals with diverse interests (Ouchi 1980). The purpose of organizational control is to obtain such cooperation.

Organizational control research has historically followed one of two directions. Early organizational theorists have interpreted organizational control as the sum of interpersonal influence relations in organizations, using "to control" as a synonym for "to direct" workers' activities (e.g., Tannenbaum 1968)[1] or treating control as the equivalent to having power over workers (e.g., Etzioni 1965). This rather narrow conceptualization of control focuses exclusively on influence and authority relationships in organizations and is responsible for the negative connotation that is often associated with organizational control. It has also been the catalyst for a small but thought-provoking literature advocating a critical perspective on organizational control (e.g., Barker 1993; Delbridge 2010; Jermier 1998).

In this book, we follow a second and broader conceptualization of organizational control. This conceptualization grants workers considerably more autonomy and focuses more broadly on any "mechanisms through which an organization can be managed so that it moves towards its objectives" (Ouchi 1979: 833). These mechanisms include a close monitoring and directing of workers' activities (from Tannenbaum's viewpoint), but they also include

---

[1] Tannenbaum (1962: 239) defined organizational control as "any process in which a person or group of persons or organization of persons determines, i.e., intentionally affects, what another person or group or organization will do."

giving workers discretion over their activities and instead monitoring the outcomes of those activities and taking corrective actions if necessary (Reeves & Woodward 1970). These mechanisms could also be more subtle, such as attempts to achieve goal congruence by selectively hiring workers who already display a high commitment to organizational objectives, or by socializing workers, with the goal of instilling and maintaining a deep commitment to organizational objectives (Ouchi 1979).

1.2   Pervasiveness, Relevance, and Timeliness of Organizational Control

The classic administration theorist Henri Fayol (1949) has emphasized control as one of the primary functions of management, along with forecasting and planning, organizing, commanding, and coordinating. However, according to Fayol, control permeates every aspect of managing, as control integrates the other primary functions. Not surprisingly, both classic (e.g., Taylor 1911; Weber 1946) and modern theories of management (e.g., March & Simon 1958; Scott 1992) recognize that organization implies control. In fact, the very starting point for agency theory (e.g., Fama & Jensen 1983; Jensen & Meckling 1976) is the separation of ownership and control characterizing modern corporations (Berle & Means 1932).

The strategic management literature considers organizational control an essential part of a strategic planning exercise, with strategic control focusing "on the dual questions of whether: (1) the strategy is being implemented as planned; and (2) the results produced by the strategy are those intended" (Schendel & Hofer 1979: 18). In many organizations, there are variations of a multistep strategic planning process in which monitoring progress and maintaining momentum and motivation is the final step. Control, along with organizational culture, structure, and human resource management, is considered an essential tool for implementing intended strategies (Anthony & Govindarajan 2001).

In line with the strategic management literature, the accounting field has also highlighted organizational control as a general management function that is concerned with the achievement of overall organizational goals and objectives (Anthony 1965) and positioned control as being sandwiched between strategic planning and operational control. If strategic planning is concerned with setting long-term goals and objectives for the entire organization, and operational control is concerned with ensuring that immediate tasks are carried out, organizational control is the process that links the two (Otley et al. 1995).

Organizational control is therefore fundamental to all organizations and one of management's essential functions (Fayol 1949; Mintzberg 1989; Van Maanen & Barley 1984). At the same time, it remains a vexing challenge, as the pursuit of larger organizational goals requires individuals to subordinate, at least to some extent, their individual goals and surrender, at least partially, their autonomy to the larger collective (Barnard 1938). This inherent tension gives rise to "the age-old management dilemma: how to cause members to behave in ways compatible with organizational goals" (Kunda 1992: 11).

Moreover, modern ways of organizing and recent technological innovation have not resolved this tension between the pursuit of individual and organizational interests. On the one hand, as we will discuss in Chapter 5, new developments in information and communication technologies allow for unprecedented abilities to monitor workers' behavior and performance. Artificial intelligence (AI) and machine learning (ML) increasingly complement and expand – and can even replace – conventional forms of organizational control. In some cases, AI and ML can even remove managers – and human supervision in general – from the scene of work. On the other hand, we are also facing key organizational changes, such as the COVID-19 pandemic-related surge in remote work and the progression of alternative work arrangements, such as temporary workers, independent contractors, and freelancers. These trends indicate a rapidly changing organizational environment that may no longer exhibit key tenets of classic control theory, such as information asymmetry, stable and hierarchical employment relationships, or shared identities, loyalties, and norms among workers.

These trends are problematic as they often have complex and even contradictory implications for organizational control, posing a conundrum for both theory and practice. For instance, we have long known that traditional behavior and outcome controls do not accommodate knowledge worker tasks characterized by elusive means-ends relationships (i.e., with low behavior observability) and ambiguous outcome assessments (i.e., with low outcome measurability) (Frenkel et al. 1995; Ouchi 1979). This is a challenge that has become even more pronounced in our increasingly virtual or remote world. What is relatively new, however, is that the often proposed alternative of informal (or clan) control – which emphasizes the role of shared identities, loyalties, and norms in guiding and influencing behavior (e.g., Kirsch 1996; Ouchi 1979) – is equally problematic for the increasing numbers of remote, temporary, and gig workers in our economies. This is because these work arrangements are not conducive to the creation of strong organizational identities and norms, and workers develop little loyalty to their often multiple simultaneous "employers" (Barley et al. 2017).

A solution to this conundrum could be the enhanced electronic monitoring capabilities accessible to organizations, which could chip away at the traditional information asymmetry in favor of workers (cf., Eisenhardt 1985). However, the increased accessibility of worker surveillance data also represents increasing challenges in terms of collecting, storing, analyzing, and sharing vast troves of information. This is because the amount of information scales faster than managers' and workers' attention and processing capabilities, leading to information overload, biased decision-making, and attention distracted from the job itself (Farr et al. 2014; Van Knippenberg et al. 2015). The economist and Nobel laureate Herb Simon (1996: 144) had it right all along when he cautioned that a "design representation suitable to a world in which the scarce factor is information may be exactly the wrong one for a world in which the scarce factor is attention." The availability of enhanced forms of control, on the one hand, and the challenges associated with managing the newly obtained information due to managers' and workers' attention being limited, on the other hand, highlight the continued importance of bounded rationality as a key constraint (cf., Eisenhardt 1989a). And it remains an open question to what extent recent advances in AI and ML can help mitigate such bounded rationality constraints.

These trends and their complex and often contradictory implications cast increasing doubts on the explanatory and predictive power of classic control theory. Prior research has started to examine these trends and challenges, but research in this area consists largely of a patchwork of articles focused on one or only a few facets of this new work environment. What is lacking is a comprehensive framework addressing what implications all these changes combined have for organizational control.

In addition, with the exception of more recent research that has examined combinations of different types of controls (e.g., Cardinal et al. 2004, 2010; Kreutzer et al. 2016; Sihag & Rijsdijk 2019), the majority of correlational research has focused on a limited selection of organizational controls, has ignored interdependencies among controls, and has resulted in net-effects thinking emphasizing the isolated effects of individual controls. Classic contingency approaches, where the relationship between organizational control and its outcomes depends on a third (moderating) variable, tend to be limited to two or three variables, and therefore also fall short of matching the complexity of the phenomenon. Hence, both correlational and contingency approaches are underspecified and do not realistically display organizational controls' coexistence in actual organizations (Cardinal et al. 2017). Despite several attempts to integrate multidimensional configurations into control theory (e.g., Bedford & Malmi 2015; Cardinal et al. 2010, 2018; Gregory et al. 2013; Kreutzer & Lechner 2010; Wiener et al. 2016), this research has only presented some of the fundamental components needed for configurational theorizing about control but "not gone far enough to create a theoretical frame for understanding how the multiple elements of control manifest into coherent patterns" (Cardinal et al. 2018: 87). A comprehensive configurational approach to organizational control, while promising, is still lacking.

1.3   What to Expect *from* This Book

Our book is intended to address these challenges by reconceptualizing organizational control theory to accommodate new and evolving technological trends, organizational practices, and organizational forms. Our book offers three related contributions to our understanding of organizational control in twenty-first-century organizations. First, we report the results of comprehensive conceptual and empirical reviews of the multidisciplinary organizational control literature, including its underlying theories and assumptions. Our review culminates in an overarching organizing framework of the dimensions, functions, outcomes, and key contingencies comprising organizational control theory, thereby integrating and synthesizing diverse insights across multiple disciplines as a starting point for our reconceptualization. Our synthesis further extends recent reviews of the field (Cardinal et al. 2017; Sitkin et al. 2020), particularly since some of the developments we outline have materialized only recently and challenge the conclusions reached by prior reviews.

Second, we illustrate how recent trends in technological, demographic, sociocultural, and organizational environments expose the limitations of traditional control practices and challenge key assumptions underlying organizational control theory. This anachronism highlights the need for a critical look at the suitability of our control approaches for contemporary and emergent organizational contexts. Specifically, we incorporate three key organizational trends that capitalize on the latest technological developments and that have direct implications for organizational control: the COVID-19 pandemic-fueled surge in remote work; the progression of alternative work arrangements, such as temporary, on-call, and contract workers, independent contractors, and freelancers, as well as the larger gig economy; and the increasingly widespread reliance on algorithmic surveillance and control. By integrating these trends, we not only expand the theoretical scope of control research but also highlight the evolving nature, as well as new forms, of organizational control.

Third, extending the literature's predominant correlational and contingency approaches, we propose a configurational approach (e.g., Furnari et al. 2021; Meyer et al. 1993). We conceptualize organizational control as multidimensional constellations that explicitly incorporate the complex interdependencies between different control dimensions and that reflect the multidisciplinary nature of the phenomenon. A configurational approach enables us to consolidate past gains by synthesizing broad patterns across multiple disciplines (cf., Meyer et al. 1993). More importantly, this approach allows us to develop new theory on how multiple controls combine in complementary – and sometimes contradictory – ways to jointly affect outcomes (i.e., acknowledging conjunction between explanatory variables), often with multiple alternative paths to the same levels of outcomes (i.e., incorporating equifinality or disjunction) (cf.,

Furnari et al. 2021). These configurations are orchestrated by the technological and organizational trends outlined earlier – as well as the implications these trends have for key assumptions underlying organizational control – serving as the central themes and integrative mechanisms. The goal of our book is to start bridging the gap between today's organizational challenges and our theoretical understanding of organizational control.

1.4   What to Expect *in* This Book

In Chapter 2, we perform a systematic, cross-disciplinary review of the most influential journal articles on organizational control to synthesize our definition of organizational control. We provide a comparison of how organizational control has been conceptualized across the disciplines of accounting, information systems (IS), management, marketing, and operations management, and present a citation network that illustrates the multidisciplinary intellectual underpinnings of our control definition as well as influential articles that have shaped the field's understanding of organizational control. We conclude our conceptualization of organizational control by discussing overlap and differences with related constructs, such as power, structure, culture, and the locus of control.

In Chapter 3, we offer a brief review of the history of organizational control – from ancient bureaucracies to the behavioral theory of the firm – as well as a discussion of the theoretical foundation underlying organizational control research. We also present the results of a co-citation analysis examining 1,148 organizational control articles published between 1938 and 2022 to illuminate the field's intellectual base and emerging research fronts. Based on the uncovered intellectual structure of the organizational control field, we review its constituent theories, outline its underlying assumptions, and briefly discuss the critical perspective on organizational control.

Building on this theoretical foundation, in Chapter 4, we review the multidisciplinary organizational control literature, synthesize its key elements, and present a comprehensive theoretical framework that includes the dimensions of organizational control (i.e., target, formality, singularity, direction, and style), the control functions or mechanisms describing how the control dimensions influence outcomes (i.e., monitoring, incentives, and coordination), the control outcomes (i.e., adaptability, human relations, process, and rational goal outcomes), as well as key contingencies. We further submit our framework to an empirical test by examining the proposed relationships with a multidisciplinary meta-analysis of 293 articles, published between 1967 and 2022, that analyzed 310 independent samples, for a total sample size of 110,585. The results of this analysis provide broad support for the key tenets of organizational control theory, including antecedents and control–outcome relationships. The results also

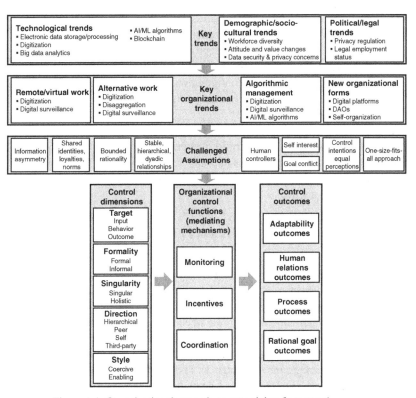

Figure 1.1 Organizational control: an organizing framework

suggest the presence of numerous context factors and contingencies, as well as significant interaction effects between controls, including both complementary and substitution effects among controls. Together, these results attest to the powerful impact, but also causal complexity, of organizational control.

Having established the theoretical and empirical foundations of organization control research, in Chapter 5, we examine key trends in the technological, demographic, sociocultural, and organizational environments that have implications for organizational control. We outline how these trends influence the future of work within and beyond organizational boundaries, challenge taken-for-granted assumptions underlying traditional control approaches, and give rise to an increasingly challenging and contested space for organizational control in contemporary organizations. Figure 1.1 provides an overview of our organizing framework.

In Chapter 6, we present our reconceptualization of organizational control. We discuss four fundamental shifts in organizations – from face-to-face work to remote work; from stable, full-time work to alternative work arrangements; from human managers to algorithmic control; and from traditional to platform-mediated gig work – and discuss the impact of these shifts on organizational control. Our reconceptualization consists of both a conceptual part, where we advance a configurational approach to model the causal complexity inherent in organizational control, and an empirical part, where we present exemplary archetypes of control configurations across a variety of twenty-first-century organizations, including trucking companies, GitLab, Amazon warehouses, Uber, and Upwork.

In Chapter 7, we conclude our reconceptualization of organizational control by discussing new forms of control, novel combinations of existing controls, new challenges to fundamental assumptions, and new forms of organizing – all of which should represent promising directions for future organizational control research and practice.

1.5   Roadmap for Researchers and Practitioners

The overall structure we just outlined provides a general roadmap for our reconceptualization of organizational control. We also recognize, however, that different audiences might benefit from following a different path through our book and may want to focus on certain chapters more than others. For our fellow researchers interested in the phenomenon, Parts I and II, Chapters 2–4, should be instructive in defining and mapping the intellectual structure of the field. In particular, the synthesis of a definition (Chapter 2), its history and theoretical background (Chapter 3), and our multidisciplinary literature review – both conceptual and (meta-)analytical (Chapters 3 and 4) – culminate in our organizing framework (Chapter 4) that we hope can provide the theoretical basis for future theory development and empirical inquiry into the phenomenon. In these first few chapters, we also provide detailed methodological descriptions of our co-citation analysis (Section 3.2) and meta-analysis (Section 4.5), to allow for future replication and extension. Chapters 5 and 6 provide insights into the changing internal and external context, including challenges to the fundamental assumptions underlying traditional organizational control research, that any future research needs to address. We also provide a detailed description of our configurational approach to reconceptualizing organizational control, including the logic behind our approach and an illustration of its application to analyzing archetypical control configurations across a range of organizations and industries (Chapter 6). Chapter 7 summarizes key theoretical implications and avenues for future research.

Managers and other practitioners, on the other hand, might be more interested in the practical implications of our reconceptualization of organizational control. For this audience, we would recommend reconciling their understanding of organizational control with our definition presented in Section 2.1, as well as familiarizing themselves with the key dimensions, mechanisms, and outcomes of organizational control in our organizing framework (the lower part of Figure 1.1 and Chapter 4). The most insightful part of our book for this audience, however, should be our discussion of the future of work inside and outside organizations, including recent technological, demographic, sociocultural, and organizational trends (Chapter 5), and their implications for organizational control (Chapter 6). Both our diverse set of case studies illustrating different archetypes of organizational control configurations (Chapter 6), as well as our discussion of new forms – and new combinations – of organizational control, new challenges to fundamental assumptions, and new forms of organizing (Chapter 7), should allow practitioners to reflect on their own organizations' control approaches. Especially the graphical representations of control configurations, and the detailed illustrations of the employed control elements and their often complex interactions, should provide a basis for such a critical reflection.

2   What Is Organizational Control?

2.1   Synthesis of a Definition

To synthesize a definition of organizational control, we reviewed the most influential (i.e., most highly cited) articles on organizational control published in top-tier journals across a variety of disciplines. To obtain these articles, we performed a key word search of article titles (TI), author keywords (AK), Keyword Plus keywords (KP), and abstracts (AB) in the *Web of Science* database[1] with Boolean combinations of relevant keywords detailed in Section 2.3. In line with prior reviews (e.g., Bergh et al. 2016), we focused on articles published in peer-reviewed journals across management, accounting, marketing, finance, operations management, ethics, and information systems (IS) that are part of the Financial Times 50 list.[2] These journals are detailed in Section 2.3 as well.

Our search on November 2, 2022, resulted in 2,118 articles published between 1938 and 2022. We sorted the resulting list of articles by discipline and by the number of citations each article has received. We then worked down the list of the most highly cited articles in each discipline, read each article's title and abstract to verify topical relevance, and then read the full text to extract the authors' definition of organizational control if available. Table 2.1 presents the definitions provided by the top-ten most-cited articles across the five disciplines of accounting, IS, management, marketing, and operations research. In addition, to represent the more recent control literature, we integrated the five most cited articles per discipline during the ten-year period from 2013 to 2022, to the extent that they provide an explicit definition of organizational control. These definitions are shaded in gray in Table 2.1.

According to these definitions, and across all disciplines, the key elements of organizational control are: (1) influencing (or: regulating, directing, governing) behavior (actions, efforts) (mentioned in 76 percent of the definitions we reviewed); (2) alignment (congruence, consistency, conformity, compliance) (65 percent); and (3) goals and objectives (outcomes, standards, interests)

[1] www.webofscience.com   [2] www.ft.com/content/3405a512-5cbb-11e1-8f1f-00144feabdc0

Table 2.1 *Organizational control definitions across disciplines*

Discipline	Author(s)	Citation count[a]	Definition of organizational control
Accounting	Chenhall (2003)	1,266	"The terms management accounting (MA), management accounting systems (MAS), management control systems (MCS), and organizational controls (OC) are sometimes used interchangeably. MA refers to a collection of practices such as budgeting or product costing, while MAS refers to **the systematic use of MA to achieve some goal**. MCS is a broader term that encompasses MAS and also includes other controls, such as personal or clan controls. OC is sometimes used to refer to controls built into activities and processes such as statistical quality control, just-in-time management" (p. 129).
	Bushman and Smith (2001)	915	"Corporate control mechanisms are **the means by which managers are disciplined to act in the investors' interest**. Control mechanisms include both internal mechanisms, such as managerial incentive plans, director monitoring, and the internal labor market, and external mechanisms, such as outside shareholder or debtholder monitoring, the market for corporate control, competition in the product market, the external managerial labor market, and securities laws that protect outside investors against expropriation by corporate insiders" (p. 238).
	Dekker (2004)	536	"the primary purpose of control can be described as **creating the conditions that motivate the partners in an IOR [interorganizational relationship] to achieve desirable or predetermined outcomes**. [...] A second purpose of control in IORs therefore can be described as the coordination of interdependent tasks between partners." (pp. 29–30)
	Henri (2006a)	502	"MCS [management control systems] are defined as **formalized procedures and systems that use information to maintain or alter patterns in an organizational activity** (Simons 1987). This definition includes planning systems, reporting systems, and monitoring procedures that are based on information use." (pp. 532–533)
	Langfield-Smith (1997)	496	"Management control was defined by Anthony (1965) as 'the process by which managers ensure that resources are obtained and used effectively and efficiently in the accomplishment of the organization's objectives.' [...] MCS have also been described as **processes for influencing behavior** (Flamholtz et al. 1985). MCS provide **a means for gaining cooperation among collectives of individuals or organizational units who may share only partially congruent objectives, and channeling those efforts toward a specified set of organizational goals** (Flamholtz 1983; Ouchi 1979)." (p. 208)
	Itner and Larcker (2001)	455	"Anthony [(1965)] described management control as **the process for ensuring that resources are obtained and used effectively and efficiently to achieve the organization's objectives**." (p. 351)

Table 2.1 (*cont.*)

Discipline	Author(s)	Citation count	Definition of organizational control
Accounting	Bisbe and Otley (2004)	434	"The term Management Control Systems (MCS) refers to the **set of procedures and processes that managers and other organizational participants use in order to help ensure the achievement of their goals and the goals of their organizations** (Otley & Berry 1994), and it encompasses formal control systems as well as informal personal and social controls (Chiapello 1996; Otley 1980; Ouchi 1977)." (p. 709)
	Widener (2007)	370	"The purpose of the management control system (MCS) is to **provide information useful in decision-making, planning, and evaluation** (Merchant & Otley 2006)." (p. 757)
	Simons (1990)	367	"management control systems are the **formalized procedures and systems that use information to maintain or alter patterns in organizational activity**. Using this definition, these systems broadly include formalized procedures for such things as planning, budgeting, environmental scanning, competitor analyses, performance reporting and evaluation, resource allocation and employee rewards (Simons 1987)." (p. 128)
	Simons (1987)	353	"control systems refer to **formalized procedures and systems that use information to maintain or alter patterns in organizational activity**." (p. 358)
	Bedford et al. (2016)	115	"The primary function of MC [management control] is the **alignment of individual and group behaviours towards intended objectives** (Speklé 2001). [...] At a top management level, these control problems are neatly summarized by Otley and Berry (1980, p. 232), who define MC as: '[T]hose procedures which act to maintain viability through goal achievement, those concerned with the coordination and integration of differentiated parts, and those which promote adaptation to both internal and external change.'" (p. 14)
	Chenhall and Moers (2015)	112	"We define MCS [management control systems] as a set of many formal and informal input, process and output controls that are **used by management to achieve organizational goals**." (p. 1)
	Fullerton et al. (2013)	71	"Management accounting controls **monitor and direct behavior in order to achieve goal congruence**." (p. 51)
	Grabner (2014)	54	"The purpose of an incentive system is to **establish goal congruence between management and employees** in the absence of direct monitoring devices (Baiman 1982, 1990; Merchant & Otley 2006; Merchant & Van der Stede 2012)." (p. 1732)
	Cooper (2015)	51	"management control systems should **direct and motivate employees to act in accordance with organizational strategy**." (p. 17)

Information systems	Choudhury and Sabherwal (2003)	327	"This paper views control broadly, in a behavioral sense (Jaworski 1988; Kirsch 1996, 1997), as **attempting to ensure individuals act in a manner that is consistent with achieving desired objectives**. This view of control draws upon agency and organization theories in a way consistent with prior studies in organization design (e.g., Eisenhardt 1985), IS (Henderson & Lee 1992; Kirsch 1996, 1997; Kirsch et al. 2002) and marketing (Jaworski 1988; Jaworski & MacInnis 1989)." (p. 292)
	Kirsch (1997)	322	"control is viewed in a *behavioral sense*, that is, as **attempts to ensure that individuals working on organizational projects act according to an agreed upon strategy to achieve desired objectives** (Jaworski 1988; Merchant 1988)." (p. 216, emphasis in original)
	Stewart and Gosain (2006)	315	"ideology may be important as the vehicle of clan control (Barker 1993). Rather than dictating specific actions or manipulating tangible rewards, **clan control occurs when shared understandings define appropriate ways to behave and respond to situations in the group** (Kirsch 1997; Ouchi 1979). In order for it to result in positive team outcomes, ideology should motivate behaviors and responses that are likely to be productive for the team, constrain opportunistic behavior, and apply in a broad variety of situations to orient team members." (p. 293)
	Constantinides et al. (2018)	220	"**control mechanisms let platform owners enforce rules that reward and punish behavior, and establish best practices on the platform** (Evans & Schmalensee 2007). These controls can be informal or formal and may include tasks such as gatekeeping, process, metrics, and relational control (Tiwana 2013)." (p. 384)
	Kirsch (2004)	206	"control, which is viewed broadly to mean **any attempt to motivate individuals to behave in a manner consistent with organizational objectives** (Cardinal 2001; Das & Teng 1998; Jaworski 1988; Ouchi 1979)." (p. 374)
	Maruping et al. (2009)	201	"In the context of software development, control is defined as management's '**attempts to ensure that individuals working on organizational projects act according to an agreed-upon strategy to achieve desired objectives**' (Kirsch 1996, p. 1). Control is generally exercised through the monitoring and evaluation of behaviors or outcomes, and has been identified as an important antecedent of project team performance in terms of both efficiency and effectiveness (Henderson & Lee 1992; Nidumolu & Subramani 2003)." (p. 379)
	Piccoli and Ives (2003)	201	"Following Kirsch (1997), we conceptualize control as **attempts to ensure that individuals working on organizational projects act in conformity with pre-defined strategies**. Thus, control is exercised via mechanisms that, when successfully implemented, lead to the regulation of behavior (Kirsch 1997)." (p. 368)
	Tiwana (2015)	153	"Control refers to **the mechanisms used by a platform owner to encourage extension developers to act in ways that further the interests of the platform**." (p. 269)

Table 2.1 (cont.)

Discipline	Author(s)	Citation count	Definition of organizational control
Information systems	Chen et al. (2012)	145	"From a control perspective, **both reward and punishment are control mechanisms to achieve organizational goals** [(Eisenhardt 1985)]." (p. 159)
	Tiwana (2010)	141	"control mechanisms are intended to enhance alignment in outsourced systems development. [...] Control refers to **how the actions by the vendor are governed in a manner that furthers the interests of the client** [(Choudhury & Sabherwal 2003)]." (pp. 88 and 90)
	Huber et al. (2013)	109	"While contractual governance emphasizes the importance of contracts and their exercise as formal control [(Faems et al. 2008; Goo et al. 2009; Nidumolu & Subramani 2003)], relational governance relies on trust and informal control [(Goo et al. 2009; Lee & Kim 1999; Poppo & Zenger 2002)]. Both types of governance have their unique strengths [(Adler & Borys 1996; Goo et al. 2009; Poppo & Zenger 2002; Sydow & Windeler 2003)]. Contractual governance prescribes expected outcomes **and behaviors for the client and vendor, and thus is an effective safeguard against opportunism.** Relational governance is particularly suitable to cope with unforeseen events as it allows flexible reactions to issues not covered by the contract." (p. 82)
	Wiener et al. (2016)	87	"In the IS project control literature (e.g., Choudhury & Sabherwal 2003; Kirsch 1996, 1997; Tiwana & Keil 2009), as well as in related literature in contributing disciplines (e.g., Das & Teng 1998; Jaworski 1988; Ouchi 1979), *control is defined as any attempt to align individual behaviors with organizational objectives.*" (p. 742; emphasis in original)
	Gregory et al. (2013)	77	"In order for organizations, including temporary organizations such as projects, to achieve their objectives, **some type of strategy must be implemented that 'effectively controls members' activities in a manner functional for the organization'** (Barker 1993, p. 409). Ouchi (1977, 1979; Ouchi & Maguire 1975) proposed one of the most widely adopted control frameworks, which focuses on formal behavioral and outcome controls as well as informal clan controls. An extension of this framework to the context of IS projects was proposed by Kirsch (1996, 1997), who built upon this work as well as related studies (e.g., Henderson & Lee 1992)." (pp. 1212–1213)
	Khansa et al. (2017)	45	"Controls not officially dictated by the company are generally dubbed informal controls. Such controls could consist of individual ethical beliefs and self-control [(Chatterjee et al. 2015; Hu et al. 2015)] or social norms [(Galletta & Polak 2003; Hsu et al. 2015)] – that is, **informal signals and cues that give insights into what is or is not socially acceptable by others in the organization, including coworkers and superiors.** On the other hand, formal controls are officially imposed and generally consist of **rules and policies, monitoring, and penalties in the event of policy violations** [(Chen et al. 2012; D'Arcy et al. 2009; Hsu et al. 2015; Liang et al. 2013)]." (pp. 142–143)

Information systems	Di Tuillio and Staples (2013)	28	"Governance is needed to establish and manage procedures, policies, and decision rights that **motivate and allow project stakeholders to work effectively and efficiently to reach the project goals** [(Midha & Bhattacherjee 2012)]. Governance is implemented through various mechanisms and control modes. IS project control has been defined as activities (i.e., mechanisms) designed to align individuals' activities to be consistent with organizational goals, objectives, and a project plan [(Kirsch et al. 2002; Tiwana & Keil 2009)]." (p. 50)
Management	Ouchi (1980)	2,040	"From the perspective of Mayo (1945) and Barnard (1968), the fundamental problem of cooperation stems from the fact that individuals have only partially overlapping goals. Left to their own devices, they pursue incongruent objectives and their efforts are uncoordinated. Any collectivity which has an economic goal must then find **a means to control diverse individuals efficiently**." (p. 130)
	Das and Teng (1998)	1,731	"we consider control as '**a regulatory process by which the elements of a system are made more predictable through the establishment of standards in the pursuit of some desired objective or state**' (Leifer & Mills 1996: 117)." (p. 493)
	Ouchi (1979)	1,625	"Organizational control has many meanings and has been interpreted in many ways. Tannenbaum [(1968)], whose view has dominated organizational theory, interprets control as the sum of interpersonal influence relations in an organization. In a similar vein, Etzioni [(1965)] finds it useful to treat control in organizations as equivalent to power. Other than the power-influence approach to control, organization theorists have also treated control as a problem in information flows (Galbraith [(1973)]; Ouchi and Maguire [(1975)]), as a problem in creating and monitoring rules through a hierarchical authority system as specified by Weber [(1947)] and interpreted by Perrow [(1972)], Blau and Scott [(1962)], and many organizational sociologists, and as a cybernetic process of testing, measuring, and providing feedback (Thompson [(1967)]; Reeves and Woodward [(1970)]). This paper considers a more simple-minded view of organizational control stated in the following two questions: What are **the mechanisms through which an organization can be managed so that it moves towards its objectives?** How can the design of these mechanisms be improved, and what are the limits of each basic design?" (p. 833)
	Arthur (1994)	1,520	"The goal of control human resource systems is to reduce direct labor costs, or improve efficiency, by **enforcing employee compliance with specified rules and procedures and basing employee rewards** on some measurable output criteria (Eisenhardt 1985; Walton 1985)." (p. 672)

Table 2.1 (cont.)

Discipline	Author(s)	Citation count	Definition of organizational control
Management	Gulati and Singh (1998)	1,319	"Prior research on contract choices in alliances and the extent of hierarchical controls they embody has been influenced primarily by transaction cost economists, who have focused on the appropriation concerns in alliances, which originate from pervasive behavioral uncertainty and contracting problems (Balakrishnan & Koza 1993; Pisano 1989; Pisano et al. 1988). Following this perspective, scholars have suggested that **hierarchical controls are an effective response to such [appropriation] concerns at the time the alliance is formed**." (pp. 781–782)
	Alvesson and Willmott (2002)	1,227	"we are here concerned primarily with how organizational control is accomplished through **the self-positioning of employees within managerially inspired discourses about work and organization with which they may become more or less identified and committed**." (p. 620)
	Barker (1993)	1,136	"For any organization to move toward its goals and purposes, its 'particular outcomes,' **its members must interactively negotiate and implement some type of strategy that effectively controls members' activities in a manner functional for the organization**." (p. 409)
	Das and Teng (2001)	1,013	"Control is generally viewed as a process of regulation and monitoring for the achievement of organizational goals. [...] In this article, we adopt the definition of control as '**a regulatory process by which the elements of a system are made more predictable through the establishment of standards in the pursuit of some desired objective or state**' (Leifer & Mills 1996: 117)." (p. 258)
	Eisenhardt (1985)	981	"Recent organizational approaches to control (e.g., Ouchi 1979) suggest two underlying control strategies. On the one hand, control can be accomplished through performance evaluation. Performance evaluation refers to the cybernetic process of monitoring and rewarding performance. This strategy emphasizes the information aspects of control. Namely, to what degree can the various aspects of performance be assessed? Alternatively, control can be achieved by minimizing the divergence of preferences among organizational members. That is, members cooperate in the achievement of organizational goals because the members understand and have internalized these goals. This strategy emphasizes people policies such as selection, training, and socialization. [...] the role of control is **to provide measures and rewards such that individuals pursuing their own self-interest will also pursue the collective interest**." (pp. 135 and 137)
	Gupta and Govindarajan (1991)	832	"To use Williamson's (1985) terminology, corporate control over a specific subsidiary can be thought of as **a governance mechanism instituted by the corporation to regulate transactions between it and the focal subsidiary**." (p. 770)

Management	Misangyi and Acharya (2014)	345	"Corporate governance research and practice […] has been 'most concerned with describing the governance mechanisms that solve the agency problem' (Eisenhardt 1989a: 59). That is, the concern is with how to constrain executives of publicly traded corporations to run the firms for the shareholders' benefit." (p. 1681)
	Handley and Angst (2015)	103	"Contractual governance involves the extent to which formal incentives/disincentives (typically financial) are used clearly to specify and control service activities between a buyer (i.e., customer firm) and supplier (i.e., service provider). […] Relational governance, on the other hand, assesses the extent to which a business relationship involves commitment and cooperation from both parties, and performance targets that are less clearly specified. Both mechanisms are consistently argued to be effective at bringing the service provider's behaviors into better alignment with the interests of the customer, and improving the performance of interorganizational relationships (Goo et al. 2009; Kirsch et al. 2002; Poppo & Zenger 2002)." (p. 1413)
	Kreutzer et al. (2015)	56	"Organizational control addresses the fundamental managerial problem of managers seeking 'to align employee capabilities, activities, and performance with organizational goals and aspirations' (Sitkin et al. 2010b: 3)." (p. 1317)
	Stanko and Beckman (2015)	52	"organizational control in which, often through rules, norms, and technical systems, organizations exert control over how employees work (Edwards 1979; Kunda 1992; Ouchi & Maguire 1975)." (p. 713)
	Kownatzki et al. (2013)	51	"corporate control – defined as corporate headquarters' attempts to manage or influence the process, content, and/or outcome of strategy making in their SBUs [strategic business units]." (p. 1296)
Marketing	Hartline and Ferrell (1996)	961	"Jaworski (1988, p. 26) calls these activities formal controls and defines them as 'management-initiated mechanisms that influence the probability that employees or groups will behave in ways that support the stated marketing objectives.'" (p. 56)
	Jap and Gensan (2000)	817	"Control mechanisms are safeguards that firms put in place to govern interorganizational exchange, minimize exposure to opportunism, and protect TSIs [transaction-specific investments]. In general, social control involves designing mechanisms that either inhibit opportunistic behavior or induce behaviors that promote the continuance of a given relationship (Coleman 1990; Stump & Heide 1996)." (p. 230)
	Anderson and Oliver (1987)	564	"A control system is an organization's set of procedures for monitoring, directing, evaluating, and compensating its employees. By accident or design, such a system influences employee behavior, ideally in a way that enhances the welfare of both the firm and the employee." (p. 76)

Table 2.1 (cont.)

Discipline	Author(s)	Citation count	Definition of organizational control
Marketing	Mohr et al. (1996)	517	"When one party exerts control over another, it has **influenced or specified a partner's actions in order to achieve desired outcomes** (Frazier 1983; Pfeffer & Salancik 1978; Skinner & Guiltinan 1985). Although power is commonly expressed as the ability of one party to influence another (for a review, see Gaski 1984), control is best viewed as an outcome of power and results when a firm is successful in modifying its partner's behaviors (e.g., Anderson & Narus 1984; El-Ansary & Stern 1972; Etgar 1976; Skinner & Guiltinan 1985)." (p. 104)
	Jaworski et al. (1993)	469	"'Control' refers to **attempts by managers or other stakeholders within the SBU [strategic business unit] to influence the behavior and activities of marketing personnel to achieve desired outcomes.**" (p. 58)
	Jaworski (1988)	447	"Control of marketing personnel refers to **attempts by management or other stakeholders within the organization to influence the behavior and activities of marketing personnel to achieve desired outcomes** (similar in spirit to the approaches of Tannenbaum [(1968] and Flamholtz [(1983)]). The control device is designed to affect individual action which, in turn, is expected to influence performance." (p. 24)
	Stump and Heide (1996)	435	"Such [transaction-specific] investments give rise to a problem of *social control* (Coleman 1990). In general, social control involves **designing mechanisms that either inhibit opportunistic action or induce behaviors that promote the continuance of a given relationship.**" (p. 432, emphasis in original)
	Oliver and Anderson (1994)	400	"As stated in our previous work (Anderson & Oliver 1987, hereafter A&O) a control system is '**an organization's set of procedures for monitoring, directing, evaluating, and compensating its employees'** (p. 76)." (p. 53)
	Hartline et al. (2000)	385	"Marketing control refers to **management's attempts to influence the behavior and activities of marketing personnel to achieve desired outcomes** (Jaworski 1988; Jaworski et al. 1993)." (p. 36)
	Bello and Gilliland (1997)	368	"In an export context, unilateral controls refer to specific, **manufacturer-initiated directives aimed at influencing foreign distributors to perform marketing actions in ways that support manufacturer objectives** (Jaworski 1988; Sachdev et al. 1995)." (p. 25)

Marketing	Miao and Evans (2012)	113	"Companies typically employ sales control systems – the formalized policies, rules, and procedures – to direct the sales force to reach desired organizational objectives (Anderson & Oliver 1987)." (p. 73)
	Crosno and Brown (2015)	51	"Control refers to an organization's set of procedures for monitoring, directing, evaluating, and compensating agents (e.g., employees, trading partners) (Anderson & Oliver 1987)." (p. 298)
	Katsikeas et al. (2018)	43	"A sales control system is defined as 'the organization's set of procedures for monitoring, directing, evaluating, and providing feedback to its employees' (Anderson & Oliver 1987, p. 76)." (p. 45)
	Grewal et al. (2013)	38	"Output control 'approximates a market contracting arrangement' (Anderson & Oliver 1987, p.76) that firms use to assess the observable consequences of an exchange partner's actions against predetermined standards (Heide et al. 2007). [...] Process control entails offering helpful suggestions or 'guidance' (Bello & Gilliland 1997, p. 25) to influence a partner's marketing activities, such as selling procedures, promotional practices, and product management, to achieve desired outcomes (Celly & Frazier 1996)." (pp. 380–381)
	Kim and Tiwana (2016)	13	"Control refers to mechanisms used by a controller to encourage controlees (the agents) to act in a manner that furthers the controller's (the principal) interests (Jaworski et al. 1993; Ouchi 1979)." (p. 318)
Operations research	Choi et al. (2001)	817	"controls, such as rules and regulations or institutional and budgetary restrictions, ensure that an individual agent's behavior is greatly limited, thus, changing the complexity of aggregate behavior and helping the CAS [complex adaptive system] to behave more predictably and cybernetically." (pp. 354–355)
	Cao and Lumineau (2015)	427	"**Contractual governance**, also called 'formal contract' (Li et al. 2010), 'legal contract' (Achrol & Gundlach 1999), 'explicit contract' (Zhou & Poppo 2010), or 'legal safeguards' (Lui & Ngo 2004), **refers to the extent to which one IOR [interorganizational relationship] is governed by a formal and written contract which explicitly stipulates the responsibilities and obligations of each party** (Abdi & Aulakh 2012; Ryall & Sampson 2009). By specifying each party's rights and duties, **contractual governance may reduce opportunism and safeguard IORs** (Williamson 1985). [...] **Relational governance**, also named 'relational mechanism' (Jayaraman et al. 2013) or 'social control' (Li et al. 2010), **refers to the extent to which one IOR is governed by social relations and shared norms** (Poppo et al. 2008; Zhou & Xu 2012). Different from contractual governance relying on formal structure and third party enforcement, relational governance relies on informal structure and self-enforcement of each party (Dyer & Singh 1998; Malhotra & Murnighan 2002)." (p. 17)

Table 2.1 (cont.)

Discipline	Author(s)	Citation count	Definition of organizational control
Operations research	Cousins and Menguc (2006)	344	"The purpose of this study is to examine the role of two governance mechanisms on the supply chain setting: integration and socialization. We propose that the **buyer's use of supplier integration and socialization mechanisms will enhance the supplier's communication and operational performance** and in turn, it will **enhance the buyer's perceived level of supplier's contractual conformance.**" (p. 604)
	Li et al. (2010)	198	"Control mechanisms in interfirm cooperation – **structural arrangements deployed to regulate partners' behavior** – greatly influence the success of buyer–supplier relationships (Fryxell et al. 2002)." (p. 333)
	Germain et al. (2008)	134	"Formal control refers to devices used to monitor systems on a written, codified, and rational basis (Khandwalla 1974; Workman et al. 1998). Developing and enforcing performance control and behavioral prescriptions **improves decisions and increases the predictability of performance** (Pierce & Delbecq 1977)." (p. 558)
	Goodale et al. (2011)	124	"the control function in organizations exists, at least in part, to counteract the adverse effects of uncertainty on the organizational system, **ensure conformity to established routines, correct deviations from expected behaviors, and promote efficiency and exploitative learning within the confines of established operations** (Boyer & Lewis 2002; Devaraj et al. 2004; Krajewski et al. 2010)." (p. 117)
	Koufteros et al. (2014)	118	"PM [performance management] systems are by their very nature conducive towards better performance because they can be used to **benchmark operations against targets and abet the organization orchestrate resources to enhance future performance.**" (p. 315)
	Handley and Benton (2013)	111	"In the present paper's context, control is aimed at **aligning the service provider's behaviors with the customer firm's interests.**" (p. 110)
	Li et al. (2008)	98	"Control is intended to **reduce goal incongruence and preference divergences among alliance participants,** and is widely acknowledged as essential for alliances (Geringer & Hebert 1989)." (p. 260)
	Liu (2015)	96	"Control refers to the **rules and processes that govern the actions of controlees employed by controllers to foster desirable controlee behavior** (Tiwana & Keil 2009)." (p. 48)

Operations research	Netland et al. (2015)	84	"management control [...] has been defined as 'the process by which managers ensure that resources are obtained and used effectively and efficiently in the accomplishment of the organization's objectives' (Anthony 1965, p. 17)." (p. 91)
	Jayaraman et al. (2013)	48	"The transaction cost perspective suggests that organizations must consider the costs and resources required to effectively coordinate activities within the firm and with the external party to mitigate the risks inherent in any outsourcing engagement. Both inter-organizational and the intra-organizational governance control mechanisms enable the firm to reduce transaction costs in the relationship and achieve higher performance (Govindarajan 1988; Klein et al 1978)." (p. 317)
	Handley and Gray (2013)	43	"the use of behavioral monitoring and outcome-based contracts and the independent and interactive effectiveness of the two mechanisms in aligning the quality-related interests of the two organizations." (p. 1541)
	Akkermans et al. (2019)	19	"performance-based contracts (PBCs) (Guajardo et al. 2012). These contracts support collaboration by aligning incentives of suppliers and buyers (Eisenhardt 1989a; Selviaridis & Wynstra 2015)." (p. 23)
	MacCormack and Mishra (2015)	12	"agency theorists (e.g., Eisenhardt 1989a; Gibbons 1998; Holmstrom & Milgrom 1991) have shown that formal contracts provide a framework by which to align the incentives of a firm and its partners, so that each acts in a manner that benefits all parties. [...] while formal contracting provides the foundation for governing partnering relationships, relational contracting can fill critical gaps in these contracts by reducing information asymmetry and reconciling differences in the incentives of a firm and its partners (Poppo & Zenger 2002)." (pp. 1552–1553)

We highlight the most important part of the definition in bold. To ensure that each definition remains embedded in its original context, we also present parts of the text that go beyond the definition itself. The most highly cited articles of all times are listed first for each discipline, and articles resulting from our search of the most recent ten-year period between 2013 and 2022 are shaded in gray.

[a] *Web of Science Core* citations, retrieved on December 2, 2022.

(61 percent). These key elements are followed by other common but less frequently mentioned elements: (4) incentives (motivation, encouragement, compensation, reward, punishment) (28 percent); (5) monitoring (20 percent); (6) evaluating (assessing) (15 percent); (7) information (9 percent); and (8) coordination (5 percent). There are more definitions that explicitly mention formal controls (27 percent) than definitions that mention informal controls (13 percent), or both (12 percent). Three percent of definitions mention third parties as controllers, 4 percent explicitly focus on owners controlling top executives, 24 percent on managers controlling workers, and 28 percent on organizations controlling their external partners (e.g., suppliers, alliance partners).

There are also noteworthy differences between disciplines. Given its focus on product and process design, operations, and supply chains, it is not surprising that operations management mentions organizational goals and objectives significantly less than the other four disciplines (33 percent versus 60–80 percent). The accounting discipline puts less emphasis (53 percent) on influencing behavior than operations (73 percent), management (73 percent), IS (80 percent), and marketing (100 percent). Another cross-disciplinary difference is evident in who controls whom. Of the articles that explicitly mention such a focus, in accounting (27 percent), management (27 percent), and especially marketing (53 percent), the dominant focus is on managers controlling their organizations' workers. Reflecting their research interest in the management of external relationships, operations management (60 percent), marketing (33 percent), and IS (27 percent) predominantly focus on managers controlling their organizations' external partners. Accounting and management are, furthermore, the only disciplines in which definitions mention owners controlling executives (13 and 7 percent, respectively) and organizations controlling their SBUs (strategic business units) (7 and 13 percent, respectively). Building on these similarities and differences, we synthesized the following definition:

Organizational control comprises all formal and informal organizational attempts to enable, motivate, and direct organizational members and partners to individually and collectively act in a way that aligns with an organization's goals and aspirations. These attempts can originate from owners, managers, and the workers themselves and involve specifying, monitoring, evaluating, and rewarding inputs, behaviors, or outcomes, or any combination of those.

Our view of control builds on agency and organizational theories in the management literature (e.g., Eisenhardt 1985) and is also in line with conceptualizations of control in accounting (e.g., Chenhall 2003), IS (e.g., Kirsch 1997), marketing (e.g., Jaworski 1988), and operations management (e.g., Li et al. 2010). In keeping with the cross-disciplinary definitions in Table 2.1, our conceptualization views organizational control in a behavioral sense; that is, organizational control is focused on monitoring inputs, behaviors, and/or outcomes and motivating organizational members and partners to act in a manner consistent with desired goals and objectives (e.g., Choudhury & Sabherwal 2003). In addition to these monitoring and incentive functions, organizational control can also have a coordination function, which enables workers to accomplish task objectives efficiently and effectively by providing important task-related information and by directing and coordinating workers' attention and task-related efforts (see Section 4.2 for details on these three functions of organizational control).

Our conceptualization of organizational control is multifaceted (Sitkin et al. 2010a). It is not restricted to one or even a few organizational practices but encompasses a diverse array of practices that comprise both formal (i.e., explicit, codified, and officially sanctioned) and informal (i.e., unwritten, uncodified, and unofficial) approaches. These formal and informal approaches range from early bureaucratic, authoritative, and coercive control regimes (Taylor 1911) to control mechanisms that empower workers, provide them with broad autonomy regarding the means to complete a given task, and increase their perceived self-determination. Our conceptualization strives to balance workers' desires for personal control, on the one hand, and the accomplishment of organizational goals, on the other hand (Adler & Borys 1996; Simons 1995a). Our conceptualization of organizational control therefore recognizes both organizational authority and individual agency. It also acknowledges organizational control mechanisms and worker agency as mutually constitutive (Emirbayer & Mische 1998; Giddens 1984). While workers are subject to and affected by organizational control, their engagement also reproduces – and may even transform – organizational control arrangements. Workers can take actions that influence the efficacy of organizational control (e.g., by gaming organizational reward systems), and they can become a constituting force of organizational control, for example, by engaging in monitoring themselves (in the form of self-control) and their colleagues (in the form of peer control). In that sense, organizational control is not simply a coercive, top-down function but the consequence of workers' and managers' sense-making and meaning-giving processes (Sitkin et al. 2020). On the flipside, our conceptualization is also not naïve with regards to the problematic issues associated with organizational control (e.g., Barker 1993; Delbridge 2010; Jermier 1998). Section 4.3 will discuss unintended outcomes, such as stymied creativity and innovation; negative outcomes, such as worker stress, dissatisfaction, and turnover; as well as workers' active resistance to organizational control efforts.

Most organizational control researchers consider control to be manager-centric, that is, hierarchical or top-down (see Cardinal et al. 2017, for a review of the literature). Extending that focus, our conceptualization includes self-control (e.g., Kirsch 1996), lateral or peer control (e.g., Loughry 2010), and control emanating from third parties, such as customers (e.g., Fuller & Smith 1991). Our control conceptualization also applies across levels of organizations – from managers overseeing workers and corporate headquarters managing their SBUs, to boards of directors overseeing the organization's top executives, companies managing their supplier and interfirm alliance relationships, and digital platforms brokering relationships between clients and gig workers.

For simplicity, we use the terms "manager" and "worker" throughout our book to signify controller and controlee, respectively. However, our discussion applies equally to the other control relationships mentioned earlier. It encompasses managers' control over workers (e.g., Hartline & Ferrell 1996), workers' control over their peers (e.g., Walter et al. 2021), corporate headquarters' control over their SBUs (e.g., Gupta & Govindarajan 1991), investors' control over executives (e.g., Bushman & Smith 2001), and organizations' control over their alliance partners (e.g., Gulati & Singh 1998) and suppliers (e.g., Cousins & Menguc 2006). However, our conceptualization excludes bottom-up influence attempts, such as workers lobbying their managers (see, e.g., Kipnis & Schmidt 1988). These bottom-up influence attempts in the pursuit of individual agendas are unlikely to contribute to an alignment of individual and organizational interests and therefore do not fall under our conceptualization of organizational control.

Irrespective of its origin and direction, our conceptualization of organizational control is goal oriented, with control mechanisms directly tied to specific organizational goals (Cardinal et al. 2017; Sitkin et al. 2010b). We are aware, however, that this places organizational control in complex territory, as organizational goals can be fluid, divergent, or even conflicting (Bourgeois 1985; Cyert & March 1963), and organizational goals may be shaped by both managerial intentions and workers' autonomous (e.g., Burgelman 1983), emergent (e.g., Mintzberg & Waters 1985), or political activities (e.g., Bower & Doz 1979; Pfeffer & Salancik 1974).

Last, our conceptualization is reflective of both foundational and recently published research in the "mainstream" literature on organizational control (to borrow the term used by Delbridge [2010: 80], Ezzamel & Willmott [1998: 358], and Sitkin et al. [2010a: 6]). However, the mainstream literature's focus on the alignment between individual and organizational goals represents a conceptual worldview that is fundamentally different from a critical perspective on control, which focuses on the power relations and inequalities inherent in organizational control practices and emphasizes normative and ethical implications of control (e.g., Barker 1993; Delbridge 2010; Jermier 1998). Addressing Ezzamel and Willmott's (1998: 360) critique that in much of the administrative science literature on control ideologies and practices, "there is little recognition of their political construction and representation in relations of domination," in Section 3.5, we review this perspective and integrate its ideas and arguments into our theorizing.

As a simple illustration of the intellectual underpinnings of our control definition, Figure 2.1 shows a citation network we created using UCINET version 6.752 (Borgatti et al. 2002). The nodes in this network consist of both the most influential articles across disciplines listed in Table 2.1 and the articles they cite as part of their organizational control definitions. The directed lines connecting nodes in the network represent citation patterns, with each article being connected to the sources it cites, and the arrow pointing toward the cited reference.

As evident from Figure 2.1, the overall network is composed of a main component of connected articles that reference each other in their definitions of organizational control as well as several smaller, unconnected clusters of articles that only cite each other and individual articles that are not citing any articles in their control definition. It is encouraging to see that the main component is multidisciplinary, with articles from IS, management, and marketing frequently citing articles from other disciplines in their definition of organizational control.

The exceptions to this are the disciplines of accounting and operations management, with articles from those two disciplines only rarely being part of the main component. Articles from these two disciplines tend to appear in smaller, unconnected clusters of articles citing each other, such as the clusters around Grabner (2014) and around Simons (1987). Sometimes, articles in these two disciplines cite other articles in their own discipline but remain isolated from the main component, such as Goodale et al. (2011) and Mohr (1996). And oftentimes, articles in these two disciplines appear as isolates, such as the articles listed in Figure 2.1 as a column on the left.

To illustrate cross-disciplinary connections among organizational control definitions, Figure 2.2 presents the same citation network, but with articles grouped by discipline. This figure confirms that the disciplines of management and IS are densely connected, which means that they tend to cite each other frequently when defining organizational control. The same applies, although to a lesser extent, to the disciplines of management and operations management. In contrast, when it comes to drawing on other disciplines when defining organizational control, accounting is comparatively isolated from the other disciplines, with only very few connections to management and marketing, and none to the other disciplines.

We also analyzed the influence of individual articles on organizational control definitions by calculating each article's network centrality (see Table 2.2 for a ranked list of the most central articles). An article's *indegree centrality* – or the number of citations it received as part of other articles' control definitions – represents its popularity or influence on future control definitions, whereas its *betweenness centrality* – or the number of times an article falls on the shortest path between other pairs of articles – reflects an article's importance as a bridge between articles within and across disciplines (cf., Bonacich 1987; Freeman 1977).

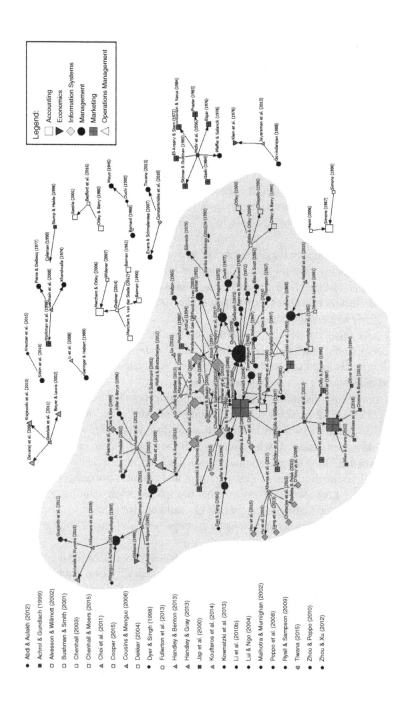

Figure 2.1 Citation network of organizational control definitions

Notes: Node size is determined by indegree centrality or the number of articles citing the focal article in their control definition. The main component of connected articles is shaded in gray.

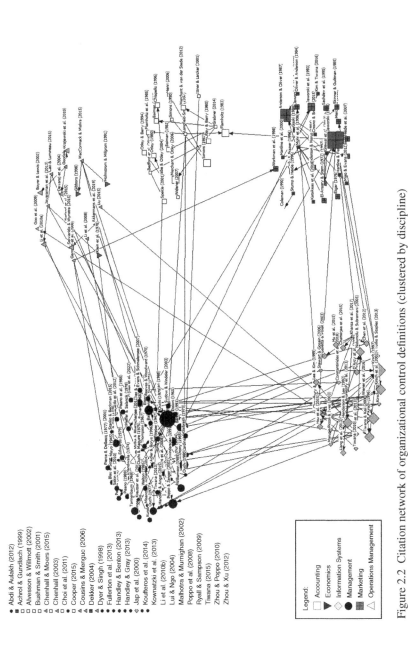

Figure 2.2 Citation network of organizational control definitions (clustered by discipline)

Note: Node size is determined by indegree centrality or the number of articles citing the focal article in their control definition.

Table 2.2 *Most highly cited articles in organizational control definitions*

Indegree centrality (3+ citations) (discipline)		Betweenness centrality (undirected, normalized) (discipline)	
Jaworski (1988) (MKT)	7	Choudhury and Sabherwal (2003) (IS)	0.102
Ouchi (1979) (MGMT)	7	Ouchi (1979) (MGMT)	0.101
Anderson and Oliver (1987) (MKT)	5	Jaworski (1988) (MKT)	0.082
Kirsch (1997) (IS)	5	Eisenhardt (1985) (MGMT)	0.066
Kirsch (1996) (IS)	4	Kirsch et al. (2002) (IS)	0.064
Anthony (1965) (MGMT)	3	Handley and Angst (2015) (OPS)	0.056
Eisenhardt (1985) (MGMT)	3	Bello and Gilliland (1997) (MKT)	0.053
Eisenhardt (1989a) (MGMT)	3	Gregory et al. (2013) (IS)	0.051
Henderson and Lee (1992) (IS)	3	Poppo and Zenger (2002) (MGMT)	0.051
Kirsch et al. (2002) (IS)	3	Wiener et al. (2016) (IS)	0.047
Ouchi and MaGuire (1975) (MGMT)	3	Grewal et al. (2013) (MKT)	0.043
Poppo and Zenger (2002) (MGMT)	3	MacCormack and Mishra (2015) (OPS)	0.043
Tiwana and Keil (2009) (IS)	3	Chen et al. (2012) (IS)	0.042

Disciplines: Information Systems (IS), Management (MNGT), Marketing (MKT), Operation Research (OPS).

Based on their indegree centrality scores in Table 2.2, marketing and management are the most popular disciplines serving as references for control definitions, followed by IS. As evident from its betweenness centrality scores and its position in Figure 2.1, Jaworski's (1988) article serves as the main connection of the marketing discipline's definitions to the main component. Ouchi's (1979) article serves in a similar position for the management discipline, as do Choudhury and Sabherwal's (2003) and Kirsch et al.'s (2002) articles for the IS discipline. Poppo and Zenger's (2002) article connects work on inter-organizational control (e.g., between alliance partners or in buyer–supplier relationships) with the main component, which is also reflected in its high betweenness centrality. Last, it is notable that no accounting article is among the top-cited articles, further supporting the relative isolation of this discipline when it comes to organizational control definitions.

2.2   What Organizational Control Is Not

Despite our broad and multifaceted conceptualization of organizational control, we want to be clear about its demarcation to other concepts that are related but fall outside the focus of our book. One such concept that is frequently invoked in connection with control is *power*. Defined as "the potential ability to influence behavior, to change the course of events, to overcome resistance, and to get people to do things that they would otherwise not do" (Pfeffer 1992: 30), it is easy to understand why early theorists have treated control as equivalent to power over workers (e.g., Etzioni 1965). While power is a necessary condition for many forms of control,[3] the use of power does not necessarily guarantee an alignment of interests – in fact, it can be used for unilateral or even nefarious purposes. We therefore consider power and control as two distinct constructs, and in line with Otley and colleagues (1995: S33), we "exclude the exercise of power for its own sake, restricting ourselves to those activities undertaken by managers which have the intention of furthering organizational objectives (at least, insofar as perceived by managers). We are, thus, primarily concerned with the exercise of legitimate authority rather than power."

A specific form of power that is prominent in the corporate governance, finance, and entrepreneurship literature is *control of organizations* in the form of stock ownership. In line with our position on power in general, we acknowledge such control over organizations as the foundation of owners' legitimate authority over managers and workers and, hence, a precondition for bureaucratic forms of control (cf., Ouchi 1979). However, control via stock ownership remains distinct from our conceptualization of organizational control.

Another concept to distinguish is *organizational structure*, which consists of aspects such as vertical and horizontal diversification, centralization, and formalization. While early research has viewed structure as isomorphic with control (e.g., March & Simon 1958; Weber 1947), later research has clarified that structure and control are related but distinct. Control represents an evaluation process rather than an attribute of structure, while structural attributes of the organization specify the reliability and validity with which such evaluations can be made (Ouchi 1977). A similar distinction can also be made to distinguish between organizational control and *organizational culture*. While culture provides a set of values that may form the foundation of control, culture is not identical with control, because culture does not entail an evaluative component (Sitkin et al. 2020).

Last, organizational control is distinct from the social psychological concepts of *locus of control*, or an individual's beliefs about control over life events (Rotter 1954), as well as the related concept of *personal control*, which is defined as "the individual's beliefs, at a given point in time, in his or her ability to effect a change, in a desired direction, on the environment" (Greenberger & Strasser 1986: 164). While both constructs share the control label, this body of research focuses on dispositional personality characteristics and therefore does not fall under our conceptualization of organizational control.

---

[3] Power (in the form of legitimate authority) is easily apparent in hierarchical or bureaucratic control (Ouchi 1979), but it is similarly at play in lateral and peer control as the reason for peers' compliance with established norms is related to peers' ability to pressure and/or ostracize deviant team members (Loughry & Tosi 2008).

2.3 Appendix: Web of Science Search Query for Control Definition

Keyword List

("organizational control*" OR "organisational control*" OR "organization's control*" OR "organisation's control*" OR "organizations' control*" OR "organisations' control*" OR "organization control*" OR "organisation control*" OR "organizations control*" OR "organisations control*" OR "firm control*" OR "company control*" OR "management control*" OR "managerial control*" OR "hierarchical control*" OR "input control*" OR "personnel control*" OR "behavior control*" OR "behavioral control*" OR "behaviour control*" OR "behavioural control*" OR "process control*" OR "output control*" OR "outcome control*" OR "results control*" OR "formal control*" OR "informal control*" OR "culture control*" OR "cultural control*" OR "diagnostic control*" OR "interactive control*" OR "belief system*" OR "boundary system*" OR "market control*" OR "bureaucratic control*" OR "clan control*" OR "clan*" OR "concertive control*" OR "enabling control*" OR "normative control*" OR "integrative control*" OR "control system*" OR "control mechanism*" OR "control target*" OR "control theory*" OR "theory of control*" OR "strategic control*" OR "financial control*" OR "peer control*" OR "self control*" OR "control dynamics*" OR "organizational-control*" OR "organisational-control*" OR "firm-control*" OR "company-control*" OR "management-control*" OR "managerial-control*" OR "hierarchical-control*" OR "input-control*" OR "personnel-control*" OR "behavior-control*" OR "behavioral-control*" OR "behaviour-control*" OR "behavioural-control*" OR "process-control*" OR "output-control*" OR "outcome-control*" OR "results-control*" OR "formal-control*" OR "informal-control*" OR "culture-control*" OR "cultural-control*" OR "diagnostic-control*" OR "interactive-control*" OR "belief-system*" OR "boundary-system*" OR "market-control*" OR "bureaucratic-control*" OR "clan-control*" OR "concertive-control*" OR "enabling-control*" OR "normative-control*" OR "integrative-control*" OR "control-system*" OR "control-mechanism*" OR "control-target*" OR "control-theory*" OR "strategic-control*" OR "financial-control*" OR "peer-control*" OR "self-control*" OR "control-dynamics*" OR "self-managing team*" OR "value-based control*")

Journal List

("Academy of Management Journal" OR "Academy of Management Review" OR "Accounting Organizations and Society" OR "Accounting Review" OR "Administrative Science Quarterly" OR "American Economic Review" OR "Contemporary Accounting Research" OR "Econometrica" OR "Entrepreneurship

Theory and Practice" OR "Harvard Business Review" OR "Human Relations" OR "Human Resource Management" OR "Information Systems Research" OR "Journal of Accounting & Economics" OR "Journal of Accounting Research" OR "Journal of Applied Psychology" OR "Journal of Business Ethics" OR "Journal of Business Venturing" OR "Journal of Consumer Psychology" OR "Journal of Consumer Research" OR "Journal of Finance" OR "Journal of Financial and Quantitative Analysis" OR "Journal of Financial Economics" OR "Journal of International Business Studies" OR "Journal of Management" OR "Journal of Management Information Systems" OR "Journal of Management Studies" OR "Journal of Marketing" OR "Journal of Marketing Research" OR "Journal of Operations Management" OR "Journal of Political Economy" OR "Journal of the Academy of Marketing Science" OR "Management Science" OR "Marketing Science" OR "MIS Quarterly" OR "M&SOM-Manufacturing & Service Operations Management" OR "Operations Research" OR "Organization Science" OR "Organization Studies" OR "Organizational Behavior and Human Decision Processes" OR "Production and Operations Management" OR "Quarterly Journal of Economics" OR "Research Policy" OR "Review of Accounting Studies" OR "Review of Economic Studies" OR "Review of Finance" OR "Review of Financial Studies" OR "Sloan Management Review" OR "Strategic Entrepreneurship Journal" OR "Strategic Management Journal")

Search Query

(TI = [*keyword list*] OR AK = [*keyword list*] OR KP = [*keyword list*] OR AB = [*keyword list*]) AND SO = [*journal list*]

3 A History of Organizational Control

This chapter provides an overview of the history of organizational control. After a brief review of organizational control's origins in ancient bureaucracies and its roots in scientific management, the human relations paradigm, and Weberian bureaucracy, we report the results of a document co-citation analysis examining 1,148 organizational control articles published between 1938 and 2022 to illuminate the field's intellectual base and emerging research fronts. We further examine the extent to which the disciplines that have examined organizational control – accounting, information systems, management, marketing, and operations management – have done so in isolation from each other, potentially depriving the field of important cross-disciplinary insights. Based on this in-depth mapping of the organizational control field, we review its constituent theories, outline the assumptions underlying organizational control research, and briefly discuss the critical perspective on organizational control.

3.1 Origins of Organizational Control

3.1.1 Ancient Bureaucracies

Ever since human societies gathered to collaborate on joint projects, people grappled with the classic problem of organizational control, which is ensuring that individuals look past their self-interests and support collective goals. Contrary to widespread belief, the concept of organizational control did not emerge in modern societies starting with the Industrial Revolution. The origins of organizational control trace back to Sumerian city-states around 2500 BC, where the Agricultural Revolution increased both population and social complexity, which triggered the growth of specialization and a rudimentary administrative hierarchy (Schott 2000). Ancient Chinese texts from 1100 BC similarly attest to the existence of a well-articulated bureaucracy and provide detailed instructions for leaders to:

(a) define departments, (b) allocate responsibilities among departments, (c) specify coordination links among officials, (d) define standard operating procedures and exceptions to these, and (e) audit officials' performance. Standardizing operating procedures would enhance efficiency, and formalizing procedures would ensure stability. The available incentives included ranks of positions, compensation, recognition, favors from the sovereign, reappointment, fines, removal from office, and reprimand (Rindova & Starbuck 1997: 152–153).

These ancient Chinese texts illustrate a surprisingly sophisticated understanding of rewards, punishments, and social norms and advocate for an approach to organizational control that is very similar to the one found in modern bureaucracies (cf., Weber 1978). Ancient Chinese leaders saw workers not only as energetic, intelligent, and capable but also as independent, self-interested, calculating, and deceitful. Moreover, control and power were considered as closely intertwined, and control approaches were expected not only to motivate subordinates but also to guard against their attempts to take over superiors' power (Dunbar & Statler 2010). Accordingly, leaders reasoned that an appropriate control system needs to foster competition by pitting workers against each other, define clear behavioral boundaries, and use rewards and punishments to induce desired behaviors (Rindova & Starbuck 1997). The ancient Chinese appreciated the power of incentives, such as monetary rewards and promotions, for inducing subordinates to support organizational interests, but they also cautioned that such incentives could trigger self-interested and deceitful manipulation on the part of subordinates (Dunbar & Statler 2010). Ancient Chinese texts also advised leaders to consider two kinds of contingencies in their control approaches – the social context (i.e., turbulent versus more tranquil situations) and workers' character and motivation – foreshadowing modern contingency models of organizational control (Rindova & Starbuck 1997).

3.1.2   Scientific Management

Many centuries later, the scientific management approach pioneered by Frederick Taylor (1911) similarly sought to achieve workers' subordination to organizational interests. By studying and analyzing individual tasks, as well as workers' capacities to perform them, Taylor set out to determine the optimal, "scientific" way to perform a task. This included breaking down a task into its simplest components and formalizing the task into a set of rules and procedures for all workers to follow. Armed with such an understanding of each task, managers could then set minimum output levels that workers had to attain before they would be entitled to additional rewards based on a piece-rate system. Taylor's approach is characterized by a clear hierarchical separation between managers, who have the prerogative to design work tasks based on their superior knowledge and skills, and workers, who are expected to do as directed and to be motivated to do it faster by a piece-rate incentive schedule (Haveman & Wetts 2019).

However, the extreme specialization of jobs and mechanistic principles of scientific management resulted in a dehumanization of work by deskilling and degrading workers (Haveman & Wetts 2019). Its disregard for workers generated boredom, low morale, absenteeism, conflict, and turnover (Mayo 1945), and the delays and costs resulting from resistance and labor disputes ultimately destroyed the economic value this approach had promised (Dunbar & Statler 2010).

3.1.3   The Human Relations Paradigm

The human relations paradigm emerged as a pragmatic attempt to rectify these problems by trying to balance organizational efficiency needs with the human needs of the workforce. A series of field experiments, among them the well-known Hawthorne studies (Mayo 1945; Roethlisberger & Dickson 1939), examined the impact of managerial interventions and organizational control and signaled a shift from an exclusive focus on task design and reachable output levels to how organizational control efforts influence workers' reaction, and how workers attribute meaning to them. These studies found that when workers were happy as a team with no sense of coercion, feelings of autonomy emerged, and workers would simply do whatever it took to help themselves, their teams, and their organizations. One of the key implications for organizational control that emerged from these studies was that organizational control does not necessarily require close supervision and direction (Dunbar & Statler 2010). By modeling and supporting desirable behavior rather than commanding, managers can allow workers discretion in determining goals and how best to achieve them. Managers' leadership and social skills can therefore substitute for continuous behavior control, thereby enabling ongoing cooperation on the job while simultaneously defusing worker alienation.

3.1.4   Weber's Bureaucracy

Max Weber's (1946) seminal research on bureaucracy constitutes the "rule platform" (Dunbar & Statler 2010: 19) underlying the majority of organizational control approaches. Weber's theory of bureaucracy emphasizes the merits of administrative structures and hierarchical authority based on meritocracy, universalism, and neutrality – in contrast to traditional control regimes' reliance on power, patronage, or charisma – as a foundation for efficiently and reliably coordinating and governing organizational tasks. The Weberian bureaucracy's main attributes are (1) a fixed division of labor by specialization, (2) qualification by examination, (3) thorough and expert training of personnel, (4) administration based on written documents and coordination by impersonal rules, and (5) authority legitimated by hierarchical office (Van Maanen & Barley

1984; Walton 2005). By the 1950s, the ascendance of large corporations and the growing importance of the public sector have made bureaucracy the standard organizational template and paradigmatic form of organization in both Europe and the United States (Dunbar & Statler 2010). Bureaucracy continues to flourish despite the economic, technological, and political changes of recent decades and can be found in increasingly diverse organizational settings, such as grassroots initiatives, hippie collectives, terrorist groups, technology start-ups, and online communities (see Monteiro & Adler 2022, for a recent review).

Despite its widespread adoption, bureaucracy has attracted considerable criticism, and it has long been a synonym for rigidity, conformism, and disenfranchisement (e.g., Crozier 1964; Merton 1940), making it appear outdated or even irrelevant for twenty-first-century organizations (Child & McGrath 2001). Metaphors such as "machine" (Mintzberg 1979), "mechanistic system" (Burns & Stalker 1961), and "iron cage" (Barker 1993) reflect the inflexible and lifeless character often ascribed to bureaucracies. Such criticism has proved persistent despite evidence of creativity and flexibility (e.g., Bigley & Roberts 2001; Klein et al. 2006) and of the empowering potential of bureaucracy (e.g., Adler & Borys 1996). Such criticism also appears hypocritical. As Perrow (1972) pointed out decades ago, "while people may lament the proliferation of red tape, in the next breath, many complain that 'there ought to be a rule;' they grumble about hierarchy, but in the next breath ask, 'who's in charge around here?'" The dramatic failures of de-bureaucratization efforts in the name of agility and market responsiveness – such as Turco's (2016) ethnography of a fast-growing social media marketing company that invested considerable effort in avoiding bureaucracy (defined in narrow and pejorative terms) only to rediscover its relevance – remind us that we should not take the benefits of bureaucracy's meritocratic and universalistic values for granted (Monteiro & Adler 2022).

In sum, far from being a product of modern industrial societies, ancient Sumerian and Chinese societies had already developed surprisingly sophisticated bureaucracies several millennia ago. In the early twentieth century, Frederick Taylor's scientific management approach and Max Weber's seminal work heralded the advent of modern bureaucracies. The human relations paradigm provided a counterweight to these efficient, but often dehumanizing, approaches and relaxed the assumption that organizational control always requires close supervision and direction. Last, despite persistent criticism, bureaucracies remain the prevailing form of organizing across a wide range of industries and organizations.

3.2   Document Co-citation Analysis of the Organizational Control Literature

To develop a more systematic understanding of the intellectual foundation of organizational control, we conducted a document co-citation analysis of the literature. A co-citation analysis uses bibliometric methods to examine how disciplines, fields, specialties, and individual publications are related to one another. More specifically, it analyzes the frequency with which two publications are cited together, which serves as a proxy for the similarity between them (Small 1973; White & Griffith 1981). A co-citation analysis therefore relies on a population of subject matter experts (i.e., published authors) to cluster publications together, based on their expert judgments of what they deem valuable or interesting and thus worthy of being cited in their own research (Zupic & Čater 2015). Frequently cited publications represent the key concepts and ideas in a scientific field, and document co-citation analysis maps out in great detail the relationship between these key ideas (Small 1973).

A co-citation analysis allows us to map the organizational control field's *intellectual structure*, which is the spatial representation of the interrelationships among published research, analogous to a geographic map (cf., Zupic & Čater 2015). More specifically, it reveals the *intellectual base* of organizational control, which is the relatively stable citation and co-citation footprint in the scientific literature over time (cf., Chen 2006). It also reveals the organizational control's *research front* (Price 1965) at a given time, which is the emergent and transient grouping of concepts and underlying research issues that represent the state-of-the-art thinking published in the most recent publications actively citing the field's intellectual base. In contrast to our narrative literature review at the beginning of this chapter, our co-citation analysis aims to produce a systematic, transparent, and reproducible review of organizational control by employing a quantitative approach to describe and evaluate the body of published control research.

Moreover, our derivation of an organizational control definition in Section 2.1 has further substantiated the cross-disciplinary nature of organizational control research. While that makes control theory widely applicable, and to a diverse range of phenomena, the question remains if new insights gained in one discipline quickly diffuse across disciplinary boundaries, or if the disciplines remain largely isolated from each other, with their own terminologies and their unique insights into the phenomenon. Such an insular approach would prevent research in any of the disciplines from capitalizing on insights from the others, thereby undermining the entire field's progress. In addition to mapping the organizational control field's intellectual structure, a co-citation analysis also allows us to assess the degree of fragmentation of this field and, if necessary, to suggest avenues of cross-disciplinary integration.

3.2.1   Data Collection and Analysis

For our co-citation analysis, we relied on the same key word search we conducted in Section 2.1 (see Section 2.3 for details on our search terms). Our search on September 15, 2022 resulted in 2,093 articles published between 1938 and 2022 in the peer-reviewed journals across management, accounting, marketing, finance, operations management, ethics, and information systems (IS) that are part of the Financial Times 50 list.[1] Of these articles, we reviewed titles, abstracts, and full texts to ascertain topical relevance for our document co-citation analysis and eliminated articles that did not contain at least one cited reference. Our selection process resulted in 1,148 articles that together contained 79,913 citations. We used OpenRefine (version 3.6.1) to clean and correct cited author and journal names before manually cleaning the remaining citation data, following recommendations in Zupic and Čater (2015). Given our focus on the intellectual structure of organizational control research, we also excluded references to highly (co-)cited methods papers (e.g., Aiken & West 1991; Nunnally 1978; Podsakoff et al. 2003; Podsakoff & Organ 1986).

We analyzed and visualized the complete set of bibliographical records, using CiteSpace version 6.2.R3 (Chen 2006). CiteSpace takes these bibliographic records – including terms from the citing and cited publications' titles, abstracts, key words, and subject categories – and models the field's intellectual structure as a synthesized network of cited references, with connections between references representing the strength of co-citation (Chen 2017).[2] By sequentially integrating structural and content-analysis components, CiteSpace supports the identification and analysis not only of clusters of publications, which reflect patterns in the overall body of knowledge, but also of key publications. Together, these provide insights into transient patterns and emerging trends of organizational control research over time (Chen 2004).

3.2.2   Results

There are eighty-four clusters in the co-citation network of the organizational control literature. Figure 3.1 shows the twenty largest clusters as a node-and-link diagram, with the cited publications being represented as nodes, and the co-cited publications being connected by lines. Figure 3.2 presents the same network but highlights the most-cited publications. Strongly connected publications are clustered together, and loosely connected publications are assigned to different clusters. To improve the clarity of our co-citation network, we used CiteNet's Pathfinder network scaling algorithm, which relies on a triangle inequality test to determine whether a particular link should be preserved or

---

[1] www.ft.com/content/3405a512-5cbb-11e1-8f1f-00144feabdc0

[2] More specifically, CiteSpace employs a progressive network analysis method: It uses a time-slicing technique to construct a series of network models over time before synthesizing these individual networks to construct an overall network for the systematic review of the literature. These networks are visualized with the help of a modified spring-embedder node placement algorithm, either as a cluster view or as a time-zone view.

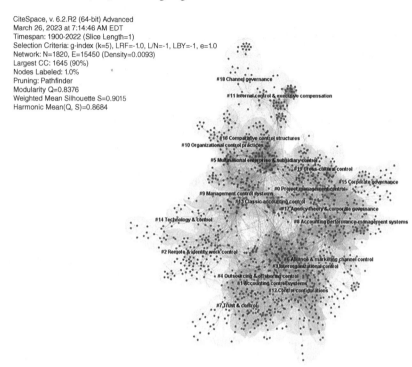

CiteSpace, v. 6.2.R2 (64-bit) Advanced
March 26, 2023 at 7:14:46 AM EDT
Timespan: 1900-2022 (Slice Length=1)
Selection Criteria: g-index (k=5), LRF=-1.0, L/N=-1, LBY=-1, e=1.0
Network: N=1820, E=15450 (Density=0.0093)
Largest CC: 1645 (90%)
Nodes Labeled: 1.0%
Pruning: Pathfinder
Modularity Q=0.8376
Weighted Mean Silhouette S=0.9015
Harmonic Mean(Q, S)=0.8684

Figure 3.1 Largest co-citation clusters in the organizational control literature (1963–2022)

eliminated, with the selection criterion being that a single-link path's weight should not exceed that of alternative paths of multiple links.[3]

The co-citation network of the organizational control literature has a high modularity Q score[4] of 0.84, which indicates a network that is reasonably divided into loosely coupled clusters, and a high weighted mean silhouette S score[5] of 0.90, which indicates that the homogeneity of clusters is, on average, very high (Chen et al. 2010). Clusters are arranged such that those connected by

---

[3] The Pathfinder scaling algorithm preserves the chronological growth patterns in co-citation networks better than multidimensional scaling (Chen & Morris 2003).

[4] The modularity Q measures the extent to which a network can be divided into independent modules. The modularity score ranges from 0 to 1. A low modularity suggests a network that cannot be reduced to clusters with clear boundaries, while a high modularity implies a well-structured network (Chen et al. 2010).

[5] The weighted average silhouette value of a cluster, ranging from −1 to 1, indicates the average homogeneity of a cluster. A value of 1 represents the perfect separation of a cluster from other clusters (Chen et al. 2010).

CiteSpace, v. 6.2.R2 (64-bit) Advanced
March 26, 2023 at 7:14:46 AM EDT
Timespan: 1900-2022 (Slice Length=1)
Selection Criteria: g-index (k=5), LRF=-1.0, L/N=-1, LBY=-1, e=1.0
Network: N=1820, E=15450 (Density=0.0093)
Largest CC: 1645 (90%)
Nodes Labeled: 1.0%
Pruning: Pathfinder
Modularity Q=0.8376
Weighted Mean Silhouette S=0.9015
Harmonic Mean(Q, S)=0.8684

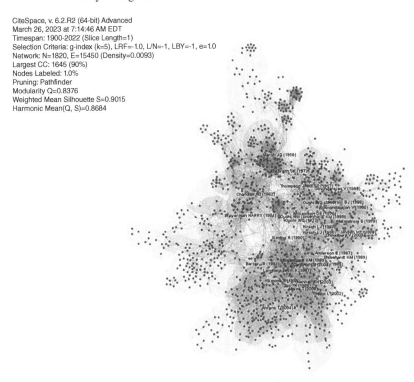

Figure 3.2 Most-cited intellectual base publications in the organizational control literature (1963–2022)

many publications are in close proximity to each other. For instance, Cluster 3 ("Interorganizational control") and Cluster 6 ("Alliance & marketing channel control") are relatively close to each other within the overall network and are connected by many publications. This suggests that publications written by authors in these two clusters were cited by many of the same articles, and significant overlap exists within these two knowledge domains.

Figure 3.3 shows the timeline view of the same co-citation network, which arranges its clusters along horizontal timelines. The time zones are arranged chronologically from left to right, such that a research front points back to its intellectual base (Chen 2006).[6] Each publication is positioned based on the earliest year in which it was cited in our dataset. Cluster labels are shown at the end of each cluster's timeline.

---

[6] The layout algorithm of the timeline view is a modified spring-embedder algorithm; the horizontal movement of a publication is restricted to its own time zone, and its vertical movement is determined by its connections to publications in other time zones (Chen 2006).

CiteSpace, v. 6.2 R2 (64-bit) Advanced
March 26, 2023 at 7:14:46 AM EDT
Timespan: 1900-2022 (Slice Length=1)
Selection Criteria: g-index (k=5), LRF=1.0, L/N=1, LBY=1, e=1.0
Network: N=1820, E=15450 (Density=0.0093)
Largest CC: 1645 (90%)
Nodes Labeled: 1.0%
Pruning: Pathfinder
Modularity Q=0.8576
Weighted Mean Silhouette S=0.9015
Harmonic Mean(Q, S)=0.8684

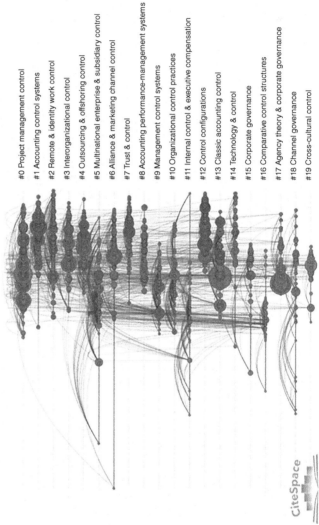

#0 Project management control
#1 Accounting control systems
#2 Remote & identity work control
#3 Interorganizational control
#4 Outsourcing & offshoring control
#5 Multinational enterprise & subsidiary control
#6 Alliance & marketing channel control
#7 Trust & control
#8 Accounting performance-management systems
#9 Management control systems
#10 Organizational control practices
#11 Internal control & executive compensation
#12 Control configurations
#13 Classic accounting control
#14 Technology & control
#15 Corporate governance
#16 Comparative control structures
#17 Agency theory & corporate governance
#18 Channel governance
#19 Cross-cultural control

Figure 3.3 Timeline view of largest co-citation clusters in the organizational control literature (1963–2022)

Influential publications. To identify gatekeepers (i.e., pivotal points between different specialties and disciplines) and tipping points in the evolving network, we calculated the cited publications' centrality metrics. The *betweenness centrality score* measures the extent to which the cited publication is on the shortest path that connects other publications in the network, which highlights publications that serve as a bridge connecting different clusters with each other. A publication's indegree centrality is the number of citations for this publication, indicating the degree to which a publication is popular, and therefore important in this knowledge domain (Chen et al. 2010).

We also identified influential research front publications for different time periods using CiteNet's burst detection algorithm, which detects whether and when the citation count of a particular publication has surged, allowing us to identify emergent areas in this literature even before they attract enough citations to be integrated into the field's intellectual base (Chen et al. 2010). Table 3.1 provides the twenty most-cited publications' citation counts; betweenness centralities; *citation burstness* (τ), which is an indicator of the most active areas of research and is conceptualized as the time span between a research front and its intellectual base measured as the difference between their average years of publications; and its novelty indicator Σ, which is measured as $(centrality + 1)^{burstness}$ (Chen et al., 2010). Table 3.2 provides the top-20 publications with the highest betweenness centrality scores, and Figure 3.4 lists all publications with citation bursts over time.

Cluster analysis. Table 3.3 summarizes the twenty largest clusters in the network. The cited publications in each cluster constitute the intellectual base of the organizational control literature, the citing articles represent the research front (Chen 2006). CiteSpace offers the capability to automatically characterize the nature of a co-citation cluster in terms of salient noun phrases extracted from the titles, abstracts, and index terms of those publications that cite a cluster (i.e., the research front), using two term-ranking algorithms: Labels selected by term frequency-inverse document frequency (TFIDF) weighting represent the most salient aspects of a cluster, whereas labels selected by log-likelihood ratio (LLR) tests tend to reflect a unique aspect of a cluster (Chen et al. 2010). In addition to these automatically extracted phrases, we examined the most-cited publications constituting both the research front and the intellectual base for each cluster to derive each cluster label.

Cluster 0 ("Project management control") represents the cluster with the largest intellectual base of 152 publications, which includes seven of the twenty most-cited publications in the organizational control literature's intellectual base (Eisenhardt 1985; Kirsch 1996, 1997; Ouchi 1977, 1980; Thompson 1967; Williamson 1975). This cluster's intellectual base is predominantly rooted in traditional management research (e.g., Eisenhardt 1985; Ouchi 1980; Thompson 1967) and, to a lesser extent, information systems

Table 3.1 *Twenty most influential publications*

Cited publications	Discipline	Cluster ID	Citation count	Betweenness centrality	Citation burstness (τ)	Novelty (Σ)
Ouchi (1979)	MGMT	13	160	0.03	n/a	n/a
Eisenhardt (1985)	MGMT	0	102	0.07	n/a	n/a
Ouchi (1980)	MGMT	0	86	0.06	5.77	1.43
Chenhall (2003)	ACCT	1	73	0.02	12.94	1.33
Thompson (1967)	MGMT	0	70	0.10	6.83	1.96
Williamson (1975)	MGMT	0	66	0.06	5.45	1.35
Williamson (1985)	MGMT	3	63	0.01	10.85	1.13
Eisenhardt (1989a)	MGMT	6	55	0.03	5.44	1.15
Barker (1993)	MGMT	4	53	0.08	5.80	1.57
Das and Teng (1998)	MGMT	4	47	0.07	8.40	1.74
Ouchi (1977)	MGMT	0	46	0.06	7.03	1.49
Simons (1995b)	ACCT	12	44	0.01	8.45	1.05
Eisenhardt (1989b)	MGMT	12	41	0.01	n/a	n/a
Langfield-Smith (1997)	ACCT	1	36	0.03	5.18	1.18
Cardinal et al. (2004)	MGMT	12	34	0	8.17	1.03
Braverman (1974)	MGMT	9	34	0.07	7.28	1.61
Kirsch (1997)	IS	0	33	0	8.69	1.02
Kirsch (1996)	IS	0	32	0	8.66	1.03
Chandler (1962)	MGMT	9	31	0.14	6.08	2.16
Galbraith (1973)	MGMT	5	30	0.07	4.86	1.40

Notes: τ = time span between a research front and its intellectual base, measured as the difference between their average years of publications; Σ = scientific novelty indicator, measured as the combined strength of structural and temporal properties of a node, that is, its betweenness centrality and citation burst: $(centrality + 1)^{burstness}$ (Chen et al. 2010).

(e.g., Choudhury & Sabherwal 2003; Kirsch 1996, 1997) and marketing (e.g., Jaworski 1988; Jaworski & MacInnis 1989; Weitz 1981). Across the three disciplines, this cluster's publications focus primarily on various control objectives and their applicability to project management or software/IS development. Its 1982 intellectual base contains eighteen publications with citation bursts, including key organizational control publications from the mid-1970s (e.g., Ouchi 1977; Ouchi & Maguire 1975; Williamson 1975) and 1980s (e.g., Ouchi 1980), and another citation burst with Kirsch's (1996, 1997) influential work on organizational control in the context of information system development, which indicates that this cluster as a whole captures a previously active area of research and indicates a former trend in the literature.

The research front citing this cluster consists of ninety-five articles across the management, information systems, accounting, and marketing disciplines that are focused broadly on management control systems (e.g., Baliga & Jaeger 1984; Chenhall 2003; Jaeger & Baliga 1985), control of outsourcing/offshoring

Table 3.2 *Top twenty publications with the highest betweenness centralities*

Cited publications	Discipline	Cluster ID	Citation count	Betweenness centrality	Citation burstness (τ)	Novelty (Σ)
March and Simon (1958)	MGMT	16	27	0.17	8.87	4.04
Chandler (1962)	MGMT	9	31	0.14	6.08	2.16
Anthony (1965)	MGMT	13	24	0.13	7.14	2.32
Blau and Scott (1962)	MGMT	5	9	0.11	5.49	1.80
Burns and Stalker (1961)	MGMT	9	21	0.10	n/a	n/a
Thompson (1967)	MGMT	0	70	0.10	6.83	1.96
Barker (1993)	MGMT	4	53	0.08	5.8	1.57
Barnard (1938)	MGMT	11	5	0.07	n/a	n/a
Galbraith (1973)	MGMT	5	30	0.07	4.86	1.40
Braverman (1974)	MGMT	9	34	0.07	7.28	1.61
Eisenhardt (1985)	MGMT	0	102	0.07	n/a	n/a
Das and Teng (1998)	MGMT	4	47	0.07	8.4	1.74
Etzioni (1961)	MGMT	5	8	0.06	n/a	n/a
Burchell et al. (1980)	ACCT	10	21	0.06	n/a	n/a
Andrews (1980)	MGMT	17	2	0.06	n/a	n/a
Ouchi (1980)	MGMT	0	86	0.06	5.77	1.43
Tichy et al. (1982)	MGMT	0	2	0.06	n/a	n/a
Williamson (1975)	MGMT	0	66	0.06	5.45	1.35
Ouchi (1977)	MGMT	0	46	0.06	7.03	1.49
Alchian and Demsetz (1972)	MGMT	18	18	0.06	n/a	n/a

Notes: τ = time span between a research front and its intellectual base, measured as the difference between their average years of publications; Σ = scientific novelty indicator, measured as the combined strength of structural and temporal properties of a node, that is, its betweenness centrality and citation burst: $(centrality + 1)^{burstness}$ (Chen et al. 2010).

projects (e.g., Gregory et al. 2013; Handley & Benton 2013; Srivastava & Teo 2012), and, to a lesser extent, corporate governance (e.g., Baysinger & Hoskisson 1990; Gómez-Mejía & Wiseman 1997), with an average publication year of 2001.

With 147 publications, the intellectual base of *Cluster 1 ("Accounting control systems")* is similar in size to Cluster 0, but it was published, on average, almost 20 years later, in 2000. More than half of its publications (and its most influential ones) are in the accounting discipline and comprise the influential reviews of Chenhall (2003) on contingency-based control research and of Langfield-Smith (1997) on management control systems and strategy, both among the top-20 publications. Malmi's (2008) editorial piece on typologies of control, Ahrens and Chapman's (2004) case study on enabling control, and Bisbe and Otley's (2004) survey research on the interactive use of

References	Year	Strength	Begin	End	1900 - 2022
March JG, 1958, ORGANIZATIONS, V0, P0	1958	8.87	1963	1995	
Blau PM, 1962, FORMAL ORG, V0, P0	1962	5.49	1963	1983	
Cyert RM, 1963, BEHAV THEORY FIRM, V0, P0	1963	5.77	1965	1994	
Tannenbaum AS, 1968, CONTROL ORG, V0, P0	1968	6.81	1972	1993	
Anthony RN, 1965, PLANNING CONTROL SYS, V0, P0	1965	7.14	1973	1991	
Chandler AD, 1962, STRATEGY STRUCTURE C, V0, P0	1962	6.08	1973	2000	
Ouchi WG, 1975, ADMIN SCI QUART, V20, P559, DOI 10.2307/2392023, DOI	1975	8.69	1981	1997	
Ouchi WG, 1977, ADMIN SCI QUART, V22, P95, DOI 10.2307/2391748, DOI	1977	7.03	1981	2004	
Otley DT, 1980, ACCOUNT ORG SOC, V5, P413, DOI 10.1016/0361-3682(80)90040-9, DOI	1980	6.06	1984	2004	
Mintzberg H, 1978, STRUCTURING ORG, V0, P0	1978	5.73	1984	1995	
Hayes RH, 1980, HARVARD BUS REV, V58, P67	1980	7.38	1985	1996	
Porter ME, 1980, COMPETITIVE STRATEGY, V0, P0	1980	7.33	1985	2003	
Otley DT, 1978, J ACCOUNT RES, V16, P122, DOI 10.2307/2490414, DOI	1978	4.88	1985	2003	
Merchant KA, 1985, CONTROL BUSINESS ORG, V0, P0	1985	5.73	1990	1996	
Porter ME, 1985, COMPETITIVE ADVANTAG, V0, P0	1985	5.64	1990	1993	
Lawrence PR, 1967, ORGAN ENV MANAGING DIF, V0, P0	1967	5.52	1990	1994	
Galbraith JR, 1973, DESIGNING COMPLEX OR, V0, P0	1973	4.86	1991	2004	
Govindarajan V, 1990, ACAD MANAGE J, V33, P259, DOI 10.2307/256325, DOI	1990	6.43	1992	2006	
Ouchi WG, 1980, ADMIN SCI QUART, V25, P129, DOI 10.2307/2392231, DOI	1980	5.77	1992	2004	
Williamson OE, 1985, ECON I CAPITALISM, V0, P0	1985	10.25	1993	2008	
Jaworski BJ, 1988, J MARKETING, V52, P23, DOI 10.2307/1251447, DOI	1988	5.49	1993	1997	
Hofstede GH, 1980, CULT CONSEQUENCE, V0, P0	1980	4.92	1994	2007	
Dimaggio PJ, 1983, AM SOCIOL REV, V48, P147, DOI 10.2307/2095101, DOI	1983	4.86	1994	1999	
Granovetter MS, 1985, AM J SOCIOL, V91, P481, DOI 10.1086/228311, DOI	1985	6.16	1996	2010	
Simons R, 1987, ACCOUNT ORG SOC, V12, P357, DOI 10.1016/0361-3682(87)90024-9, DOI	1987	4.93	1997	2011	
Dent JF, 1990, ACCOUNT ORG SOC, V15, P3, DOI 10.1016/0361-3682(90)90010-R, DOI	1990	4.92	1997	2006	
Braverman HARRY, 1974, LABOR MONOPOLY CAPIT, V0, P310	1974	7.28	1998	2006	
Edwards R, 1979, CONTESTED TERRAIN, V0, P0	1979	5.09	1998	2004	
Langfield-smith K, 1997, ACCOUNT ORG SOC, V22, P207, DOI 10.1016/S0361-3682(95)00040-2, DOI	1997	5.18	2000	2004	
Das TK, 1998, ACAD MANAGE REV, V23, P491, DOI 10.5465/AMR.1998.926623, DOI	1998	8.4	2001	2017	
Thompson JAMESD, 1967, ORGAN ACTION SOCIAL SC, V0, P0	1967	6.83	2002	2005	
Kunda G, 1992, ENG CULTURE CONTROL, V0, P0	1992	5.02	2002	2007	
Chenhall RH, 1986, ACCOUNT REV, V61, P16	1986	5.86	2003	2007	
abernethy MA, 1995, ACCOUNT ORG SOC, V20, P241, DOI 10.1016/0361-3682(94)E0014-L, DOI	1995	5.49	2003	2005	
Chenhall RH, 2003, ACCOUNT ORG SOC, V28, P127, DOI 10.1016/S0361-3682(01)00027-7, DOI	2003	12.94	2004	2020	
Barker JR, 1993, ADMIN SCI QUART, V38, P408, DOI 10.2307/2393374, DOI	1993	5.8	2004	2014	
Williamson OE, 1975, MARKETS HIERARCHIES, V0, P0	1975	5.45	2004	2009	
Briers M, 2001, ACCOUNT ORG SOC, V26, P237, DOI 10.1016/S0361-3682(00)00029-5, DOI	2001	4.85	2005	2011	
Dekker HC, 2004, ACCOUNT ORG SOC, V29, P27, DOI 10.1016/S0361-3682(02)00056-9, DOI	2004	8.62	2006	2012	
Cardinal LB, 2004, ORGAN SCI, V15, P411, DOI 10.1287/ORSC.1040.0084, DOI	2004	8.17	2007	2022	
Ahrens T, 2004, CONTEMP ACCOUNT RES, V21, P271, DOI 10.1506/VJR6-RP75-7GUX-XH0X, DOI	2004	7.56	2007	2019	
Poppo L, 2002, STRATEG MANAGE J, V23, P707, DOI 10.1002/SMJ.249, DOI	2002	7.4	2007	2020	
Tomkins C, 2001, ACCOUNT ORG SOC, V26, P161, DOI 10.1016/S0361-3682(00)00018-0, DOI	2001	5.73	2007	2011	
Cardinal LB, 2001, ORGAN SCI, V12, P19, DOI 10.1287/ORSC.12.1.19.10119, DOI	2001	5.56	2007	2019	
Uzzi B, 1997, ADMIN SCI QUART, V42, P35, DOI 10.2307/2393808, DOI	1997	5.26	2008	2015	
Das TK, 2001, ORGAN STUD, V22, P251, DOI 10.1177/0170840601222004, DOI	2001	5.06	2008	2020	
Coletti AL, 2005, ACCOUNT REV, V80, P477, DOI 10.2308/ACCR.2005.80.2.477, DOI	2005	4.87	2008	2022	
Choudhury V, 2003, INFORM SYST RES, V14, P291, DOI 10.1287/ISRE.14.3.291.16563, DOI	2003	8.85	2009	2019	
Kirsch LJ, 1997, INFORM SYST RES, V8, P215, DOI 10.1287/ISRE.8.3.215, DOI	1997	8.69	2009	2013	
Kirsch LJ, 1996, ORGAN SCI, V7, P1, DOI 10.1287/ORSC.7.1.1, DOI	1996	8.66	2009	2019	
Bisbe J, 2004, ACCOUNT ORG SOC, V29, P709, DOI 10.1016/J.AOS.2003.10.010, DOI	2004	6.45	2009	2020	
Adler PS, 1996, ADMIN SCI QUART, V41, P61, DOI 10.2307/2393986, DOI	1996	6.44	2009	2019	
Henri JF, 2006, ACCOUNT ORG SOC, V31, P529, DOI 10.1016/J.AOS.2005.07.001, DOI	2006	6.95	2010	2020	
Kirsch LJ, 2002, MANAGE SCI, V48, P484, DOI 10.1287/MNSC.48.4.484.204, DOI	2002	6.58	2010	2015	
Widener SK, 2007, ACCOUNT ORG SOC, V32, P757, DOI 10.1016/J.AOS.2007.01.001, DOI	2007	5.85	2010	2020	
Ahrens T, 2007, ACCOUNT ORG SOC, V32, P1, DOI 10.1016/J.AOS.2006.09.013, DOI	2007	5.68	2010	2018	
Diamantopoulos A, 2001, J MARKETING RES, V38, P269, DOI 10.1509/JMKR.38.2.269.18845, DOI	2001	4.93	2010	2011	
Anderson SW, 2005, MANAGE SCI, V51, P1734, DOI 10.1287/MNSC.1050.0456, DOI	2005	6.49	2011	2017	
Merchant KA, 2007, MANAGE CONTROL S, V2ND, P0	2007	5.31	2011	2019	
Jensen MC, 1976, J FINANC ECON, V3, P305, DOI 10.1016/0304-405X(76)90026-X, DOI	1976	5.01	2011	2014	
Jap SD, 2000, J MARKETING RES, V37, P227, DOI 10.1509/JMKR.37.2.227.18735, DOI	2000	4.91	2011	2015	
Holmstrom B, 1991, J LAW ECON ORGAN, V7, P24, DOI 10.1093/JLEO/7.SPECIAL_ISSUE.24, DOI	1991	4.91	2011	2015	
Eisenhardt KM, 1989, ACAD MANAGE REV, V14, P57, DOI 10.2307/258191, DOI	1989	5.44	2012	2015	
Snell SA, 1992, ACAD MANAGE J, V35, P292, DOI 10.2307/256375, DOI	1992	6.03	2013	2019	
Baumeister RF, 1998, J PERS SOC PSYCHOL, V74, P1252, DOI 10.1037/0022-3514.74.5.1252, DOI	1998	5.7	2015	2020	
Malmi T, 2008, MANAGE ACCOUNT RES, V19, P287, DOI 10.1016/J.MAR.2008.09.003, DOI	2008	15.28	2016	2022	
Grabner I, 2013, ACCOUNT ORG SOC, V38, P407, DOI 10.1016/J.AOS.2013.09.002, DOI	2013	12.21	2016	2020	
Simons R, 1995, LEVERS CONTROL, V0, P0	1995	8.45	2016	2020	
Milgrom P, 1995, J ACCOUNT ECON, V19, P179, DOI 10.1016/0165-4101(94)00382-F, DOI	1995	5.12	2016	2020	
Bonner SE, 2002, ACCOUNT ORG SOC, V27, P303, DOI 10.1016/S0361-3682(01)00052-6, DOI	2002	4.98	2016	2020	
Grabner I, 2014, ACCOUNT REV, V89, P1729, DOI 10.2308/ACCR-50756, DOI	2014	7.48	2019	2020	
Bedford DS, 2016, ACCOUNT ORG SOC, V51, P12, DOI 10.1016/J.AOS.2016.04.002, DOI	2016	5.61	2019	2020	
Bedford DS, 2015, MANAGE ACCOUNT RES, V28, P12, DOI 10.1016/J.MAR.2015.04.003, DOI	2015	5.61	2019	2020	
Bedford DS, 2015, MANAGE ACCOUNT RES, V27, P2, DOI 10.1016/J.MAR.2015.04.002, DOI	2015	5.61	2019	2020	
Cardinal LB, 2017, ACAD MANAGE ANN, V11, P559, DOI 10.5465/ANNALS.2014.0086, DOI	2017	5.39	2019	2022	

Figure 3.4 Publications with citation bursts

management control systems and its influence on product innovation complement the influential accounting base in this cluster. All of these publications form the core of this cluster's eight publications with citation bursts, starting in the early 2000s with Langfield-Smith (1997) and continuing until 2020 (Baumeister et al. 1998; Chenhall 2003), highlighting this cluster as an active area of research and indicating an emerging trend in the literature. Slightly less than a third of the publications in this cluster's intellectual base are foundational works in the broader management literature (e.g., Baumeister et al. 1998; Kaplan & Norton 1996). The research front citing this cluster consists of sixty-four articles predominantly from the accounting field, which include

Table 3.3 *Top-ranked clusters representing intellectual bases and research fronts in organizational control*

		Intellectual base					Research front			
ID	Label	Size	Silhouette	Mean year	Discipline (%)	Representative publications	Size	Mean year	Discipline (%)	Representative articles
0	Project management control	152	0.749	1982	MGMT (76), IS (10), MKT (6)	Eisenhardt (1985); Kirsch (1997); Ouchi (1980)	95	2001	MGMT (53), IS (24), ACCT (11), MKT (8)	Baysinger and Hoskisson (1990); Chenhall (2003); Gregory et al. (2013)
1	Accounting control systems	147	0.819	2000	ACCT (57), MGMT (31)	Chenhall (2003); Kaplan and Norton (1996); Langfield-Smith (1997)	64	2011	ACCT (83), ETHICS (6), MGMT (6), MKT (5)	Braumann et al. (2020); Caglio and Ditillo (2008); Chenhall (2003)
2	Remote & identity work control	120	0.869	1996	MGMT (65)	Barley and Kunda (1992); Edwards (1979); Kunda (1992)	33	2009	MGMT (91), ACCT (6)	Huber and Brown (2017); Rahman and Valentine (2021); Sewell (1998)
3	Interorganizational control	89	0.930	1992	MGMT (77), MKT (7), OPS (7)	Gulati (1995); Poppo and Zenger (2002); Williamson (1985)	38	2004	MGMT (63), OPS (18), ACCT (11), MKT (5)	Cao and Lumineau (2015); Dekker (2008); Luo et al. (2008)
4	Outsourcing & offshoring control	80	0.899	1996	MGMT (51), ACCT (17)	Barker (1993); Das and Teng (1998); Dekker (2004)	46	2008	ACCT (43), MGMT (43), OPS (7)	Caglio and Ditillo (2008); Cobb et al. (2001); Vélez et al. (2008)
5	Multinational enterprise & subsidiary control	79	0.933	1968	MGMT (67)	Galbraith (1973); Hofstede (1980); Lawrence and Lorsch (1967)	27	1993	MGMT (74), ACCT (11), OPS (7)	Baliga and Jaeger (1984); Chow et al. (1994); Gupta and Govindarajan (1991)
6	Alliance & marketing channel control	78	0.872	1991	MGMT (79), MKT (13)	Anderson and Oliver (1987); Eisenhardt (1989a); Ring and Van de Ven (1994)	43	2007	MGMT (49), MKT (23), ACCT (12), IS (7), ETHICS (5), OPS (5)	Grewal et al. (2013); Shah and Swaminathan (2008); Vélez et al. (2008)

Table 3.3 (cont.)

					Intellectual base				Research front	
ID	Label	Size	Silhouette	Mean year	Discipline (%)	Representative publications	Size	Mean year	Discipline (%)	Representative articles
7	Trust & control	70	0.905	2001	MGMT (36), ACCT (33), MKT (16)	Bello and Gilliland (1997); Coletti et al. (2005); Das and Teng (2001)	31	2015	ACCT (68), MKT (19), MGMT (6)	Long (2018); Shah and Swaminathan (2008); Vélez et al. (2008)
8	Accounting performance-management systems	69	0.936	1991	ACCT (81), MGMT (10)	Kaplan and Norton (1992); Merchant (1981); Otley (1978)	24	2000	ACCT (92)	Chenhall (2003); Luft and Shields (2003); Merchant et al. (2003)
9	Management control systems	69	0.941	1975	MGMT (55), ACCT (5)	Braverman (1974); Burns and Stalker (1961); Chandler (1962)	25	1995	MGMT (56), ACCT (40)	Baliga and Jaeger (1984); Hoskisson and Hitt (1988); Neimark and Tinker (1986)
10	Organizational control practices	67	0.957	1976	MGMT (39), ACCT (29), MKT (5)	Ahrens and Chapman (2002); Bower (1970); Burchell et al. (1980)	12	1986	ACCT (58), MGMT (25), MKT (17)	Ahrens and Mollona (2007); Collins (1982); Hofstede (1981)
11	Internal control & executive compensation	65	0.971	1962	MGMT (50), ACCT (13), OPS (5)	Barnard (1938); DeCoster and Fertakis (1968); Simon (1957)	4	1973	ACCT (50), MGMT (50)	Gonedes (1970); Lowe (1971); Zannetos (1964)
12	Control configurations	61	0.904	2005	ACCT (55), MGMT (38)	Cardinal et al. (2004); Grabner and Moers (2013); Simons (1995b)	48	2016	ACCT (58), MGMT (23), IS (13), ETHICS (6)	Braumann et al. (2020); Chown (2021); Wiener et al. (2016)
13	Classic accounting control	61	0.894	1986	ACCT (45), MGMT (43), IS (6)	Otley (1980); Ouchi (1979); Simons (1990)	69	2000	ACCT (72), MGMT (20)	Bhimani (1999); Giglioni and Bedeian (1974); Henri (2006b)

No.	Topic	Count	Value	Year	Codes	References	No.	Year	Codes	References
14	Technology & control	53	0.946	1999	MGMT (57), ACCT (20)	Barley (1986); Briers and Chua (2001); Drazin and Van de Ven (1985)	14	2012	ACCT (50), MGMT (50)	Anthony (2021); Massa and O'Mahony (2021); Quattrone and Hopper (2005)
15	Corporate governance	51	0.924	1985	MGMT (65), ACCT (10)	Daniel and Reitsperger (1991a); Hayes and Abernathy (1980); Hoskisson and Hitt (1988)	13	1996	MGMT (85), ACCT (15)	Baysinger and Hoskisson (1990); Hitt et al. (1996); Ittner et al. (1997)
16	Comparative control structures	50	0.957	1960	MGMT (68)	Brehm (1966); Likert (1961); March and Simon (1958)	10	1975	MGMT (100)	Levine (1973); McMahon and Perritt (1973); Smith and Tannenbaum (1963)
17	Agency theory & corporate governance	48	0.935	1988	MGMT (60), ACCT (11)	Beatty and Zajac (1994); Healy (1985); Jensen and Meckling (1976)	38	2005	MGMT (76), ACCT (13)	Baysinger and Hoskisson (1990); Merchant et al. (2003); Walsh and Seward (1990)
18	Channel governance	45	0.925	1974	MGMT (53), MKT (12)	Alchian and Demsetz (1972); Heide and John (1988); Mintzberg et al. (1976)	14	1997	MGMT (79), MKT (21)	Celly and Frazier (1996); Giglioni and Bedeian (1974); Gómez-Mejía and Wiseman (1997)
19	Cross-cultural control	43	0.943	1982	MGMT (72), ACCT (16), OPS (7)	Crozier (1964); Govindarajan and Gupta (1985); Lorange et al. (1986)	17	1991	ACCT (59), MGMT (41)	Bhimani (1999); Daniel and Reitsperger (1991b); Harrison and McKinnon (1999)

reviews (e.g., Caglio & Ditillo 2008) and articles on a range of control topics, such as work building on Simons's (1995b) levers of control framework (e.g., Braumann et al. 2020; Gerdin et al. 2019; Mundy 2010). Notably, this research front also contained a number of articles from the business ethics discipline that examine, for instance, the impact of organizational control on social (e.g., Lisi 2018) and environmental performance (e.g., Wijethilake et al. 2018), as well as a small number of articles from management (e.g., Shi et al. 2017) and marketing (e.g., Katsikeas et al. 2018).

The intellectual base of *Cluster 2 ("Remote & identity work control")* dates back to 1996 and consists of 120 publications, with almost two-thirds from the management discipline (e.g., Barley & Kunda 1992; Edwards 1979; Kunda 1992), with the latter two publications being the only ones in this cluster with citation bursts, and the rest coming from across a wide disciplinary spectrum, including accounting, sociology, and philosophy, but not containing any of the top-20 intellectual base publications. This cluster's research front of thirty-three articles (with a mean year of 2009) is almost entirely in the management discipline and focuses on diverse organizational control settings, such as remote work (e.g., Hafermalz 2021; Rahman & Valentine 2021; Wilner et al. 2017), and the implications of organizational control for worker identity and resistance (e.g., Alvesson & Willmott 2002; Huber & Brown 2017; Sewell 1998).

Besides a small number of publications in marketing (e.g., Heide & John 1992; Jap & Ganesan 2000) and operations management (e.g., Jayaraman et al. 2013; Liu et al. 2009), the intellectual base of *Cluster 3 ("Interorganizational control")* is predominantly in the management discipline and ranges from Williamson's (1985) seminal work on transaction cost economics, which is one of four publications in this cluster with citation bursts and the only top-20 reference in this intellectual base, to Gulati's (1995) and Poppo and Zenger's (2002, another publication with a citation burst) influential publications on interfirm governance, with an average publication year of 1992. As is evident from its associated 2004 research front, this intellectual base has influenced subsequent research in management (e.g., Das & Teng 1998; Handley & Angst 2015; Luo et al. 2008), operations management (e.g., Cao & Lumineau 2015; Li et al. 2008; Stouthuysen et al. 2012), and accounting (e.g., Chalos & O'Connor 2004; Dekker 2004, 2008), that focused on interorganizational control in buyer–supplier relationships, joint ventures, and via contractual governance.

Cluster 4's ("Outsourcing & offshoring control") intellectual base from 1996 is dominated by management and, to a lesser extent, accounting, and goes back to two top-20 control publications – Barker's (1993) work, which is part of a critical perspective on organizational control (see Section 3.5 for details), and Das and Teng's (1998) study on the interplay of trust and control in interorganizational relationships – as well as an influential publication in the accounting discipline, that is, Dekker's (2004) study on the control of interorganizational relationships. These publications further represent four of the total of six publications in this cluster with citation bursts. This work has influenced a 2008 research front on interorganizational work similar to Cluster 3 that focuses on outsourcing and offshoring in the accounting literature (e.g., Caglio & Ditillo 2008; Free 2007; Vélez et al. 2008) as well as other interfirm control issues in the management discipline (e.g., Das & Teng 2001; Fryxell et al. 2002; Luo et al. 2008).

The 1968 intellectual base *of Cluster 5 ("Multinational enterprise & subsidiary control")* is in the early management field going back to work on contingency and information processing theory (e.g., Galbraith 1973, which is another top-20 intellectual base publication; as well as Lawrence & Lorsch 1967) and Hofstede's (1980) work on international differences in organizational culture. These publications are three of the total of four publications in this cluster with citation bursts. This cluster's intellectual base has influenced a 1993 research front in the management and accounting disciplines, on the control of multi-national enterprises and on headquarters' control of their (internationally) dispersed subsidiaries (e.g., Baliga & Jaeger 1984; Chow et al. 1994; Gupta & Govindarajan 1991).

Cluster 6's ("Alliance & marketing channel control") intellectual base from 1991 is predominantly in management, represented by foundational publications on agency theory (e.g., Eisenhardt 1989a, which is the only top-20 publication and the only publication with a citation burst in this cluster), and on the governance of interorganizational relationships (e.g., Ring & Van de Ven 1994). The remainder of this cluster's intellectual base consists mostly of marketing publications, such as Anderson and Oliver's (1987) publication contrasting behavior-based and outcome-based salesforce controls, and Jaworski et al.'s (1993) publication on marketing control. Cluster 6's 2007 research front covers three disciplines – management, marketing, and accounting – and can be characterized by its focus on the governance of interfirm alliances (e.g., Luo et al. 2008; Shah & Swaminathan 2008; Vélez et al. 2008) and firms' marketing channels (e.g., Grewal et al. 2013; Gundlach & Cannon 2010).

The intellectual base of *Cluster 7 ("Trust & control")* is balanced across management, accounting, and, to a lesser extent, marketing. With a mean publication year of 2001, it is the second most recent cluster. Key publications focus on trust and control in strategic alliances (e.g., Coletti et al. 2005; Das & Teng 2001, which are also two of the total of four publications in this cluster with citation bursts) as well as control and flexibility in export channels (e.g., Bello & Gilliland 1997). This cluster's 2015 research front mainly consists of accounting (e.g., Bonner & Sprinkle 2002; Merchant & Van der Stede 2007, two additional publications with citation bursts) and marketing articles (e.g., Anderson & Weitz 1992; Bergen et al. 1992), with a similar focus on trust and control (e.g., Long 2018; Shah & Swaminathan 2008; Vélez et al. 2008).

Cluster 8 ("Accounting performance-management systems") is an almost exclusively accounting cluster. Its 1991 intellectual base features classic accounting control (e.g., Hirst 1983; Merchant 1981; Otley 1978, which we will discuss in Section 4.1.7) and management control work (e.g., Kaplan & Norton 1992), with Otley (1978) being the only publication with a citation burst in this cluster. This cluster has further influenced a 2000 research front predominantly in the accounting discipline, on incentive and management control systems (e.g., Chenhall 2003; Chow et al. 1999; Merchant et al. 2003).

With a mean year of 1975, *Cluster 9 ("Management control systems")* is one of the oldest clusters in terms of its intellectual roots. A little more than half of its intellectual base consists of management publications, most notably three seminal books: Burns and Stalker's (1961) contingency-theoretic typology distinguishing organic and mechanistic organizational structures; Chandler's (1962) analysis of the interplay of strategy and structure; and Braverman's (1974) discussion of management's and technology's influence on labor (with the latter two being among the top-20 publications and comprising the two publications total in this cluster with citation bursts). A small number of accounting publications (e.g., Cammann 1976) are also part of this cluster's intellectual base. The 1995 research front citing this cluster includes both management (e.g., Baliga & Jaeger 1984; Cheng & McKinley 1983; Hoskisson & Hitt 1988) and accounting work (e.g., Langfield-Smith 1997; Neimark & Tinker 1986; Quattrone & Hopper 2005), and is focused broadly on management control systems.

Cluster 10's ("Organizational control practices") intellectual base from 1976 is situated in early management (e.g., Argyris 1952; Bower 1970) and accounting research (e.g., Ahrens & Chapman 2002; Burchell et al. 1980) and contains a small number of marketing publications (e.g., Anderson 1985). It has influenced a 1986 research front dominated by accounting (e.g., Ahrens & Chapman 2007; Ahrens & Mollona 2007; Collins 1982) and a few management (e.g., Dermer 1974; Lorange 1974; Markham et al. 1984) and marketing articles (e.g., Anderson & Oliver 1987; Jaworski & MacInnis 1989), focused on organizational control practices.

With a mean publication year of 1962, *Cluster 11 ("Internal control & executive compensation")* is the second oldest cluster in terms of its intellectual base and goes back to Barnard's (1938) and Simon's (1957) work in management and DeCoster and Fertakis's (1968) work in accounting, with a small number of operations management publications (e.g., Hillier 1967). This base is cited by the oldest (1973) and smallest research front, with only four articles that are equally balanced between management and accounting, and focused on internal controls (Gonedes 1970; Lowe 1971; Zannetos 1964) and executive compensation (Gómez-Mejía et al. 1987).

Cluster 12 ("Control configurations") is the most recent cluster both in terms of its intellectual base and its research front. It is also the cluster we will build on most closely to develop our reconceptualizing of organizational control in Chapter 6. This cluster reflects the control literature's shift from focusing on single controls and contingency-theoretic approaches to acknowledging the interactive nature of controls and analyzing configurations of controls and their impact on (performance) outcomes. This cluster's 2005 intellectual base is focused on balanced, holistic forms of control, often with a configurational perspective that accounts for complementarities among control elements. It consists of predominantly accounting publications (e.g., Simons's (1995b) influential levers of control framework we will discuss in Section 4.1.7) and, to a lesser extent, management publications (e.g., Cardinal et al. 2004), with both of these being among the top-20 publications. Its twelve publications with citation bursts (Adler & Borys 1996; Bedford 2015; Bedford & Malmi 2015; Bedford et al. 2016; Cardinal 2001; Cardinal et al. 2004, 2017; Grabner 2014; Grabner & Moers 2013; Holmstrom & Milgrom 1991; Simons 1995b; Widener 2007), the second highest for any cluster in this literature, are evidence that the research in this cluster represents an emerging trend in the organizational control literature. This intellectual base is cited by a 2016 knowledge front consisting of accounting (e.g., Braumann et al. 2020; Gerdin et al. 2019; Posch 2020), management (e.g., Chown 2021; Stendahl et al. 2021; Walter et al. 2021), and information systems articles (e.g., Gregory et al. 2013; Rustagi et al. 2008; Wiener et al. 2016) that is focused, like its intellectual base, on complementarities among organizational controls. Like Cluster 1, this cluster's research front also contains a number of ethics publications that, among others, examine the impact of organizational control on firms' environmental capabilities (Albertini 2019) and review the literature on the ethical implications of organizational control systems (Endenich & Trapp 2020).

Cluster 13's ("Classic accounting control") intellectual base from 1986 is in accounting (e.g., Otley 1980; Simons 1990, with the former being part of this cluster's five total publications with citation bursts) and management (e.g., Anthony 1965, which is another publication in this cluster with a citation burst; Ouchi 1979, which is one of the top-20 highest-cited publications), and contains a small number of publications in information systems (e.g., Benbasat & Taylor 1978). Its associated 2000 research front is predominantly in the accounting field (e.g., Bhimani 1999; Henri 2006a, 2006b) and, to a lesser extent, in management (e.g., Daft & Macintosh 1984; Giglioni & Bedeian 1974; Goold & Quinn 1990), and it consists mainly of organizational control research in the classic agency theory tradition.

Cluster 14's ("Technology & control") intellectual roots from 1999 are based on management (e.g., Barley 1986; Drazin & Van de Ven 1985) and accounting disciplines (e.g., Briers & Chua 2001, this cluster's only publication with a citation burst), and have induced a 2012 research front equally balanced between accounting (e.g., Ahrens & Chapman 2007; Chua & Mahama 2007; Quattrone & Hopper 2005) and management (e.g., Anthony 2021; Massa & O'Mahony 2021; Rahman & Valentine 2021). Topics that are covered in this cluster are the implications of new technologies for organization structure and control.

Cluster 15's ("Corporate governance") intellectual base from 1985 is primarily in management (e.g., Hayes & Abernathy 1980, which is also this cluster's only publication with a citation burst; Hill & Hoskisson 1987; Hoskisson & Hitt 1988), including Hoskisson et al.'s (1993) macro control framework we will discuss in Section 4.1.7, complemented by a few publications in accounting (e.g., Daniel & Reitsperger 1991a). Its 1996 research front is similarly management-focused with a few accounting publications and focuses broadly on corporate governance issues (e.g., Baysinger & Hoskisson 1990; Hitt et al. 1996; Kochhar & David 1996).

The oldest intellectual base from 1960 can be found in *Cluster 16 ("Comparative control structures")* and consists mostly of management research (e.g., Brehm 1966; Likert 1961; March & Simon 1958, this cluster's only publication with a citation burst). This cluster also contains Tannenbaum's (1962) influential work on control graphs, which we will discuss in more detail in Section 4.1.7. The relatively small associated research front from 1975 is entirely management-centered and focuses on comparing the efficacy of internal control structures (e.g., Levine 1973; McMahon & Perritt 1973; Smith & Tannenbaum 1963).

Although *Cluster 17's ("Agency theory & corporate governance")* 1988 intellectual base is dominated by management (e.g., Banker et al. 1996; Beatty & Zajac 1994; Rumelt 1974) and a few accounting publications (e.g., Healy 1985), the most highly cited publications in this base contain many foundational agency theory publications (e.g., Fama & Jensen 1983; Holmstrom 1979; Jensen & Meckling 1976, this cluster's only publication with a citation burst). This cluster's associated 2005 research front is similarly management-dominated (e.g., Baysinger & Hoskisson 1990; O'Connell & O'Sullivan 2014; Walsh & Seward 1990), complemented by a few accounting publications (e.g., Arya et al. 1997; Christie & Zimmerman 1994; Merchant et al. 2003), and focuses broadly on corporate governance issues from an agency theory perspective.

Cluster 18's ("Channel governance") intellectual base from 1974 is in the management discipline (e.g., Bazerman et al. 1998; Brech 1965; Mintzberg et al. 1976) and, to some extent, in marketing (e.g., Heide & John 1988), but the most highly cited publication is Alchian and Demsetz's (1972) seminal paper on transaction cost economics. Mirroring its intellectual base, this cluster's 1997 research front is predominantly in management (e.g., Giglioni & Bedeian 1974; Gómez-Mejía & Wiseman 1997; Sharma 1997) and, to some extent, marketing (e.g., Sivadas & Dwyer 2000), both with a notable focus on the governance of buyer–supplier or channel relationships (e.g., Celly & Frazier 1996; Lassar & Kerr 1996; Stump & Heide 1996).

Cluster 19's ("Cross-cultural control") intellectual base from 1982 is in management (e.g., Crozier 1964; Lorange et al. 1986) and, to a lesser extent, in accounting (e.g., Govindarajan & Gupta 1985) and operations management (e.g., Buffa 1984). Its associated 1991 research front provides a cross-cultural comparison of organizational control systems in both management (e.g., Daniel & Reitsperger 1991b; Goold 1991; McMahon & Perritt 1973) and accounting (e.g., Bhimani 1999; Chow et al. 1999; Harrison & McKinnon 1999).

3.2.3 Reflection on the Intellectual Structure of Organizational Control

When we embarked on our quest to map the organizational control literature, we expected to encounter the often-lamented fragmentation of the field, with disciplinary silos, and with little cross-fertilization between the disciplines. We were encouraged to find, however, that only three of the twenty largest clusters were dominated by just one discipline, and that all others contained significant numbers of publications from across multiple disciplines. The same was true for the research fronts associated with each cluster, with only two out of twenty dominated by just one discipline. These results suggest that both the intellectual bases and the research fronts in the organizational control literature are formed around phenomena – such as project management control (Cluster 0) and outsourcing and offshoring control (Cluster 4) – and are built on, and tend to attract interest from, researchers across disciplinary boundaries. Management is the dominant discipline across intellectual bases (with 51 percent of all publications across all twenty intellectual bases), followed by accounting (20 percent across thirteen bases), marketing (3 percent across six bases), information systems (2 percent across two bases), and operations management (1 percent across three bases). The associated research fronts are slightly more diverse, with management representing 44 percent of all publications across nineteen out of twenty research fronts, followed by accounting (39 percent across eighteen fronts), marketing (6 percent across seven fronts), information systems (6 percent across three fronts), and operations management (3 percent across four fronts). The most frequently encountered combination, by far, is management and accounting, which occurred in thirteen out of twenty intellectual bases and seventeen out of twenty research fronts, followed by management and marketing (in six bases and seven fronts), accounting and marketing (in six fronts), and management and operations management (in three bases and four fronts).

Moving from the clusters to individual publications, the most-cited publications represent seminal works on organizational control (e.g., Chenhall 2003;

Eisenhardt 1985; Ouchi 1979, 1980), complemented by works on transaction cost theory (Williamson 1975, 1985) and contingency theory (Galbraith 1973; Thompson 1967), predominantly in the management discipline, with a few works in accounting and information systems (see Table 3.1 for details). The most central publications, in contrast, are classic management books (e.g., Anthony 1965; Barnard 1938; Blau & Scott 1962; Burns & Stalker 1961; Chandler 1962; Galbraith 1973; March & Simon 1958; Thompson 1967) that serve as bridges between the different clusters. Moreover, Barker's (1993) critical study of concertive control, which has the highest betweenness centrality score of all publications focused on organizational control, and Das and Teng's (1998) article on trust and control in alliances serve as bridges between their own Cluster 4 (Outsourcing & offshoring control) and Cluster 1 (Accounting control systems), Cluster 2 (Remote & identity work control), Cluster 3 (Interorganizational control), and Cluster 6 (Alliance & marketing channel control). Four central management publications in Cluster 0 (Eisenhardt 1985; Ouchi 1977, 1980; Williamson 1975) serve as bridges to the surrounding clusters (Clusters 5, 9, 15, 17, and 19) and the rest of the co-citation network. Burchell et al.'s (1980) work on the role of accounting in practice connects their own Cluster 10 (Organizational control practices) with Cluster 5 (Multinational enterprise & subsidiary control) and Cluster 16 (Comparative control structures). Furthermore, Alchian and Demsetz's (1972) seminal work on transaction cost economics connects Cluster 18 (Channel governance) via Cluster 10 (Organizational control practices), Cluster 11 (Internal control & executive compensation), and Cluster 16 (Comparative control structures) to the rest of the co-citation network.

As evident from Figure 3.4's list of publications with citation bursts, which allows us to identify emergent areas in this literature over time, the management discipline dominated early citation bursts (1963–1984), before the emergence of accounting bursts in 1984 triggered by Otley's (1978) control framework, followed by marketing bursts in 1993 triggered by Jaworski (1988), and, much later, the information system bursts in 2009 triggered by Choudhury and Sabherwal (2003) and Kirsch (1996, 1997). Since 2016, citation bursts shifted to an almost exclusive focus on accounting work, with the notable exception of Cardinal and colleagues' (2017) recent review of the organizational control literature. It is further notable that several publications experienced a long lag between their initial publication and their subsequent influence on the field. Thompson's (1967) contingency-theoretic publication, for instance, took more than 30 years to influence a research front on project management control (Cluster 0). Braverman's (1974) discussion of the degradation of work in the twentieth century experienced a citation burst almost 25 years later and inspired Cluster 9's research front on management control systems. And Simons's (1995b) publication highlighting complementarities between organizational control types inspired a 2016 research front on control configurations (Cluster 12).

And last, early citation bursts reflect foundational organizational control frameworks and their underlying theories. Examples of the former are Tannenbaum's control graph and Simons's levers of control (both of which we will discuss in Section 4.1.7), Ouchi's control framework (Section 3.4), and Otley's control framework (Section 4.1.7). Examples of the latter include March and colleagues' behavioral theory (Section 3.3.1), Jensen and colleagues' agency theory (Section 3.3.2), Williamson's transaction cost theory (Section 3.3.3), contingency theory (Section 3.3.4), and information processing theory (Section 3.3.5). In Section 3.3, we will build on this intellectual map of the organizational control literature and review the key theories underlying organizational control.

3.3   Key Theories and Assumptions Underlying Organizational Control

3.3.1   Behavioral Theory

The behavioral theory of the firm[7] set out to address the criticism of the machine-like and mechanistic character of Weber's bureaucracy and to provide a more realistic account of human constraints in organizations. This theory is based on the premise that "decision-making is the heart of administration" (Simon 1947: xiv), but it also acknowledges that human beings are not the perfect calculators and decision-makers that economists had assumed. Instead, "the vocabulary of administrative theory must be derived from the logic and psychology of human choice" (Simon 1947: xiv) and be "concerned with the limits of rationality, and the manner in which organizations affect these limits for the person making a decision" (Simon 1947: 241). Herbert Simon's key insight was that decision-makers lack access to perfect information, do not have fully fleshed-out preferences, and, as a result, cannot consider all possible options when making choices, nor can they anticipate the consequences of each choice. Instead of maximizing by searching for and selecting the optimal alternative, boundedly rational decision-makers *satisfice*, that is, they engage in limited search and choose the first alternative they expect to be satisfactory given their aspiration level. Alternatively, decision-makers resort to coping mechanisms in the form of repertoires of simple, automatic rules or mental shortcuts (i.e., heuristics) that avoid foresight by capitalizing on insights gained from prior experience (Cyert & March 1963).

---

[7] The behavioral theory of the firm originated at Carnegie Mellon University, where Herbert Simon, James March, Richard Cyert, and other faculty members at the Graduate School of Industrial Administration (known today as the Tepper School of Business) developed a new school of economic thought, which is why behavioral theory is often referred to as the "Carnegie School."

Extending Simon's ideas on bounded rationality, March and Simon (1993: 2) depict organizations as "systems of coordinated action among individuals and groups whose preferences, information, interests, or knowledge differ. Effective control over organizational processes is limited by the uncertainties and ambiguities of life, by the limited cognitive and affective capabilities of human actors, by the complexities of balancing trade-offs across time and space, and by threats of competition." According to behavioral theory, organizations can overcome the constraints of bounded rationality and reconcile individual and organizational goals – however imperfectly – by having managers set clear goals and define standard operating procedures for subordinates, monitor and reward their performance, and adjust goals and procedures as necessary. Workers agree to participate as long as the perceived value of the rewards they receive – both material and nonmaterial, including psychological and social benefits accruing from organizational membership – exceeds the perceived opportunity costs of their contributions (Gavetti et al. 2007). In sum, the behavioral theory of the firm complemented prior approaches by emphasizing both workers' and managers' cognitive constraints as central to understanding organizational control.

3.3.2   Agency Theory

Agency theory is the first of two contractual theories of the firm underlying organizational control research. Agency theorists have conceptualized organizations as "legal fictions which serve as a nexus for a set of contracting relationships among individuals" (Jensen & Meckling 1976: 310), with managers brokering and coordinating these contracts between shareholders, creditors, workers, customers, suppliers, and other stakeholders (Fama 1980; Fama & Jensen 1983). The starting point of agency theory is the separation of ownership and control characterizing modern corporations (Berle & Means 1932), with principals (i.e., owners or shareholders) delegating decision-making authority to agents (i.e., managers). This type of delegation is efficient, as those with the best understanding of the task, that is, professional managers, can make the decisions. And it allows for specialization advantages, with owners focusing on managing their wealth, and professional managers focusing on decision-making (Fama & Jensen 1983). The delegation of decision-making authority also results in monitoring and control costs for principals, especially when there are (1) conflicting interests or at least some divergence of interests between principals and agents and (2) information asymmetries between principals and agents, with principals having incomplete information to verify agents' behaviors (Eisenhardt 1989a; Fama & Jensen 1983; Jensen & Meckling 1976). Under those circumstances, agents may not always act in the principals' best interest. Agents may not put forth the agreed-upon effort, which constitutes a hidden action or moral hazard problem, and/or misrepresent their abilities, which constitutes a hidden information or adverse selection problem (Arrow 1985; Eisenhardt 1989a). In a sense, we can understand agency theory as a neoclassical economic response to the questions the Carnegie School has raised regarding the behaviors of an organization of self-interested agents with at least partially conflicting goals and with asymmetrically distributed information (Levinthal 1988).

The focus of agency theory is to determine the optimal (i.e., cost-efficient) contract for the agents' services (Eisenhardt 1985). However, since principals have only incomplete information on agents' behaviors, they are left with three options when it comes to determining the optimal contract. The first option is to invest in information systems revealing agents' behaviors, thereby mitigating information asymmetries, and allowing principals to rely on a contract based on agents' behaviors (Arrow 1985; Jensen & Meckling 1976; Pratt & Zeckhauser 1985). This option constitutes behavior control. The feasibility of this option hinges on *task programmability*, or the degree to which it is possible to specify appropriate agent behavior in advance, with more programmable tasks being easier to observe and evaluate (Eisenhardt 1989a). Monitoring and rewarding agents based on their behavior is also the preferred option considering risk. Specifically, outcomes are only partly a function of agents' behaviors, and in contrast to principals who are capable of diversifying their investments, agents are unable to diversify their employment, making them more risk averse (Eisenhardt 1989a).

The problem of information asymmetry is particularly pronounced when it comes to knowledge work, or the increasing share of work tasks across all industries that entail problem-solving and the production of knowledge. In the case of knowledge workers, the usual division of labor between managers and workers is further complicated by a division of knowledge (Sharma 1997). Unlike traditional work arrangements, the resources that are critical for the success of knowledge work reside in workers' heads and are largely tacit and intangible, which implies that workers own and control the means of production (Drucker 1999). Moreover, knowledge work is typically characterized by a high degree of autonomy and the limited involvement of managers (Sharma 1997). As a result, managers are both dependent on knowledge workers and lack the required knowledge or technical skills to understand and evaluate knowledge workers' jobs, which increases their agency costs and places severe constraints on their abilities to harness traditional managerial methods of control (Mitchell & Meacheam 2011). As Barley (1996: 437) put it: "When those in authority no longer comprehend the work of their subordinates, hierarchical position alone is insufficient justification for authority, especially in technical matters."

The second option is to contract not on the agents' behaviors, but on the outcomes of those behaviors. This type of outcome control, in turn, incentivizes agents' behaviors by aligning their interests with those of the principals, as the rewards for both now depend on the same outcomes (Jensen & Meckling 1976; Pratt & Zeckhauser 1985). A prerequisite for this option is the *availability of readily measurable outcomes* (Eisenhardt 1985), while the transfer of risk to agents represents an important caveat. In sum, the focus of these first two options is on choosing between controlling agents' behaviors and controlling their outcomes. The deciding factor between the two is the costs of measuring the behavior and the outcomes of the behavior rather than the ability to do so, with information being a purchasable commodity rather than a characteristic of the task itself (Eisenhardt 1985).

The third control option is to align agents' interests with principals' interests *ex ante*, that is, before agents get to work on a task. This alignment can be achieved by either searching for and selecting agents who embrace and are committed to the principals' objectives and goals or investing in socialization mechanisms that instill a "deep level of common agreement between members on what constitutes proper behavior, and it requires a high level of commitment on the part of each individual to those socially prescribed behaviors" (i.e., input control) (Ouchi 1979: 838). With such goal congruence, agents will behave in the principal's best interest, regardless of whether or not behaviors and their outcomes are monitored (Eisenhardt 1989a; Pratt & Zeckhauser 1985).

The domain of agency theory extends beyond a firm's owners and its top executives, and includes any relationship that mirrors the basic agency structure of a principal and an agent engaged in cooperative behavior, but with, at best, only partially congruent goals (Eisenhardt 1989a). Agency theory represents the dominant theoretical tenet underlying organizational control research (see Cardinal et al. 2017, for a review), and the underlying assumptions of agency theory have served as the foundation for organizational control research. In a nutshell, organizational controls are designed to address agency problems between managers and workers in organizations (Sitkin et al. 2020).

3.3.3 Transaction Cost Theory

The second contractual theory of the firm is transaction cost theory. This theory considers a transaction as the basic unit of organizational analysis and focuses on the decision of whether to contract on the outside market or internalize a given transaction by integrating it into the organizational hierarchy (Williamson 1975, 1985). Transaction cost theory rests on two behavioral assumptions. Bounded rationality prevents parties from including all relevant contingencies in their contracts. Opportunism – or "self-interest seeking with guile" (Williamson 1975: 255) – suggests that the exchange partners may take advantage of the incomplete contract. Owing to the potential for opportunism and due to their bounded rationality constraints, organizations incur costs associated with any transactions they engage in and will attempt to minimize these costs by internalizing those transactions that are particularly vulnerable to opportunism. Vulnerable transactions (1) are uncertain, complex, or exhibit information asymmetries and are thus difficult to specify ex ante; (2) occur infrequently and are thus more likely to justify the high overhead costs of hierarchical governance; and (3) exhibit high degrees of asset specificity, defined as the difference between an asset's value in the current transaction (i.e., its best use) versus its value in a transaction with an alternative party (i.e., its next best use) (Williamson 1979).

Similar to the concept of agency costs in agency theory, firms incur transaction costs when negotiating, monitoring, and enforcing contracts between parties to ensure that their interests are protected, and the main objective centers around minimizing these transaction costs. When transaction hazards are negligible, spot markets and their price mechanisms for rewarding agents based on their outputs represent the most efficient (i.e., least costly) form of governance. In contrast, when transactions are uncertain and infrequent, and assets are transaction specific, the most efficient solution is hierarchical governance (Williamson 1975). While the initial transaction cost theory focused on the choice between either market or hierarchy, subsequent research has also acknowledged intermediate governance modes between markets and hierarchies, such as long-term contracts (Williamson 1979), relational contracting (Williamson 1979, 1981), and interfirm alliances or "hybrids" (Williamson 1991).

Transaction cost theory shares several assumptions with agency theory, such as the preeminence of efficiency, self-interest, and bounded rationality. The two theories also predict corresponding dependent variables: hierarchies (i.e., behavior control) versus markets (i.e., outcome control) (Eisenhardt 1989a). In contrast to agency theory, which focuses on the contract between cooperating parties regardless of organizational boundaries, transaction cost theory is concerned with predicting organizational boundaries based on its maxim to minimize transaction costs (Williamson 1975). Moreover, instead of agency theory's focus on risk preferences, outcome uncertainty, and information systems, transaction cost theory focuses on opportunism, asset specificity, and the frequency of transactions as key determinants (Williamson 1979).

3.3.4 Contingency Theory

In its basic form, contingency theory suggests that organizational effectiveness depends on the fit between formal organizational structures, on the one hand, and contingencies, such as an organization's size, strategy, technology, and external environment, on the other hand (Lawrence & Lorsch 1969; Thompson 1967). According to this theory, there is no single, ideal way to organize, and the best way depends on the nature of the environment in which an organization is embedded. Contingency theory further emphasizes the information processing requirements of different organizational environments (Galbraith 1973). As environmental uncertainty and complexity increase, and as interdependences among the organization's tasks increase, so does the amount of information needed to perform those tasks. Those enhanced information requirements, in turn, call for organizations to increase their ability to process information, for instance, by forging lateral relations between organizational members to foster interactions.

Early approaches to organizational control (e.g., Ouchi & Maguire 1975) built on this contingency logic to suggest that the choice between behavior and outcome control depends on a given task's information requirements, that is, the knowledge of the process of transforming inputs into outputs (i.e., controller knowledge or task programmability) and the ability to measure outputs. When managers lack an understanding of the transformation process, behavior control becomes ineffective, and outcome control would be the preferred choice. When reliable and valid outcome measures are not available, outcome control is no longer feasible, and behavior control would be the preferred choice (Ouchi 1977). If neither behavior nor outcomes are observable and/or measurable, the only feasible control choice would be to select workers who embrace and are committed to the principals' objectives and goals, or to invest in socialization mechanisms to align workers' interests with the organization's interests (i.e., input control) (Ouchi 1979).

The key insight contingency theory contributed to organizational control research is that there is no universally applicable system of control. Instead, the choice of an appropriate organizational control regime depends on the characteristics of a specific organization and the characteristics of the tasks that are controlled. While contingency theory provides a rich theoretical foundation for organizational control studies, researchers have criticized it as a rather simplistic, reductionist, and static approach and suggested taking a more complex, complementary, dynamic, and configurational approach (e.g., Van de Ven et al. 2013). This approach, which we will pursue for our reconceptualization of organizational control in Chapter 6, is especially promising for organizations that are complex and face multiple conflicting environmental demands, internal design configuration trade-offs, and diverse performance expectations.

3.3.5   Information Processing Theory

Closely related to contingency theory, information processing theory maintains that the role of organizational structure and control is to increase the organization's information processing capacity in order to deal with both the organization's internal complexity and the uncertainty in the organization's external environment (Galbraith 1977; Tushman & Nadler 1978). According to this theory, the role of organizational control is twofold. On the one hand, and in line with agency, transaction cost, and contingency perspectives, managers use control to gather information about their workers' task performance. On the other hand, organizational control allows managers to ensure that their workers obtain the information they need to accomplish their assigned tasks, thereby decreasing their workers' task-related uncertainty and increasing their ability to achieve high task performance (Leifer & Mills 1996; Tushman & Nadler 1978).

3.3.6 The Attention-based View

The attention-based view of the firm (Ocasio 1997) builds on the Carnegie School's notion of bounded rationality as well as insights from psychological research about human attention processes to propose that the decisions and behavior of organizations are shaped by their members' limited attentional capabilities. The attention-based view is built on three interrelated premises. First, organizational actors' decision-making and behavior depend on the issues they focus their attention on. Second, what actors focus their attention on depends on the situational influences they find themselves in. Third, and most relevant for organizational control, the situational influences that actors are subject to depend on how the organization's resources, rules, and relationships come together to shape specific communication and decision-making channels (Ocasio 1997). These organizational attention structures, in turn, govern the allocation and distribution of time and effort through three separate mechanisms: by generating a set of values that order the legitimacy, importance, and relevance of issues; by channeling and distributing decision-making activity into a concrete set of procedures and communications; and by providing decision-makers with a structured set of interests and identities that shapes their understanding of the situation and that motivates their actions (Ocasio 1997).

The attention-based view is relevant for organizational control research as the control regime that workers are embedded in provides them with important information to use in their sense-making and decision-making processes (Sitkin et al. 2020). Effective organizational control requires the structuring and management of attention. After all, "[a]n organization must succeed at directing members' minds or it never will manage to direct their actions" (Ocasio & Wohlgezogen 2010: 191). In line with this idea, some definitions of organizational control explicitly mention focusing and directing attention as a key feature of organizational control (e.g., Cardinal et al. 2017; Long et al. 2015; Simons 1991), and it is part of our definition of organizational control as "organizational attempts to enable, motivate, and *direct* organizational members and partners" (see Section 2.1, emphasis added).

From an attention-based perspective, organizational controls serve as intermittent reminders, directing and redirecting distracted actors' attention back toward organizational goals (Ocasio & Wohlgezogen 2010). Specifically, behavior control affects actors' selective attention by influencing which stimuli they are more likely to attend to. Outcome control, in contrast, sets explicit expectations that can have a powerful, regulative effect and that direct attention to organizational goals and objectives. Whereas behavior control's effect on actors' attention is more situational, outcome controls also have a normative effect, guiding and monitoring compliance with values and ideals that go beyond the specific tasks for which they are set. Outcome control can therefore have a pervasive, subconscious effect on behavior and decision making by shaping attentional selection, with outcome goals not functioning as "a compass instrument that is occasionally consulted, but as a moral compass that operates constantly" (Ocasio & Wohlgezogen 2010: 201). Last, actors who have developed shared identities, loyalties, and norms subconsciously translate the organization's values into rules on how to allocate their attention (Ocasio & Wohlgezogen 2010). The impact of assimilated values and beliefs can also go beyond filtering and directing actors' attention: It can compel them to actively direct their peers' behavior; it can enhance their attentional alertness to any deviant behavior and motivate its sanctioning; and it can thereby ensure conformity to organizational norms (Ouchi 1979).

The theories discussed above are summarized in Table 3.4. These theories, including their underlying assumptions, provide the basis for organizational control theory as well as the determinants of organizational control choices.

3.4   Organizational Control Theory

In his seminal paper on organizational control, William Ouchi (1979) synthesized key insights from the human relations paradigm, Weberian bureaucracy, and the Carnegie School, in addition to insights from transaction cost economics, contingency theory, and information processing theory, to distill three fundamentally different options for organizations to align individual and organizational interests: markets, hierarchies, and clans.

Under *market control*, any transaction between two parties is mediated by a price mechanism, and competition among buyers and sellers guarantees both parties' equitable terms of exchange (Ouchi 1980). In their pure (i.e., frictionless) form, markets are very efficient control mechanisms (Arrow 1974). Prices convey all of the information necessary for efficient decision-making, and by rewarding each party in direct proportion to their contributions, prices provide a mechanism for solving the problem of goal incongruity (Ouchi 1979). Under market control, managers examine the results that workers generate in order to assess and comparatively evaluate the performance of particular workers, with workers acting more like independent contractors who pursue their individual economic interests, actively compete with other workers, and aim at maximizing their personal productivity (Sitkin et al. 2020).

Table 3.4 *Theoretical perspectives with their assumptions and control determinants*

Theory	Assumptions	Key determinants of control choice
Behavioral theory	• Firms as coalitions of individuals or groups that participate in goal setting (conflict potential) • Bounded rationality results in satisficing (instead of maximizing) behavior • Information gathering is not costless and requires resources	• Uncertainty, limited cognitive and affective capabilities of managers and workers, and complexities of balancing trade-offs across time and space • Perceived value of rewards in relation to perceived opportunity costs of workers' contributions
Agency theory	• Self-interest • Diverging (partly conflicting) interests between principals and agents • Information asymmetries between principals and agents • Preeminence of efficiency	• Task programmability • Availability of readily measurable outcomes • Costs of measuring behavior and its outcomes • Risk preferences
Transaction cost theory	• Self-interest • Bounded rationality • Opportunism • Preeminence of efficiency	• Opportunism • Asset specificity • Frequency of transactions

Contingency theory	• No universally applicable system of control
	• The appropriate control choice depends on the characteristics of a specific organization and its tasks
		• Task information requirements:
		  • Task programmability
		  • Outcome measurability
		  • Task uncertainty and complexity
		• Task interdependence

Information processing theory	• Control designed to increase the organization's information processing capacity to deal with internal complexity and environmental uncertainty • Control gathers information about workers' task performance • Control ensures that workers obtain the information they need to accomplish their assigned tasks	• Workers' task-related uncertainty • Organizations' information processing capacity

Attention-based view	• Bounded rationality
	• Limited attentional capabilities
	• Organizational actors' decisions and behaviors depend on the issues they pay attention to
	• What actors pay attention to depends on situational influences
	• Situational influences depend on how organizational resources, rules, and relationships shape communication and decision-making channels
		• Situational influences
		• Organizational attention structures govern by:
		  • generating a set of values that order the legitimacy, importance, and relevance of issues
		  • channeling and distributing decision-making activity into a concrete set of procedures
		  • providing decision-makers with a structured set of interests and identities that shapes their understanding of the situation and motivates their actions

If markets were completely frictionless, however, there would be little reason for formal organizations to exist (Coase 1937). The proliferation of organizations therefore signals an alternative control mechanism: bureaucratic (Weber 1947) or hierarchical control (Williamson 1975). Under *bureaucratic control*, workers contribute their labor to an organization, and managers possess the legitimate authority to utilize formal rules and regulations, specialized jobs, and hierarchical mandates to direct workers' actions and specify outcome or quality standards. Managers further monitor the extent to which workers adhere to these rules and task directives in order to place a value on each worker's contribution and to compensate it fairly (Ouchi 1980).

Both market and bureaucratic control are distinct means to address incongruent individual goals in the pursuit of cooperative objectives. It is conceivable, however, that organizations could also achieve goal congruence by selectively hiring workers who are already committed to organizational objectives and by maintaining their commitment via high-contact, face-to-face socialization, which Ouchi (1979) refers to as *clan control*. Managers in clan control systems create an environment where subordinates share and enact common values and perspectives to account for their actions (O'Reilly & Chatman 1996). The risk of social ostracism and professional peril allows an organization under clan control to manage with a very light bureaucratic touch, as workers' natural (or socialized) inclination is to act in the organization's best interest, which greatly reduces the need for explicit surveillance and evaluation (Barker 1993; Ouchi 1980).

Building on agency and contingency theories, Ouchi's research also advances normative implications for organizational control. Specifically, Ouchi and Maguire (1975) suggest that the choice between different control options should be based on the aspect of the controlled task that managers have better information on. If valid and reliable outcome measures are available, the preferred choice would be outcome control. If managers have a sound understanding of the monitored tasks (i.e., the monitored tasks are largely programmable), control should focus on the surveillance of workers' behaviors. Clan control is intended for cases where neither behavior nor outcome control work, because managers have too little knowledge about the process *and* the outcomes (Ouchi 1979, 1980).

3.5   A Critical Perspective on Organizational Control

As is evident from our review of organizational control definitions, key theories, and assumptions, the vast majority of publications in the mainstream literature on organizational control subscribes to our focus on the alignment between individual and organizational goals. There is, however, a small but insightful literature advancing a different, critical perspective on organizational control (see, e.g., Delbridge 2010; Jermier 1998, for reviews of this literature). The critical perspective questions the mainstream literature's view of organizational control as inevitable, criticizes its narrow focus on performance in economic or profit-maximizing terms, and objects to its goal of helping design efficient and effective organizations. In contrast, the critical perspective views organizational control as socially constructed and seeks to understand the effects of control on workers, including its ethical implications and shortcomings. However, the critical perspective also assumes a normative stance. It pledges to expose inequalities, abuses of power, and mistreatment inherent in organizational control practices, and contrasts these practices with "Utopian states that are free from exploitation, oppression, and social injustice" (Jermier 1998: 237). In a nutshell, the critical perspective encourages a reflection on who or what controls whom, as well as why, that is, on the *purpose* of control – its focus is less on what control is, and more on what it could be (Jermier 1998).

Another key difference between mainstream and critical perspectives on organizational control is the responsibility of researchers. According to the critical perspective, social scientists cannot strive for impartiality or ignore the normative implications of their theories and findings – by doing so, they assist, often unwittingly, in the social reproduction of repressive control regimes. Instead, scientists should aspire to serve the public interest by capturing and portraying the perspectives of individuals or groups whose perspectives are ordinarily devalued or neglected. By giving voice and credence to individuals who are unable to articulate their situation – because they either do not comprehend the conditions that are responsible for their situation or they are socialized into accepting them as part of the natural order – scientists' aspirations should be to subvert the repressive conditions they find (Jermier 1998). The critical perspective not only targets "the insidiousness of bureaucratic mechanisms of control (and the threat they pose to democracy and freedom)," but it is equally set on unraveling the "iron fist of power [clad in a] velvet glove to reveal the mettle of well-hyped, 'humanistic' strategies [that] disguise control in the rhetoric of emancipation" (Jermier 1998: 245–246, 235).

Despite these differences, the critical perspective has influenced the organizational control literature more broadly. This is especially evident in Barker's (1993) critical ethnography, which highlights the tendency of self-managing teams – despite being freed from hierarchical control – to develop value-based normative rules that control their actions even tighter than bureaucratic organizations. Although representative of the critical perspective, our co-citation analysis found that this article is among the most cited and therefore influential articles in the organizational control literature. It has the highest betweenness centrality score of all publications focused on organizational control, which indicates that it serves as a central bridge between numerous intellectual bases constituting the organizational control literature. And it has seen a surge in citations (i.e., a citation burst) between 2004 and 2014, attesting to the attention Barker's (1993) article has received from the broader organizational control field.

While our book remains situated in the mainstream perspective on organizational control, we acknowledge and incorporate the critical perspective in several ways. First, we highlight the importance of identity – both workers' sense of self and their socially constructed identities (Delbridge 2010) – as well as workers' agency for understanding the effects of organizational control. Second, we acknowledge the socially constructed nature of control and integrate it into our discussion, for instance, of the managerial intent behind control versus workers' perceptions of control (Section 7.3.2). Third, we acknowledge the blurring lines between work and non-work lives (Sections 5.3.2 and 5.3.3) as well as the increasingly pervasive and coercive surveillance of workers, both inside and outside the workplace, and often supported by algorithms (Sections 5.3.1 and 5.3.4). Fourth, we examine the effects of control on a broad range of outcomes – including environmental and social goals as well as unintended and detrimental consequences of control – and for different stakeholders, such as organizational performance versus worker satisfaction (Section 4.3).

3.6   Organizational Control across the Ages

From their origins in ancient bureaucracies, approaches to organizational control have evolved over time, and sometimes dramatically so. Early research in the traditions of scientific management, Weberian bureaucracy, agency theory, and transaction cost theory has framed workers as rational actors who seek to maximize pleasure and minimize pain as the extrinsic outcomes of work activity and who are therefore amenable to control via extrinsic incentives. In response to such assumptions about human nature and agency, early research has advanced autocratic and dictatorial (Taylor 1911) or bureaucratic, authoritative, and coercive (Weber 1946) methods of control, administered by organizations in a machine-like, instrumental manner.

The Carnegie School, contingency and information processing theory, and, most recently, the attention-based view have relaxed the assumption of human rationality and instead emphasized information constraints, internal and external complexity, and the organizational context as key contingency factors for the efficacy of organizational control approaches. The human relations paradigm represents another fundamental shift in both assumptions about human agency and corresponding approaches to organizational control. This approach maintains that the essence of control is tied to human affect and motivation rather than logic and rationality. It attempts to balance the need for organizational efficiency with worker empowerment and self-determination, which has led to control approaches that recognize both extrinsic economic and financial incentives and intrinsic rewards, such as autonomy, recognition, and (self-)fulfilment.

However, it appears as if organizational control has come full circle. Recent technological and organizational advances enable organizations to engage in more intrusive, coercive, and all-encompassing control approaches than ever before. As we will discuss in Chapter 5, in an echo of Taylorism and Fordism at the turn of the twentieth century, these recent advances have started to remove workers' knowledge of and control over the work tasks, and the execution of work is rationalized into discrete piecework that is organized and overseen by managers in an increasingly scientific process (Braverman 1998; Duggan et al. 2020). Moreover, analyzing electronic surveillance data with the help of increasingly sophisticated artificial intelligence (AI) and machine learning (ML) algorithms has enabled organizations to digitize and further disaggregate tasks that are increasingly removed from managerial oversight and instead subject to algorithmic control. To better understand the implications of these recent developments for organizational control, however, we will first develop and test an overarching organizing framework of organizational control – its dimensions, mechanisms or functions, outcomes, and key contingencies.

Part II

Current State of Organizational Control

4   An Organizational Control Framework

In this chapter, we present our multidisciplinary organizing framework providing a contemporary view on organizational control. Building on our discussion of the underlying theories and assumptions of control research (Chapter 3), we cluster prior research into five control dimensions, namely: target, formality, singularity, direction, and style. We also distill three mechanisms – monitoring, incentivizing, and coordinating – through which organizational control influences a range of outcomes clustered into four categories (adaptability, HR, process, and rational goal outcomes) and discuss several key contingencies. Our framework provides the basis for both organizing the existing literature and outlining the future of organizational control research.

4.1   Dimensions of Organizational Control

We differentiate between five dimensions – target, formality, singularity, direction, and style – that together cover the range of options for organizational control.

4.1.1   Control Target

Traditional control research (e.g., Ouchi 1977; Ouchi & Maguire 1975) has distinguished between two targets of organizational control: behavior control and output control. *Behavior control* (also called process control or action control, e.g., Merchant & Van der Stede 2007) consists of explicitly setting operating procedures and rules coupled with direct, personal surveillance of ongoing worker behavior to monitor, evaluate, and reward (punish) workers' compliance (noncompliance) with these rules and procedures.[1] Behavior control therefore focuses on the means by which outcomes are achieved. In contrast, output or *outcome control* (also called results control, e.g., Merchant &

---

[1] It is important to note that control can involve both contingent rewards and contingent punishments for workers' behavior and for the outcomes of those behaviors (e.g., Challagalla & Shervani 1996).

Van der Stede 2012) is focused on setting targets, such as financial results, for workers to pursue; measuring how well outcomes align with these targets; and providing rewards and penalties, respectively, for success and failure in achieving these targets (Eisenhardt 1985).

More recent research (e.g., Cardinal 2001) has extended the aspects of an organization's task environment that managers intend to influence to include not just behavior and outcomes, but also inputs. *Input control* (also referred to as personnel or cultural control, e.g., Merchant 1982, 1985; Speklé 2001) is an ex ante control that focuses on managers selecting workers for specific teams or the organization at large, and/or providing workers with appropriate training, developing, and socializing opportunities to ensure that the workers' identities, loyalties, and norms are aligned with those of the organization (Cardinal 2001; Chatman 1991; Harrison & Carroll 1991; Snell 1992).

Input control through the selective assignment of workers to specific teams and/or tasks also offers an opportunity for what some authors have referred to as *identity control* (e.g., Alvesson & Kärreman 2007; Alvesson & Willmott 2002). Workers derive value from their social identities but require opportunities to enact their desired identities at work, ostensibly with the hope of being (or becoming) who they desire to be. Workers' desires for such opportunities to live out their occupational identities, in turn, allow managers to use the granting and withdrawing of opportunities – such as assigning interesting work or special projects to select individuals – as a form of organizational control (Anteby 2008).

In contrast to our conceptualization, which differentiates three theoretically and empirically distinct control targets, some early research (e.g., Anderson & Oliver 1987; Krafft 1999; Makhija & Ganesh 1997; Oliver & Anderson 1994), as well as a few more recent studies (e.g., Zhong et al. 2022), have depicted the target of control as a continuum ranging from high behavior control on the one end to high outcome control on the other end. This alternative view assumes an inherent trade-off between outcome control and behavior control, and also assumes that no more than one control target can be present at the same time. However, neither of these two assumptions corresponds to the empirical reality in organizations (see our discussions of control singularity in Section 4.1.3), and we therefore retain our differentiation of the three distinct control targets that organizations can implement either individually or in conjunction with each other. For an overview of the three control targets, their main control elements, and examples, see Table 4.1.

4.1.2   Control Formality

When it comes to the second dimension, control formality, traditional control research (e.g., Ouchi 1977; Ouchi & Maguire 1975) has focused largely

Table 4.1 *Control targets*

Control target (synonyms)	Control elements	Examples
Input control (personnel control, cultural control)	• Selecting workers who are a good fit for the organization	• Defining competences, skills, and abilities necessary to perform a task • Using these criteria for recruiting new workers
	• Socializing workers	• Offering social events, off-site meetings, and (casual) lunches or dinners
	• Training and developing workers	• Training and development opportunities for workers who might not (yet) meet the required competencies, skills, and abilities
Behavior control (process control, action control)	• Setting explicit operating procedures and rules • Monitoring ongoing worker behavior (i.e., engaging in personal surveillance)	• Standard operating procedures • Procedural manuals • Directly observing workers on their job
	• Evaluating workers' compliance with rules and procedures	• Commenting on workers' rule compliance and providing suggestions for improvement
	• Providing incentives for compliance with rules and procedures	• Adherence to procedural requirements as a prerequisite for monetary rewards and promotions
Outcome control (output control, results control)	• Defining and assigning targets for workers to pursue	• Setting performance targets • Setting revenue targets
	• Measuring how well outcomes align with these targets	• Engaging in interim and final results control
	• Providing rewards and punishment, respectively, for success and failure in the achievement of these targets	• Making variable pay (i.e., performance-based) a significant part of workers' total pay

on formal controls. Formal controls are characterized by explicit and codified institutional rules, policies, and procedures that are officially sanctioned. Examples of formal controls are written goal requirements and performance standards, job descriptions, behavioral or process specifications, and standard operating procedures (see Cardinal et al. 2017, for a review of the literature). As outlined in Section 3.4, however, Ouchi's (1979) influential control framework also acknowledges informal *clan control*, which emphasizes the role of shared identities, loyalties, and norms in influencing behavior and allowing workers to be managed with a light administrative touch. Clan control includes aspects of input control, such as selection, socialization, and training (Cardinal 2001; Kirsch 1996; Snell & Youndt 1995; Turner & Makhija 2006), and it also includes aspects of behavior control, such as providing an informal guide to what is acceptable and proper, and what is outside the set boundaries (Kirsch et al. 2010). While it is often managers who intentionally design clan control (Kirsch et al. 2010; Loughry 2010; Walter et al. 2021), workers who are all at the same hierarchical level help ensure that their peers adhere to shared norms and values. Workers achieve this by rewarding behavior that is consistent with team values and norms, and by sanctioning deviant behavior (Errichiello & Pianese 2016; Kirsch 2004; Kirsch et al. 2010).

Owing to its multifaceted character, conceptualizing informal control as clan control has also faced criticism, especially in more recent research. As is evident from the description earlier, despite being labeled as informal by early research, clan control exhibits both formal and informal aspects (Sihag & Rijsdijk 2019). For instance, both informal gatherings between individuals and small groups and formal company events, off-site meetings, and casual lunches or dinners, can serve as opportunities for socializing workers (Choudhury & Sabherwal 2003; Kirsch et al. 2010). Further conflating different aspects of control, clan control also contains elements of input control and peer control (Section 4.1.4). For these reasons, we follow Cardinal et al. (2004, 2010) and differentiate the same control targets as the literature on formal control does, which are input control, behavior control, and outcome control. More specifically, *formal control* refers to "officially sanctioned (usually codified) institutional mechanisms, such as written rules, standard operating systems, and procedural directives – visible, objective forms of control," whereas *informal control* refers to "unwritten, unofficial [...,] less objective, uncodified forms of control" (Cardinal et al. 2004: 414). Formal control and informal control are not the opposite ends of a single formality continuum as some research has suggested (e.g., Barnard 1938), but represent distinct dimensions of organizational control (Cardinal et al. 2010), with visibility and explicitness being the key differentiators between formal and informal controls. Consequently, informal control, like formal control, can focus on all three control targets – input, behavior, and outcome – leading to a total of six control types.

4.1.3   Control Singularity

While it is broadly recognized that few organizations use individual controls in isolation, the majority of traditional studies on organizational control have been based on *singular* views of control. Table 4.2 displays the commonly assumed ideal, which is a singular control target, contingent on whatever

Table 4.2 *Conditions that determine organizational control targets*

		Knowledge about the transformation process/ task programmability	
		Perfect	Imperfect
Outcome measurability	High	Formal behavior or formal outcome control	Formal outcome control
	Low	Formal behavior control	Informal clan control

This framework is adapted from Ouchi (1979) and Eisenhardt (1985).

managers have accurate and complete information on. Specifically, and in line with Ouchi's research on organizational control (Section 3.4), agency theory (Section 3.3.2), and contingency theory (Section 3.3.4), the most efficient and effective target of control depends on a given task's information characteristics, such as knowledge about the process transforming inputs into outputs (i.e., task programmability) and the ability to measure outputs (i.e., outcome measurability). With limited knowledge about the transformation process, control of workers' behaviors becomes less effective; and as outcome measures' reliability and validity decline, outcome control becomes increasingly problematic (Ouchi 1977). When neither behavior nor outcomes are observable and/or measurable, control must focus on minimizing the incongruence between workers' and the organization's preferences and goals via selection, socialization, and training (Ouchi 1979, 1980).

In addition to managers' understanding of the controlled processes and the availability of outcome measures – or, in agency theoretic terms, the costs of measuring behaviors and their outcomes – a third factor that determines the optimal choice between control targets is risk (see our discussion in Section 3.3.2). While managers can mitigate information asymmetries regarding workers' behaviors by focusing their control efforts on outcomes, outcomes are only partially determined by workers' behaviors, and workers might resist, or need to be compensated for, being on the receiving end of this transfer of risk (Eisenhardt 1985).

In a notable break with this contingency approach, more recent organizational control research has examined how different controls can complement each other instead of serving as substitutes. This research proposes a more *holistic* approach, acknowledging that combinations of formal and informal controls coexist in organizations (Cardinal et al. 2010; Joseph et al. 2019). According to this view, blending different controls – each with their distinct advantages and disadvantages – helps mitigate the limitations of individual control and should thereby be more effective than relying on singular controls (Kreutzer et al. 2016). This approach therefore advocates for a balanced and integrated mix of formal and informal control approaches. Researchers have referred to those control combinations as control systems (Jaworski et al. 1993; Simons 1995b), control archetypes (Caglio & Ditillo 2008), and, more recently, control configurations (Cardinal et al. 2010).

Jaworski and colleagues (1993), for instance, distinguished between bureaucratic systems (with mostly formal controls), clan systems (with mostly informal controls), low control systems (with few formal and informal controls), and high control systems (with a combination of formal and informal controls). They also found high control systems to be superior for job satisfaction and to reduce both person-role conflict and role ambiguity but found no significant influence on job performance. Later research, taking a control configurational approach, found complementary effects between formal behavior and formal outcome controls (Kreutzer et al. 2015), between formal and informal controls on the performance of strategic initiative teams (Kreutzer et al. 2016), and also between norm strength and peer pressure on team performance (De Jong et al. 2014).

Cardinal et al. (2017) further distinguished between weak and strong holistic control approaches. In contrast to singular control approaches, which are characterized by a theoretical and empirical focus on one type of control only, *weak holistic control* approaches examine multiple types of control, but present a theoretical preference for one type. Cardinal (2001), for instance, theorized a contingency effect by proposing input control as effective, and behavior control and output control as counterproductive, for new pharmaceutical drug innovation. More recently, control researchers have turned to theorizing *strong holistic control* approaches, such as interactions, configurations, or blends of different types of control. These studies emphasize the advantages of strong holistic approaches for understanding control dynamics (e.g., Cardinal et al. 2004, 2017) and control–outcome relationships in the increasingly complex, ambiguous, and fluid environment that twenty-first century organizations have to face (McGrath 2014).

4.1.4   Control Direction

Hierarchical and lateral control. As a consequence of its agency-theoretic heritage, the traditional focus of control has been on *hierarchical control*, with higher-ranked managers monitoring and enforcing subordinate workers' compliance (Ouchi & Maguire 1975). In a departure from the traditional hierarchical approach, more recent research has acknowledged that control can also be exercised laterally between co-workers who have no formal authority over one another, resulting in a fledgling literature on *peer control* (e.g., De Jong et al. 2014; Loughry & Tosi 2008; Walter et al. 2021). Workers can exert peer control over each other both formally and informally (Loughry

2010), and can direct their peer control efforts at any control target – inputs, behaviors, and outcomes.

The literature has long recognized that peer control has advantages compared to top-down control. Specifically, peers interact much more frequently with their co-workers and therefore enjoy information advantages over their managers (Fama & Jensen 1983; Welbourne & Ferrante 2008), which will become even more pronounced in the future, as the increasingly complex nature of teamwork makes it difficult for managers to identify members' individual contributions (Kirsch 2004). An important caveat is that the positive productivity impact of peer control is contingent on peers' observing each other and on frequent interactions among peers (Mas & Moretti 2009). Research has further differentiated peer control approaches both by their origin and whether they are direct or indirect. Peer control can be designed by management, for example, in 360-degree feedback systems, or by the workers themselves, for example, in self-managed teams that create explicit rules for working together (Loughry 2010). It is important to note that this captures only who is responsible for the design of the peer control system, and not the question of who controls whom. Therefore, even in management-designed peer controls, the peers are the ones who control their co-workers. An additional distinction is between *direct peer control* – which includes noticing, praising, correcting, reporting, and discussing what co-workers do – and *indirect peer control*, which happens behind co-workers' backs and includes gossiping about certain co-workers and avoiding them (Loughry & Tosi 2008; Walter et al. 2021). While direct peer control can be formal and informal, indirect peer control is by nature informal. Table 4.3 provides examples for the different origins, targets, and formality of peer control.

Self-control. A third direction of control is *self-control*, where workers set their own goals for a particular task and then monitor, evaluate, reward, and sanction themselves (Errichiello & Pianese 2016; Jaworski 1988; Kirsch 1996). Considering our target-formality logic, we would expect self-control to comprise all three control targets. A worker might opt in for certain projects she sees as the best fit, sign up for appropriate training (input control), monitor her behavior and activities (behavior control), and/or monitor the achievement of self-assigned objectives (output control). Across all three control targets, self-control grants workers high degrees of autonomy, with workers themselves determining both goals – such as a timetable with project milestones – and the behaviors through which these goals should be achieved, by setting behavioral expectations or standards (Choudhury & Sabherwal 2003; Henderson & Lee 1992). While the distinction between formal and informal self-controls seems possible – for example, a worker might set a goal and write it down (formal) or just have it in mind (informal) – we consider it to be less relevant in the self-control context.

Table 4.3 *Examples of peer control by origin, target, and formality*

Peer control		Designed by	
Formality	Target	Management	Workers
Formal	Input	• Inviting peer participation in hiring decisions	• Formal peer onboarding activities
	Behavior	• Formal behavior-focused peer evaluations (such as in 360-degree feedback systems) • Whistle-blowing hotlines • Management-designed on-the-job training or mentoring systems among peers	• Explicit work rules (and any explicitly associated rewards/sanctions) that teams create for themselves • Workers explicitly noticing what peers do and how they behave at work • Workers openly correcting peers when they make mistakes • Workers formally informing supervisors about peer misbehavior
	Outcome	• Formal outcome-focused peer evaluations (such as in 360-degree feedback systems)	• Worker-initiated rules for posting/sharing comparative performance data • Formal discussions about everyone's performance at work among peers • Formal recognition and appreciation of above-average performance among peers
Informal	Input	• Training workers in techniques for cooperating with each other (e.g., conflict-management techniques)	• Rejecting/avoiding peers who are perceived to not fit the organization/team • Informal peer onboarding activities
	Behavior	• Management structuring the work context to facilitate peer control (e.g., creating open offices) • Management's attempts to manage the organization's culture	• Rejecting/avoiding peers who do not adhere to work rules and cultural norms • Gossiping about co-workers' behavior • Implicit work rules
	Outcome	• Management-initiated public posting/sharing of comparative performance data, allowing workers to recognize each other's achievements	• Rejecting/avoiding underperforming peers • Gossiping about poorly performing co-workers • Informal discussions about everyone's performance at work among peers

Note: Direct peer control is not shaded; indirect peer control is shaded.
Adapted and extended from Loughry (2010).

Third-party control. *Third-party control* complements top-down, lateral peer, and self-control as a fourth direction of control. It refers to control in which the dyadic control relationship between a manager and a worker in the same organization is extended to include a third party from outside the organization. The most common third party exercising control over workers is the customer. In fact, even foundational work on organizational control has acknowledged especially high-income, demanding clients as "an important part of the control system [...] by providing direct control over a large range of nonoutput measured goals" (Ouchi 1977: 108).

An example of such customer-centered, third-party control is the ubiquitous feedback organizations request from their customers, such as from hotel guests (Banker et al. 2000; Orlikowski & Scott 2014), from patients about hospital workers' care (Pope 2009), or from passengers about airline workers' contribution to flight and nonflight experiences like the boarding process (Saha & Theingi 2009). In addition to the information and disciplinary advantages resulting from customer feedback, it can also be beneficial for worker motivation. Customer feedback makes workers aware of their impact on customers' lives, which can lead them to take ownership of their clients' problems and thereby regulate themselves (Schepers et al. 2012).

With the rise of digital platforms, the availability and influence of third-party feedback, evaluations, ratings, reviews, and rankings have skyrocketed (see Section 5.3.5 for a more detailed discussion). Digital platforms such as Airbnb, eBay, or Uber are becoming the "evaluative infrastructure" (Kornberger et al. 2017) on which users (as third parties) constantly assess workers' activities and performance, and which determine workers' access to resources, recognition, and job opportunities provided by the platform (Newlands 2021; Rahman 2021). In that sense, algorithmic management by platform-based rating and reputation represents an extension of earlier customer management strategies, which employed customers as "agents in the management circuit," so that "customers, rather than managers, are set up as the ones who must be pleased, whose orders must be followed, whose ideas, whims and desires appear to dictate how work is performed" (Fuller & Smith 1991: 11). Since customer ratings sometimes reflect reasons unrelated to the quality of the work, and since platform workers can no longer rely on managers to intervene and buffer the effect of negative customers, workers feel pressure to anticipate their customers' actions, decipher how the platform's algorithm collects and uses their data, and look for ways to maintain or increase their ratings (Cameron & Rahman 2022). Workers on the grocery-delivery platform Instacart, for example, purchase out-of-stock items out of their own pockets in other stores to keep customers satisfied (Cameron 2021; Milkman et al. 2021).

An indirect form of third-party control takes place when organizations collect information and monitor their customers' behavior to control their workers indirectly, a phenomenon referred to as *"refractive surveillance"* (Levy & Barocas 2018). In that instance, observation is decoupled from control, and information collected about one party (e.g., customers) is used to influence parties other than the target of the surveillance (e.g., workers). Refractive surveillance happens, for example, in retail stores, where data on consumer preferences and customers' in-store behaviors are commonly tracked and collected. This information – which was originally collected without the intent to control workers – nevertheless provides a new and much more exhaustive basis for the evaluation of individual workers: "By piggybacking on systems developed initially to monitor customers' movements, retailers can track how associates move around the store over the course of a shift, when they interact with customers, and whether those encounters are converted into sales" (Levy & Barocas 2018: 10). This form of refractive surveillance provides more fine-grained information on a specific purchase, which allows retailers to assess the performance of individual sales associates in their stores (Levy & Barocas 2018).

A special case of third-party control is *professional control*, in which control is exerted through a code of conduct that is shared by workers who belong to the same professional category (e.g., sales representatives, accountants, lawyers, and other professional services), but who often work for different organizations. This type of control is effective especially, and perhaps only, among workers who care about preserving their own professional image among colleagues (Errichiello & Pianese 2016), such as the workers who belong to the professional categories listed earlier. Professional control is similar to Ouchi's (1979) notion of clan control, in that it is mostly informal and based on social and self-control processes (Orlikowski 1991) in which responsibility is enforced by ethical systems, internalized during the education process, and enforced by formal punishment and the reputational game (Arrow 1985). In contrast to informal clan control, professional control is an external (i.e., third-party) form of control that is not confined to workers controlling each other in the same organization, and it may also entail formal standards of professional conduct.

The view that professional control is sufficient because professionals can be trusted to always serve the public good instead of using their expertise to pursue their own goals, however, has received a significant amount of criticism. Concerns about the viability of professional control are exacerbated by a potential clash between professional controls, on the one hand, and the organizational controls used by the firms that professionals work for, on the other hand, which are often difficult to reconcile (Abernethy & Stoelwinder 1995).

From our discussion of these different directions of control – hierarchical, lateral/peer, self, and third-party control – it is obvious that "the surveillant gaze is multivalent and can point in many directions, sometimes even more than one at the same time" (Levy & Barocas 2018: 2). In professional service firms, for instance, a partner's activities and performance are monitored by the firm's managing partner and the consulting firm's established norms (hierarchical control), by fellow partners (peer control), by the partner herself (self-control), by the professional standards of conduct for a professional consultant (professional control), and by the firm's clients (third-party control) (Empson 2021). Platforms such as Apadua,[2] which was established to provide transparency in an opaque market for professional services, further use consulting firms' client feedback to provide information on fee structures, expertise, and quality of services provided by the firm and by individual partners, thereby acting as another third-party control.

From an organizational control perspective, normative pressures from outside stakeholders, such as stakeholder activism to increase corporate social or environmental responsibility (Durand et al. 2017; Oliver 1991), do not constitute third-party control. Like bottom-up influence inside organizations, these outside pressures are not necessarily aligned with an organization's goals and aspirations, and we therefore do not include them into our conceptualization of third-party control.

4.1.5   Control Style

Building on agency theory's assumption of conflicting goals between workers and managers (Eisenhardt 1989a), traditional studies have further conceptualized organizational control as *coercive*, which involves heavy-handed, bureaucratic, and authoritative attempts to ensure workers' efforts and compliance through threats or force (Ouchi & Maguire 1975). In this view, organizational control is designed to counteract breakdowns of work processes. Any deviation from standard procedure is seen as suspect. Accordingly, this approach to control is focused on conformity, consistency, and a narrow division of labor (Adler & Borys 1996).

Contemporary research has offered an alternative to the traditional view of coercive control. In the *enabling* view, control does not need to be designed to make processes foolproof but should enable intelligent workers to deal more effectively with inevitable contingencies. This view therefore emphasizes clarifying responsibilities and providing guidance. Managers use control to coordinate workers' activities by enhancing information exchange in ways that provide workers with an understanding of the rationale for the control system as well as a wide range of contextual information, particularly on how a given worker's task fits into the broader organization (Adler & Borys 1996; Ahrens & Chapman 2004). This enabling view seeks frequent interaction between

---

[2] https://apadua.com/

Figure 4.1 Five dimensions of organizational control

managers and workers (Adler 1999; Gregory et al. 2013; Wiener et al. 2016) and goes hand in hand with transparency and worker empowerment to enable workers to be more efficient and effective in their assigned tasks (Cram & Wiener 2020).

4.1.6   Organizational Control Framework

These five dimensions together form the framework we propose as a basis for advancing organizational control research (Figure 4.1 provides an overview). The target (input, behavior, and outcome) and formality (formal and informal) provide the six control approaches available to superiors (top-down control), co-workers (peer control), the workers themselves (self-control), and third parties (third-party control) to use in a unique combination (holistic approach) to enable and/or coerce the worker and thereby achieve organizational objectives.

4.1.7   Alternative Control Frameworks

In their literature review of the last fifty years' research on organizational control, Cardinal and colleagues (2017) identified seven control frameworks. In addition to the four we have already discussed earlier – the control systems framework (market, bureaucracy, clan), the behavior-output framework, the formal control targets framework, and the formal and informal control targets framework – we will briefly outline the other three frameworks in Cardinal et al. (2017), as well as other prominent frameworks in the literature.

Control graph. Tannenbaum's (1962) control graph conceptualizes organizational control as the sum of interpersonal influence relations and focuses on assessing how control is developed and deployed at different hierarchical levels. A control graph plots the amount of control exercised at various hierarchical levels, thereby capturing both the total sum of interpersonal influence relations in an organization and the distribution of control throughout that organization (Tannenbaum 1962, 1968). Echoing the human relations paradigm (Section 3.1.3), Tannenbaum's research argues that control should be shared across different levels of the organization to generate positive psychological outcomes by enhancing self-esteem through identification, motivation, and job satisfaction. Although Tannenbaum's social psychological emphasis resonated with subsequent researchers and resulted in an identifiable research stream based on his ideas (e.g., work in Cluster 16 of our co-citation analysis in Section 3.2.2), his work never spread broadly across the organizational control field.

Macro controls. Hoskisson and colleagues' (1993) macro control framework maintains that the decisions senior-level corporate managers are confronted with are more uncertain, and their specific behaviors are not as programmable, as regular workers' tasks. Instead of differentiating behavior control and outcome control, the authors therefore propose the terms *strategic control*, which refers to the evaluation of managers based on their understanding of strategic priorities before implementation (i.e., ex ante), and *financial control*, which refers to evaluating managers based on financial performance after their decisions were implemented (i.e., ex post). They further recommend an emphasis on strategic control, as a focus on short-term financial incentives could lead to less risk taking and lower investment in research and development, which could jeopardize the organization's long-term performance. While this framework has not been widely adopted in organizational control research, it has influenced subsequent research on corporate governance (see Cardinal et al. 2017, for a summary), as evident from its prominent role in Cluster 15's intellectual base (see Section 3.2.2 for details).

Levers of control. Simons's (1995b) *levers of control (LoC) framework* originated in the accounting discipline and became the most influential alternative control framework, justifying a more in-depth discussion here. This framework distinguishes between four types of top-down, formal control systems that are considered in a holistic way to balance opposing forces and help organizations implement their strategies. *Belief systems* consist of the explicit set of organizational definitions that are formally communicated and systematically reinforced by managers to provide basic values, purpose, and direction for the organization (Simons 1995b). They are deliberately designed to lead workers to align themselves with the organization's core values and mission, especially as they engage in nonroutine, creative tasks and seek out new opportunities. *Boundary systems* identify and communicate areas, actions, behaviors, and risks that workers must avoid. *Diagnostic control* is simple, feedback-based control focused on monitoring critical performance variables, such as costs and revenues, and rewarding goal achievement. Last, *interactive control* focuses on monitoring activities that represent strategic uncertainties by communicating concerns and promoting the vertical exchange of information to help workers avoid pitfalls. Diagnostic and interactive control systems combined thus represent feedback and performance measurement systems, with the difference between the two being the personal attention they receive from managers (Simons 1995b).

Table 4.4 *Correspondence of Simons's (1995b) LoC systems with our control framework*

Control lever	Definition	Correspondence with our top-down control dimensions
Belief systems	Explicit sets of shared beliefs that define basic values, purpose, and direction	Formal input control
Boundary systems	Formally stated limits and rules that must be respected	Formal behavior control
Diagnostic control systems	Output target setting, assessments, and corrections of negative deviations	Formal outcome control
Interactive control systems	Intensive top management (in contrast to line management or staff) attention and involvement in deploying or adapting one or more of the other control systems	Not explicitly captured as it overlaps with multiple control dimensions (e.g., target, direction, and style). The difference between interactive and diagnostic control systems is based on the controller (top manager versus line manager) and the control focus (routine tasks versus novel/uncertain tasks)

In contrast to earlier contingency frameworks (e.g., Ouchi & Maguire 1975), LoC is an explicitly holistic control framework, with the four control levers complementing each other in strategy implementation. Specifically, "the interplay of positive and negative forces creates a dynamic tension between opportunistic innovation and predictable goal achievement that is necessary to simulate and control profitable growth" (Simons 2000: 301). This overarching tension is evident in three specific tensions that the LoC should balance: intended versus emergent strategy, workers' self-interested versus stewardship behavior, and unlimited opportunity space versus limited attention (Simons 1995b). Simons considers belief and interactive control systems as positive and inspirational forces that serve as a catalyst for the emergence of new ideas and worker learning, and boundary and diagnostic systems as limits to opportunity-seeking behavior and as an insurance that workers are compliant with managers' directions. Based on this description, the LoC framework entails both enabling and coercive control elements. Simons's (1995b) first three levers map well onto our control dimensions (see Table 4.4). Interactive control adds another dimension to the control discussion by capturing the degree of management attention and involvement.

Apart from a few attempts to establish the LoC framework in the management and strategy field (e.g., Marginson 2002; Simons 1991, 1994), it has almost exclusively been adopted and further developed in the managerial accounting discipline. Simons's work is part of Cluster 0's research front on project management control (Simons 1994) as well as Cluster 13's research front on classic accounting control (Simons 1987, 1990) (see Section 3.2.2 for details). It is also included in five clusters' intellectual bases: Cluster 1 on accounting control systems (Simons 2000), Cluster 6 on alliance and marketing channel control (Simons 1994), Cluster 12 on control configurations (Simons 1995b), Cluster 13 on classic accounting control (Simons 1987, 1990), and Cluster 15 on corporate governance (Simons 1991). However, some researchers have criticized the conceptualization and operationalization of especially the interactive control system, which studies found to be unstable in exploratory factor analyses, operationalized inconsistently throughout the literature, and both context-dependent and time-dependent (Bisbe et al. 2007; Grafton et al. 2010; Gray 1990). In response, as the construct of interactive control overlaps with some of our control dimensions – in particular, the enabling logic of the style dimension – we do not consider it in our framework.

Performance management. In addition to the seven frameworks Cardinal et al. (2017) have distinguished, another class of organizational control frameworks that has emerged in the accounting discipline is performance management frameworks. These frameworks rely mainly on formal behavior and outcome control and are closely related to balanced scorecard approaches (Kaplan & Norton 1996). Otley's (1999) performance management framework, for example, examines the comprehensive design of control systems in light of five central issues – starting with the key organizational objectives, the strategies and plans for their attainment, target setting, incentive and reward structures, and information feedback loops. This framework has been widely adopted in the managerial accounting literature and is part of the intellectual base of two clusters in our co-citation analysis in Section 3.2.2: Cluster 8 on accounting performance-management systems (Otley 1978) and Cluster 13 on classic accounting control (e.g., Otley 1980). It focuses on how control systems can address reward, performance, planning, and organizational learning issues by aligning the components of a control system with a firm's strategic demands.

Strategic control. Another organizational control framework was developed by Schreyögg and Steinmann (1987) and is part of Cluster 8's (accounting performance-management systems) intellectual base (see Section 3.2.2). This framework rests on a three-part critique of traditional control systems. First, the corrective measures for a necessary plan revision based on feedback are usually too late, which means that traditional control suffers from a temporal problem. Second, traditional control focuses primarily on the means of goal achievement, and not on the appropriateness of the goals and standards, and therefore, traditional control also has a factual problem. Third, the predictability and controllability that are required for traditional control frameworks are unrealistic in increasingly dynamic and complex environments. In these environments, the importance of strategic planning decreases in favor of strategic control, which focuses on organizational adaptation and learning processes. Instead of seeing control as a downstream and subordinate function, this framework proposes planning and control as simultaneous and complementary processes of corporate management.

Schreyögg and Steinmann (1987) conceptualize strategic control as comprising three components. The ongoing monitoring of progress and results during strategy implementation (labeled *implementation control*) remains the essential first component, and is in line with our formal behavior and formal outcome controls. However, the validity of the strategy content, or more precisely, the planning premises, is monitored already during strategy formulation, making *premise control* the second component of strategic control. The third component, *strategic surveillance*, is focused on identifying possible internal and external threats to the selected strategy at an early stage. The strategic control system's focus therefore expands from internal control to include aligning the organization with its environment. Classic feedback control is supplemented by feedforward control.

In addition to these prominent organizational control frameworks (see Table 4.5 for an overview), there are several others that are worth noting and are also listed in the table. These include the distinction between organic and mechanistic control (Burns & Stalker 1961), between problem-solving and judicial control (Gavin et al. 1995), between restrictive and promotive control (Scholl 1999), between technocratic and socio-ideological control (Alvesson & Kärreman 2004), and between different types of peer control (Loughry & Tosi 2008) and function-specific control, such as salesforce control (Kohli et al. 1998).

4.2   Functions and Purpose of Organizational Control

Functions of organizational control refer to *how* the five organizational control dimensions – target, formality, singularity, direction, and style – influence outcomes (Cardinal et al. 2017). Building on its agency-theoretic foundation, organizational control can improve task performance and other outcome variables via two key mediating mechanisms. The *monitoring function* gives organizations better information about workers' behavior and performance and reduces opportunities to engage in hidden action. The *incentive function* motivates workers to engage in behaviors that are beneficial to the organization in order to earn rewards or avoid negative consequences (Loughry & Tosi 2008).

Building on key tenets of information processing theory (see Joseph & Gaba 2020, for a review), recent research in the management discipline has added a third control function, *coordination*. According to this view, organizational

Table 4.3 *Comparison of organizational control frameworks*

Frameworks	Target	Formality	Singularity	Style	Direction	Distinctive feature(s) of this framework
Organic and mechanistic control (Burns & Stalker 1961)	• Behavior (mechanistic) • Input, clan (organic)	• Formal (mechanistic) • Informal (organic)	• Weak holistic	• Coercive	• Top-down	• Organic and mechanistic control distinction can be used to classify controls but cannot be unambiguously mapped on target and formality dimensions
Control graph (Tannenbaum 1962)	• n/a	• Formal	• Singular	• Enabling	• Top-down	• Total amount of control • Distribution of control
Behavior-output control (Ouchi & Maguire 1975)	• Behavior • Outcome	• Formal	• Weak holistic	• Coercive	• Top-down	• Means-ends contingency theory
Organization design (Mintzberg 1981)	• Input (professional bureaucracy) • Behavior (simple structure, machine bureaucracy) • Outcome (divisionalized form)	• Formal (machine bureaucracy, divisionalized form) • Informal (simple structure, professional bureaucracy, adhocracy)	• Weak holistic	• Coercive	• Top-down (simple structure, machine/professional bureaucracy, divisionalized form) • Peer (adhocracy) • Self (professional bureaucracy)	• Five configurations as combinations of control, structure, and situation: simple structure, machine bureaucracy, professional bureaucracy, divisionalized form, and adhocracy
Strategic control (Schreyögg & Steinmann 1987)	• Behavior and outcome (implementation control)	• Formal	• Weak holistic	• Enabling and coercive	• Top-down	• Forward-looking feedforward controls: • Premise control • Strategic surveillance
Control systems (Ouchi 1979)	• Input (clan) • Behavior (bureaucracy) • Outcome (market)	• Formal • Informal	• Weak holistic	• Coercive	• Top-down	• Control systems as ideal organizational arrangements driven by contextual factors

Table 4.5 (*cont.*)

Frameworks	Target	Formality	Singularity	Style	Direction	Distinctive feature(s) of this framework
Macro controls (Hoskisson et al. 1993)	• Outcome (financial control)	• Formal	• Weak holistic	• Coercive	• Top-down	• Relevance in corporate governance research • Strategic control (evaluation based on strategic criteria) as an alternative to financial control
Levers of control (Simons 1994)	• Input (belief systems) • Behavior (boundary systems) • Outcome (diagnostic)	• Formal	• Strong holistic	• Enabling and coercive	• Top-down	• Interactive control: intensive top-management attention and involvement using and adapting one or more of the other control systems
Judicial and problem-solving control (Gavin et al. 1995)	• n/a	• Formal	• Singular	• Enabling (problem-solving) or coercive (judicial control)	• Top-down	• Judicial control focused on "punitive measures as a deterrent to future poor performance incidents" (p. 209) • Problem-solving control "more interactive, cooperative, and nonpunitive in nature" (p. 209)
Salespeople's learning and performance orientation (Kohli et al. 1998)	• Input/behavior (capability orientation) • Behavior (activity orientation) • Outcome (end-results orientation)	• Formal	• Weak holistic	• Enabling and coercive	• Top-down	• Capability-orientation focused on "the development of salespeople's skills that enhance the quality of their behaviors" (p. 264); the supervisor's role is more like a coach, and it thus resembles interactive control
Performance management (Otley 1999)	• Behavior • Outcome	• Formal	• Weak holistic	• Coercive	• Top-down	• Comprehensive question list for strategy implementation

	Control targets	Formal/Informal	Holistic	Enabling/Coercive	Direction	Description
Restrictive and promotive control (Scholl 1999)	• n/a	• Formal	• Singular	• Enabling and coercive	• Top-down	• Distinction between restrictive and promotive control takes worker interests into account and whether they are aligned with the managers' (promotive) or not (restrictive control, in which the manager exerts power)
Formal control targets (Cardinal 2001)	• Input • Behavior • Outcome	• Formal	• Weak holistic	• Enabling and coercive	• Top-down	• Formal input, behavior, and outcome control
Interfaces of control (Alvesson & Kärreman 2004)	• Behavior and outcome control (technocratic control) • Clan/peer/self-control (socio-ideological control)	• Formal (technocratic) • Informal (socio-ideological)	• Strong holistic	• Coercive	• Top-down • Peer • Self	• Socio-ideological control can be classified as input control; like clan control, it also relies on shared meanings indirectly achieving self-control of workers and peer control among workers
Formal and informal control targets (Cardinal et al. 2004)	• Input • Behavior • Outcome	• Formal • Informal	• Strong holistic	• Enabling and coercive	• Top-down	• Formal and informal input, behavior, and outcome control
Peer control (Loughry & Tosi 2008)	• n/a	• Formal • Informal	• Strong holistic	• Enabling and coercive	• Peer	• Direct versus indirect peer control • Management-induced versus peer-induced peer controls
Our control framework	• Input • Behavior • Outcome	• Formal • Informal	• Strong holistic	• Enabling and coercive	• Top-down • Peer • Self • Third-party	• Integrates all control dimensions

control can foster the exchange of important task-related information that allows workers to accomplish task objectives more efficiently and effectively (Long et al. 2015). Organizational control can thus enhance task performance by helping "inform [workers] of the requirements they are obligated to achieve, provide them with ways to make their goals congruent with broader objectives, and direct them to resources (e.g., physical resources, information) necessary to achieve desired results" (Sitkin et al. 2020: 343).

The coordination and monitoring functions are echoed in the accounting literature. Following Anthony's (1965) seminal research, this literature maintains that organizational control is aimed at ensuring that the tasks performed by all members of an organization come together in a coordinated set of actions. In addition, observations and reports on the actual achievement are used to ensure that the planned actions really achieve the desired results (Otley et al. 1995).

This conceptualization of organizational control functions overlaps with the two functions of organizations in general: the division of labor and the integration of effort (March & Simon 1958; Puranam et al. 2014). The first, division of labor, refers to the breakdown of an organization's goals into contributory tasks and the allocation of these tasks to individual members within the organization, and falls outside our focus on organizational control. The second, however, concerns the integration of effort and consists of two subfunctions that closely reflect two of the three functions of organizational control. The provision of rewards, which consists of monetary and nonmonetary rewards to motivate members to cooperate by taking costly actions toward executing the tasks they have been allocated (Puranam et al. 2014), maps onto organizational control's incentive function. The provision of information, which refers to workers having access to the information needed to execute their tasks and coordinate actions with others (Puranam et al. 2014), maps onto control's coordination function.

These three functions of organizational control are conceptually distinct from the concept of *subordination*, which Sitkin et al. (2020) added as an additional control function in their recent review of the organizational control literature. This view resonates with critical control theorists (e.g., Barker 1993; Delbridge 2010; Jermier 1998), who have long conceptualized control as a means that powerful authorities use to accomplish their goals by subjugating workers, and who set out to unmask the more nefarious aspects of organizational control (see Section 3.5 for a discussion of this view). As discussed in that chapter, the critical perspective also encourages a reflection on the purpose of control, which is less focused on what control is, and more on what it could be (Jermier 1998). However, both purpose and subordination contain value judgments about the purpose of control, and therefore do not fall under our conceptualization of control functions as the mechanisms for *how* organizational control influences outcomes.

4.3   Outcomes of Organizational Control

Another key element in our framework is the outcomes of control. We follow Cardinal et al.'s (2017) classification of organizational control outcomes based on the competing values approach, which differentiates outcomes on two dimensions. The internal/external dimension distinguishes processes and people inside the organization from external outcomes that are more closely aligned with stakeholders in the outside environment. The stability/flexibility dimension differentiates stability outcomes that are focused on routinized aspects of the organization from flexibility outcomes that are focused on adaptation and change (Quinn & Rohrbaugh 1983).

We further extend Cardinal et al.'s (2017) framework by considering unintended or negative consequences for each of the four outcome categories. As Chen and colleagues (2022: 309) have pointed out, there are two possible types of unintended consequences: "(1) where performing behaviors in accordance with tight control directly decreases project success, and (2) where tight control causes workplace resistance." In addition, we extend previous research by acknowledging that organizational control can have different, and even contrary, effects on outcomes at different levels of analysis, such as behavior control being beneficial for performance at the team level, but detrimental to job satisfaction at the individual team member level, as well as in the short run versus the long run.

4.3.1   Outcome Categories

Adaptability outcomes. Adaptability outcomes focus on an organization's ability to survive and prosper in the long run, with organizational learning, innovation, and change serving as examples of such outcomes. Around 21 percent of the organizational control studies reviewed by Cardinal et al. (2017) focused on such adaptability outcomes.

Going back more than half a century (Burns & Stalker 1961; Thompson 1967), the organizational behavior and social psychology literatures have positioned adaptability and control as opposing forces. In this view, workers' autonomy and freedom over their own work breed innovation, whereas control constitutes a barrier to any creative endeavor (e.g., Amabile et al. 1996; Shalley et al. 2000, 2004). Especially behavior control, with its tendency to suppress any deviation from standardized processes, can compress the very variation and experimentation that are at the heart of innovation (March & Simon 1958). The opposing forces of control and creativity also present a challenge for organizations: While organizations are dependent on control systems, standardized practices, and routines to ensure smooth and efficient operations, these systems can also have the unintended consequence of inhibiting workers' creative propensities (Zhou & George 2003).

However, these arguments and findings should be examined very carefully, as the majority of studies on the relationship between control and creativity focused on controls that explicitly limit behavior, such as monitoring or rewards (e.g., Gilson et al. 2005; Hirst et al. 2011; Shalley et al. 2000). In addition, more recent research has argued (e.g., Adler & Chen 2011) and found (e.g., Speklé et al. 2017) that creativity and control can, in fact, coexist, as there are no inevitable trade-offs between creativity and control, and that organizations can achieve both. Managers are able to design organizational control systems that provide both space to be creative and boundaries and direction for problems that need innovative solutions, as well as the incentives to engage in creative thought (Speklé et al. 2017). Research building on Simons's holistic LoC framework (see Section 4.1.7), for example, studied adaptability outcomes from an enabling perspective (e.g., Marginson 2002), leading to a "growing consensus that formal controls, when activated in an enabling, facilitative, and interactive fashion, increase the capacity of an organization to derive benefits from innovation" (Bedford 2015: 12).

Human relations (HR) outcomes. Building on the positive organizational scholarship movement (e.g., Cameron & Caza 2004; Cameron & Spreitzer 2012; Dutton et al. 2006), the focal point of HR outcomes is worker well-being and growth. Examples of such outcome variables are increased worker satisfaction, morale, effort, and citizenship (Cardinal et al. 2017). Forty-four percent of the studies that Cardinal et al. (2017) reviewed focused on these intended HR outcomes. On the flipside are unintended HR outcomes, such as dissatisfaction, stress, lack of effort in the form of loafing or freeriding, misbehavior, and even illegal activities, such as worker theft. Additional unintended HR outcomes are discussed in the burgeoning literature on workplace resistance (e.g., Anteby & Chan 2018; Cameron & Rahman 2022; Maffie 2022), with workers reacting to organizational controls with cynicism (Fleming & Spicer 2003) or open resistance in the form of strikes (Rennstam & Kärreman 2020).

These negative effects of organizational control on HR outcomes can be explained by work in psychology and microeconomics suggesting that extrinsic motivation – such as the promise of rewards and recognition in behavior and outcome control – tends to crowd out intrinsic motivation, or people pursuing an activity for its inherent satisfaction, and not to obtain some external reward (Deci 1971). Indeed, experimental studies, such as Enzle and Anderson (1993), have found that surveillance, when it is perceived as controlling, threatens people's personal autonomy and decreases their intrinsic motivation. While clearly not all organizational tasks are intrinsically motivating, some of them are, at least to a certain extent, and those could be susceptible to such a crowding-out effect.

Some meta-analyses have found mixed or even no effects of extrinsic rewards on intrinsic motivation (e.g., Cameron & Pierce 1994; Eisenberger &

Cameron 1996), but others have provided evidence that properly accounting for the treatment of moderating and dependent variables – for example, the kind of reward or class of dependent variable measure – reveals a robust effect of motivation crowding (e.g., Deci et al. 1999; Rummel & Feinberg 1988; Tang & Hall 1995; Wiersma 1992). Accordingly, increasing organizational control might lead to the unintended consequence of undermining workers' intrinsic motivation for a task, with negative consequences for both HR outcomes (e.g., dissatisfaction, lack of effort, perfunctory compliance, and decreasing extra-role behavior) and rational goal outcomes.

Process outcomes. The focus of process outcomes, examined in 36 percent of control research reviewed by Cardinal et al. (2017), is on order and regularity, as is evident from examples, such as smooth workflow processes, effective information flows, and task coordination. Studies examining these outcomes were historically limited to processes within the organization, but more and more studies have broadened their focus and included processes cutting across organizational boundaries, such as information flows and coordination with alliance partners (e.g., Li et al. 2010), although the focal organization and its needs remain central.

Rational goal outcomes. The most frequently examined control outcomes are rational goal outcomes, with close to 50 percent of research focused on this aspect (Cardinal et al. 2017). These outcomes have efficiency and productivity as focal points, and they aim at the attainment of short-term performance goals that are of interest to shareholders, customers, and other stakeholders. Examples are profitability, risk-adjusted returns, and other core business outcomes, as well as product or service quality.

However, a focus on rational goal outcomes must be qualified by also considering the financial costs associated with organizational control. Prior research has provided ample examples of managers tightening organizational controls to the point where increasing costs outweighed controls' benefits (e.g., Bonner et al. 2002; Cardinal 2001). Mankins et al. (2014), for instance, provide astonishing numbers for how much time a single weekly performance review meeting can consume across the organization they studied: the actual performance review meeting time among the executive committee (7,000 person hours); meetings of the executives' respective reporting units (20,000 hours); unit team meetings to generate and cross-check critical information in anticipation of the executive committee meetings (63,000 hours); as well as preparatory meetings (210,000 hours). Accounting for all these meetings, the company's performance review cumulatively consumed about 300,000 person hours a year. Compliance with self-imposed rules and regulations is similarly costly: Deloitte (2015) estimated that Australian businesses spent $155 billion a year to satisfy internal organizational requirements – $21 billion to develop and administer these rules, and a stunning $134 billion a year in compliance costs – often with little to show for it. Furthermore, we all have become only too familiar with the steep increase in virtual meetings since the widespread shift to remote work at the start of the COVID-19 pandemic (Feintzeig 2021), despite our collective realization that most of those meetings "could have been an email" (Dill 2022).

In addition to these direct costs of control, and in line with our discussion of unintended HR outcomes, increasing workers' extrinsic motivation via organizational control might also undermine their intrinsic motivation for a task (Deci 1971), which likely results in lower satisfaction and effort, which, in turn, could jeopardize rational goal outcomes, such as task performance.

4.3.2 Level of Analysis Differences

Most organizational control studies have examined outcome variables at the intraorganizational level, which comprises individual-level outcomes (e.g., worker satisfaction), team-level outcomes (e.g., team success), business unit- or divisional-level outcomes (e.g., divisional performance), and firm-level outcomes (e.g., firm performance). In contrast to intraorganizational studies, interorganizational studies examine how control influences alliance, franchise, joint venture, or ecosystem partners and their pursuit of both individual and collective goals.

Moreover, organizational control can simultaneously affect multiple outcomes at different levels, often in different, even opposite, ways. Case in point, even as managers tout the efficiency gains from the surveillance of workers (a positive rational goal outcome at the organizational level), what often remains unmeasured is the cost to the workers themselves (an unintended HR outcome at the individual level). More specifically, the demand to meet electronically monitored goals often leads to workers taking risks and pushing themselves physically in ways that result in more injuries, lower morale, and higher staff turnover. At the global shipping company UPS, the "mental whip" of constant surveillance by the telematics system has led drivers to "beat the system" by disregarding safety rules, putting themselves and others in danger (Ajunwa et al. 2017). Another example is one of our own studies of volunteer workers (Walter et al. 2021), which found indirect peer control – that is, the prevalence of gossiping about and avoiding certain co-workers – to have a positive effect on the performance of their respective teams. However, indirect peer control's team-level benefits came with negative consequences at the individual level, as workers expressed lower levels of job satisfaction. From these and other examples of a given control choice's differential effects on outcomes at different levels of analysis, it becomes evident that managers can face inherent trade-offs when it comes to their organizational control choices.

4.3.3   Temporal Considerations

It is further conceivable that organizational control might affect outcomes in different temporal patterns, although there is only little research to inform us about these patterns. Going back to our study of volunteer workers (Walter et al. 2021), accepting indirect peer control's positive effect on team performance might be shortsighted, as its detrimental effect on job satisfaction might lead to workers decreasing their efforts and/or leaving the organization in the long run, especially in a volunteer context, which would subsequently lower team performance. Along the same lines, the short-term efficiency benefits of standardizing and streamlining organizational processes with the help of behavior control could have the unintended long-term consequence of undermining creative variation and, hence, organizational innovation (Zhou & George 2003).

Together, the differential effects of a given organizational control choice – both at different levels of analysis and regarding different time horizons – make it even more important to consider combining different types of control into more balanced or holistic control approaches.

4.4   Key Contingencies

Organizational controls' influence on outcome variables further depends on the context in which the controls are enacted. While a comprehensive review of all theoretically hypothesized and empirically supported contingencies is beyond the scope of this chapter, we will briefly list several key contingencies across different levels of analysis. Along with the individual characteristics of the manager and worker, the task, the organization, and the external environment represent crucial context factors.

At the individual level, personality differences, such as the locus of control (e.g., Cameron & Rahman 2022; Elias 2009),[3] the experience and familiarity with the task, the organization, and the control approach, affect the relationships between controls and outcomes (Ouchi 1978), as could – at the dyadic level between manager and worker – their experience working together and their prior familiarity and closeness. At the task level, prior research has predominantly examined controller knowledge or knowledge about the transformation process (e.g., Kirsch et al. 2010), as well as task programmability, behavior observability, and outcome measurability (e.g., Liu & Wang 2014). Prior research has shown that the distinction between routine and nonroutine

---

[3] Individuals differ in the extent to which they believe they can control their environment, and in the ways they attribute success and failure to internal or external causes, which is commonly referred to as the *locus of control* (Rotter 1966; Spector 1982).

work, between exploitative and exploratory tasks, as well as task uncertainty, complexity, and interdependence influence the effectiveness of organizational controls (e.g., Kirsch 1997; Kirsch & Choudhury 2010; Kreutzer et al. 2016; Richter et al. 2023).

At the organizational level, the size of the firm, its resources (or resource constraints), culture, and micro-political context, as well as the interrelatedness and distance (mainly cultural or geographic distance) among its units/ divisions and external partners, have been the focus of inquiry (e.g., Handley & Benton 2013). At the interorganizational level, general alliance experience, partner-specific experience, and partner relative dependence, as well as performance risk and relational risk, have been studied as potential moderators (e.g., Zeng et al. 2021). Furthermore, at the external environment level, industry dynamism, turbulence, complexity, and munificence as well as national and regional institutions, laws, and cultural preferences have proved to influence control-outcome relationships (e.g., Zeng et al. 2021).

In line with our discussion of control outcomes, these key contingencies can also create challenges for organizational control across different levels of analysis. For example, the existence of task interdependencies constrains the feasibility of outcome control (such as compensation based on individual performance) at the individual level, as outcomes depend on other workers' contributions to the task, and individuals will likely not want to accept sole responsibility for joint outcomes. At the same time, however, such task interdependencies also create a need for outcome control at the organizational level, which helps direct individual activities toward the achievement of organizational objectives (Adler & Chen 2011; Grabner 2014).

4.5   Meta-analytical Review of the Organizational Control Literature

Having assembled the key elements of our organizational control framework, we conducted a meta-analytical review of the literature to substantiate key relationships between these elements: between antecedents and controls, between controls and outcomes, interactions between individual controls, and contingency effects on control-outcome relationships. A meta-analysis allows us to accomplish two main goals: to estimate the overall strength and direction of these relationships and to estimate the across-study variance in the relationship estimates as well as the factors (i.e., moderator variables) that explain this variance (cf., Hunter & Schmidt 2015). It is important to note, however, that a meta-analytical review of largely cross-sectional studies can only provide insights about correlations, but not causal relationships between the examined variables (Aguinis et al. 2011). In the following, we first summarize our expectations for key relationships, making use of the existing literature, before testing them based on 293 top-tier, peer-reviewed journal articles, published between 1967 and 2022. Compared to the most recent meta-analysis on organizational control by Sihag and Rijsdijk (2019), which includes 108 studies published up to May 2017, our meta-analysis covers both a broader set of studies and more recent studies, which better represent contemporary organizational realities (see Chapter 5 for a discussion of such realities).

4.5.1   Expected Organizational Control Relationships

Given the complexity of our organizing framework (see Figure 1.1) as well as contradictory predictions, and sometimes ambiguous empirical findings, across the control literature, we do not propose formal hypotheses. Instead, we briefly summarize the key relationships between antecedents, controls, and outcomes and identify key contingencies before we examine those relationships meta-analytically.

Relationships between antecedents and control. As outlined in Sections 3.4 and 4.1.3, classic control theory has maintained that the accuracy with which behavior or outcomes can be observed or measured should determine the choice of the control target (Ouchi 1977). In line with that logic, when workers' behavior can be observed, and the manager has sufficient knowledge about the task, control should focus on workers' behavior. When results can be measured accurately, and when unclear or ambiguous performance standards are not a problem, control should focus on outcomes (Jaworski & MacInnis 1989; Kirsch 1996, 1997; Kirsch et al. 2002). Similarly, classic control theory has assumed input control and informal control to fill the void if a task is characterized by an incomplete understanding of cause–effect and ambiguous performance standards, and thus neither reliable behavior nor valid outcome measures are available (Choudhury & Sabherwal 2003; Eisenhardt 1985; Kirsch et al. 2010; Snell & Youndt 1995). In line with these arguments, we would expect behavior observability, managers' knowledge of the task, and outcome measurability to influence the target of control.

Relationships between control and outcomes. As outlined in Section 4.2, organizational control can improve task performance and other outcome variables via three key mediating mechanisms: monitoring, which gives organizations better information about workers' behavior and performance and reduces opportunities to engage in hidden action; incentives that motivate workers to engage in behaviors that are beneficial to the organization in order to earn rewards or avoid negative consequences; and coordination, or the exchange of important task-related information, that allows workers to accomplish task objectives more efficiently and effectively. In line with this logic, we would expect organizational control (input, behavior, outcome, peer, and self-control) to have a positive effect on organizational outcomes (adaptability, HR, process, and rational goal outcomes).

Moderators. Our review of the literature on organizational control also suggests a number of boundary conditions on the relationships discussed earlier. With organizational control comprising organizational attempts to align members' actions with an organization's goals (see Section 2.1), we expect both the *organizational setting* – intra- versus interorganizational – and the *level of analysis* – for example, individual, project, team, SBU, or firm – to act as potential moderators of our examined relationships. The organizational control literature's early emphasis on task characteristics for control choices (e.g., Ouchi & Maguire 1975) suggests that accounting for the variability in *task types* – for example, manufacturing, sales, research and development, or service – might help further qualify our meta-analytical results. Given their respective advantages and disadvantages – self-reported data may be subject to a host of human biases but tend to be more fine-grained, whereas archival measures may be less biased but often represent more distant proxies (Venkatraman & Ramanujam 1986) – we would expect the *nature of the dependent variable* to influence organizational control relationships. We further added a fairly common *industry* control to our moderator analysis. In light of the well-established influence of language and cultural differences on organizational control processes and outcomes – see, for example, the literature that comprises Cluster 19 on "Cross-cultural control" in our co-citation analysis (Section 3.2.2) – we considered the *geographic location* of a sample as an additional boundary condition. While the *size* of a team or organization is often considered as a boundary condition in meta-analyses, given the variability of this construct in our sample – which comprises settings ranging from individual transactions and projects to multinational organizations and interorganizational alliances – size is not comparable in a meaningful way across samples, and we did not consider it in our analysis.

Control as substitutes versus complements. As outlined in Section 4.1.3, classic control theory has assumed equifinality between the targets of control, with behavior control and outcome control serving as substitutes for one another (Ouchi 1977), and formal control and informal control serving as substitutes for each other (Eisenhardt 1985). Contrary to this classic view, recent theoretical arguments and empirical evidence point toward a complementary relationship among controls. For example, some studies have found that both behavior control and outcome control are positively associated with performance outcomes (e.g., Cardinal 2001; Kirsch 1997), which is in line with the holistic control approach (Cardinal et al. 2017). This research explicitly acknowledges interdependencies among controls (Cardinal 2001) and the need for balance between different control types (Cardinal et al. 2004). In addition, more recent studies have also provided empirical support for the argument that the simultaneous use of behavior control and outcome control can mitigate their respective disadvantages and, thus, enhance performance outcomes (Kreutzer et al. 2015), providing additional support for the holistic view. For our meta-analysis, we do not take a position on this debate but will examine whether controls act as substitutes, or whether they complement each other in their influence on outcomes.

4.5.2 Data Collection

To investigate these relationships meta-analytically, we built on our literature reviews in Chapters 2 and 3 and performed searches of article titles, keywords, and abstracts in the *Web of Science*, with Boolean combinations of relevant keywords detailed in Section 4.7. We further supplemented our *Web of Science* search with a similar search of the *Proquest Central* database, which is detailed in Section 4.8. Both databases have recently been recommended as "well-suited to evidence synthesis in the form of systematic reviews in that they met all necessary performance requirements" and therefore "can be used as principal search systems" (Gusenbauer & Haddaway 2020: 208). In keeping with prior meta-analytic reviews (Bergh et al. 2016), we focused on articles published in the top peer-reviewed journals across management, accounting, marketing, information systems, operations management, finance, economics, and business ethics, that are part of the Financial Times 50 list, which is detailed in Table 4.6. We focused on articles published in these journals to ensure the high quality of the studies we included in our analysis and to capture those articles that are likely to have the largest influence on the field (Bergh et al. 2016). Since our meta-analysis requires empirical results to be reported in an article, we excluded the *Academy of Management Review*, the *Harvard Business Review*, and the *MIT Sloan Management Review*. Following Bergh et al.'s (2016) recommendation, we did not consider unpublished studies, as we were unable to ascertain that we would obtain a representative sample of the population of unpublished studies, or control for study quality absent a full peer review. Prior research has further found that excluding unpublished studies has no influence on meta-analytic findings (Dalton et al. 2012).

Our key word searches on October 21 and 26, 2022, resulted in 6,143 *Web of Science* articles and 4,141 *Proquest Central* articles, published over the period from 1900 to 2022. Excluding duplicate articles with the help of HubMeta[4] resulted in a total of 7,844 articles, for which we manually screened titles and abstracts. We excluded 6,426 articles based on their titles and abstracts,[5] and

---

[4] www.hubmeta.com/
[5] Cohen's (1960) kappa statistic for interrater reliability of this process was 0.987, and any disagreements were resolved via discussion.

then conducted a full-text screening of the remaining 1,418 articles. Of these 1,418 articles, 1,108 turned out to be irrelevant for our study purpose or did not contain effect sizes we could extract. We also excluded seventeen articles that exhibited an overlap in their samples (cf., Wood 2007), and included two independent samples reported in the same article for fifteen articles, and three independent samples for one article. Our final sample consists of 293 articles published between 1967 and 2022, containing 310 independent samples, with a total of 24,359 effect sizes, and a total sample size of 110,585.

4.5.3   Data Coding

Following Villiger et al.'s (2022) guidelines, we relied on a coding scheme for all independent, dependent, and moderating variables, which we developed based on the existing control literature (see Table 4.7 for examples), and which we further refined after coding a first batch of studies as a pretest, before re-coding both the initial batch and coding the remaining studies. Each of us coded a part of the sample independently, and then the other coder performed a second coding, such that every study was double-coded. For 1.5 percent of coded variables, we initially disagreed, and we resolved any discrepancies in a discussion.

To code our variables, we further focused on the measurement items that were listed in the coded studies, and not on the labels the authors used, which allowed us to attribute variables to the correct coding categories. All categories are mutually exclusive and have distinct theoretical scope and boundaries.

Table 4.6 *Coded articles by journal*

Journal	#	Journal	#
Accounting Organizations and Society	35	Journal of Management Studies	8
Journal of Marketing	19	Contemporary Accounting Research	7
Strategic Management Journal	19	Journal of Management Information Systems	7
Academy of Management Journal	18	Accounting Review	6
Journal of the Academy of Marketing Science	16	Management Science	6
Journal of Marketing Research	15	Journal of Accounting Research	5
Journal of Business Ethics	14	Organization Studies	5
Organization Science	14	Production and Operations Management	5
Journal of International Business Studies	13	Entrepreneurship Theory & Practice	4
Administrative Science Quarterly	11	Human Resource Management	4
Journal of Applied Psychology	11	Accounting, Organizations & Society	3
Journal of Management	11	MIS Quarterly	3
Journal of Operations Management	11	Journal of Business Venturing	2
Human Relations	10	Research Policy	1
Information Systems Research	9	Strategic Entrepreneurship Journal	1

Table 4.7 *Definition of study constructs and exemplary measures*

Constructs	Definitions and exemplary measures
Antecedents	
Behavior observability	*Definition*: The extent to which the behavior of workers, the procedures they follow, and the way they implement the transformation process can be observed by the manager (Kirsch 1996).
	Measure: Kirsch (1996) developed four items to measure behavior observability, including the time and effort spent monitoring the project leader, the frequency of participating in formal reviews, the frequency of formal and informal discussions with the project leader, and the frequency of written reports received from the project leader.
Controller knowledge	*Definition*: The manager's knowledge of the task and the required transformation process (Kirsch 1996).
	Measure: Kirsch (1996) developed two items to measure the controller's knowledge of the systems development process: the controller's number of prior projects with outcome responsibility, and the extent of practical or academic experience to design, program, and implement comparable projects.
Outcome measurability	*Definition*: The extent to which the results of a task, project, initiative, etc., can be quantified and tracked (Kirsch 1996).
	Measure: Kirsch (1996) developed three items that measure the possibility to accurately and reliably measure whether project goals were met.
Controls	
Input control	*Definition*: Ex ante control, focused on managers selecting workers for specific teams or the organization at large and/or providing workers with appropriate training, development, and socializing opportunities to ensure workers' identities, loyalties, and norms are aligned with the organization's (Cardinal 2001; Snell 1992).
	Measure: Snell and Youndt (1995: 719) used one item to measure input control: "the degree of emphasis placed on staffing procedures and the opportunity provided for training and development."
Behavior control	*Definition*: Explicitly setting operating procedures and rules coupled with direct, personal surveillance of ongoing worker behavior to monitor and evaluate workers' compliance with these rules and procedures (Eisenhardt 1985).
	Measure: Snell (1992: 305) used a nine-item scale measuring "the degree to which standards and procedures are imposed top-down and performance is evaluated via superiors' observation of subordinates' behavior."
Outcome control	*Definition*: Focused on setting targets, such as financial results, for workers to pursue; measuring how well outcomes align with these targets; and providing rewards and penalties, respectively, for success and failure in achieving these targets (Eisenhardt 1985).
	Measure: Cardinal (2001) measured outcome control with a combination of goal specificity, emphasis on output, rewards and recognition, and emphasis on professional output.
Clan control	*Definition*: Emphasizes the role of shared identities, loyalties, and norms in influencing behavior and allowing workers to be managed with a light administrative touch (Ouchi 1979).
	Measure: Kirsch et al. (2002: 497) developed a four-item clan control measure "in which the client liaison becomes part of the project team clan by instilling, embracing, and fostering shared values and goals among the project team, and common approaches to working on the project."

Table 4.7 (*cont.*)

Constructs	Definitions and exemplary measures
Peer control	*Definition*: Exercised laterally between co-workers with no formal authority over each other; both direct, including noticing, praising, correcting, reporting, and discussing what co-workers do, and indirect, including gossiping about and avoiding certain co-workers (Loughry & Tosi 2008).
	Measure: De Jong et al. (2014) developed a four-item measure of peer pressure, including the extent of expressed dissatisfaction, confrontation, information, and feedback when a team member behaves inappropriately, unprofessionally, and fails to meet performance expectations.
Self-control	*Definition*: Workers set their own goals for a particular task and then monitor, evaluate, reward, and sanction themselves (Errichiello & Pianese 2016; Jaworski 1988; Kirsch 1996).
	Measure: Kirsch et al. (2002: 497) developed a two-item measure of self-control capturing the extent to which the "project leader autonomously defines goals and behaviors for the project."
Formal control	*Definition*: Officially sanctioned, explicit, and codified institutional mechanisms, such as written procedures and rules and directions (Cardinal et al. 2017).
	Measure: Kreutzer et al. (2015) developed a seven-item scale that includes both formal behavior control and formal outcome control.
Informal control	*Definition*: Unwritten, unofficial, and less objective forms of control (Cardinal et al. 2004).
	Measure: Four-item scale developed by Kreutzer et al. (2016), containing two items for informal behavior control, and two items for informal outcome control.
Outcomes	
Adaptability outcomes	*Definition*: Focused on an organization's ability to survive and prosper in the long run via organizational learning, innovation, and change (Cardinal et al. 2017).
	Measures: Team creativity (Grabner et al. 2022); innovation rate (Müller-Stewens et al. 2020); alliance formation (Gulati & Westphal 1999); exploration/distal search (Speckbacher & Wabnegg 2020).
HR outcomes	*Definition*: Focused on worker well-being and growth (Cardinal et al. 2017).
	Measures: Cohesion (Courtright et al. 2017); counterproductive work behavior (Tyler & Blader 2005); effort (De Jong et al. 2014); job satisfaction (Walter et al. 2021); organizational citizenship (Lemoine et al. 2015); organizational identification (Hughes & Ahearne 2010); worker health (Xie et al. 2008).
Process outcomes	*Definition*: Focused on order and regularity of work processes (Cardinal et al. 2017).
	Measures: Communication (Chalos & O'Connor 2004); coordination (Dahlstrom & Nygaard 1999); information flow (Homburg et al. 2020).
Rational goal outcomes	*Definition*: Focused on efficiency and productivity, aimed at the attainment of short-term performance goals of interest to shareholders, customers, and other stakeholders (Cardinal et al. 2017).
	Measures: Alliance performance (Posch 2020); competitive advantage (Nidumolu & Subramani 2003); customer satisfaction (Lui & Ngo 2004); financial performance (Koufteros et al. 2014); project performance (Liu 2015).

For each study, we recorded the Pearson correlation coefficient r and the sample size n. We also recorded the composite reliability or Cronbach's alpha, if available, to represent each construct's reliability. Whenever a study measured a construct in different ways, we followed Hunter and Schmidt's (2015) recommendation and used the correlations between the different measures to calculate composite scores, which have better coverage of the underlying construct and higher reliability (Steel et al. 2021). Last, we coded several moderators: *organizational setting* (intra- or interorganizational), *level of analysis* (individual, project, team, SBU, firm, or other), *task types* (manufacturing, sales, research and development (R&D), information systems development (ISD), service, or other), *nature of the dependent variable (DV)* (self-reported, archival, or both), *industry* (services, manufacturing, healthcare, pharma, or other), and *geographic location* (North America, Europe, Asia, or other).

4.5.4   Data Analysis

In line with the majority of meta-analyses (see Aguiniset et al. 2011, for a review), we relied on a random-effects model using Hunter and Schmidt's (2015) procedures, which allow us to correct for range restrictions in both the independent and dependent variables, and to correct for measurement error in the independent variable. To help account for measurement error, we corrected the obtained study correlations for attenuation whenever the study's authors reported the reliabilities for a construct. For studies that did not report reliabilities, we used the average reliability to replace the missing values (cf., Lipsey & Wilson 2001). We then transformed the corrected correlations to Fisher's z scores, which we subsequently weighted by sample size to adjust for sampling error. Weighting correlations by sample size reflects the rationale that an effect size obtained from a study with a large sample offers greater precision than an effect size obtained from a study with a small sample. Once averaged, Fisher's z scores were transformed back to correlation coefficients for ease of interpretation.

For each relationship between our key constructs, we report k, the number of independent effect sizes (i.e., correlations) used to compute the mean effect; N, the total sample size; r, the estimate of the population correlation coefficient; r_c, the sample size-weighted, reliability-corrected estimate of the population correlation coefficient; and SE, the standard error of r_c. We also calculated the 95 percent confidence interval for r_c (Hunter & Schmidt 2015). We were also concerned about the potential impact of unpublished studies that were not included in our literature search. To address this so-called file-drawer problem, we calculated Rosenthal's (1979) *fail-safe N*, which is the number of unpublished studies with statistically nonsignificant effects that would be needed to nullify the meta-analytically derived mean effect size.

To account for heterogeneity, or systematic variability, between studies that cannot be attributed to sampling error, we calculated four additional statistics (cf., Gonzalez-Mulé & Aguinis 2018). First, the Q statistic is the sum of squared deviations of each study's effect size from the mean effect size across studies, with each study weighted by its inverse variance (Hunter & Schmidt 2015).[6] A statistically significant Q test allows us to reject the null hypothesis that effect sizes are constant across studies, and suggests the presence of boundary conditions. Second, we calculated the credibility interval (*CrI*), which provides upper and lower bounds of the population effect size, representing another estimate of variability around the population effect size, after within-study variance and the effects of other methodological and statistical artifacts have been removed. The typical decision rule is that tests for boundary conditions are justified if the *CrI* is sufficiently wide or includes zero (Whitener 1990). Third, we computed τ^2, the between-study variance, which is the Q statistic minus the degrees of freedom (i.e., $k-1$), divided by a scaling factor. Fourth, we calculated the I^2 statistic, or the ratio of between-study variance to total variance, which indicates the proportion of dispersion that can be attributed to real differences in effect sizes as opposed to within-study error. Hence, an I^2 statistic of zero would mean that all variability in effect size estimates is due to sampling error within studies, whereas an I^2 statistic of >0.50 would mean that more than 50 percent of the variance in effect sizes is attributable to between-study effects that should be explored further (Higgins & Thompson 2002). Together, these four measures provide evidence of the statistical significance (Q statistic) as well as the absolute (*CrI*, and τ^2) and relative (I^2) degree of heterogeneity between studies, which would justify the search for moderating variables.

To examine the extent to which boundary conditions predict the relationship between two variables, or potential moderating effects, we conducted meta-regression analyses (Stanley & Jarrell 2005). More specifically, we estimated the following equation:

$$y_i = B_0 + \sum_{j=1}^{J} B_j x_{ij} + u_i + e_i,$$

where y_i denotes the effect size estimate (r) in the ith study; B_0 is the model intercept; x_{ij} denotes the value of the jth boundary condition in the ith study; B_j denotes the unstandardized regression coefficient associated with boundary condition j that indicates the extent to which the effect size y changes because of a one-unit change in x_{ij}; u_i denotes the random-effects variance components with distribution $N(0, \tau^2_{res})$; and e_i denotes the within-study variances with distribution

---

[6] The Q statistic follows a χ^2-distribution with $k-1$ degrees of freedom, with k being the number of studies (Huedo-Medina et al. 2006).

$N(0, v_i)$ (Gonzalez-Mulé & Aguinis 2018). We estimated this equation as a mixed-effects model, which assumes that our sample of studies is a random draw from the population, and that not every possible boundary condition is included in the model, allowing for residual heterogeneity in effects not accounted for by the boundary conditions that are included in the model (Gonzalez-Mulé & Aguinis 2018). We further used a weighted least-squares estimator, which accounts for correlated moderators, assigns proper weighting to studies based on the inverse of the sampling error variance, and avoids dichotomization of continuous modera-tors (Steel & Kammeyer-Mueller 2002).[7] Positive (negative) coefficients indicate an increase (decrease) in effect size with increasingly large values of the moder-ator x. The statistical significance of each individual moderator can be assessed by computing a Z-statistic for each coefficient in the meta-regression model (e.g., $Z_1 = B_1 / SE_{B1}$) (Aguinis et al. 2011).

Given that only very few studies have reported information on interactions between control variables, we followed previous meta-analyses (Cao & Lumineau 2015; Sihag & Rijsdijk 2019) and used meta-analytic structural equation modeling (MASEM) to test for complementarities and substitutions between control variables. We used the meta-analytic correlations matrix as input for subsequent structural equation modeling (SEM) analyses. In line with recommendations in the literature (Bergh et al. 2016; Landis 2013), we used the harmonic mean for sample size. We then tested the simultaneous effects of different organizational controls on our outcome variables to examine whether their total effects are greater (suggesting complementarity) or smaller (sug-gesting substitution) than their direct effects (cf., Alwin & Hauser 1975).

4.5.5   Results

Bivariate correlations. Table 4.8 summarizes the bivariate meta-analytic cor-relations between antecedents and controls, if there are at least two primary studies that have reported a given correlation. In line with our expectations, behavior observability is positively and significantly correlated with behavior control, whereas the correlations with outcome, clan, and self-control are not significant, as indicated by their confidence intervals including zero. Controller knowledge is positively and significantly correlated with both behavior and outcome control, although the correlation is higher for behavior control, with the difference being statistically significant at $p < 0.001$. Input, clan, and self-control do not have significant meta-analytical correlations with controller knowledge, lending additional support to our expectations. Also in line with

---

[7] The weights are calculated as $w_i = 1 - [v_i + \tau_{res}^2]$, where w_i is the weight assigned to the ith study; v_i is the within-study variance of the ith study; and τ_{res}^2 is an estimate of the residual heterogene-ity after accounting for the moderators included in the model (Gonzalez-Mulé & Aguinis 2018).

our expectations, outcome measurability is positively and significantly corre-lated with outcome control. Although several other correlations for outcome measurability are positive and significant, the explained variance for outcome control is the highest (explained variance of 16 percent versus 6 percent for behavior control),[8] with all differences – except the one between input and self-control's correlations with outcome measurability – being statistically sig-nificant at $p < .05$ or better. High values for the fail-safe K further corroborate these significant results. For instance, fifty-four studies with nonsignificant results would be required to make the reported mean effect size for the cor-relation between behavior observability and behavior control no longer sig-nificant. However, some of the effect sizes reported in our results should be interpreted with caution, as they are derived from a limited number of primary studies (e.g., only two studies have reported correlations between behavior observability and self-control). The low fail-safe K values associated with the nonsignificant results also suggest that caution is warranted when interpreting these results.

Table 4.9 summarizes the bivariate meta-analytic correlations between orga-nizational control and outcomes. Overall, input, behavior, and outcome con-trol, as well as formal and informal controls, are the most highly and positively correlated with process outcomes, followed by adaptability (for input and behavior control), rational goal outcomes (for outcome, formal, and informal control), and HR outcomes (for informal control), with all differences statisti-cally significant at $p < 0.01$ or better. Clan control is the most highly correlated with HR outcomes, followed by adaptability and process outcomes, with all differences being statistically significant at $p < 0.01$ or better. Peer control is more highly correlated with rational goal outcomes than with HR outcomes, but the difference is not statistically significant at $p = 0.11$. Aggregated across all outcome dimensions, clan control has the highest positive correlation, fol-lowed by self-control, input and informal control, behavior, and peer control, whereas outcome and formal control have the lowest positive correlations.

With only two exceptions (input and formal control's correlations with HR outcomes), the results provide broad support for a positive relationship between organizational control and a diverse range of outcomes, albeit with large differences between their explained variances. Moreover, large and significant Q values, large amounts of unexplained variance (I^2), as well as many credibility intervals including zero suggest the presence of boundary conditions.

Moderation analyses. Table 4.10 presents the results from our meta-regression examining moderation effects. We did not analyze combinations of control and outcomes with fewer than ten observations and have shaded those

---

[8] The explained variance can be obtained by squaring the effect size (Aguinis et al. 2011).

Table 4.8 Overview of antecedent–organizational control relationships

Relationships		k	N	r	r_c	SE	CI	FSK	Q	CR	τ^2	I^2
Behavior observability	Behavior	5	746	0.24	0.37	0.06	0.25 to 0.49	54	6.67	0.29 to 0.45	0.01	0.40
	Outcome	4	629	0.23	0.33	0.17	0.00 to 0.66	38	49.15***	−0.08 to 0.74	0.20	0.94
	Clan	3	352	0.10	0.12	0.11	−0.09 to 0.33	1	8.93*	−0.07 to 0.31	0.05	0.78
	Self	2	257	0.00	0.00	0.16	−0.32 to 0.32	−2	9.43**	−0.26 to 0.26	0.13	0.89
Controller knowledge	Input	6	1,266	0.06	0.08	0.07	−0.05 to 0.22	−2	19.1**	−0.09 to 0.26	0.03	0.74
	Behavior	18	3,608	0.17	0.22	0.05	0.12 to 0.32	451	106.82***	−0.02 to 0.47	0.05	0.84
	Outcome	16	3,013	0.11	0.14	0.06	0.02 to 0.26	116	120.98***	−0.14 to 0.43	0.06	0.88
	Clan	4	488	0.18	0.21	0.14	−0.05 to 0.48	18	31.58***	−0.11 to 0.54	0.11	0.91
	Self	5	1,090	0.06	0.08	0.12	−0.16 to 0.32	−4	46.31***	−0.25 to 0.41	0.09	0.91
Outcome measurability	Input	10	1,976	0.12	0.15	0.06	0.04 to 0.26	62	42.64***	−0.05 to 0.35	0.03	0.79
	Behavior	17	3,076	0.19	0.25	0.07	0.11 to 0.38	384	179.78***	−0.10 to 0.59	0.09	0.91
	Outcome	14	2,444	0.33	0.40	0.07	0.27 to 0.53	762	115.11***	0.11 to 0.70	0.07	0.89
	Clan	4	566	0.13	0.15	0.10	−0.04 to 0.35	5	17.48***	−0.07 to 0.37	0.05	0.83
	Self	4	954	0.14	0.17	0.05	0.08 to 0.27	10	5.08	0.12 to 0.23	0.01	0.41

Notes: $n = 310$ (number of studies included); $k =$ number of correlations (if less than two correlations exist, no analysis was conducted); $N =$ total sample size; $r =$ estimate of the population correlation coefficients; $r_c =$ sample size-weighted, reliability-corrected estimate of the population correlation coefficients (with significant correlations shaded); $SE =$ standard error of r_c; $CI = 95$ confidence interval for r_c, lower and upper limit; $FSK =$ fail-safe K, that is, number of studies with null results needed to make the reported mean effect size insignificant; $Q =$ heterogeneity test; $CR = 80$ percent credibility interval for r_c, lower and upper limit; $\tau^2 =$ between-studies variance; $I^2 =$ percentage of unexplained variance. p-values: * $p < 0.05$, ** $p < 0.01$, *** $p < 0.001$

Table 4.9 *Overview of organizational control–outcome relationships*

Relationships		k	N	r	r_c	SE	CI	FSK	Q	CR	τ^2	I^2
Input control	Aggregate outcomes	42	10,529	0.22	0.27	0.05	0.18 to 0.37	5,240	913.48***	−0.11 to 0.66	0.12	0.96
	Adaptability	7	1,283	0.24	0.30	0.08	0.15 to 0.46	121	43.70***	0.05 to 0.55	0.06	0.86
	HR	14	5,365	0.10	0.14	0.12	−0.09 to 0.36	99	1322.29***	−0.41 to 0.69	0.38	0.99
	Process	14	4,003	0.32	0.37	0.05	0.27 to 0.46	1,245	118.14***	0.15 to 0.58	0.04	0.89
	Rational goal	27	5,786	0.20	0.24	0.04	0.16 to 0.33	1,492	234.33***	−0.02 to 0.50	0.05	0.89
Behavior control	Aggregate outcomes	109	31,081	0.20	0.23	0.03	0.18 to 0.28	28,264	1955.73***	−0.11 to 0.56	0.08	0.94
	Adaptability	16	3,854	0.24	0.28	0.04	0.20 to 0.36	783	85.19***	0.09 to 0.47	0.03	0.82
	HR	42	17,126	0.19	0.23	0.04	0.15 to 0.30	4,828	798.77***	−0.08 to 0.53	0.07	0.95
	Process	25	4,488	0.29	0.36	0.03	0.29 to 0.42	2,250	131.99***	0.17 to 0.55	0.04	0.82
	Rational goal	82	18,491	0.13	0.15	0.03	0.09 to 0.21	6,967	1305.30***	−0.19 to 0.48	0.09	0.94
Outcome control	Aggregate outcomes	126	56,113	0.13	0.16	0.02	0.12 to 0.19	32,177	1632.68***	−0.07 to 0.38	0.04	0.92
	Adaptability	24	31,187	0.11	0.12	0.02	0.08 to 0.17	2,510	281.37***	0.00 to 0.25	0.02	0.92
	HR	41	12,082	0.13	0.16	0.04	0.08 to 0.24	2,481	611.76***	−0.16 to 0.47	0.07	0.93
	Process	22	3,288	0.23	0.30	0.06	0.17 to 0.42	1,090	229.38***	−0.06 to 0.65	0.10	0.91
	Rational goal	89	22,447	0.16	0.19	0.02	0.15 to 0.23	10,755	769.21***	−0.05 to 0.43	0.04	0.89
Clan control	Aggregate outcomes	28	6,208	0.32	0.37	0.04	0.29 to 0.45	3,567	286.38***	0.10 to 0.64	0.06	0.91
	Adaptability	3	315	0.26	0.29	0.12	0.05 to 0.54	14	13.99***	0.05 to 0.54	0.07	0.86
	HR	14	4,114	0.37	0.43	0.06	0.31 to 0.56	1,309	211.63***	0.13 to 0.73	0.08	0.94
	Process	3	490	0.22	0.28	0.08	0.13 to 0.44	15	6.23*	0.16 to 0.41	0.03	0.68
	Rational goal	19	4,096	0.19	0.22	0.06	0.10 to 0.34	922	296.47***	−0.11 to 0.56	0.09	0.94
Peer control	Aggregate outcomes	14	3,275	0.19	0.23	0.07	0.09 to 0.36	318	170.82***	−0.09 to 0.54	0.08	0.92
	HR	12	3,138	0.12	0.15	0.06	0.02 to 0.27	116	112.47***	−0.11 to 0.41	0.06	0.90
	Rational goal	8	692	0.18	0.20	0.07	0.07 to 0.34	47	27.36***	0.01 to 0.40	0.04	0.74

		k	N	r	r_c	SE	CI	FSK	Q	CR	τ^2	I^2
Self-control	Aggregate outcomes	13	3,818	0.22	0.29	0.07	0.16 to 0.42	531	151.40***	0.00 to 0.58	0.07	0.92
	HR	9	3,174	0.18	0.24	0.07	0.11 to 0.37	198	76.14***	0.01 to 0.48	0.05	0.89
	Rational goal	7	1,970	0.24	0.28	0.07	0.14 to 0.43	150	70.09***	0.04 to 0.52	0.07	0.91
Formal control	Aggregate outcomes	196	76,971	0.12	0.13	0.02	0.09 to 0.16	78,276	4223.03***	−0.16 to 0.41	0.06	0.95
	Adaptability	31	33,214	0.10	0.10	0.02	0.06 to 0.14	3,019	530.61***	−0.05 to 0.25	0.02	0.94
	HR	66	23,944	0.01	0.02	0.04	−0.05 to 0.10	2,410	1978.09***	−0.37 to 0.41	0.11	0.97
	Process	42	6,962	0.30	0.34	0.03	0.27 to 0.40	6,576	369.03***	0.07 to 0.61	0.07	0.89
	Rational goal	144	34,590	0.17	0.19	0.02	0.15 to 0.22	36,663	1890.48***	−0.09 to 0.46	0.06	0.92
Informal control	Aggregate outcomes	49	12,753	0.24	0.27	0.04	0.20 to 0.34	8,694	775.62***	−0.04 to 0.58	0.07	0.94
	Adaptability	6	1,109	0.17	0.19	0.08	0.04 to 0.35	49	37.46***	−0.03 to 0.42	0.05	0.87
	HR	21	7,631	0.19	0.22	0.06	0.11 to 0.34	1,076	482.00***	−0.11 to 0.56	0.09	0.96
	Process	13	3,632	0.33	0.36	0.05	0.25 to 0.46	1,116	138.36***	0.12 to 0.59	0.05	0.91
	Rational goal	29	6,383	0.20	0.22	0.04	0.13 to 0.31	2,219	402.60***	−0.08 to 0.51	0.07	0.93

Notes: $n = 310$ (number of studies included); k = number of correlations (if less than two correlations exist, no analysis was conducted); N = total sample size; r = estimate of the population correlation coefficients; r_c = sample size-weighted, reliability-corrected estimate of the population correlation coefficients (with significant correlations shaded); SE = standard error of r_c; CI = 95 confidence interval for r_c, lower and upper limit; FSK = fail-safe K, that is, number of studies with null results needed to make the reported mean effect size insignificant; Q = heterogeneity test; CR = 80 percent credibility interval for r_c, lower and upper limit; τ^2 = between-studies variance; I^2 = percentage of unexplained variance; *p*-values: * $p < 0.05$, ** $p < 0.01$, *** $p < 0.001$

Table 4.10 *Statistically significant meta-regression results*

Outcome	Moderator		Input control	Behavior control	Outcome control	Clan control	Peer control	Self-control	Formal control	Informal control
Aggregated outcomes	*n*		62	165	176	39	21	18	283	69
	Org. setting	Interorganizational		0.069†			0.097†			
	Level of analysis	Individual					−0.184†	−0.221**		−0.277**
		Project	−0.279*							−0.255*
		Team								−0.326*
		SBU		−0.193***					−0.090†	−0.234*
		Firm								
	Task type	Manufacturing								
		Sales								0.240*
		R&D			0.089*					
		ISD					0.287*			0.223*
		Service								
	Nature of DV	Self-report		0.132†						
		Archival						−0.363†		
	Industry	Manufacturing	0.148*	−0.106*	0.105*					
		Healthcare								
		Pharma	0.140*							
		Services							0.117*	−0.158†
	Geographic location	North America								
		Europe							0.098†	
		Asia	0.190†	0.114†						
Adaptability outcomes	*n*		7	16	24	3	0	1	31	6
	Org. setting	Interorganizational			−0.123***				−0.298†	
	Level of analysis	Individual							0.322†	
		Project								
		Team								

		14	42	41	14	12	9	66	21
	SBU							0.343†	
	Firm								
Task type	Manufacturing								
	Sales							0.155†	
	R&D								
	ISD								
	Service								
Nature of DV	Self-report		−0.196**						
	Archival								
Industry	Services			−0.201***					
	Manufacturing								
	Healthcare								
	Pharma								
Geographic location	North America								
	Europe								
	Asia								
HR outcomes									
	n	14	42	41	14	12	9	66	21
Org. setting	Interorganizational				−0.371***				−0.249***
Level of analysis	Individual				0.372*	−0.268*			
	Project								
	Team					0.275**			
	SBU				0.350*				
	Firm				0.483†				0.355†
Task type	Manufacturing				0.260†				
	Sales							0.260†	
	R&D							−0.368**	−0.340**
	ISD								
	Service								
Nature of DV	Self-report			−0.184*				−0.246†	
	Archival			−0.239*				−0.314*	−0.443*

Table 4.10 (*cont.*)

Outcome	Moderator		Input control	Behavior control	Outcome control	Clan control	Peer control	Self-control	Formal control	Informal control
	Industry	Services	0.227†		0.173†				0.240*	
		Manufacturing								
		Healthcare								
		Pharma								
	Geographic location	North America					−0.312**			
		Europe					−0.396**			
		Asia					−0.485*			
Process outcomes	*n*		14	25	22	3	1	1	42	13
	Org. setting	Interorganizational								
	Level of analysis	Individual								0.194†
		Project								
		Team	−0.180†		−0.273**				−0.355***	−0.230*
		SBU	−0.300**	−0.214***						−0.350*
		Firm	−0.250**							−0.300**
	Task type	Manufacturing								
		Sales								
		R&D	0.307**							0.324*
		ISD								
		Service								
	Nature of DV	Self-report		0.211***					0.186**	
		Archival		0.125*						
	Industry	Manufacturing		−0.183***					−0.181†	
		Services								
		Healthcare		−0.213***					−0.211**	
		Pharma								
	Geographic location	North America								
		Europe	0.363**		0.453**					0.310†
		Asia								

		27	82	89	19	8	7	144	29
Rational goal outcomes	*n*								
Org. setting									
Level of analysis	Interorganizational								
	Individual	$-0.242^{\dagger}$	-0.224^{**}	$-0.150^{\dagger}$	$-0.447^{\dagger}$			-0.173^{***}	$-0.307^{\dagger}$
	Project								
	Team								
	SBU								
	Firm								
Task type	Manufacturing								
	Sales	$0.175^{\dagger}$							
	R&D								
	ISD								
	Service								
Nature of DV	Self-report	0.200^{**}	0.273^{***}		0.359^{**}				0.313^{**}
	Archival		$0.127^{\dagger}$		0.241^{*}				
Industry	Manufacturing	0.184^{*}		0.162^{*}	0.425^{*}				
	Healthcare							$0.127^{\dagger}$	
	Pharma								
	Services								
Geographic location	North America		$0.133^{\dagger}$						
	Europe								
	Asia		0.260^{**}		$0.277^{\dagger}$			$0.128^{\dagger}$	

Notes: n = sample size; † $p < 0.10$, * $p < 0.05$, ** $p < 0.01$, *** $p < 0.001$

gray in the table. Given the mixed pattern of significant interaction effects as well as the small sample sizes underlying some combinations, we are hesitant to provide a definitive interpretation of these results. Instead, we will highlight a few interesting patterns. Our results show, for instance, that the *level of analysis* both enhances and diminishes the positive effects between controls and outcomes. For example, at the individual level, clan control's positive influence is enhanced for HR outcomes but marginally diminished for rational goal outcomes. There may be an interesting trade-off here. While clan control may support individual worker's perceptions of cohesion, morale, and commitment, it may hurt rational goal outcomes, such as individual performance. Similarly, at the SBU level, formal control's positive influence is marginally reduced for aggregated outcomes, but marginally enhanced for adaptability outcomes.

At the *industry level*, manufacturing firms enhance both outcome and formal control's positive influence on aggregated, HR, and rational goal outcomes. In the manufacturing industry, the classic reliance on setting performance targets and formally monitoring their achievement seems to be paying off.

Regarding *geographic location*, for Asian firms, the positive influence of input, behavior, and formal control on aggregated outcomes is marginally strengthened, as are the positive links between behavior, clan, and formal control and rational goal outcomes. The positive relationship between peer control and HR outcomes is negatively moderated by all three major regions of the world, that is, North America, Europe, and Asia, which could suggest that, in these regions, the hierarchical control regimes appear to work effectively, and additional peer control may be redundant or even act as a distraction with potentially negative effects.

Although we have offered cautious interpretations for some of the observed empirical patterns in our moderation analysis, we caution against overinterpreting their theoretical significance. The number of samples that included all required variables to test for such moderating effects was often very small and might not have yielded enough statistical power to support moderating effects. The results are therefore not conclusive evidence against the existence of additional moderating effects, even among those we tested. However, it seems fair to say that there is evidence for boundary conditions having a significant effect on control–outcome relationships. Future research should expand the analyzed sample, for example, by integrating more journals, and thereby allow for a more comprehensive search for moderating relationships.

Substitution versus complementarity. Tables 4.11 and 4.12 presents our meta-analytic correlation matrix, which provides the data for our MASEM analyses. Since MASEM requires a complete correlation matrix with no missing values (Viswesvaran & Ones 1995), we had to exclude those combinations of variables from our analysis that did not have correlations due to a lack of articles examining this combination. Specifically, *peer and outcome control* were not tested together in any of the samples, and neither were peer and self-control, as well as peer control and adaptability outcomes. In line with Bergh et al.'s (2016) recommendation, we therefore omitted peer control from our analysis. For the same reason – that is, no sample examined adaptability outcomes and process outcomes together – we split our analysis into the four outcome categories.

Figures 4.2 to 4.7 present the results of our MASEM analyses. Figure 4.2 shows that, across all outcomes, all control dimensions (input, behavior, outcome, clan, and self-control) are positively and significantly related to each other, with the one exception of a negative correlation between clan and self-control ($r = -0.030$, $p < 0.001$). Moreover, behavior, clan, and self-control are positively and significantly associated with all outcomes, with the exception of behavior control's association with rational goal outcomes ($r = 0.015$, $p < 0.550$). Input controls' influence ranges from negative ($r = -0.089$, $p < 0.01$, for adaptability outcomes; and $r = -0.177$, $p < 0.001$, for HR outcomes), and nonsignificant ($r = 0.021$, $p = 0.398$ for aggregated outcomes; and $r = 0.045$, $p = 0.102$ for rational goal outcomes), to positive ($r = 0.185$, $p < 0.01$, for process outcomes). The effects of outcome control similarly range from negative ($r = -0.118$, $p < 0.001$ for adaptability outcomes) and nonsignificant ($r = -.030$, $p = .176$ for aggregated outcomes; $r = -0.014$, $p = 0.532$ for HR outcomes) to positive ($r = 0.131$, $p < 0.01$ for process outcomes; $r = 0.056$, $p < 0.05$ for rational goal outcomes). Moreover, Figure 4.7 shows that formal and informal control are positively and significantly correlated with each other ($r = 0.210$, $p < 0.001$). Both formal and informal control further have a positive and significant influence on all outcomes, except for the negative and significant effect of formal control on HR outcomes ($r = -0.026$, $p < 0.01$).

To examine interaction effects between control variables, we examined whether their total effects are greater (suggesting complementarity) or smaller (suggesting substitution) than their direct effects (cf., Alwin & Hauser 1975). For rational goal outcomes (Figure 4.6), except for clan and self-control, the total effects of all controls are larger than their direct effects, which provides support for a complementary effect of these controls in their influence on rational goal outcomes. For instance, the direct effect of behavior control is .015, its indirect effect via outcome control is $0.236 * 0.056 = 0.013$, and its total effect is the sum of the direct effect and the indirect effect $0.015 + 0.013 = 0.028$. Since the total effect is higher than its direct effect, these two controls complement each other in their influence on rational goal outcomes. The same path analyses for the indirect effects via multiple controls (e.g., input control via behavior and outcome control) also suggest complementary effects due to the positive signs for all controls, except clan and self-control. In contrast, the direct effect of clan control (0.197) is larger than the total effect via self-control

Table 4.11 *Meta-analytic correlations table*

Constructs	Input control	Behavior control	Outcome control	Clan control	Peer control	Self-control	Aggregate outcomes	Adaptability	HR	Process	Rational goal
Input control	1.00	38(11,610)	38(7,649)	6(1,348)	1(329)	2(303)	42(10,529)	7(1,283)	14(5,365)	14(4,003)	27(5,786)
Behavior control	0.26	1.00	90(23,528)	16(3,157)	5(1,171)	9(1,838)	109(31,081)	16(3,854)	42(1,7126)	25(4,488)	82(18,491)
Outcome control	0.29	0.24	1.00	17(3,316)	n/a	10(1,776)	126(56,113)	24(31,187)	41(12,082)	22(3,288)	89(22,447)
Clan control	0.29	0.35	0.26	1.00	3(518)	5(666)	28(6,208)	3(315)	14(4,114)	3(490)	19(4,096)
Peer control	0.56	0.16	n/a	0.23	1.00	n/a	14(3,275)	n/a	12(3,138)	1(1,210)	8(692)
Self-control	0.48	0.16	0.25	−0.03	n/a	1.00	13(3,818)	1(270)	9(3,174)	1(33)	7(1,970)
Aggregate outcomes	0.27	0.23	0.16	0.37	0.23	0.29	1.00	n/a	n/a	n/a	n/a
Adaptability	0.30	0.28	0.12	0.29	n/a	0.55	n/a	1.00	9(1,986)	n/a	21(5,713)
HR	0.14	0.23	0.16	0.43	0.15	0.24	n/a	0.34	1.00	15(5,253)	50(15,368)
Process	0.37	0.36	0.30	0.28	0.40	0.26	n/a	n/a	0.31	1.00	30(4,165)
Rational goal	0.24	0.15	0.19	0.22	0.20	0.28	n/a	0.24	0.28	0.32	1.00

Notes: Numbers below the diagonal report correlations; numbers above the diagonal report the number of studies (k) and sample size (N) in the form of $k(N)$.

Table 4.12 *Meta-analytic correlations table (formal versus informal control)*

Constructs	Formal control	Informal control	Aggregate outcomes	Adaptability	HR	Process	Rational goal
Formal control	1.00	48(13,591)	196(76,971)	31(33,214)	66(23,944)	42(6,962)	144(34,590)
Informal control	0.21	1.00	49(12,753)	6(1,109)	21(7,631)	13(3,632)	29(6,383)
Aggregate outcomes	0.13	0.27	1.00	n/a	n/a	n/a	n/a
Adaptability	0.10	0.19	n/a	1.00	9(1,986)	n/a	21(5,713)
HR	0.02	0.22	n/a	0.29	1.00	15(5,253)	50(15,368)
Process	0.34	0.36	n/a	n/a	0.24	1.00	30(4,165)
Rational goal	0.19	0.22	n/a	0.21	0.20	0.31	1.00

Notes: Numbers below the diagonal report correlations; numbers above the diagonal report the number of studies (k) and sample size (N) in the form of $k(N)$.

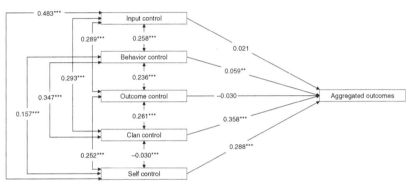

Figure 4.2 MASEM results for aggregated outcomes ($n = 1,853$; $\chi^2(5) = 483.32$, $p < 0.001$)

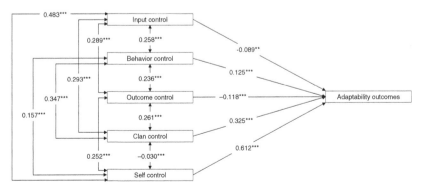

Figure 4.3 MASEM results for adaptability outcomes ($n = 969$; $\chi^2(5) = 536.91$, $p < 0.001$)

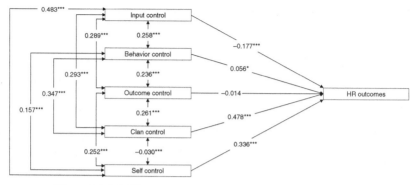

Figure 4.4 MASEM results for HR outcomes ($n = 1,783$; $\chi^2(5) = 570.04$, $p < 0.001$)

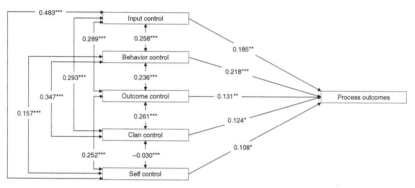

Figure 4.5 MASEM results for process outcomes ($n = 369$; $\chi^2(5) = 104.83$, $p < 0.001$)

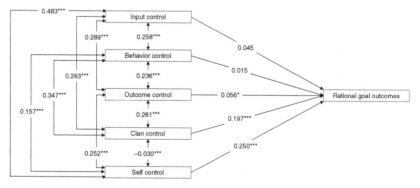

Figure 4.6 MASEM results for rational goal outcomes ($n = 1,754$; $\chi^2(5) = 260.28$, $p < 0.001$)

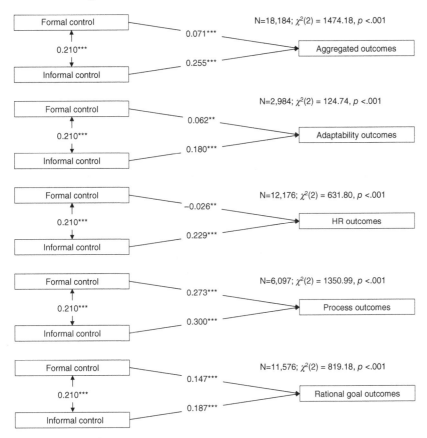

Figure 4.7 MASEM results for formal and informal controls

$(0.197 + (-0.030) * 0.250 = 0.190)$, suggesting that clan and self-control act as substitutes for each other in their influence on rational goal outcomes. We found a similar pattern of mostly complementary effects among controls for process outcomes (Figure 4.5).

There are some notable differences, however, when we consider adaptability outcomes (Figure 4.3). In addition to complementary effects, driven by all positive direct and total effects, we found substitute effects as well. For example, outcome control (with a direct effect of -0.118) acts as a substitute for behavior control, as their total effect $(0.125 + 0.236 * -0.118 = 0.097)$ is smaller than the direct effect of behavior control (0.125).

For formal and informal control, with the exception of HR outcomes, all correlations are positive and, as a result, formal and informal control complement each other in their effects on control outcomes. For HR control, the direct effect of formal control (−0.026) is smaller than the total effect (−0.026 + 0.210 * 0.229 = 0.022), suggesting that formal and informal control act as substitutes for each other in their effects on HR outcomes.

Overall, we found evidence for mostly complementary effects between different controls, but we also found instances of substitute effects, especially for some combinations of input, outcome, clan, and self-control on certain outcomes, and also for the influence of formal and informal control on HR outcomes. The effects found in our exploratory analysis are not intended to resolve the theoretical and empirical ambiguity with regard to the interactive effects of controls, but to provide initial evidence for such effects being conditional upon both the type of control and the type of outcome under consideration.

4.6   Conclusion

In this chapter, we have developed, and meta-analytically tested, a comprehensive framework representing the state-of-the-art of organizational control research, which comprises five dimensions (target, formality, singularity, direction, and style), three functions (monitoring, incentives, and coordination), four outcome categories (adaptability, HR, process, and rational goal outcomes), and contingencies at the individual, team, SBU, firm, and temporal levels. However, as Barley and Kunda (2001: 76) have reminded us more than twenty years ago:

Work and organization are bound in dynamic tension because organizational structures are, by definition, descriptions of and templates for ongoing patterns of action. When managers impose new organizational structures, they invariably alter patterns of work. Conversely, when the nature of work in an organization changes, perhaps because of new technologies or markets, organizational structures either adapt or risk becoming misaligned with the activities they organize. Because work and organizing are so interdependent, eras of widespread change in the nature of work in society should lead to the emergence and diffusion of new organizational forms and institutions.

In the next section of our book, we will discuss several fundamental changes inside and outside organizations, including in the nature of work itself, to serve as the backdrop for our reconceptualization of organizational control.

4.7   Appendix: Web of Science Search Query for Meta-analysis

Title, Keyword, and Abstract Search [6,192 Results on 10/21/2022]

(**TI** = (control* OR belief system* OR boundary system* OR clan* OR belief-system* OR boundary-system* OR self-managing team*) **OR AK** = (control* OR belief system* OR boundary system* OR clan* OR belief-system* OR boundary-system* OR self-managing team*) **OR KP** = (control* OR belief system* OR boundary system* OR clan* OR belief-system* OR boundary-system* OR self-managing team*) **OR AB** = ("organizational control*" OR "organisational control*" OR "organization's control*" OR "organisation's control*" OR "organizations' control*" OR "organisations' control*" OR "organization control*" OR "organisation control*" OR "organizations control*" OR "organisations control*" OR "firm control*" OR "company control*" OR "management control*" OR "managerial control*" OR "hierarchical control*" OR "input control*" OR "personnel control*" OR "behavior control*" OR "behavioral control*" OR "behaviour control*" OR "behavioural control*" OR "process control*" OR "output control*" OR "outcome control*" OR "results control*" OR "formal control*" OR "informal control*" OR "culture control*" OR "cultural control*" OR "diagnostic control*" OR "interactive control*" OR "belief system*" OR "boundary system*" OR "market control*" OR "bureaucratic control*" OR "clan control*" OR "clan*" OR "concertive control*" OR "enabling control*" OR "normative control*" OR "integrative control*" OR "control system*" OR "control mechanism*" OR "control target*" OR "control theory*" OR "theory of control*" OR "strategic control*" OR "financial control*" OR "peer control*" OR "self control*" OR "control dynamics*" OR "organizational-control*" OR "organisational-control*" OR "firm-control*" OR "company-control*" OR "management-control*" OR "managerial-control*" OR "hierarchical-control*" OR "input-control*" OR "personnel-control*" OR "behavior-control*" OR "behavioral-control*" OR "behaviour-control*" OR "behavioural-control*" OR "process-control*" OR "output-control*" OR "outcome-control*" OR "results-control*" OR "formal-control*" OR "informal-control*" OR "culture-control*" OR "cultural-control*" OR "diagnostic-control*" OR "interactive-control*" OR "belief-system*" OR "boundary-system*" OR "market-control*" OR "bureaucratic-control*" OR "clan-control*" OR "concertive-control*" OR "enabling-control*" OR "normative-control*" OR "integrative-control*" OR "control-system*" OR "control-mechanism*" OR "control-target*" OR "control-theory*" OR "strategic-control*" OR "financial-control*" OR "peer-control*" OR "self-control*" OR "control-dynamics*" OR "self-managing team*" OR "value-based control*")) **AND SO** = ("Academy of Management Journal" OR "Accounting Organizations and Society" OR "Accounting Review" OR "Administrative Science Quarterly" OR "American Economic Review" OR "Contemporary Accounting Research" OR "Econometrica" OR "Entrepreneurship Theory and Practice" OR "Human Relations" OR "Human Resource Management" OR "Information Systems Research" OR "Journal of Accounting & Economics" OR "Journal of Accounting Research" OR "Journal of Applied Psychology" OR "Journal of Business Ethics" OR "Journal of Business Venturing" OR "Journal of Consumer Psychology" OR "Journal of

Consumer Research" OR "Journal of Finance" OR "Journal of Financial and Quantitative Analysis" OR "Journal of Financial Economics" OR "Journal of International Business Studies" OR "Journal of Management" OR "Journal of Management Information Systems" OR "Journal of Management Studies" OR "Journal of Marketing" OR "Journal of Marketing Research" OR "Journal of Operations Management" OR "Journal of Political Economy" OR "Journal of the Academy of Marketing Science" OR "Management Science" OR "Marketing Science" OR "MIS Quarterly" OR "M&SOM-Manufacturing & Service Operations Management" OR "Operations Research" OR "Organization Science" OR "Organization Studies" OR "Organizational Behavior and Human Decision Processes" OR "Production and Operations Management" OR "Quarterly Journal of Economics" OR "Research Policy" OR "Review of Accounting Studies" OR "Review of Economic Studies" OR "Review of Finance" OR "Review of Financial Studies" OR "Strategic Entrepreneurship Journal" OR "Strategic Management Journal")

4.8   Appendix: ProQuest Central Search Query for Meta-analysis

Keyword List

"organizational control*" OR "organisational control*" OR "organization's control*" OR "organisation's control*" OR "organizations' control*" OR "organisations' control*" OR "organization control*" OR "organisation control*" OR "organizations control*" OR "organisations control*" OR "firm control*" OR "company control*" OR "management control*" OR "managerial control*" OR "hierarchical control*" OR "input control*" OR "personnel control*" OR "behavior control*" OR "behavioral control*" OR "behaviour control*" OR "behavioural control*" OR "process control*" OR "output control*" OR "outcome control*" OR "results control*" OR "formal control*" OR "informal control*" OR "culture control*" OR "cultural control*" OR "diagnostic control*" OR "interactive control*" OR "belief system*" OR "boundary system*" OR "market control*" OR "bureaucratic control*" OR "clan control*" OR "clan*" OR "concertive control*" OR "enabling control*" OR "normative control*" OR "integrative control*" OR "control system*" OR "control mechanism*" OR "control target*" OR "control theory*" OR "theory of control*" OR "strategic control*" OR "financial control*" OR "peer control*" OR "self control*" OR "control dynamics*" OR "organizational-control*" OR "organisational-control*" OR "firm-control*" OR "company-control*" OR "management-control*" OR "managerial-control*" OR "hierarchical-control*" OR "input-control*" OR "personnel-control*" OR "behavior-control*" OR "behavioral-control*" OR "behaviour-control*" OR "behavioural-control*" OR "process-control*" OR "output-control*"

OR "outcome-control*" OR "results-control*" OR "formal-control*" OR "informal-control*" OR "culture-control*" OR "cultural-control*" OR "diagnostic-control*" OR "interactive-control*" OR "belief-system*" OR "boundary-system*" OR "market-control*" OR "bureaucratic-control*" OR "clan-control*" OR "concertive-control*" OR "enabling-control*" OR "normative-control*" OR "integrative-control*" OR "control-system*" OR "control-mechanism*" OR "control-target*" OR "control-theory*" OR "strategic-control*" OR "financial-control*" OR "peer-control*" OR "self-control*" OR "control-dynamics*" OR "self-managing team*" OR "value-based control*"

Journal List

"Academy of Management Journal" OR "Academy of Management Journal (pre-1986)" OR "Accounting, Organizations and Society" OR "Administrative Science Quarterly" OR "The American Economic Review" OR "Contemporary Accounting Research" OR "Econometrica" OR "Econometrica (pre-1986)" OR "Econometrica (1986–1998)" OR "Entrepreneurship Theory and Practice" OR "Human Relations" OR "Human Resource Management" OR "Human Resource Management (pre-1986)" OR "Human Resource Management (1986–1998)" OR "Information Systems Research" OR "Journal of Accounting & Economics" OR "Journal of Accounting Research" OR "Journal of Applied Psychology" OR "Journal of Business Ethics" OR "Journal of Business Ethics (pre-1986)" OR "Journal of Business Ethics (1986–1998)" OR "Journal of Business Venturing" OR "Journal of Consumer Psychology" OR "Journal of Consumer Research" OR "Journal of Consumer Research (pre-1986)" OR "Journal of Consumer Research (pre-1986)" OR "The Journal of Finance" OR "Journal of Financial and Quantitative Analysis" OR "Journal of Financial Economics" OR "Journal of International Business Studies" OR "Journal of International Business Studies (pre-1986)" OR "Journal of Management" OR "Journal of Management Information Systems" OR "The Journal of Management Studies" OR "Journal of Marketing" OR "Journal of Marketing (pre-1986)" OR "JMR, Journal of Marketing Research" OR "JMR, Journal of Marketing Research (pre-1986)" OR "Journal of Operations Management" OR "The Journal of Political Economy" OR "Journal of the Academy of Marketing Science" OR "Journal of the Academy of Marketing Science (pre-1986)" OR "Management Science" OR "Management Science (pre-1986)" OR "Management Science (1986–1998)" OR "Manufacturing & Service Operations Management" OR "Marketing Science" OR "Marketing Science (pre-1986)" OR "Marketing Science (1986–1998)" OR "MIS Quarterly" OR "Operations Research" OR "Organization Science" OR "Organization Studies" OR "Organizational Behavior and Human Decision Processes" OR

"Production and Operations Management" OR "The Quarterly Journal of Economics" OR "Research Policy" OR "Review of Accounting Studies" OR "The Review of Economic Studies" OR "Review of Finance" OR "The Review of Financial Studies" OR "The Review of Financial Studies (1986–1998)" OR "Strategic Entrepreneurship Journal" OR "Strategic Management Journal" OR "Strategic Management Journal (pre-1986)" OR "Strategic Management Journal (1986–1998)" OR "The Accounting Review"

Title Search [3,822 Results on 10/26/2022]

TI("control*" OR "belief system*" OR "boundary system*" OR "clan*" OR "belief-system*" OR "boundary-system*" OR "self-managing team*") AND PUB.EXACT([*insert journal list*])

Abstract Search [1,991 Results on 10/26/2022]

AB([*insert keyword list*]) AND PUB.EXACT([*insert journal list*])

Keyword Search [1,401 Results on 10/26/2022]

SU([*insert keyword list*]) AND PUB.EXACT([*insert journal list*])

Part III

Quo Vadis Organizational Control?

5   The Future of Work Inside and Outside Organizations

[T]oday, paradigm-shifting forces seem to be driving significant changes in both work and the workforce. New digital and communications technologies are changing how work gets done. The growth of the gig economy and advances in artificial intelligence are changing who does the work. Even the question of what work looks like is coming under examination as a continually evolving marketplace drives organizations to explore new business models. In the face of these technological and social forces, it could be imperative for businesses to rethink their approaches to the how, who, and what of work in fundamental, perhaps even transformative ways. (Stockton et al. 2018: 2)

Over the past quarter century, we have witnessed dramatic changes in technology, society, and in organizations. Technology is now mediating every step of the work process, and the global COVID-19 pandemic has further accelerated this trend. As Microsoft's CEO Satya Nadella framed it at the start of the pandemic, "[w]e've seen two years' worth of digital transformation in two months" (Microsoft 2020). This breakneck speed of technological developments is unlikely to slow down anytime soon, with many experts anticipating that we will experience more progress in the next decade than in the last 100 years (e.g., Diamandis & Kotler 2020). These technological changes are accompanied by equally important shifts in demographics and socio-culture, leading to profound changes in organizations and the nature of work more generally. In this chapter, we will discuss important technological, demographic, sociocultural, and organizational trends. We will outline how these trends influence the future of work within and outside organizational boundaries, challenge taken-for-granted assumptions underlying traditional control approaches, and, as a consequence, require a new perspective on organizational control.

5.1   Technological Trends

Two key technological trends are particularly relevant for our reconceptualization of organizational control: advances in information and communication technology, especially in data storage and processing, digitization (i.e., transforming social life into quantitative data), and big data analytics; and the renaissance of artificial intelligence (AI), especially machine learning (ML) algorithms (see Table 5.1 for an overview of these technological trends and their implications).

5.1.1   Advances in Information Technology

> [T]he relentless improvement in the power of computing; the increasing speed of broadband access; the dramatic spread of sensors; and the birth of cloud computing. The combination of these four developments is giving us a new kind of world – a world that is hyperconnected and data saturated, a world in which the Internet of everyone is linked to an Internet of everything. (Wooldridge 2015: 29)

For several decades, we have witnessed exponential increases in information processing speed and electronic data storage capacity, with their associated costs falling quickly. In line with Moore's law, first articulated in 1965, our technological information processing capacity roughly doubles every 14–18 months, our telecommunication capacity every 34 months, and our storage capacity every 40 months, all on a per capita basis (Hilbert & Lopez 2011). In more recent years, we have also seen increasing access to and speed of broadband (and mobile) Internet, paving the way for a proliferation of cloud computing, which permits applications to be delivered with minimal local software or processing power (World Economic Forum 2016).

Capitalizing on these technological developments are increasing efforts in *digitization* (or datafication), defined as the transformation of artifacts of social life into computerized, quantitative data (Cukier & Mayer-Schoenberger 2013; Galliers et al. 2017; McKinsey Global Institute 2020). Our mobile phones, online activities, electronic communication, smart ID badges, and wearable global positioning systems all produce torrents of data, often as a by-product of their ordinary operation, transforming each and every one of us into a "walking data generator" (McAfee & Brynjolfsson 2012). These developments have been coupled with advances in remote sensing technologies, giving rise to the "Internet of Things" (IoT) (Ashton 2009). Computer sensors are integrated not just into portable electronic equipment – such as smart watches, tablets, and mobile phones – but also into industrial equipment and everyday objects – which can be anything from light switches and thermostats to chairs sensing ergonomic postures (Wang & MacLellan 2018) and "smart" toilets that can identify health- and drug-related issues (Petre 2018). The IoT connects objects, people, information, and computers, thereby unleashing "an enormous amount of data and the opportunity to see patterns and design systems on a scale never before possible" (World Economic Forum 2016: 7). These ubiquitous and low-cost data collection technologies are increasingly

Table 5.1 *Key technological trends*

Technological trends	Underlying development and logic	Implications
5.1.1 Advances in information technology	• Advances in electronic processing speed and data storage capacity at reduced costs • Proliferation of cloud computing • Digitization or datafication • Internet of Things (IoT) • Emotion-sensing technologies • Big data analytics (distinct by the volume of data, the velocity of new data creation, and the variety of previously disjoint data that can be aggregated)	• Allowing for the tracking and recording of all everyday life activities of everyone • Tracking and recording of people's internal emotional and physiological states becomes possible • Reduced costs of tracking and recording data (due to steadily declining costs of storage, memory, processing, and bandwidth) make big data analytics economical • Attention of individuals, groups, and organizations represents a key constraint on utilizing the full potential of big data analytics
5.1.2 Renaissance of artificial intelligence	• Enabled by advances in information processing and electronic data storage • Machine learning (ML) enables the consideration of information that might otherwise be too costly or time-consuming to collect and analyze	• Automation of knowledge worker tasks possible • Human managers might be replaced by algorithms • Algorithms are often criticized as opaque, biased, and unaccountable • Algorithms may introduce new inaccuracies or even biases (for both designers and users)

in continuous use and are capable of tracking and recording "the minutiae of an individual's everyday life" (Newell & Marabelli 2015: 3). The IoT is expected to continue growing, with an early white paper on the topic predicting $14.4 trillion of new value associated with IoT applications (Cisco 2013). Moreover, applications are no longer restricted to tracking and recording externally observable behavioral data. Recent developments in emotion-sensing technologies – which focus on eye movements, facial expressions, and skin conductance – allow for the tracking of people's internal emotional and physiological states (Whelan et al. 2018).

These advances in electronic processing speed and storage capacity, broadband and mobile Internet, cloud computing, datafication, and ubiquitous computing have culminated in *big data analytics*. Three key differences distinguish big data analytics from earlier forms of business analytics (McAfee & Brynjolfsson 2012). The first is the sheer *volume* of data. More data circulate the Internet every second than were stored in the entire Internet just 20 years ago. The US retailer Walmart, for instance, collects more than 2.5 petabytes of data every hour from its customer transactions, which is the equivalent of about 20 million filing cabinets' worth of text.

Second, even more important than its volume is big data's *velocity*, or the speed of new data creation. Big data sets are often composed of and continuously expanded by real-time data streams. For example, a group of researchers at the MIT Media Lab used smartphone location data to track the number of customers in the parking lots of the US department store chain Macy's, allowing the researchers to estimate the retailer's sales even before the company itself had recorded those sales (McAfee & Brynjolfsson 2012). Such real-time digital data creation can also happen autogenically, when the very act of engaging with data creates new data (Adner et al. 2019). The act of requesting a database search and browsing its results, for instance, by itself creates new data about the requesters as well as their interests, needs, and habits. Similarly, when people engage with everyday technologies (e.g., mobile phones or automobiles), they generate data exhaust, or passively collected, non-core data as a by-product of their daily activities. While such ambient data may have limited or no value to the original data collection party, it can be recombined with other data sources to create new sources of value (George et al. 2014).

Third, beyond the quantitative growth and speed of data, a qualitative shift arises from the ability to aggregate a large *variety* of previously disjoint data. Besides traditional databases and text documents, big data can include messages, updates, and images posted to social networks, readings from electronic sensors, location signals from smartphones, and other digital data streams (Alharthi et al. 2017). Big data are not just interconnected, which means that data from various sources can be synthesized, but also portable, that is, remotely accessible and transferrable from one context or application to another (Günther et al. 2017).

Unlike traditional business analytics, big data is vastly more voluminous and ever-expanding, its sources and types of data are significantly more varied, and big data analytics often obtains its relevance from real-time processing (Galliers et al. 2015). The structured databases and IT systems that handle traditional types of data are therefore ill-suited to storing and processing big data. While big data sets are often massive, unstructured, and rapidly evolving, they can contain "a huge amount of signal in the noise, simply waiting to be released" (McAfee & Brynjolfsson 2012: 63). Combinations of previously disjoint information allow us to answer questions that used to be impossible to address (Adner et al. 2019; George et al. 2014). In addition, the steadily declining costs of storage, memory, processing, and bandwidth mean that data-intensive approaches have become more economical (Alharthi et al. 2017). In sum:

[T]he big data of this revolution is far more powerful than the analytics that were used in the past. We can measure and therefore manage more precisely than ever before. We can make better predictions and smarter decisions. We can target more-effective interventions, and can do so in areas that so far have been dominated by gut and intuition rather than by data and rigor. (McAfee & Brynjolfsson 2012: 62)

In a sense, big data analytics is the logical twenty-first-century extension of scientific management. Slow motion capture techniques in Taylor's scientific management approach (Section 3.1.2) and the Hawthorne studies (Section 3.1.3) are reproduced in the big data age, but "with a commensurate increase in speed and a lack of direct intrusion; [and] with an increase in overall intrusion, such as through work outside of the workplace in the form of expected use of email and other applications" (Evans & Kitchin 2018: 46).

Despite their potential for mitigating the constraints of human-bounded rationality (Adner et al. 2019), big data analytics are constrained by the sheer volume of data that are produced and their associated storage costs. For instance, a printout of telematics gathered from a single shift of a UPS delivery driver – for example, speed, whether the engine is off or on, whether the back door is open or closed, whether the seat belt is engaged, whether the driver is backing up, and more – covers up to forty pages (Kaplan 2015). Another example is self-driving cars, which accumulate enormous amounts of data even during short trips, from interior and exterior video feeds, GPS locations, and vehicle component diagnostics. The costs of storing such massive amounts of data have reached as much as $350,000 per year for a single vehicle, forcing companies to reign in their storage costs by retaining only a sliver of data they deem most useful (Paresh 2023).

Big data analytics are also bound by a constraint that does not scale up as easily as our IT infrastructures: the attention of individuals, teams, and organizations. The abundance of information creates increasing competition for our attention and bears the risk that the constant flood of information distracts us from more relevant information or from the actual task at hand. The key challenge of the information age is to manage the wealth of available information and channel it to productive ends (Van Knippenberg et al. 2015). Fortunately, a promising solution to this challenge has emerged in recent years, and it has the potential to revolutionize big data analytics: AI and ML.

5.1.2   *Renaissance of Artificial Intelligence*

Advances in information processing and electronic data storage have paved the way for a renaissance of AI. AI was first espoused in the 1950s, but has only recently found its way into mainstream organizational applications (Baum & Haveman 2020). One of the most active areas within AI is ML, which comprises computer algorithms that quickly and automatically produce models to classify and predict without using explicit human instructions (Jordan & Mitchell 2015). Such algorithms are starting to take over even knowledge worker tasks that have long been regarded as impossible or impractical for machines to perform:

These include reading and parsing text, recognizing images and speech, translating languages, and uncovering intricate patterns in complex data (e.g., biochemical data, mobile phone records, social media posts, internet search records, and financial transactions). For business organizations, ML algorithms ease document and data handling, improve sales forecasts, facilitate cross-selling, accelerate drug discovery, improve customer targeting and communications, and manage executive recruitment and human resources systems, along with myriad other tasks. (Baum & Haveman 2020: 268)

Applied to ever-larger and ever-richer data sets, and in almost real time, ML algorithms also make it possible to consider information that might otherwise be too costly or time-consuming to collect and analyze (e.g., decision-making records or social media posts) and to uncover intricate patterns in complex data that remain invisible to the human eye.[1] In this way, ML enhances – and possibly replaces – existing organizational tasks by lowering costs, reducing uncertainty, and increasing the accuracy of predictions (Baum & Haveman 2020).

Despite their promise, AI and ML algorithms can also introduce new inaccuracies or even biases (Kellogg et al. 2020). Algorithms may reinforce social and racial inequalities, because they direct people's attention to particular inferences and classes of people in ways that are biased (Angwin et al. 2016). Algorithms could also lead to the reproduction of inequalities due to biased training data, which means the data that is used to allow the ML algorithm to find patterns between inputs and outputs. If training data are biased – either due to historical training data reflecting existing patterns of discrimination (Angwin et al. 2016) or due to algorithms drawing inferences from a biased sample of the population, thereby systematically disadvantaging those who are underrepresented or overrepresented in the training dataset (Brayne & Christin 2021) – it can lead to discriminatory models (Barocas & Selbst 2016). Furthermore, big data sets make it harder to spot inaccuracies and biases, as it is more difficult to reverse-engineer the data or cross-check it with related information to ensure its accuracy (Bodie et al. 2017).

It is not surprising, then, that algorithms have often been critiqued as biased. However, as Miller (2018: para. 11, emphases in original) points out, a "not-so-hidden secret behind the algorithms […] is that they actually *are* biased.

---

[1] Examples are Deloitte's discovery that the extent of grammatical errors on resumes predicted the performance of salespeople to a greater degree than academic grades; Xerox's finding that personality type predicts turnover, such that those workers identified as creative tend to stay longer than those regarded as being inquisitive; and IBM's insight that workers who worked overtime without rewards or promotion were more likely to leave the organization (Cheng & Hackett 2021).

But the humans they are replacing are *significantly more biased*. After all, where do institutional biases come from if not the humans who have traditionally been in charge?" In line with that argument, some recent research suggests that algorithms – although not without flaws – are actually less biased and more accurate than the humans they replace (e.g., Kleinberg et al. 2017). This research would suggest that, compared to human decision-makers, algorithms are capable of more objective and precise predictions provided in real time, which can help mitigate the constraints of human-bounded rationality (Adner et al. 2019).

Another source of bias, which is plaguing humans and ML technologies equally, is input incompleteness (Choudhury et al. 2020). It occurs when information that is relevant for ML predictions is missing, and it leads to decisions being biased toward what is most salient, rather than what is most relevant. Biased or incomplete training data can also be provided intentionally by strategic actors, resulting in what computer scientists call adversarial ML (Choudhury et al. 2020).

A special case of missing information arises from incomplete contracting in the AI context (Hadfield-Menell & Hadfield 2019). Economists and legal scholars have long recognized that writing complete contracts is prohibitively costly or simply impossible because of unobservable, unpredictable, and unverifiable contingencies, as well as the bounded rationality of the involved parties (e.g., Williamson 1975). This insight can also be applied to the alignment between ML algorithms' reward functions and their designers' intended outcomes. In particular, reinforcement ML uses iterative scoring to improve AI decision-making. Designers specify a reward function, and algorithms generate decisions, which are rewarded based on how well they perform in relation to this reward function, and the algorithm then draws inferences on what was successful and what was not, in order to improve itself. Misspecification problems arise because reward functions may accurately reflect the designer's preferences in the circumstances the designer had in mind when designing a particular algorithm, but fail to accurately reflect how humans value all state and action combinations. As a result, algorithms make decisions in self-interest (i.e., to maximize reward functions) without any regard to external consequences, such as social or environmental constraints. Hadfield and Hadfield (2019: 10) provide an insightful example for problems stemming from AI algorithms pursuing their own self-interest:

When a robot is given a reward function that specifies a reward only based on moving boxes, it will ignore a vase that appears in the path (Amodei et al., 2016). If a human agent is given a contract that pays only for moving boxes, she will interpret her contract to include an implied term that penalizes knocking over the vase. This is because the human contract is embedded in a normative environment in which institutions such as courts and culture impose formal sanctions (such as money damages) or informal sanctions (such as exclusion from valuable economic and social relationships) for violating formal rules and informal norms. The human agent will naturally refer to this environment to determine the true contract. Achieving a similar result for the robot will require building the technical tools that allow the robot to make a similar appeal to external sources of norms and values to address misspecification.

In addition to these biases and misspecification potential, algorithms suffer from another important constraint. Human learning – although famously fallible – is varied, rich in social context, forward-looking, and based on sentient judgment and understanding (Lindebaum et al. 2020). As they learn, humans actively engage with and develop diverse understandings of their environments. ML, in contrast, lacks any knowledge of causal relationships among variables, relies solely on past, codifiable data, neglects other non-codifiable but relevant aspects of the problem when making decisions, and cannot foresee future consequences. Machines "learn" over time by computing more predictively accurate solutions to well-codified problems as additional data become available (Balasubramanian et al. 2022). Especially when organizations substitute ML for human learning (instead of complementing it), they risk fundamentally decreasing the richness inherent in human learning, resulting in a form of learning myopia:

ML replaces the diversity in routines arising from human learning with a small, homogenous set of variants selected based on conformance with historical data ("selection effect"). This, combined with the lower richness of background knowledge ("nescience effect") and the consequent reduction in the ability to engage in substantive rationality, makes organizations susceptible to ignoring environmental changes, within-organizational interdependencies across routines, and extreme outcomes. (Balasubramanian et al. 2022: 449)

ML's vast computational capabilities further exacerbate this problem. In contrast to human selection processes, which are slow, and often the result of a trial-and-error process, ML's ability to rapidly process large volumes of data allows it to quickly identify and select the predictively most accurate variant, reducing any remaining variability (Balasubramanian et al. 2022).[2]

For all their potential, AI and ML algorithms also present an important conundrum for their designers and users. Relying on complex webs of correlational inference, ML algorithms are often opaque and inscrutable, even to their architects (Burrell 2016; Demetis & Lee 2018). Humans are often incapable of fully understanding "what happens as data move between the multiple, interdependent 'hidden' layers of ML algorithms" (Baum & Haveman 2020: 270),

---

[2] In fact, a recent study reveals a fundamental challenge of developing artificial intelligence: Attempts to improve one part of the enormously complex AI models make other parts of the models perform worse (Chen et al. 2023). This phenomenon, called drift, is responsible for recent press articles proclaiming that "ChatGPT is getting dumber at basic math" (Zumbrun 2023).

resulting in situations in which even their designers "may not understand, or be fully responsible for, what their algorithms do" (Markus 2017: 235). A downside of relying on such opaque algorithms is that it restricts people to a superficial understanding and prevents them from building cumulative knowledge of a phenomenon, and there will be few, if any, opportunities to learn from mistakes (Newell & Marabelli 2015). Adner and colleagues (2019: 259) have succinctly summarized this balance as follows:

Cutting-edge techniques such as machine learning produce an additional qualitative shift in how data are used – from representing data to improving human perception of phenomena to prediction, which may or may not involve or be subject to human comprehension. There is a delicate balance that managers may have to strike in this area: they may need to let go of the need to understand in order to satisfy the need to predict. Yet, the risks of ethically repellant outcomes and regulatory constraints and the desire to satisfy sheer human curiosity make this balancing act far from trivial.

Last, some authors have cautioned to not overestimate AI and ML capabilities (e.g., Bettis & Hu 2018). In contrast to many of the problems managers are facing, algorithms require mathematically precise input-output functions. And because of the processing speed and memory constraints of even our most sophisticated (and still largely experimental) quantum computers, algorithmic computation is forced to rely on heuristics – and not optimization – for many problems it is tasked to solve. While capable of handling vastly more complexity than human cognition, even AI algorithms are therefore subject to some form of bounded rationality.

5.2   Demographic and Socio-cultural Trends

Along with technological advances, recent demographic and socio-cultural trends have important implications for organizational control, and the nature of work more generally. Three trends are especially important: an increase in workforce diversity and changing attitudes and values within and between generations. Table 5.2 provides an overview of these demographic trends and their implications.

5.2.1   Increasing Workforce Diversity

Changes in demographics have had a profound impact on the workforce. In most societies, life expectancy is increasing. By 2020, people over the age of sixty five outnumbered children under the age of five worldwide (Economist 2019), and made up about 17 percent of the population in the United States (Statista 2023). In line with that trend, the median age of the global workforce has increased from about 34 years in 1990 to 39 years in 2020 (Statista 2023), and the median age of the US workforce is projected to increase from 42 in 2020 to 43 in 2030 (US Bureau of Labor Statistics 2021). With longer lifespans, productive work time and careers are extended, allowing people to stay in the workforce longer than ever before. For example, 72 percent of baby boomers, which is the generation born between 1946 and 1964, plan to delay their retirement beyond the official retirement age (Mercer 2020). People remaining in the workforce for a larger portion of their lives, in turn, leads to greater age and generational diversity in the workplace (e.g., Birkinshaw et al. 2019). In 2020, the global workforce was composed of four main generations, that is, cohorts based on shared experiences at similar ages: 6 percent baby boomers (born 1946–1964), 35 percent Generation X (born 1965–1979), 35 percent Generation Y or millennials (born 1980–1996), and 24 percent Generation Z (born after 1996) (Statista 2016).

Workforce diversity has further increased in terms of gender, race/ethnicity, and nationality. For instance, the share of leadership positions held by women globally has increased from 21 percent in 2012 to 29 percent in 2019 (Grant Thornton 2019). And workforce diversity is expected to further increase over the next decade. Millennials are already racially and ethnically diverse (Gallup 2016), and Generation Z is predicted to be the most diverse generation yet, with nearly half (48 percent) identifying as racial or ethnic minorities (Cilluffo & Cohn 2019). And progressively globalized economies will continue to hire people of different nationalities into organizations (Mercer 2020).

Moreover, across the world, many organizations increasingly embrace virtual teams, in which members are no longer physically collocated, and which frequently cross geographical, cultural, and time boundaries (Cascio & Montealegre 2016; Farr et al. 2014). Since virtual teams are often geographically dispersed, they are more likely to be culturally diverse, exhibiting a variety of attitudes, preferences, and values resulting from individuals being socialized in different cultural settings (Gibson et al. 2014; Malhotra et al. 2007). In sum, workers socialized in different generations and across geographic, national, and cultural settings are likely to result in more heterogenous organizational identities, values, and norms than organizations have faced before.

Contrary to popular belief, however, the female employment rate has not changed significantly in the last 30 years. In the United States, it was at 53.3 percent in 1990, peaking at 57.5 percent in 2020, and declining from a recent high of 55.4 percent in 2019 to 53.2 percent in 2021 (Statista 2022). The COVID-19 pandemic is responsible for the recent drop (Novacek et al. 2022), and a widening professional inequality that represents a setback of at least 2 years (PwC 2022). Worldwide, the female employment rate decreased from about 51 percent in 2000 to about 46 percent in 2020 (International Labour Organization 2019).

Table 5.2 *Key demographic and socio-cultural trends*

Demographic trends	Underlying development and logic	Implications
5.2.1 Increasing workforce diversity	• Generational diversity: Increasing life expectancy extends the workforce's productive work time, and careers are extended; results in a more diverse workplace composed of four generations • Gender diversity: Share of leadership positions held by women globally has increased • Racial/ethnic diversity: Millennials are racially/ethnically diverse; Generation Z is predicted to be the most diverse generation yet • Diversity in terms of geography, nationality, and culture	• Workers socialized in different generations and across geographic, national, and cultural settings results in heterogenous organizational identities, values, and norms
5.2.2 Generational differences in attitudes and values	• Differences in attitudes and values regarding careers, work–life balance, retirement, and, more generally, the way people want to work, and the type of organization they want to work for • Diversity regarding technological savviness among digital natives, digital immigrants, and non-digitals • Millennial workers' preference for clear individual expectations and ongoing and detailed feedback and guidance • Disengagement especially among Generation Z and young millennials	• Traditional one-size-fits-all approach to managing workers becomes untenable, and managers have to adjust their approaches to meet diverse backgrounds and expectations • Millennial workers' preferences contrast with companies' traditional annual face-to-face feedback meetings • Managers' roles need to shift from a generalized command-and-control approach to a more customized approach, in which they act more as personal coaches and career developers
5.2.3 Changes in attitudes and values across generations	• Traditional careers (often in the same organization) are replaced by weakening temporal, physical, and administrative attachments between workers and organizations • Quiet quitting • Increasing relevance of meaning, purpose, and sensegiving at work • Increasing demands for flexibility in terms of what tasks to work on, when to work, and where to work • Less central relevance of work in people's lives; increasing demand for leisure, personal well-being, and work–life balance	• Increase in virtual teams, remote work, and the gig economy • Organizations drawn into competition for talent amidst the "Great Resignation"

5.2.2   Generational Differences in Attitudes and Values

An increasingly diverse workforce brings with it growing differences in attitudes and values regarding careers, work–life balance, retirement, and, more generally, the way people want to work, and the type of organization they want to work for (Birkinshaw et al. 2019; Stockton et al. 2018). Take technological savviness as an example:

> Perhaps the most apparent difference between Millennials and other generations in the workplace is their distinctive relationship with technology. This should not be surprising. By birth year, the Internet itself is a member of the Millennial generation. The TCP/IP suite that enables the Internet as we know it was established in 1982 – the same year the first Millennials were born. [...] Two icons of the millennial lifestyle, cell phones and online social networks, also grew up alongside the generation. (Hershatter & Epstein 2010: 212)

No surprisingly, digital natives – who cannot even remember the first time they accessed the Internet (Prensky 2001) – rely heavily on technology, and almost constantly use an electronic device, almost immediately after waking up (Colbert et al. 2016). Digital natives are comfortable multitasking, such as monitoring Twitter feeds and Snapchat messages while watching a video on YouTube. For many digital natives, technology use is a constant, with 44 percent reporting that they never fully "unplug" (Colbert et al. 2016). As a result, they are better at multitasking, reacting to visual stimuli, and filtering information, which allows them "to effectively utilize broadly networked digital communication technologies to quickly and seamlessly accomplish a wide variety of tasks" (Gorman et al. 2004: 257). On the flipside, digital natives are less skilled in in-person communication and reading nonverbal clues (Small & Vorgan 2008).

Digital natives may even be wired differently because of their digital immersion, with neuroscience studies providing evidence of a brain gap, or significant variations in cerebral circuitry that result from the learning and practice of technological abilities (Tapscott 2009). Digital natives are therefore likely to respond differently to management approaches than digital immigrants – those workers who have readily adopted newly available technologies (Prensky 2001) – and especially non-digitals. Consequently, the traditional one-size-fits-all approaches to managing workers become increasingly untenable, and managers have to adjust their approaches to meet workers' diverse backgrounds and expectations.

Another example of growing differences between generations can be attributed to millennials (born between 1980 and 1996) taking over the workplace. Millennials are now the largest living adult generation (Gallup 2016), making up around 35 percent of the global workforce in 2020 (Statista 2016; Tilford 2018), and more than two thirds of the workforce in some global professional service firms like EY or Accenture. Millennials are predicted to represent 75 percent of the global workforce in 2025 (Albanese 2018). Thus, it is important to understand their unique attitudes and values, and especially those that differ from prior generations based on which classic control theory was built.

Millennials demand a structured work environment "with centralized decision-making, clearly defined responsibilities, and formalized procedures" (Hershatter & Epstein 2010: 217). They flourish when a clear road to success based on expected skills is outlined for them (Hershatter & Epstein 2010). Compared to other generations, millennial workers are perceived as more motivated by extrinsic rewards (Krahn & Galambos 2014), technology (Hershatter & Epstein 2010), and work–life balance (Ng et al. 2010). Moreover, millennials as a generation are characterized by their optimism about the future of their companies, their preference for teamwork, community, and customer engagement, as well as their tendency to care about, and naturally align themselves, with corporate missions (Hershatter & Epstein 2010).

On the flipside, millennials expect appreciation for their specific strengths and the contributions they can make at work. They are used to real-time communication and continuous feedback from their families and (virtual) friends on social media (Gallup 2016), and when they consume (Gruber et al. 2015). Unsurprisingly, they expect communication and feedback to function in a similar way at work (Colbert et al. 2016), by setting clear individual expectations, providing ongoing and detailed guidance – preferably in bite-sized chunks – continuous reinforcement and correction, and ideally, the use of multiple (including online and social media) channels. According to Gallup's (2016: 3–4) research, "millennials don't want bosses – they want coaches. [...] Millennials don't want annual reviews – they want ongoing conversations." However, those preferences clearly contrast with the still widely used annual, face-to-face feedback meetings (Van Knippenberg et al. 2015).

Stemming from their experience growing up and the degree to which institutions, such as schools, have made themselves malleable to the needs and desires of this cohort, millennials expect organizations to accommodate them, their needs, and their desires. While prior generations, especially Generation X, may perceive them as entitled, millennials view themselves as having grown up under pressure and with expectations of high achievement. Furthermore, they have grown accustomed to supportive, nurturing environments that provide them with every opportunity to succeed (Hershatter & Epstein 2010). However, in their search for jobs that enable personal growth and development by offering flexible and multifaceted tasks, millennials frequently encounter workplaces characterized by stifling hierarchies and high levels of routinization (Gruber et al. 2015).

Even more problematic, according to a study by Gallup (2016), millennials are the least engaged generation in the workplace. Only 29 percent of millennials report that they are emotionally and behaviorally connected to their job and company, whereas the majority of millennials (55 percent) is "checked out" – they are indifferent about work and show up just to put in their hours without energy or passion for their jobs – which is higher than any other generation. Not engaging millennial workers is a big miss for organizations, and Gallup (2016) estimates the cost of millennials' lack of engagement for the US economy to fall between $284 and $469 billion annually in lost productivity. And worker engagement has further declined since the pre-pandemic years, with the reported engagement of Generation Z and younger millennial workers – those below age 35 – dropping by six percentage points from 2019 to 2022 (Harter 2022).

Acknowledging such differences between millennials and earlier generations, some observers have cautioned that the rising generation might grow up to be "a very demanding workforce" (Zemke et al. 2000). Managers leading millennials might have to shift from a generalized command-and-control approach to a more customized approach in which managers act more as personal coaches and career developers (Colbert et al. 2016; Gallup 2016). Inspiration could come from games, in which stretch goals and corresponding rewards are set and adjusted to the specific needs and abilities of individual workers (McGonigal 2011).

We should also share a note of caution regarding generational differences. In contrast to the popular press, which often highlights generational stereotypes and prominently features the clash of generations at work (e.g., Zemke et al. 2000), academic research that controls for age and period effects has often found only marginal differences between generations with regard to work attitudes, such as job satisfaction, perceived job security, and recognition at work (e.g., Costanza et al. 2012; Deal et al. 2010; Kowske et al. 2010). Similarly, a recent study by McKinsey of over 33,000 workers across sixteen industries in eighteen countries across Australia, Asia, North America, Europe, and the Middle East found that work preferences are more similar than different across age groups, suggesting that many generation-based stereotypes are more myth than fact (De Smet et al. 2023). According to this research, while generational differences exist, they are often modest at best, and many are "brought about just as any prejudice is created, through fear of change" (Smith & Nichols 2015: 42). Instead of taking a generational perspective, recent research has recommended a more nuanced perspective. This perspective is grounded in social constructivism – which does not consider generations as tangible and demonstrable units but as socially constructed entities – as well as in lifespan development – which, instead of focusing on deterministically grouping people into generations, emphasizes that development follows a continuous and multidirectional process (Rudolph et al. 2021). A recent cross-country and cross-industry survey of more than 10,000 managers, for instance, found no support for common generational stereotypes, such as that millennials are more purpose-driven or less traditionally career-minded than older workers (Birkinshaw et al. 2019). However, even generational stereotypes are relevant for our discussion, as these stereotypes and personal biases may affect both managers' choice of, and workers' reaction to, organizational approaches to managing workers (cf., King et al. 2019).

5.2.3   Changes in Attitudes and Values across Generations

Other trends in attitudes and values are commonly associated with millennials, but are actually more broadly shared across generations. We see three trends in particular – independent of generations – that mark a significant transition from the past and thus need to be considered when reflecting on organizational control in the twenty-first century: traditional careers being eroded by weakening attachments between workers and organizations; the increasing relevance of meaningfulness, purpose, and sensegiving at work; and the trend toward work-related flexibility.

Concerning the first trend, traditional careers (often in the same organization) are "replaced by weakening temporal, physical, and administrative attachments between employees and organizations" (Grant & Parker 2009: 342). This trend is further accelerated by the rise of organizational arrangements, such as virtual teams and remote work, and alternative work arrangements, such as gig work, which we will discuss in Section 5.3. However, weakening attachments between workers and organizations have also changed the nature of careers. According to LinkedIn co-founder Reid Hoffman, careers are now simply "tours of duty." New degree-holders have, on average, twice as many jobs in their first five post-college years now as they did in the mid-1980s, and 58 percent of companies expect their new workers to stick around for less than 10 years (Bersin 2017). More recently, pandemic-related shut-downs led to an even more fundamental disruption in the labor market, with millions of workers quitting their jobs, sometimes even without having a new job lined up – a phenomenon the organizational psychologist Anthony Klotz dubbed the "Great Resignation" (Cohen 2021). Recent surveys have found that 40 percent of workers globally, and 26 percent of workers in the United States, are actively looking for new employment opportunities and are considering leaving their current employers by the end of the year (De Smet et al. 2021). And even if they are not actively looking for another job, workers across all generations are increasingly disengaged at work, as evident from the recent phenomena of "quiet quitting" (Ellis & Yang 2022) and "lazy-girl jobs" (Mogg 2023). These workers reject the idea of going above and beyond in their careers. They largely coast at work, draw a paycheck, and focus their time and energy on the things they do outside the workplace. Quiet quitters are looking to reduce their work hours, are no longer interested in training and development, and stop trying to socialize with their co-workers. According to a recent Gallup study, quiet quitters make up at least half of the US workforce, and probably more (Harter 2022). These trends force organizations to engage in an increasingly competitive market for talent (Freeman 2021), turning the "Great Resignation" into the "Great Renegotiation" (De Smet et al. 2022), with many firms finding themselves having to make substantial concessions regarding working conditions to appeal to sought-after talent (Morath & Ip 2021).

The second change in attitudes represents both opportunities and challenges for organizations trying to stay competitive in the ongoing war for talent. Workers no longer look for financial reward only, but increasingly for purpose, meaningful work, and ways of making sense of their work (Bailey et al. 2019). Recent reports found meaningful work to be among the five most important factors that make workers join an employer and among the top six factors that make them stay (Mercer 2020). Furthermore, recent reports also found that more than 90 percent of workers are willing to trade (with 23 percent a significant) part of their life income for permanently meaningful work (Achor et al. 2018). Workers increasingly ask for an organization's purpose, expect managers to help them understand it, and want to see a clear and direct link between their strengths, individual contributions, and the overall purpose (Gallup 2016). This trend reflects the recent move from a predominant shareholder value orientation toward a stakeholder view intending a balance between financial, environmental, and social goals (De Man et al. 2019). As a result, organizational approaches to motivating workers may need to adjust the predominant focus on financial incentives to include aspects of shared meaning (e.g., Sewell 1998), or pursue hybrid approaches that incorporate both bureaucratic and post-bureaucratic logics about worker motivation (e.g., Hodgson 2004).

The third change in attitudes is a higher demand for flexibility at work. According to a recent McKinsey report (Fuller et al. 2022), flexibility has become the number one driver of attrition in frontline retail and hospitality jobs, which employ more than 30 million workers in the United States. However, the desire for work–life balance is strong among people of all generations, with about 63 percent of job seekers calling work–life balance a top priority when selecting a new job, according to LinkedIn's (2022) global talent report. For working parents, for example, work flexibility is the most important factor in a potential job, ahead of work–life balance (Flexjobs 2016). The growing workforce of millennials is also more likely to demand work–life balance and, due to technological possibilities, to live it (Hershatter & Epstein 2010).

People are increasingly asking for flexibility in terms of *when* and *where* they work. This general trend toward more flexible and remote work arrangements, such as telecommuting, co-working spaces, virtual teams, etc., is facilitated by technology and has been accelerated by the recent COVID-19 pandemic (IBM Institute for Business Value 2020), forcing most firms to require workers to temporarily work from home. Of course, remote work is not possible for certain tasks and workers, such as production (e.g., assembly-line manufacturing) or service workers (e.g., bedside nursing, hair dressing). According to the economist Nicholas Bloom, only 51 percent of people responding to his survey can work from home – mostly managers, professionals, and financial workers who can carry out their jobs on computers, and reported an efficiency rate of 80 percent or more (Wong 2020). That leaves nearly half of the workforce that cannot work remotely, with many lacking the space or sufficient internet capacity to work effectively from home. More than half of the respondents working from home were doing so in shared rooms or their bedrooms. Only 65 percent reported having fast enough internet speed to support workable video calls, with the remaining 35 percent having such poor internet connections – or having no internet at all – that it prevents them from effectively telecommuting (Wong 2020). For the workforce that is able to, however, flexible work arrangements is a trend that seems to be here to last: more than 75 percent of surveyed workers indicated that they would like to continue to work remotely at least occasionally, while slightly more than half would like this to be their primary way of working (IBM Institute for Business Value 2020).

People are also demanding flexibility in terms of *what* they work on. If organizations are unwilling or unable to comply, people are more likely to voluntarily change jobs, referred to as job-hopping (Lake et al. 2017). A recent study by Mercer (2020) finds developmental opportunities to be among the top three reasons why workers join, stay at, and leave organizations. This is in line with prior research that found today's workers to expect more from their organization, in particular, in terms of customizing tasks, roles, and responsibilities to their specific skills and preferences (Rousseau et al. 2006; Twenge 2006). Workers may even engage in "job crafting," defined as altering tasks, relationships at work, and their interpretation of tasks to make work more meaningful (Dutton & Wrzesniewski 2020).

The demand for flexibility regarding when and where to work is in line with a decline in the central relevance of work in people's lives, and meets the increasing demands for leisure, personal well-being, and work–life balance (Lyons & Kuron 2014). These are not only important to Generation X and millennials (around 57 percent of respondents), but also to baby boomers (49 percent) (Gallup 2016). The trend toward flexibility is also reflected in the higher prevalence of freelance and gig work arrangements. According to a recent study (Mercer 2020), 77 percent of executives believe freelancers will substantially replace full-time workers within the next 5 years.

Whether flexible work arrangements in terms of time, place, and style are ultimately effective remains an open question. While autonomy is perceived to be higher, and while family and work tasks might be better balanced (e.g., Duxbury et al. 1998; Raghuram & Wiesenfeld 2004), perceived conflict between more blurred and interwoven roles could also have negative effects, including stress and burnout (e.g., Igbaria & Guimaraes 1999; Standen et al. 1999). However, empirical studies on this trade-off have not come to a clear conclusion (Gajendran & Harrison 2007).

5.3   Organizational Trends

We live in a global world where technology, especially information and communication technology, is changing the manner in which businesses create and capture value, how and where we work, and how we interact and communicate. [...] These technologies are not just helping people to do things better and faster, but they are enabling profound changes in the ways that work is done in organizations. (Cascio & Montealegre 2016: 350)

Another challenge in studying work is that both work and the workplace are ever-changing. Although some occupations and organizations have largely disappeared [...], many older forms of work, professions, and organizations remain. And as they remain, they are constantly reorganized, reformed, and reconstituted such that the people doing the work, the arrangements around the work, the technology used in the performance of the work, and even the purpose of the work may change. (Okhuysen et al. 2013: 492)

Piggybacking on the technological advances and demographic and socio-cultural trends we discussed are several fundamental changes in organizations. The digitization of work and work-related processes not only enables unprecedented levels of worker surveillance, both inside and outside the workplace, but it also facilitates the disaggregation or disintermediation of work. Coupled with advances in information and communication technologies, digitization and disaggregation of work increase flexibility with regards to where and when we work, thereby enhancing the feasibility of remote and virtual work arrangements, and leading to a proliferation of alternative work arrangements, such as temporary work, contingent work, and independent contract (or freelance) work. The increasing digitization of work and enhanced electronic surveillance capabilities have also allowed recent advances in ML algorithms to complement – and even supplant – established forms of management. In some cases, ML algorithms have even removed managers – and human supervision in general – from the scene of work. Last, technological developments have also paved the way for entirely new forms of organizations, such as digital platforms and the emergence of the gig economy. Table 5.3 provides an overview of these organizational trends and their implications.

5.3.1   Electronic Surveillance at Work and Beyond

Given the technological advances we discussed earlier, the potential for monitoring every move of every worker every second of the day has arrived and extends far beyond the workplace, as organizations' abilities to engage in such continuous monitoring are no longer restricted to the workplace, or to observable behaviors.

Reactive versus proactive surveillance. Electronic surveillance can be differentiated into two approaches. The first approach is reactive and is typically employed *after* an organization has received indications of illicit or illegal activity, such as the distribution of e-mails with questionable content or defamation of the organization. After receiving complaints from staff members about improper e-mails, for instance, Dow Chemical started monitoring workers and penalized them after computer records showed violations of the company's e-mail policy. The company dismissed at least 60 workers because of concerns that e-mail abuse could lead to sexual harassment claims, and punished hundreds more for sending e-mails that were deemed aggressive or sexually explicit (Kidwell 2005). Many other firms are also using electronic surveillance to protect themselves from legal liability, as evident from incidents at well-known companies like Xerox, the New York Times, and Merck (Kidwell & Sprague 2009).

A second approach to electronic surveillance is more proactive and independent of suspicious occurrences. This approach involves the general electronic monitoring of some or all activities of the company's workers. Along with tracking the content of workers' e-mails, organizations can record keystrokes and time spent on the computer or phone handling customer inquiries. While avoiding legal liability may sometimes be a justification for this general monitoring approach, the main goal is to increase worker productivity, followed by worker safety (Kidwell & Sprague 2009).

An example of this second approach is electronic performance monitoring (EPM), which allows organizations to "track individual employees continuously, randomly, or intermittently; discreetly or intrusively; and with or without warning or consent" (Ravid et al. 2020: 102). This includes companies taking screenshots of their workers' computers at regular intervals, and recording when and for how long they use which applications and websites, virtually tracking their workers logging or clocking in and out, and tracking their workers' location or movements (Gartner 2020). Organizations can also target specific tasks for surveillance. Some hospital nurses, for instance, have been asked to wear electronic badges that record how often they wash their hands

Table 5.3 *Key organizational trends*

Organizational trends	Underlying development and logic	Implications for organizational control
5.3.1 Electronic surveillance at work and beyond	• Justifications for electronic surveillance include legal liability, productivity gains, and worker safety • *Reactive surveillance* after suspicious occurrences to protect the organization from legal liability versus *proactive surveillance* to monitor some or all activities of the organization's workers • Surveillance beyond behavior to analyze emotional/physiological data • Surveillance beyond the workplace, including private social media and health data	• Risk of morale-eroding micromanagement • Surveillance reaches deep into private aspects of workers' lives and moves from panopticon (one organization watching many workers) to omniopticon (everyone watching everyone else), with potential negative implications, like new forms of workplace bullying
5.3.2 Remote and virtual work arrangements	• Information and communication technologies provide more flexibility in terms of *where* and *when* to work • Organizations are experimenting with different working models, from completely remote to completely in the office, as well as hybrid models	• Remote and virtual teams allow organizations to tap a larger and more diverse pool of talent • Virtual teams and remote work also have the potential to negatively affect organizational culture and workers' identification with the organization • Organizations have to manage trade-offs between providing flexibility and work–life balance for workers, retaining a sense of commitment to the organization, and providing managers with tools to fulfill their responsibilities
5.3.3 Alternative work arrangements	• Digitization of work facilitates task standardization and information sharing, which reduces transaction costs associated with contracting out job tasks, and supports the disaggregation of work • The result is a proliferation of three alternative work arrangements: temporary work, contingent work, and freelance work	• Traditional assumptions of stable, hierarchical, and dyadic control relationships are no longer valid for alternative work arrangements • Shared identities, loyalties, and norms are challenging • Mixed teams of traditional and alternative workers may require different arrangements to govern their work

Table 5.3 (*cont.*)

Organizational trends	Underlying development and logic	Implications for organizational control
5.3.4 Management by algorithms	• Advances in ML algorithms enable (partial or full) automatization of organizational control • In many organizations, computer algorithms schedule, monitor, and evaluate workers	• Algorithms allow more fine-grained specification and prediction of worker behavior and its outcomes • Algorithmic control can remove managers and human supervision • Algorithms reduce the cost, and offer new forms, of talent section (i.e., input control) • Gamification (e.g., of performance management) gaining in importance
5.3.5 Digital platforms and gig work	• Gig workers combine characteristics of all four technology-enabled organizational trends (Sections 5.3.1–5.3.4) • Digital platforms match supply and demand through algorithms and administer payments, manage performance, monitor and control gig workers, and track their reputation	• Increasing importance of gig workers for both unskilled and semiskilled micro tasks • While platform organizations actively engage in monitoring and controlling gig workers, they insist that they are not legally employing these gig workers

(Ajunwa et al. 2017). Despite their productivity and safety rationales, critics have disparaged such EPM systems as morale-eroding micromanagement – akin to a manager looking over a worker's shoulder at every moment of the day – and have referred to them as "bossware" (Mims 2022).[3]

An example of proactive surveillance is the US-based global shipping company UPS. Starting in 2009, UPS has been installing around 200 sensors in each of its delivery trucks, which record everything from driving speed to idle times, allowing the company to rank drivers by their daily deliveries and identify those who took unauthorized breaks. Over 4 years, UPS was able to deliver 1.4 million additional packages a day with 1,000 fewer drivers (Ajunwa et al. 2017).

As this example illustrates, the technological opportunities presented by the IoT have further accelerated the collection of worker data. Moreover, if

---

[3] The evolution of worker surveillance coupled with big data analytics has also given rise to the organizational control-related field of *human resource analytics*, which "involves sophisticated analyses including internal (from HR area) and external (from the firm or the market) data collected and manipulated with information technologies to support decisions related to the personnel linked to business results and organizational performance" (Garcia-Arroyo & Osca 2021: 4338).

history teaches us anything, then is it likely that many of the novel and highly intrusive surveillance technologies that were hastily introduced to combat the COVID-19 pandemic can and will be converted into a new generation of workers surveillance regimes (Aloisi & De Stefano 2022). Their hurried adoption and opaque nature often limit workers' understanding of their objectives, and thereby further erode meaningful consent and human agency. Especially the collection of passive data – which is data collected without workers' active involvement – stands in stark contrast to people's desire for at least partial privacy, leading Ellen Bayer of the American Management Association to conclude that "[p]rivacy in today's workplace is largely illusory" (quoted in Ajunwa et al. 2017: 743). Even more problematic is that many workers may be unaware of the extent to which they are being tracked by their employer (Ajunwa et al. 2017).

Surveillance beyond behavior. Besides the usual behavioral data – which consists of externally observable data related to what workers do; what movements they make, including packing a box or operating a machine; where they are; who they interact with; and how they interact with others and their environment – organizations now routinely collect and analyze emotional and physiological data. For example, e-mail monitoring allows organizations to track workers' thoughts, feelings, and attitudes expressed in electronic exchanges, and social media monitoring allows them to track the social networks and relationships that workers build inside and outside of the workplace (Ravid et al. 2020). Organizations also track and analyze physiological data, which comprises a person's internal, biological characteristics, such as heartbeat or neural activity, and the human body's responses to external stimuli, such as eye movements or facial expressions (Cram & Wiener 2020).

An illustrative example is the Dutch bank ABN Amro. In partnership with Philips Electronics, ABN Amro has developed a so-called "Rationalizer" technology to reduce trading risk in financial markets by alerting traders to strong emotions that can interfere with objectivity and rationality (Van Hout 2009). This technology involves measuring galvanic skin response – a change in the electrical resistance of the skin, which is also measured in polygraphs – via a wristband (called EmoBracelet), along with a saucer-shaped display (called EmoBowl). The technology detects if a trader experiences heightened emotions (e.g., due to large fluctuations in the stock price) and alerts the wearer by emitting a light pattern (e.g., deep red) on the display. The light pattern on the bracelet display changes again when the trader's emotions have normalized. By making traders aware of their heightened emotional state, which tends to be associated with underestimating their associated risks and thus overpaying for assets, the company intends to avoid irrational emotional actions on behalf of their traders and nudge them to rethink their trading decisions (Cram & Wiener 2020; Whelan et al. 2018).

In sum, EPM tools collect and store data on workers' behaviors, attitudes, and emotions in great detail, creating comprehensive, lasting records that managers can easily access and that may or may not be directly related to performance (Ravid et al. 2020). Data may now even be collected without a clear purpose as electronic monitoring, unlike traditional monitoring, does not require conscious attention, time, and effort from managers (Aiello & Svec 1993). And surveillance does not stop outside the workplace, as Section 5.3.1 has discussed.

Surveillance beyond the workplace. Employers have long collected information outside of the traditional tasks that need to be controlled to meet cost, time, and quality targets. In the early twentieth century, automobile pioneer Henry Ford did not restrict himself to only patrolling his factory floors with a stopwatch to increase worker productivity. He also recruited private investigators to snoop on workers' lives outside of the factory to find out whether they had any personal issues that might interfere with their performance (Ajunwa et al. 2017). Ford and his detectives could not be everywhere at once, however, and it was therefore impossible to monitor workers continuously. In contrast, today's workers are subject to almost limitless surveillance, with omniscient "Argus Panoptes" technologies retrieving worker data from the Internet, and collecting even private health data, all with the purported consent of the worker (Ajunwa et al. 2017). Monitoring thus reaches deep into private aspects of workers' lives, making workers wary of being psychoanalyzed by their employers' software and raising privacy and discrimination concerns (Moise 2018).

5.3.2 Remote and Virtual Work Arrangements

> [N]ew forms of technology have changed how individuals do their jobs, how employees relate to one another, and how organizations operate and are managed [… and] provide increased flexibility in terms of how, where, and when we work. (Heaphy et al. 2018)

New and evolving technologies do not just facilitate the electronic surveillance of work. They also act as catalysts for profoundly different ways for work to be done in organizations. To start with, advances in information and communication technologies, especially those allowing for the digital surveillance and digitization of work, provide increased flexibility in terms of where and when we work (Heaphy et al. 2018; Malhotra & Majchrzak 2005). No longer constrained by spatial proximity, many organizations have embraced *virtual teams*, in which members are no longer physically collocated, allowing organizations to leverage a larger pool of intellectual resources and diverse talent to complete tasks (Cascio & Montealegre 2016; Farr et al. 2014; Malhotra et al. 2007). "Just a keystroke away from work at any hour of the day or night"

(Ashford et al. 2007: 75), virtual work has been referred to as the "new normal" (Raghuram et al. 2019: 308).

Even before the forced shift to a largely remote workforce in response to the COVID-19 pandemic,[4] 43 percent of US workers reported that they have engaged in *remote work*, defined as using computer technology to work from home or another location away from the office (Gallup 2017). During the pandemic, according to economist Nicholas Bloom,

an incredible 42 percent of the U.S. labor force now working from home full-time. About another 33 percent are not working – a testament to the savage impact of the lockdown recession. And the remaining 26 percent – mostly essential service workers – are working on their business premises. So, by sheer numbers, the U.S. is a working-from-home economy. Almost twice as many employees are working from home as at work. More strikingly, if we consider the contribution to U.S. gross domestic product based on their earnings, this enlarged group of work-from-home employees now accounts for more than two-thirds of U.S. economic activity. (Wong 2020)

Moreover, remote work appears to be growing on workers and organizations alike. After the pandemic, between 48 and 60 percent of workers expect to work remotely at least some of the time, compared to about 30 percent of workers pre-pandemic (Gallup 2023; Gartner 2020). Organizations also expect to continue at least some level of remote work after the pandemic (McKinsey Global Institute 2020), in order to stay competitive and attract and retain talent amid a tightening labor market (Cutter & Dill 2021). Studies project that working from home will stick, and that about 20 percent of workdays in the United States will be at home after the pandemic ends, compared with just 5 percent before (Barrero et al. 2021). The typical firm plans for its workers to work from home one to three days a week and come into the office for the remainder of the time (Wong 2020). A number of organizations, among them Facebook, now known as Meta, and Google, now known as Alphabet, have extended their pandemic-induced remote-work policies (BBC 2020). Some companies, such as Twitter, now known as X, and Yelp, even extended their policies indefinitely (Guardian 2020; Nguyen 2022).[5] Yelp's CEO, Jeremy Stoppelman,

---

[4] On March 11, 2020, the World Health Organization (WHO) declared the novel coronavirus outbreak a global pandemic and advised governments to implement aggressive measures to combat the alarming levels of spread and severity of this public health emergency (World Health Organization 2020). In response, most countries encouraged or even mandated their directly employed, non-public-facing staff to work at home (International Labour Organization 2020), and many corporations followed shortly thereafter. More than 3 years after this announcement, one of the most profound organizational shifts in response to the pandemic is a large and lasting increase in remote work, making it the new normal for many workers and parts of the economy (Levanon 2020).

[5] However, Twitter's remote work policy has recently been reversed by its new owner, Elon Musk (Burton & Confino 2022).

wrote in a blog post on June 23, 2022: "Over time we came to realize that the future of work at Yelp is remote. It's best for our employees, and for our business" (Berger 2022).

Although many executives acknowledge that working from home because of COVID-19 has been effective, in the long term, they also fear a negative impact on organizational culture and workers' identification with their organizations. As a result, in a recent McKinsey study, more than three-quarters of executives stated that they expected the typical core employee to be at work three or more days a week (De Smet et al. 2021). This stands in direct contrast to the preferences of workers, as shown by a McKinsey survey of 5,000 workers worldwide: More than half would like to work flexibly at home at least two days a week (Alexander et al. 2021). Business leaders who urge their workers to return to the office and proclaim the end of COVID-19 work arrangements therefore risk appearing tone-deaf and widening the divide with their workers (De Smet et al. 2021). This may result in higher turnover, which has already been observed worldwide to be at all-time highs. A recent work trend index report by Microsoft (2022) shows a 3 percent increase in the likelihood of Generation Z and millennials to consider changing employers within 12 months.

At the same time, however, research has found that remote work can lead to worker fatigue; exacerbate the challenge of switching off from work, as the separation between private and professional spheres is blurred (Monteiro & Adler 2022); decrease their sense of organizational belonging (Bartel et al. 2012), with only 28 percent of fully remote workers feeling a connection to the purpose of their organizations, compared to 33 percent of on-site and 35 percent of hybrid workers (Harter 2023); and result in a lack of informal mentoring and socialization, including serendipitous face-to-face interactions, which is deteriorating their social networks (Cooper & Kurland 2002; De Smet et al. 2021; Gajendran & Harrison 2007). Meta-analytical results from before the COVID-19 pandemic confirmed that working remotely has no generally detrimental effects on the quality of workplace relationships. However, high-intensity telecommuting, defined as more than 2.5 days a week, can harm relationships with co-workers (Gajendran & Harrison 2007), in line with the more general findings of a curvilinear relationship between the frequency of remote work and job satisfaction (Allen et al. 2015).

The uncertainty about the best way forward – completely remote, completely in the office, or hybrid; mandatory requirements, or free choice by workers; and so on – is reflected in the different paths that companies are taking. As mentioned earlier, companies such as Yelp or Airbnb have chosen the path toward full remote work and giving their workers complete autonomy. Elon Musk, on the other hand, announced the following in two emails to Tesla and to SpaceX workers in early June 2022:

If you don't show up, we will assume you have resigned. [...] Anyone who wishes to do remote work must be in the office for a minimum (and I mean *minimum*) of 40 hours per week or depart Tesla. [...] This is less than we ask of factory workers. [...] If there are particularly exceptional contributors for whom this is impossible, I will review and approve those exceptions directly. [...] There are of course companies that don't require this, but when was the last time they shipped a great new product? It's been a while. [...] Tesla has and will create and actually manufacture the most exciting and meaningful products of any company on Earth. This will not happen by phoning it in. (Bursztynsky 2022)

Musk backs his demand for executive attendance with the story that if he had not "lived in the factory so much [...,] Tesla would long ago have gone bankrupt" (Bursztynsky 2022). Tesla reportedly uses access cards to check whether workers come into the office. Those who have not used their employee card to enter into any of the offices or factory buildings for more than 16 days will receive an e-mail with a reminder that all workers are expected to return to the office full-time. Workers are required to let their manager know the reason for their absence, such as vacation, business trips, or illness, and to send a copy to absence@tesla.com (Jerzy 2022). In line with Tesla's policy, after acquiring the company, Musk has recently also reversed Twitter's remote work policy, now allowing "only 'exceptional' Twitter employees [to] work from home" (Burton & Confino 2022).

Unsurprisingly, Musk has faced headwinds for his approach. He has responded by highlighting that factory workers, who must be physically present, are often forgotten in the discussion about remote work. There is also scientific support for his claim that innovation can suffer in remote settings. Brucks and Levav's (2022) experimental research, for example, indicates that videoconferencing, which is as effective as face-to-face interaction for selecting which idea to pursue, nevertheless inhibits the production of creative ideas, because it focuses communicators on a (small) screen, resulting in a narrower cognitive focus. For more routine work, however, the evidence is mixed. A recent study of workers at the US Patent and Trademark Office, for instance, showed that workers granted full remote-work privileges improved their productivity by 4 percent over workers participating in limited work-from-home programs (Choudhury et al. 2019).

Other large US technology companies, including Alphabet, Amazon, Apple, and Meta, are not (yet) forcing all workers back into the office – especially for fear of losing talent – and allowing hybrid models. Indeed, flexible hybrid solutions appear to pay off, with studies finding higher organizational commitment among workers who were free to choose whether to work in the office or at home, and commitment to mediate the positive relationship between workplace autonomy and task performance (Hunton & Norman 2010). However, in such hybrid work settings, companies must intentionally invest in providing workers with a sense of connection in order to sustain workforce performance and the intention to stay. About 40 percent of HR leaders said that they have increased their budgets related to organizational culture since the beginning of the pandemic in response to their workers, of whom two thirds said workplace culture is very or extremely important to be effective in their jobs (Gartner 2022). The key challenges of organizational remote work going forward are therefore offering workers the flexibility and work–life balance they desire, while simultaneously cultivating a sense of commitment to the organization and providing managers with avenues to fulfill their monitoring and control responsibilities.

5.3.3   Alternative Work Arrangements

> It is true that many specific, well-defined jobs continue to exist in contemporary organizations. But we presently are in the midst of what we believe are fundamental changes in the relationships among people, the work they do, and the organizations for which they do it. [...] They may be independent contractors, managing simultaneously temporary or semi-permanent relationships with multiple enterprises [...] with no single boss, no home organizational unit, and no assurance of long-term employment. (Oldham & Hackman 2010: 466)

In addition to acting as a catalyst for electronic surveillance and remote work, the increasing digitization of work also facilitates the standardization of many tasks and can make information on workers' behavior and performance widely available. This, in turn, helps reduce the transaction costs associated with contracting out job tasks, supports the disaggregation of work (Katz & Krueger 2019; Walsh et al. 2006), and leads to a proliferation of *alternative work arrangements*. These arrangements are defined as work that is not on a fixed schedule, not under an organization's administrative control, and does not entail any mutual expectation of continued employment (Ashford et al. 2007).

The alternative workforce as a whole makes up 20 to 30 percent of the working-age population in the United States and the European Union and is relatively diverse in terms of age, income levels, educational attainment, and gender (McKinsey Global Institute 2016). There are three main types of alternative work arrangements. *Temporary work*, which is short-term and often brokered by a temp agency, has long been a fixture in organizations. A more recent development is the growth of *contingent work*, which is employment tied to the completion of a specific task. Contingent work arrangements consist of on-call work (or work on an as-needed basis) and contractual work (or work for a staffing agency that provides their services to another organization on a contractual or project basis) (Katz & Krueger 2019). Organizations use contingent workers primarily to cut costs by replacing full-time positions,[6] and to

---

[6] Industry insiders estimate that relying on independent contractors rather than employees can lower direct costs by roughly 25 percent (Scheiber 2015).

fill labor shortages caused by illness (Gartner 2020). The largest group among alternative workers consists of *independent contractors* (or *freelancers*), who obtain clients on their own to provide goods and services under a specific contractual agreement (Gallup 2018; Katz & Krueger 2019). In contrast to temporary and contingent workers, these workers are not employees, but work for themselves. While the work outcome is contractually agreed upon with the client organization, the work process is controlled by the independent contractor (Cappelli & Keller 2013). Independent contractors are typically hired on a project basis and may work for multiple clients simultaneously. Similar to remote workers, independent contractors tend to work outside an organization's place of business (Ashford et al. 2007; Spreitzer et al. 2017). The key challenge of alternative work arrangements is managing teams of traditional and alternative workers often working alongside each other, despite the absence of stable, hierarchical, and dyadic reporting relationships, and despite few (if any) shared identities, loyalties, and norms.

5.3.4   Management by Algorithms

Algorithmic management has been defined as a control system that relies on machine-readable data and software algorithms that support and/or automate managerial decision-making about work (Duggan et al. 2020; Lee et al. 2015; Meijerink et al. 2021). Advanced algorithms analyzing vast repositories of digitized work process data allow for a more fine-grained description and, in many cases, prediction of worker behavior and performance, which complements and expands – and can even supplant – established forms of management (Schafheitle et al. 2020). Algorithms can *support* managerial tasks with advanced surveillance technologies and analytic capabilities, which provide useful insights to managers regarding workers' behaviors and performance. In this case, human managers remain "in the loop" (Bucher et al. 2021a: 46). But algorithms can also *remove* managers – and human supervision in general – from the scene of work (Ajunwa et al. 2017; Cram & Wiener 2020; Kellogg et al. 2020; Newell & Marabelli 2015), thereby taking human managers "out of the loop" (Bucher et al. 2021a: 46).[7] In fact, some organizations already rely on computer algorithms to schedule, monitor, and evaluate workers, with the management of humans by other humans becoming increasingly anachronistic (Davis 2015). Moreover, algorithmic input control has the potential to expand and diversify the potential talent pool and dramatically reduce the costs associated with talent selection (Garcia-Arroyo & Osca 2021). The recent COVID-19

---

[7] A third option would be algorithms making decisions that are subject to human oversight, or "humans on the loop" (Bucher et al. 2021a: 46), which, for our purposes, can be subsumed under the category "humans in the loop."

pandemic has acted as a catalyst for such algorithmic management in two ways: It increased people's willingness to embrace these technologies, and it compelled the digitization of many previously offline management acts, which then became training data for AI applications (Quaquebeke & Gerpott 2023).

Algorithms also pave the way for a broader and more sophisticated approach to gamification, defined as "the application of game systems – competition, rewards, quantifying player/user behaviour – into non-game domains, such as work, productivity and fitness" (Woodcock & Johnson 2018: 542). The increasing gamification of performance management in today's workforce created an $11 billion industry that includes not only workforce-management systems, such as CornerStone, OnDemand, BetterWorks, and Kronos, but also enterprise social platforms, such as Microsoft's Yammer, Salesforce's Chatter, and Facebook's Workplace (Kaplan 2015).

In sum, algorithms are increasingly complementing and, in some cases, even replacing managerial tasks, and they provide new opportunities for the gamification of work. The key challenge of further integrating algorithms into organizational control arrangements is that doing so requires organizations to address their accountability, both regarding potential biases algorithms might introduce, and regarding their opaqueness and inscrutable nature, which often results in a very limited understanding of how algorithms work, not just among affected workers but even among the algorithms' designers.

5.3.5 Digital Platforms and Gig Work

> In contrast to hierarchies (which centralize power), markets (which disperse it), or networks (which parcel it out to trusted collaborators), platforms exercise power over economic transactions by delegating control among the participants. They do so by establishing a digital infrastructure with which to govern the service triangle that links employers, workers, and customers. (Vallas & Schor 2020: 282)

The newest incarnation of algorithm-enabled alternative work arrangements can be found in the gig economy, where workers are automatically matched with jobs by digital platforms. These digital platforms capitalize on the ubiquity of mobile devices and the ability to harness real-time information to broker efficient matches between enormous pools of workers and clients (Baum & Haveman 2020). Gig work is typically defined by four characteristics: irregular work schedules, driven by fluctuations in demand for workers' services; workers providing some or all of the capital equipment used in their work (e.g., mobile phones, cars, bikes, or computing equipment) as well as their own place of work (e.g., cars or their home offices); piece-rate work remuneration; and the work being facilitated and mediated by digital platforms (Stewart & Stanford 2017). Gig workers can perform both unskilled and semiskilled micro tasks (e.g., Amazon's Mturk, TaskRabbit), delivery jobs (e.g., DoorDash), and ride sharing (e.g., Uber or Lyft), as well as skilled technical tasks in complex short-term projects (e.g., via Freelancer or Upwork). While about 4 percent of US adults have earned money as gig workers in 2015 (McKinsey Global Institute 2016), by 2020, the share was already at 36 percent (Kolmar 2022). Sixteen percent of US adults have earned money on an online gig platform at least once; 9 percent have earned income from online gig work in 2021 (Kolmar 2022). The rapid growth of digital platforms (Katz & Krueger 2019) suggests that we have only begun to see their impact.

In addition to matching worker supply and demand, these intermediary platforms also perform other activities, including administering payments, managing performance, monitoring and controlling gig workers, and tracking reputations (Meijerink & Keegan 2019). Digital platforms rely heavily on electronic surveillance, and some platforms go as far as deploying technology that will detect anger, raised voices, or crying children in the background on workers' home-office calls (Shellenbarger 2008). While digital platforms do not restrict surveillance to algorithmic control, it is the dominant form of control in what Newlands (2021: 722) called "a tripartite multimodal surveillance assemblage, consisting of algorithmic, managerial and customer surveillance." Platforms exercise control over workers by creating electronic reputations that typically include client feedback and other productivity metrics (Kuhn & Maleki 2017).

This situation presents somewhat of a paradox, as the digital platforms actively engage in monitoring and controlling gig workers, but at the same time, they insist that they do not legally employ these gig workers, nor are they responsible for work-related rights and benefits (Meijerink & Keegan 2019). As we will discuss in Section 7.4.1, a heated debate about the classification of gig workers is raging, both in the public arena and in court systems worldwide (Meijerink & Keegan 2019; Rosenblat & Stark 2016). For the purposes of our discussion, however, gig workers fall under the category of independent contractors. That is, gig workers are not employees but work remotely for themselves, have control over their work, are hired on a task basis, and may work for multiple clients simultaneously. Some digital platforms are designed explicitly to not trigger statutory definitions of employment, for example, by preventing workers from working continuously for a single client (Lehdonvirta 2016).

In sum, gig work combines the characteristics of all four technology-enabled organizational trends – electronic surveillance, remote work, alternative work arrangements, and management by algorithms. In addition, digital gig work platforms "strip a job down to its bare necessities" (Gray & Suri 2019: 122). There is no corporate office to go to, no traditional colleagues, and no traditional managers (Bucher et al. 2021a, 2021b), which offers both new opportunities but also challenges for organizational control.

5.4   The Contested Terrain of Organizational Control

Scholars and management practitioners alike have long considered the alignment of worker behavior with organizational goals one of the fundamental problems of organizations (Fayol 1949; Mintzberg 1989; Van Maanen & Barley 1984). From ancient Chinese bureaucracies to contemporary knowledge and gig economies, the challenge for any attempt at collective organization is inducing individuals to, at least partially, subordinate their goals and autonomy to the larger collective (Barnard 1938). However, efforts to monitor and control workers impose substantial costs on organizations and society at large. For instance, Ouchi (1980) concluded his seminal article on market, bureaucratic, and clan control by highlighting net productivity declines in the United States, 22 percent of which are attributable to increased needs for surveillance of potentially dishonest workers and other stakeholders (Denison 1978). In contrast to investments in other areas that are responsible for declining productivity, such as increased costs of air, water, and worker safety, the fact that the US devotes more of its resources to transactional matters than in prior years constitutes a net decline in its welfare (Ouchi 1980). Research since the turn of the century has come to similar conclusions. Besides ample evidence of increasing organizational control often outweighing its benefits (e.g., Bonner et al. 2002; Cardinal 2001), noteworthy examples are Mankins et al.'s (2014) astonishing finding that the organization they studied devotes 300,000 person hours per year for a single weekly performance review meeting, as well as Deloitte's (2015) estimate of $155 billion that Australian businesses spend annually to satisfy organizational control requirements.

Moreover, workers often undermine, or outright resist, organizations' attempts at controlling their behavior, jeopardizing the efficacy of organizational control efforts and further enhancing the societal costs of control. And advances in technological surveillance and novel organizational forms have not been able to resolve this tension between control and resistance. On the contrary, recent studies on electronic workplace surveillance and platform-mediated gig work (e.g., Bronowicka & Ivanova 2020; Cameron 2022; Cameron & Rahman 2022) suggest that our contemporary work environment has further reinforced the mutually constitutive nature of control and resistance. For instance, UPS delivery drivers have found a way to game the company's real-time telematics system by "sprinting to an apartment and slapping a delivery-attempt notice on the door without ringing the bell or waiting for someone to make it down a three-story walk-up," which is "a shortcut UPS's would have no way of catching" (Kaplan 2015: 33). In addition, there are reports of Amazon delivery drivers hanging their cellphones on trees located near the company's distribution centers to manipulate the location-based matching algorithm in their favor (Soper 2020). Growing concerns about the security and privacy of data about workers represent another battlefield between organizations' interest in, and workers' resistance to, invasive electronic surveillance.

Technological advances have proven to be a double-edged sword when it comes to control and resistance: They have led to new and more extensive surveillance opportunities for organizations, but they can also be a catalyst for resistance in the workplace. Social media have become a particularly powerful platform for gathering and disseminating information about organizations and for enabling workers to organize resistance.

This contest between organizational control and worker resistance is further complicated by the possibility of a "self-fulfilling prophecy whereby opportunistic behavior will increase with sanctions and incentives imposed to curtail it, thus creating the need for even stronger and more elaborate sanctions and incentives" (Ghoshal & Moran 1996: 14). Organizations can become embroiled in such a vicious cycle because the relationship between hierarchical control and opportunistic behavior consists of two distinct and contradictory effects. On the one hand, organizational control increases the costs of opportunistic behavior for workers, which, in turn, should reduce this type of behavior. On the other hand, hierarchical control creates a negative impression of the organization among workers, to whom control signals that they are neither trusted nor trustworthy enough to behave appropriately on their own. This negative impression, in turn, increases workers' propensity to behave opportunistically, which ultimately increases opportunistic behavior (Enzle & Anderson 1993; Ghoshal & Moran 1996). For managers, the use of monitoring, surveillance, and authority can further fuel their distrust of workers, leading to the perception that even more surveillance and control are required – what Strickland (1958: 201) has labeled the "dilemma of the supervisor."

Even the best efforts at surveillance and control offer no obvious way out of this vicious cycle, since they inevitably lead to more difficult-to-detect opportunistic behavior. As Ghoshal and Moran (1996: 24) put it, "when the balloon of opportunistic behavior is poked in one place by the blunt instrument of rational (i.e., hierarchical) control, it readily yields but reemerges elsewhere in ways that may make it more difficult and costly to detect and curtail."

In conclusion, organizational control has always been, and will remain for the foreseeable future, a "contested terrain" (Edwards 1979), in which managers and workers are engaged in ongoing formal and informal processes of negotiation (Barker 1993). Acknowledging control and resistance as two sides of the same coin (Hodson 1995), the question is: Where do we go from here?

6 Reconceptualizing Organizational Control

Despite its initial grounding in the organizational realities of the 1970s and 1980s (e.g., Eisenhardt 1985; Ouchi 1977, 1979; Ouchi & Maguire 1975), organizational control theory continues to be relevant in management and organizational research and has even seen a renaissance in the last few years (Cardinal et al. 2017; Sitkin et al. 2020). While recent contributions have provided new insights into the effectiveness of different approaches to organizational control (see Chapters 3 and 4), we are also witnessing seismic shifts in organizations, and even in the nature of work itself (see Chapter 5), which raise the question of whether our theoretical approaches to organizational control still reflect contemporary organizational realities. A promising way to refine and extend our conceptual framework of organizational control is by exploring the actual control configurations that exist in contemporary organizations. Such empirically derived configurations can help us develop a more comprehensive understanding of how controls combine in practice, and they can also help us reveal novel control forms that are not yet integrated in our existing frameworks.

6.1 A Configurational Approach to Organizational Control

> It can scarcely be denied that the supreme goal of all theory is to make the irreducible basic elements as simple and as few as possible without having to surrender the adequate representation of a single datum of experience. (Albert Einstein in a 1933 lecture, which is often paraphrased as: "Everything should be made as simple as possible, but no simpler.")

Both our empirical mapping of the organizational control literature – especially the most recent intellectual base (Cluster 12) and its associated research front we discussed in Section 3.2.2 – as well as our meta-analytical review of the literature (Section 4.5), suggest the existence of complex interactions among controls in their influence on outcomes. To account for these interdependencies, our reconceptualization of organizational control takes a strong holistic (Cardinal et al. 2017) or configurational approach. In contrast to traditional correlational theorizing, configurational approaches are well suited for addressing causal complexity (e.g., Doty & Glick 1994; Furnari et al. 2021;

Miller 1986; Mintzberg 1979; Misangyi et al. 2017; Short et al. 2008), as they are built on an understanding of organizations as "clusters of interconnected structures and practices, rather than as modular or loosely coupled entities whose components can be understood in isolation" (Fiss 2007: 1180). The purpose of configurational theorizing is to explain how and why multiple explanatory factors combine to bring about a phenomenon or outcome of interest, recognizing that more than one configuration of elements could lead to the outcome (Furnari et al. 2021). Configurational theorizing involves both identifying a constellation of interrelated factors and articulating the orchestrating themes that underlie how and why these factors work together (Meyer et al. 1993; Miller 1986, 1996).

A configurational approach to organizational control has several advantages over alternative approaches. Existing correlational research considers, at best, only a limited set of organizational controls and has historically ignored any interactions among them. Such net-effects thinking that emphasizes the unique contribution of individual controls, while holding all others constant, tends to result in underspecified models that do not realistically represent the coexistence of controls in organizations (Cardinal et al. 2017). Moreover, organizations and their environments are increasingly characterized by multifaceted complexity (see, e.g., our review of recent trends in Chapter 5), which cannot be represented adequately by "the more, the better" linear correlational models. In contrast, configurational theorizing acknowledges and embraces both organizational and contextual complexity (Misangyi et al. 2017).

Besides accounting for organizational and environmental complexity, configurational theorizing also allows for theoretical multiplicity, or the applicability of multiple theoretical perspectives (Park et al. 2020). While the specialization of our research agendas often encourages us to study organizational control from our own disciplinary perspectives, organizational control research, by its very nature, spans management, accounting, information systems, marketing, operations management, and other disciplines (see Chapters 2 to 4 for details) and is built on multiple theoretical perspectives (see Section 3.3 for details). A configurational approach embraces and leverages the multidisciplinary nature of organizational control research (Cardinal et al. 2018) and helps integrate the multidisciplinary literature by consolidating past gains and synthesizing broad patterns from contingency theory's fragmented concepts (Meyer et al. 1993).

6.1.1   Types of Configurational Theorizing

Configurational theorizing broadly falls into two camps (Meyer et al. 1993). The first camp focuses on developing theoretical typologies or *ideal types*, which are holistic configurations of organizational factors (Doty et al. 1993). The ideal type represents an organizational form that *might* exist, instead of an actual organization, and serves as an abstract model that can be used to analyze any deviations between the ideal type and actual organizations to explain organizational effectiveness. Ideal-type organizations exhibit optimal levels of internal consistency, or fit, among contextual, structural, and strategic factors and are therefore expected to be the most effective organizations (Van de Ven & Drazin 1985). The more an actual organization resembles an ideal type, the greater is the actual organization's effectiveness. The second camp focuses on deriving empirical taxonomies or *archetypes* (Short et al. 2008). In contrast to ideal types, archetypes are holistic configurations of organizational factors found in *actual* organizations, which may or may not exhibit high levels of fit among elements, and which are often context specific. In our discussion later, we will follow this second approach and present archetypes, or actually existing organizational control configurations, before discussing their effectiveness and potential shortcomings regarding our four outcome dimensions.

Given the large number of possible permutations of their constituent factors, the number of potential archetypes is vast. The actual number of archetypes found in any given environment is, however, rather limited, as the factors of strategy, structure, and environment tend to coalesce into a small number of common, predictively useful archetypes that describe a large proportion of existing organizations (Meyer et al. 1993; Miller 1986). This coalescence can be explained by three interrelated arguments: environmental selection, which allows effective configurations to flourish, and maladaptive ones to perish (Miller 1996); organizational tendencies to seek internal harmony or fit among elements (Miller et al. 1984); and organizational inertia, which is caused by change being all or nothing, and therefore very infrequent, as organizations avoid piecemeal change that destroys complementarities between factors of a configuration (Miller & Friesen 1982). The advantage of this coalescence is that only a small fraction of all theoretically conceivable configurations are viable and can be observed empirically (Meyer et al. 1993). Although these empirical configurations describe, rather than explain, the broader phenomenon of organizational control, they are important building blocks for theory development (Bedford & Malmi 2015; Grabner & Moers 2013). Descriptions of real-world control arrangements provide an empirical basis for refining and extending our conceptual frameworks. They help reveal interactions (i.e., complementarity or substitution) between controls and boundary conditions, and they help us develop parsimonious frameworks necessary for the design of valid empirical tests of specific relationships.

6.1.2 Control Configurations in the Existing Literature

Before we present our control configuration framework, we reviewed the literature of organizational control and control-related configurations, which includes both conceptual work presenting ideal types and empirical studies presenting archetypes (see Table 6.1 for an overview). The empirical studies further suggest that equifinal configurations exist for specific contexts, and that context matters – both in terms of environmental dimensions (e.g., dynamism) and organizational dimensions (e.g., strategy context). However, no previous study has examined twenty-first-century organizational realities. Instead, research remained situated in the traditional face-to-face, hierarchical, full-time work context of the twentieth century. In addition, prior configurational logics remain incomplete, as only a few control dimensions are included in each configuration. As is evident in our overview, the most common control dimensions in previous control configurations were control target and control formality, and most configurations were dominated by formal outcome controls.

6.1.3   Steps in Configurational Theorizing

Our configurational theorizing about reconceptualizing organizational control proceeds in three iterative steps (cf., Furnari et al. 2021): First, we identified the relevant factors that can plausibly form configurations (i.e., scoping); second, we examined how the attributes are connected (i.e., linking); and third, we labeled configurations to evoke their orchestrating themes (i.e., naming). We also added a fourth step, visualizing each configuration.

Scoping. In the *scoping stage*, our conceptual and empirical reviews of the field (see Chapters 3 and 4 for details) helped us delimit key factors that comprise the phenomenon of organizational control while acknowledging its (causal) complexity and multidisciplinary nature. Following Furnari et al.'s (2021) recommendations, we first complexified our factorial logic by incorporating multiple theoretical and disciplinary domains. To achieve theoretical parsimony and plausible coherence, we then simplified our factorial logic by subsuming lower-order factors – such as performance-related contracts, bonuses, profit-sharing plans, rewards, and recognition – under higher-order factors – in this example, outcome control – thereby limiting the total number of factors.

Figure 1.1 represents the "factorial logic" (Park et al. 2020: 9) of our organizational control configurations. It describes our configurations consisting of control choices along the five control dimensions: target, formality, singularity, direction, and style. It also outlines the factors that are important in order for the four control outcomes to occur, which are the organizational and environmental context variables and the (challenged) assumptions. Furthermore, it explains *why*, by invoking the three organizational control functions of monitoring, incentives, and coordination, and it also explains which elements are not causally relevant and can be eliminated, such as power, structure, culture, and locus of control (see Section 2.2 for details).

Table 6.1 *Comparison of prior organizational control configurations*

Source(s)	Control configurations	Underlying control dimensions and elements	Contingency logic	Research design	Implications
Burns and Stalker (1961)	Archetypes: • Mechanistic • Organic	• Formality (formal, informal) • Direction (top-down, peer) • Structural dimensions	• Uncertainty • Stability	• Empirical study of electronic firms	• Mechanistic organization suitable for stable environmental conditions; organic structure suitable for dynamic and uncertain settings
Bruns and Waterhouse (1975)	Archetypes: • Administrative • Interpersonal	• Target (behavior) • Formality (formal) • Concentration of authority (centralization, autonomy)	• Firm size • Firm dependence • Technological complexity	• Multi-industry study of twenty-six firms	• Administrative control is more common in larger, more technologically sophisticated organizations • Interpersonal control is more common in smaller organizations and those dependent on other organizations
Williamson (1975, 1979, 1991)	Ideal types: • Markets • Hierarchies • Hybrid (added in 1979)	• n/a	Costs associated with transactions depend on: • Transaction uncertainty • Transaction frequency • Asset specificity	• Conceptual and empirical	• Initially, transaction cost logic focused on choice between markets and hierarchies • Intermediate governance forms added later
Ouchi (1979)	Ideal types: • Market • Bureaucracy • Clan	• Target (input, behavior, outcome) • Formality (formal, informal)	• Ability to measure outcomes • Knowledge of the transformation process • Cost and benefits of controls • Stability of industries	• Conceptual	• Social (reciprocity, legitimate authority, shared values/beliefs) and informational requirements (prices, rules, traditions) of organizational control

Table 6.1 (cont.)

Source(s)	Control configurations	Underlying control dimensions and elements	Contingency logic	Research design	Implications
Mintzberg (1980, 1989)	Ideal types: • Simple structure • Machine bureaucracy • Professional bureaucracy • Divisionalized • Adhocracy • Missionary structure • Political organization	• Target (input, i.e., training and indoctrination; behavior, i.e., formalization and bureaucratization) • Formality (formal, informal) • Specialization of jobs • Planning and control systems • Decentralization	• Age • Size • Technical systems • Environment • Power	• Conceptual	• An effective organization "favor[s] some sort of configuration […] as it searches for harmony in its internal processes and consonance with its environment" (Mintzberg 1980: 322) • Associated design parameters (e.g., specialization, formalization, centralization)
Merchant (1981)	Archetypes: • Administrative structure • Interpersonal structure	• Target (behavior in the form of system sophistication, outcome in the form of importance of meeting budget) • Formality (formal in the form of formality of communication) • Participation	• Firm size • Firm diversification • Centralization	• Nineteen firms in the electronics industry	• Administrative structure is more commonly used by large firms
Bamberger and Fiegenbaum (1996)	Ideal types: • Eight configurations of three dimensions	• Target (behavior, outcome) • Time orientation (past, future) • External exposure of managers (low, high)	• Organizational goal consensus and process uncertainty • Nature of the firm's competitive advantage • Firm's current position	• Conceptual	• Focus on HR policies and practices • Identification of eight basic strategic reference points combinations
Speklé (2001)	Ideal types: • Market • Arm's length hierarchical • Arm's length hybrid • Machine action-oriented • Machine results-oriented • Exploratory hierarchical • Exploratory hybrid • Boundary hierarchical	• Target (behavior: standardization, monitoring and supervision, codified rules, contracts; outcome: performance standards, performance-related compensation) • Formality (formal)	Three TCE dimensions: • Ex ante programmability • Asset specificity • Ex post information impactedness	• Conceptual	• Given TCE's assumptions of bounded rationality and opportunism, the specific nature of the required contribution (the three moderators) gives rise to distinctive and predictable contractual problems that need to be solved by the organization

Vosselman (2002)	Archetypes: • Vertical management (strongly bureaucratic, weakly bureaucratic) • Horizontal management (captive buying and selling) • Free buying and selling (external buy-out or outsourcing)	• Target (behavior, outcome) • Formality (formal)	• Characteristics of the services • Extent of the user's needs • Level of uncertainty • Level of complexity	• Single case study of Leiden University	• Configurations as "templates for influencing managers" (p. 134) • Distinction between vertical management control configurations and horizontal management control configurations
Kirsch (2004)	Archetypes: • Informal mode for requirements determination phase) • Formal mode (development phase) • Hybrid mode (last implementation phase)	• Formality (formal, informal)	• Project context • Stakeholder context • Global context	• Longitudinal study of two IS projects	• Changes in control configurations from one project phase to another are triggered by the project, stakeholder, and global context
Henri (2008)	Archetypes: • Outcome surveillance • Management support tool • Institutionalized organizational process	• Design (mix of financial, customer, internal processes, innovation, and learning measures) • Use (monitoring, strategic decision making, attention focusing, legitimizing) • Revision (addition, deletion, and changes in performance indicators)	• Size • Strategy • Decentralization	• Survey data from 383 manufacturing firms	• Three aspects of performance measurement systems are used for the configurations: design, use, and revision of performance indicators • Three archetypes of the role and importance of performance measurement systems emerge
Sandelin (2008)	Archetypes: • Enabling platform • System of accountability	• Target (input, behavior, outcome) • Formality (formal, informal)	• Internal consistency • Complexity of operations	• Empirical case study of a small growth-oriented new-economy firm	• Control configurations' "functionality [...] depends on internal consistency, specifically on the reciprocal linkages of design and use between a primary mode of control and other control elements" (p. 324)

Table 6.1 (*cont.*)

Source(s)	Control configurations	Underlying control dimensions and elements	Contingency logic	Research design	Implications

Kreutzer and Lechner (2010)	Ideal types:
	• Core growth
	• Growth outside the core
	• Cost efficiency
	• Quality
	• Fixed assets
	• Net working capital
		• Target (input, behavior, outcome)
		• Formality (formal, informal)
			• Strategic initiative type	• Conceptual
				• Anecdotal cases
					• Identification of managerial traps that may prevent firms from achieving an initiative-control configuration fit:
					  • One-size-fits-all trap
					  • Inertia trap
					  • Over-reaction trap
					  • Rustiness trap
					  • Slack trap
					  • Fine-tuning trap

Lechner and Kreutzer (2010)	Archetypes: • Agenda-setting (low process coordination, high content coordination) • Context-setting (high process coordination, low content coordination) • Directing (high process coordination, high content coordination) • Self-organizing (low process coordination, low content coordination)	• Target (input, behavior, outcome) • Formality (formal as centralization and formalization, informal as social relations)	• Environmental complexity • Environmental dynamism • Degree of diversification • Existence of organizational slack	• Longitudinal, multi-case study design (Hügli, Helvetia, Lufthansa Cargo, Gamma)	• Four modes of coordinating growth initiatives in multi-unit corporations; no optimal mode • Personal and impersonal mechanisms do not substitute each other, and each configuration is characterized by a specific combination, suggesting complementary effects • Inertial forces in terms of sticking with an established configuration • Firms applied the same configuration independent of task uncertainty
Cardinal et al. (2004, 2010, 2018)	Archetypes: • Market configuration • Clan configuration • Bureaucratic • Integrative	• Target (input, behavior, outcome) • Formality (formal, informal) • Direction (hierarchical, peer, self)	• Start-up development phase • Company growth • Financial distress	• Qualitative, single case of a start-up short-haul moving company • Longitudinal study	• Market control configuration is not only associated with outcome control but also requires support from other controls (e.g., input control) • Formal outcome control is part of all configurations; that is, clan control configurations are not purely informal controls • Controls "reinforced each other by sending clear signals as to what was expected in the company" (Cardinal

Reference	Archetypes	Control mechanisms	Contingencies	Method	Findings
Kownatzki et al. (2013)	Archetypes: • Goal setting • Extrinsic incentives • Negative incentives • Decision process control • Conflict resolution • Strategy imposition	• Target (behavior, outcome) • Control over the content of decision-making	• n/a	• Multi-method study of five corporations across industries	• Identification of corporate control types' influence on SBU-level decision-making speed
Gregory et al. (2013)	Archetypes: • Authoritative control (procedural, tight, unilateral) • Coordinated control (hybrid, tight, bilateral) • Trust-based control (social, relaxed, bilateral)	• Control types • Procedural type (to improve efficiency and effectiveness) • Social type (to develop shared understanding) • Hybrid type • Control degree, including amount of control (frequency of control use and number of controls used simultaneously) and intensity of control • Control style (uni-/bilateral)	• Gaps in shared understanding • (Un)fulfilled expectations	• Longitudinal, single-case study • ISD offshoring project	• Control balancing is conceptualized as "making targeted adjustments to the control configuration periodically along three different dimensions: control types, control degree, and control style" (p. 1225)
Bedford and Malmi (2015)	Archetypes: • Simple • Results • Action • Devolved • Hybrid	Twenty-two control mechanisms: • Strategic planning (mode, participation) • Measurement (diagnostic, interactive, tightness, cost control, measure diversity) • Compensation (performance pay, subjective/objective, short/long term) • Structure (decentralization, hierarchy, communication, integrative liaison devices) • Policies and procedures (autonomy, boundary systems, standardization, pre-action reviews) • Socio-ideological (selection, socialization, belief systems, social control)	• Technology (outcome measurability, task programmability) • Environment (unpredictability, turbulence, complexity, hostility) • Strategy (low cost, innovation, customer focus)	• Cross-sectional sample of 400 medium to large firms • Cluster analysis	• Suggestive evidence of the equifinality of control configurations • Action configuration is a flexible variant of traditional bureaucracy • In hybrid configurations, multiple and seemingly conflicting control types intermesh

Table 6.1 (*cont.*)

Source(s)	Control configurations	Underlying control dimensions and elements	Contingency logic	Research design	Implications

Bedford et al. (2016)	Archetypes:
	• Two effective configurations for defenders
	  • Machine bureaucracy
	  • Wider array of performance dimensions; greater degree of autonomy and informal communication
	• Three effective configurations for prospectors
	  • Exploratory
	  • Devolved
	  • Adhocracy
		• Target (input, behavior, outcome)
		• Formality (formal)
		• Interactive
		• Control tightness
		• Measure diversity
		• Structure
			• Strategic context: Defender versus prospector (Miles & Snow 1978)	• Quantitative survey design (400 responses by top managers; cross-sectional)
				• fsQCA
					• Firms combine controls in multiple and equally effective ways
					• Not all control practices found to be relevant in isolation (e.g., performance-based pay) are relevant when examined simultaneously
					• "the effectiveness of accounting control and structural control choices are determined not only by their fit with strategic context but also by how they fit with each other." (p. 12)
					• Defender firms build on configurations with diagnostic control
					• Prospector firms build on configurations with interactive control as core practices, and formal input control as peripheral practices

Schafheitle et al. (2020)	Archetypes of datafication technology control configuration: • ORION at UPS • Starmind at Company Alpha	• Target (input, behavior, outcome) • Formality (formal, informal) • Control timing (before or after the contract) • Control scope (e.g., on premise, off premise) • Data sources (structured or unstructured) • Openness for worker participation • Possibility for opt out • Transparency • Granularity to which inference is possible • Analytical capacity • Reference group	• Conceptual	• Exploratory study, two exemplary use cases (UPS and Company Alpha) • Morphological analysis	• The datafication technology control configuration is a framework that comprises eleven technology control dimensions and thirty-six technology control elements

| Beese et al. (2023) | Archetypes:
• Three, unlabeled control configurations in different contexts, for example, in times of scarcity/crisis (formal control focus) or for innovation (focus on various informal control mechanisms) | • Target (input, behavior, outcome)
• Formality (formal, informal)
• Direction (hierarchical, self) | • Environmental jolts and changes (e.g., takeover of a major competitor, financial crisis)
• Organizational culture | • Longitudinal singe case study of Commerzbank's transformation | • Configuration "must match the situation, strategy, and top-level priorities" (p. 101)
• Configuration "must be balanced in the long term" (p. 101)
• Three control configurations comprised "very different control mechanisms at different points in time" (p. 100) |

Linking. The *linking stage* involves explicating the inherent logic or orchestrating theme that explains how and why multiple organizational controls plausibly combine or cohere with each other to explain control outcomes (cf., Furnari et al. 2021). Orchestrating themes can be considered integrating mechanisms that explain why certain control combinations co-occur in the same configuration to explain control outcomes, and that organize the factors of a configuration, thereby limiting the number of plausible configurations (cf., Furnari et al. 2021). While the scoping stage describes the individual factors of – or the factorial logic behind – control configurations, the linking stage describes how the different factors relate to each other to produce control outcomes – or the combinatorial logic behind the configurations' effects on control outcomes (cf., Park et al. 2020). Miller (1987, 1996) has highlighted these orchestrating themes as the theoretically most interesting element of configurational approaches – they best reflect important research paradigms, entail the most predictive and normative implications, and endow configurations with their stability.

The linking stage also allows us to explicitly acknowledge the causal complexity inherent in the organizational control phenomenon. Causal complexity comes in three forms. First, *conjunction* focuses on how and why multiple explanatory factors combine in complex, and sometimes even contradictory, ways to affect an outcome. Conjunction implies that factors serve either as *complements* of each other – that is, they mutually enhance each other's contributions to an outcome – or as *contingencies* – that is, the effects of one factor are a function of another factor's presence or absence (Furnari et al. 2021). Conjunctive mechanisms imply that doing more of one thing increases the benefits of doing another, that is, they involve thinking in "AND" terms. In the context of organizational control, for instance, there is evidence for holistic combinations of formal/informal and input/behavior/outcome control making up for deficiencies in singular controls, and thus acting in a complementary manner to improve control outcomes (e.g., Cardinal et al. 2004, 2010; Kreutzer et al. 2016; Sihag & Rijsdijk 2019). Similarly, enabling control approaches' emphasis on enhancing information exchanges between managers and workers, to ensure workers' comprehension of the rationale for the control system, and also of how their individual tasks fit into the broader organization, should amplify the effectiveness of peer control, clan control, and self-control (Adler & Borys 1996; Ahrens & Chapman 2004; Wiener et al. 2016). Moreover, we would expect controls' effects on the four outcome dimensions to be dependent on numerous contingencies or boundary conditions, such as the individual characteristics of the manager and the worker, the task, the organization, and the external environment (see Section 4.4 for a review). For our configurational theorizing, we will, however, focus on four distinct organizational contexts we discussed in Section 5.3 as key contingencies: remote work arrangements, alternative work arrangements, algorithmic control, and platform-mediated gig work.

Second, *disjunction* or *equifinality* allows for different configurations to reach the same outcome by a variety of different paths. In contrast to the all-else-equal framing of correlational theorizing, which relegates alternative explanatory factors to control variables and presumes that their effects need to be parceled out, equifinality in configurational theorizing considers how and why these factors may provide alternative causal pathways to the same outcome (Furnari et al. 2021). Disjunctive mechanisms imply that doing more of one thing decreases the benefits of the other, that is, they involve thinking in "OR" terms. Equifinality is also closely related to the idea of *substitution*, or the notion that one or more factors may be alternatives to bringing about an outcome (i.e., they are functionally equivalent). In the context of organizational control, for instance, the heavy-handed and authoritative nature of coercive control approaches clearly enhances the monitoring function of control. At the same time, however, coercive control has the potential to undermine the coordination function. This is especially problematic for peer control and self-control, which require workers to have access to task and performance information, as well as an understanding of the rationale behind control, to be effective (Adler & Borys 1996; Ahrens & Chapman 2004; Wiener et al. 2016). Similarly, behavior control's focus on workers' compliance with pre-established rules and procedures can improve process outcomes (e.g., smooth workflow). At the same time, however, it tends to undermine adaptability outcomes (e.g., creativity and innovation), as it is likely to suppress even creative deviations from standardized processes (e.g., Zhou & George 2003), and it tends to undermine human relations outcomes (e.g., job satisfaction), as it weakens workers' sense of autonomy (e.g., Enzle & Anderson 1993).

Third, configurational approaches challenge the assumption of symmetry inherent in correlational theorizing, which assumes that factors leading to the absence of a phenomenon are the inverse of those factors that lead to its presence. Configurational theorizing, in contrast, assumes *asymmetric causality*, or the idea that the presence (or absence) of one factor requires the absence of another factor to have an effect on the outcome, which involves thinking about incongruencies, tensions, and juxtapositions among factors (Furnari et al. 2021) – in other words, thinking in "NOT" terms. In the context of control, for instance, the shared identities, loyalties, and norms fostered by clan control can eliminate the need for bureaucratic control (Miller 1996). Table 6.2 provides an overview of different causal mechanisms inherent in configurational theorizing.

Naming. While the scoping and linking stages involved specifying key factors and explaining how and why they interact, the *naming stage* involves communicating the meaning of the configurations that explain a phenomenon. Furnari et al. (2021) propose three naming heuristics that help obtain plausible and distinctive configuration labels: (1) *articulate with simplicity*; at the same time, (2) *capture the whole*, or craft an overarching narrative that captures the different configurations, or the logical structure of the configurational theory as a whole; and (3) *evoke the essence*, which draws attention to the distinguishing feature(s) of each configuration.

Visualizing. In line with Furnari et al.'s (2021) recommendations, we further developed visualizations of the control configurations we discovered. Our visualizations resemble activity systems (cf., Porter 1996; Siggelkow 2001) and display maps of interrelated organizational control elements, with higher-order themes emerging from clusters of tightly linked control elements. Linked control elements reinforce each other if the value of each element is increased by the presence of the other element, suggesting that the two elements are complementary (cf., Siggelkow 2011). In addition, we provide a table of illustrative quotes for each control element. We also provide a heat map, classifying each element according to our control dimensions, to offer a simplified visual overview of each control configuration.

In sum, following a configurational approach in our reconceptualization of organizational control allows us to theorize how multiple controls combine in complementary – and sometimes contradictory – ways to jointly affect outcomes (which acknowledges conjunction between explanatory factors), often with multiple alternative paths to the same outcome (which incorporates disjunction or equifinality). Chapters 3 to 5 provide the factorial logic of our configurations by scoping key dimensions that explain the phenomenon of organizational control (see Figure 1.1 for an overview). As we outline later, the control configurations we discuss are orchestrated by the technological and organizational trends we identified – as well as the implications these trends have for key assumptions underlying organizational control – which serve as the central themes and integrative mechanisms. In Chapter 6, we review four fundamental shifts in our contemporary organizational environment that render our existing conceptualizations of control out of date. Table 6.3 provides an overview of four fundamental shifts and their implications for organizational control configurations, including our case studies associated with each configuration. We then present our reconceptualization of organizational control with several case study narratives that help us "reveal facts and processes running counter to current theory, undiscovered modes of functioning, significant organizational distinctions, and important new types of enterprise" (Miller 2018: 461).

Table 6.2 *Overview of causal mechanisms in configurational theorizing*

	Causal mechanism		Explanation	Sources
Conjunction	Complementary/ contingency ("AND")	Enabling	One factor providing the conditions for another	Bedford (2020), Huber et al. (2013)
		Compensating	One factor counteracting the weaknesses or limitations of another	
		Reinforcing	One factor increasing the effectiveness of another by enhancing one or more of its attributes	Bedford (2020)
Disjunction/ equifinality	Substitution ("OR")	Inhibiting	One factor hindering or attenuating the effectiveness of another	Bedford (2020)
		Exacerbating	One factor accentuating the detrimental effects of another	
		Instigating	Opposite of enabling effect; creates the conditions that trigger another factor to affect an outcome negatively	
		Replacing	Since two factors do the same thing, there is no need for the one if the other is in place	Huber et al. (2013)
		Dampening	One factor dampens the occurrence and/or effect of the other	
Asymmetry	Absence ("NOT")	Conflicting	Why and how the presence or absence of a factor requires the absence of another factor	Furnari et al. (2021)
Supplementary		Redundant	Factors have beneficial effects for one control problem, but detrimental consequences for another	Bedford (2020)
		Interchangeable	Whether or not a factor is present has no significant effect on outcomes	
			One factor can be replaced or exchanged with one or more others to achieve the same outcome	

6.2   From Face-to-Face to Remote Work

As outlined in Section 5.3.2, digitization and electronic surveillance of work provide workers with increased flexibility in terms of where and when to work. Recent socio-cultural trends, such as workers' desires for more autonomy, as well as the COVID-19 pandemic-induced lockdowns, have further fueled a sustained rise of remote and virtual work arrangements, which are expected to extend to about 20 percent of all workdays in the United States even after the

Table 6.3 *Control configurations*

	Challenged assumptions	Case study exemplars	Configuration label	Key sources
6.2 From face-to-face to remote work	• Information asymmetry • Shared identities, loyalties, norms	• US trucking companies • GitLab	• "Remote hierarchy" • "Work from anywhere"	• Levy (2015) • Sijbrandij (2023), Choudhury et al. (2020), Choudhury and Salomon (2023a, 2023b)
6.3 From stable, full-time to alternative work arrangements	• Stable, hierarchical, dyadic relationships • Shared identities, loyalties, norms	• n/a	• n/a	• n/a
6.4 From human managers to algorithmic control	• Bounded rationality • Information asymmetry	• Amazon warehouses	• "Algorithmic bureaucracy"	• Asher Hamilton and Cain (2019), Bensinger (2019), Dzieza (2020), Evans (2019), Gutelius and Theodore (2019), Kantor and Streitfeld (2015), Lecher (2019), Vallas et al. (2022)
6.5 From traditional work to platform-mediated gig work	• Bounded rationality • Information asymmetry • Stable, hierarchical, dyadic relationships • Shared identities, loyalties, norms	• Uber • Upwork	• "Remote gig work" • "Work for hire"	• Calo and Rosenblat (2017), Möhlmann et al. (2021), Rosenblat (2016), Rosenblat and Stark (2016), Scheiber (2017), Uzunca and Kas (2023) • Groysberg et al. (2011), Kinder et al. (2019), Minor and Yoffie (2018), Waldkirch et al. (2021), Zhu et al. (2017)

pandemic (Barrero et al. 2021). However, these work arrangements constitute a challenge for traditional control approaches, as they create new information asymmetries for managers and peers and undermine shared identities, loyalties, and norms.

6.2.1   New Information Asymmetries for Managers and Peers

Traditional control approaches rely on observing what people do (i.e., visibility) and on shaping their formal and informal participation in relationships with others (i.e., presence) at designated workplaces (Felstead et al. 2003). Remote and virtual work arrangements, in contrast, entail a spatial and temporal separation of managers and workers, along with a spatial and temporal separation of peers (Sewell & Taskin 2015). This separation is often accompanied by enhanced electronic surveillance and control, which remote workers, perhaps surprisingly, seem to generally accept as a legitimate part of the bargain (Felstead et al. 2003; Valsecchi 2006). Despite recent advances in digital surveillance, without face-to-face interactions and opportunities for observation and monitoring, information asymmetry is exacerbated for both managers and peers, with a higher risk of workers neglecting organizational interests, shirking, or even cheating (Allen et al. 2015; Bloom et al. 2015; Felstead et al. 2003). Moreover, remote work provides fewer opportunities to give and receive feedback (Eseryel et al. 2021). Information exchanges typically have a time lag, misunderstandings are more likely, and messages are less coherent, which increases conflict and undermines coordination (Hinds & Bailey 2003; O'Leary & Mortensen 2010; Pianese et al. 2023). As a result, control in remote environments tends to be not only more formal – such as formalizing job descriptions and requirements, performance standards, and communication – but also less informal, as the physical distance between managers and workers deprives managers of opportunities for informal, spontaneous interactions to convey information (Kurland & Egan 1999; Pianese et al. 2023).

Remote work compromises especially the effectiveness of peer control. This is because, with limited peer interactions, both the monitoring and cost advantages of peer control compared to those of hierarchical control evaporate (Mas & Moretti 2009). Moreover, when workers are no longer co-located, they have much fewer opportunities to influence each other's behavior by providing feedback or by coordinating with one another (Brocklehurst 2001; Loughry 2010), or they may not feel comfortable criticizing each other's ideas in virtual settings. As a result, remote work undermines both monitoring and coordination functions of control (Bijlsma-Frankema & Costa 2005).

To make matters worse, most managerial efforts to compensate for the loss of visibility and presence of remote workers – by enhanced digital surveillance, electronic diary requirements, manager visits, or other means – turn out to be futile (Brocklehurst 2001; Felstead et al. 2003). Moreover, recent evidence has shown that managers' tendencies to overcompensate for the forced switch to remote work during the COVID-19 pandemic have led to a dramatic increase in overtime and endless cycles of mostly unnecessary Zoom meetings, which not only decrease workers' motivation but also have questionable value in terms of organizational control (Economist 2021).

In line with classic control theory (e.g., Eisenhardt 1985; Ouchi 1977), a widely recommended approach for the management of remote workers is to monitor outcomes rather than behavior, suggesting that outcome control could be a suitable substitute for behavior control in remote work settings (Allen et al. 2015; Felstead et al. 2003; Groen et al. 2018; Illegems & Verbeke 2004; Kurland & Egan 1999; Sewell & Taskin 2015). Such outcome control entails "managers setting a series of short- to medium-term targets, the completion of which represents a rolling picture of employee productivity" (Felstead et al. 2003: 248), up to a formal charter for the remote work, including joint goals and milestones (Harvard Business Review Press 2016). For managers, relying on concrete information about remote workers' performance could offset concerns stemming from a lack of observation (Allen et al. 2015). A predominant outcome orientation could also enhance remote workers' motivation by providing them with higher perceived autonomy to do their work at their own discretion and wherever they are (Evans et al. 2007). As a side effect of their motivational benefits, managers could be tempted to use desirable remote work arrangements as input or identity controls (cf., Alvesson & Kärreman 2007; Alvesson & Willmott 2002; Anteby 2008), which means assigning remote work arrangements as a reward to select individuals. The key constraint to such an approach is, of course, the availability of measurable and reliable outcome information, suggesting that workers' eligibility for remote work arrangements may be partly determined by whether a worker's output can be measured (Sewell & Taskin 2015). In contrast to this argument, however, Groen et al. (2018) have found that workers who are allowed to work remotely report less emphasis on outcome controls compared to those workers who are not allowed to telework. Moreover, agency theory would suggest that outcome control is more costly than behavior control. This is because, in keeping with the agency theory, workers must be compensated for taking on the additional risk of being responsible for outcomes that may only be partially under their control (Eisenhardt 1985). As a result, this could force managers to pay a premium for those remote workers (Brice et al. 2011).

An alternative approach to hierarchical control could be to empower remote workers and delegate managerial control functions to them (Hertel et al. 2005). Such self-control could be effective for remote work because of its ability to handle the higher level of autonomy when workers' activities are less observable by others. Self-control could also improve remote workers' motivation, as it allows them to relax from time to time after periods of intense work in order to recharge and perform more effectively over time (Raghuram et al. 2019).

A more insidious type of control that arises in remote work arrangements stems from workers' anxiety about being overlooked, forgotten, or left out (Kurland & Cooper 2002; Kurland & Egan 1999; Sewell & Taskin 2015) – or what Hafermalz (2021) has termed the "threat of exile."[1] According to these studies, workers' primary concern about remote arrangements is about isolation, both professionally – that is, the fear of being out of sight and out of mind, meaning not being considered for promotions and other transitional rewards – and socially – that is, missing out on informal interactions that occur in the presence of colleagues (Kurland & Egan 1999). This anxiety is especially prevalent in environments that are organized, at the same time, around remote work, where workers are no longer physically co-located, and around teams that workers perceive as "family," and that are central to their sense of identity and belonging (Hafermalz 2021). This anxiety about isolation leads remote workers to feel more pressure than their office-based counterparts to meet performance expectations,[2] and it also compels them to make their accomplishments more publicly visible (Richardson & McKenna 2014). By going above and beyond in their efforts, and striving for constant visibility and recognition, remote workers become complicit in their own surveillance and control (Hafermalz 2021; Pianese et al. 2023). This emphasis on "managing the optics" also extends beyond hierarchical relationships and into remote workers' relations with their peers. To reduce their sense of isolation and reinsert themselves into their teams and organizations, remote workers engage in intensive efforts to signal their availability (Hafermalz 2021; Sewell & Taskin 2015). This shift leads to the paradoxical situation that workers "who felt they had license to roam around the traditional workplace (so long as they were available at a moment's notice) now felt shackled to their workstations when at home" (Sewell & Taskin 2015: 1519), with negative consequences for both perceived stress levels and boundaries between work and family life.

---

[1] It is ironic, however, that a quiet work environment and freedom from intrusion are two frequently mentioned reasons why workers volunteer for remote work opportunities (Sewell & Taskin 2015).

[2] This anxiety is not entirely unreasonable, however, as one study found that around 25 percent of managers with experience in supervising remote workers reported that they use written performance standards and performance feedback differently for remote workers compared to non-remote workers (Lautsch et al. 2009).

In sum, prior research has emphasized a tension inherent in remote work arrangements: Working away from traditional workplaces can give workers a greater sense of autonomy, while placing new constraints on the way they conduct themselves:

Early on, telework was presented as a way of transforming traditional ways of working, mainly through its capacity to decouple work activity from the physical constraints imposed by offices and factories where employees are physically present in the workplace and where the co-location of managers and peers exerts a disciplinary force on workers' conduct (Sewell 2012). Optimistic predictions were made that such disciplinary forces would fade as co-location no longer became necessary under conditions of telework, thus leading to a loosening of the reins of both managerial and peer control and a commensurate increase in the opportunities for employees to exercise autonomy. Detailed studies of telework (e.g., Brocklehurst 2001) quickly disabused us of such a simplistic view by showing the very ICTs [information and communication technologies] that enabled teleworking also incorporated features that allowed managers to control employees through previously unseen forms of remote surveillance. (Sewell & Taskin 2015: 1508)

Shifting information asymmetries also create uncertainty for, and new demands on, managers, who need to implement and adapt organizational policies regarding flexible work forms. These demands are even more complex for blended teams that comprise both remote and office-based members, which creates additional challenges for coordination, equity, motivation, and integration (Lautsch & Kossek 2011). While additional information asymmetries may tempt managers to monitor remote workers differently, define their tasks more rigidly, and be more directive, research has found that a more equitable approach to monitoring both types of work arrangements is more productive (Lautsch & Kossek 2011). Nevertheless, some control approaches that benefit office-based workers may harm remote workers or vice versa, challenging managers to work collaboratively and creatively with both groups to develop adaptive solutions to resolve these tensions (Lautsch et al. 2009).

6.2.2   Challenges to Shared Identities, Loyalties, and Norms

While the visibility challenge can be at least mitigated by modern digital surveillance, another control challenge in remote work settings arises from workers' lower identification with, and loyalty to, their organization (Foss 2021). In modern societies, work and occupations have become central components of people's identities, in terms of both how individuals see themselves in relation to others and how others see the individuals (Stryker & Burke 2000). Workers identify with their teams, managers, and organizations in the sense of experiencing varying degrees of affinity or oneness with them (Lehdonvirta

2016). These identities have important individual and social consequences, such as enhanced self-esteem, prosocial behavior, and solidarity with team members (Van Knippenberg & Van Schie 2000).

In Brocklehurst's (2001) study of professionals shifting from a traditional workplace to remote work arrangements, once workers started working from home, their feeling of belonging to a team dissipated. This loss of shared identities and norms in remote work can have several causes. As noted in Section 5.2.1, newly formed virtual teams tend to be geographically dispersed. As a consequence, individuals are socialized in different cultural settings, resulting in a variety of attitudes, preferences, and values (Gibson et al. 2014; Malhotra et al. 2007). Moreover, the loss of shared experience at work can induce work practices outside organizational norms that often remain unnoticed (Felstead et al. 2003) and the creation of distinct subgroups based on cultural similarities, time zones, or language (O'Leary & Mortensen 2010).

Remote work arrangements can also result in fractures between workplace-based and home-located workers, jeopardizing coordination. Envy of the spatial and temporal discretion afforded to remote workers, and the resulting resentment among on-site workers, can lead to tensions that disrupt team integration and the reproduction of corporate cultures, and further reduce remote workers' sense of loyalty to the organization (Felstead et al. 2003). As a result, in many remote environments, the "sense of belonging, common purpose, and shared identity that inspires all of us to do our best work gets lost" (Alexander et al. 2020: 2).

This lack of shared identities, loyalties, and norms creates complications for organizational control. Most importantly, informal and clan control – which classic control theory suggests as an alternative to behavior and outcome control (Ouchi 1979) – are challenging in remote work settings, as they rely on a high level of shared norms among workers (Kirsch et al. 2010; Kurland & Cooper 2002), which are either absent or more limited in remote work settings. Remote workplaces that tend to go hand-in-hand with less committed workers (Felstead et al. 2003) will also decrease peer control's motivational potential, as detached workers in teams that lack cohesion are less likely to respond to peer pressure (Brahm & Kunze 2012).

With informal control, clan control, and peer control being more challenging, a deliberate selection and socialization of workers who have sufficient fit with both organizational values and remote work arrangements become crucial for incentive alignment (Hoogeveen 2004; Kurland & Cooper 2002), and many organizations have made efforts to revise their virtual onboarding of new workers by investing in IT infrastructure, practices, systems, and values during the COVID-19 pandemic (Pfeffer 2023). In addition to bringing in new people and introducing them to the organization's norms and values through initial socialization, virtual teams could also seek to create ongoing virtual bonding moments that ensure that a sense of belonging is maintained even during continued virtual collaboration. With properly designed input control, organizations can also benefit from more heterogeneous teams in terms of cultural diversity, which have proved to be even more beneficial in virtual than in face-to-face teams (Staples & Zhao 2006).

The efficacy of self-control in remote work environments is less straightforward. On the one hand, given remote work's greater potential for loose cannons and damage that might not be detected until it is too late (Hoch & Kozlowski 2014), the increased discretion that self-control provides could be counterproductive for remote workers who, because of fewer shared norms, do not know exactly what is expected of them. On the other hand, studies examining remote work arrangements have also found a shift from workers' identities being tethered to their teams and organizations, to their identities being dependent on their own self-image. As discussed earlier, remote workers may no longer be controlled by others – whether by their managers or by their peers. Instead, what becomes important is "how one appears to *oneself*" (Brocklehurst 2001: 461, emphasis in original). As a consequence, many (newly minted) remote workers focus on (re-)inventing their identities by (re-)creating, at least to some degree, a traditional workplace. Brocklehurst (2001), for instance, described the case of a remote worker who had recreated a replica of his previous office, and even added photographs of his colleagues to give meaning to his work. Others imposed similar work times to further mimic the time, space, and physical artifacts of traditional office work, buttress their sense of belonging to the organization, and construct an image of themselves as reputable workers (Pianese et al. 2023). From an organizational control perspective, this increased focus on constructing their individual identities amounts to self-control. This tendency of remote workers to engage in self-control also explains why the prevailing managerial fear of losing control over remote workers – which may explain managers' resistance to such arrangements – appears largely unfounded (Kurland & Cooper 2002).

Last, some research has pointed to the potential for misaligned norms and incentives at different organizational levels in the context of remote work (Bélanger et al. 2013). For instance, workers may be rewarded for individual performance, but their managers may expect them to be available as a team player, which may also be an important factor in promotion. Or an individual worker may want to work remotely to increase her productivity by reducing interruptions, but at the same time, she experiences team-level incentives to collaborate, creating a wedge between her and her co-workers. Such misalignment of identities, loyalties, and norms further complicates the organizational control of remote work.

6.2.3   Case Study: US Trucking Companies

Our first case study is based on Karen Levy's (2015) fieldwork in the US trucking industry. Truckers are an example of a "spatially dispersed group of workers with a traditionally independent culture and a high degree of autonomy" (Levy 2015: 160), and therefore representative of remote workers. The International Labor Organization classifies long-haul truck drivers (ISCO 08 Code 8332) as requiring a skill level of two out of four, putting them in the middle tier regarding job skills.[3] While truck drivers can also be independent owner-operators driving their own truck, which would fall under alternative work (Section 6.3), the control configuration discussed here pertains to four US trucking companies – both top 10 companies and small operations – and their drivers who work as full-time remote workers.

Figure 6.1 presents these companies' organizational control configurations as an activity system of interrelated control elements. The core control elements (shown as rectangles) are arranged around higher-level core themes (shown as black ellipses). The control elements are further arranged according to the target of control (input, behavior, outcome), the direction of control (hierarchical, peer, self, third-party), and the formality of control (formal, informal). The color shading of the controls indicates the style of the control. Enabling control styles are white rectangles, coercive control styles are dark gray rectangles, and a combination of coercive and enabling control styles are gray-shaded rectangles. Finally, the letter "a" on the left side of the rectangle suggests algorithm-supported control (with humans in the loop), and the letter "A" indicates algorithmic control (with humans out of the loop). A solid line connecting core themes and/ or control elements represents a reinforcing link (i.e., conjunction or complementarity) between themes and/or elements, whereas a broken line represents a trade-off (i.e., disjunction or substitution) between themes and/or elements. Table 6.4 presents a heat map of the control configuration and Table 6.5 provides illustrative quotes for each element in the control configuration.

Discussion. In the traditional US trucking industry, the "lone wolf" nature of the job – which has historically allowed truckers to make their own day-to-day decisions about how to accomplish their work tasks and to work hard without having a boss peering over their shoulder – has attracted a notoriously independent group of workers who are resistant to any type of social control. In fact, some interviewed truckers mentioned that they came to trucking after having conflicts with authority figures in more traditional employment settings and that, as one informant put it, "[t]ruckers ain't organization people!" (Levy 2015: 162). Truckers' derisive attitude toward bureaucratic rules and authority figures, combined with the spatially dispersed and uncertain nature

---

[3] https://ilostat.ilo.org/resources/concepts-and-definitions/classification-occupation/

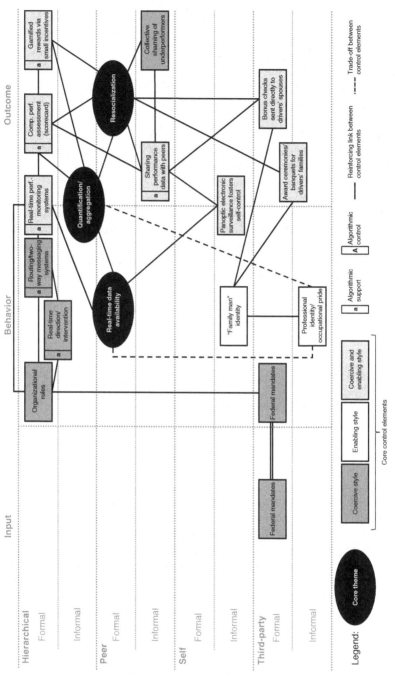

Figure 6.1 US trucking companies' control configuration

Table 6.4 *US trucking companies' control configuration heat map*

Control dimension	Target			Formality		Direction				Style		Controller	
Control element	I	B	O	F	I	H	P	S	T	C	E	H	A
Federal mandates	X	X		X					X	X		X	
Organizational rules		X		X						X		X	
Routing/two-way messaging systems		X		X		X				X		X	X
Real-time direction/intervention		X		X	x	X				X		X	X
Real-time performance-monitoring systems		X	x	X		X					X	X	X
"Family man" identity		X			X			X			X	X	
Panoptic electronic surveillance fosters self-control		X	x		X			X			X	X	
Professional identity/occupational pride			X		X				X		X	X	
Comparative performance assessment (scorecard)			X	X		X				X	X	X	X
Gamified rewards via small incentives			X	X		X	P			X	X	X	X
Sharing performance data with peers			X		X		X			X		X	X
Collective shaming of underperformers			X		X		X			X		X	
Bonus checks sent directly to drivers' spouses			X	X	X				X	X	X	X	
Award ceremonies/banquets for drivers' families			X	X	X				X	X	X	X	

Legend: Columns from left to right: target (I = input, B = behavior, O = outcome); formality (F = formal, I = informal); direction (H = hierarchical, P = peer, S = self, T = third-party); style (C = coercive, E = enabling); controller (H = human, A = algorithm); X = heavy focus on this control dimension; x = partial focus on this control dimension; empty cell = no focus on this control dimension.

Table 6.5 *Illustrative quotes for elements in the US trucking companies' control configuration*

Control element	Exemplary quote(s)
Input control	
Federal mandates	• "dozens of details of the trucker's workday regulated by the federal government – from strict licensure requirements, to required medical screenings, to the thorough vehicle inspection a driver must perform each day." (Levy 2015: 162–163)
Behavior control	
Federal mandates	• "truckers' daily work takes place largely on federal highways; it is on the system of public roads – with their speed limits and traffic controls, insurance and licensure requirements, and laws about seatbelt and cell phone use – that most of us feel the presence of behavioral rules most directly. Add to this the additional highway rules that apply specifically to truckers (designated 'no-truck' routes, weight and height clearance limitations, fuel tax regimes) and the dozens of details of the trucker's workday regulated by the federal government." (Levy 2015: 162)
Organizational rules	• "truckers encounter more day-to-day involvement with behavioral regulation than the average person. Some of these entanglements are based on firms' organizational rules and employment and/or leasing arrangements." (Levy 2015: 162)
Routing/two-way messaging systems	• "In addition to monitoring and transmitting this performance data, fleet management systems typically contain additional modules that provide services like routing and two-way messaging." (Levy 2015: 164)
Real-time direction/ intervention	• "Some systems' dispatcher portals turn a driver's data cell red when he is within a few minutes of a violation, visually flagging the driver so that a dispatcher can respond immediately by communicating with and directing him as to his next course of action. Drivers accordingly have less decision-making autonomy to determine how to handle the situation if a violation is about to occur." (Levy 2015: 169)
	• "The temporal shift [in information flows, as information is distributed in real time] also enables putative harassment of drivers by employers. Even when drivers are off-duty, employers can see where they are, and can contact them using systems' communication functions – which sometimes lack a 'mute' function for drivers to silence employer attempts at communication, even during sleep breaks." (Levy 2015: 169)
Real-time performance-monitoring systems	• "fleet management systems are capable of monitoring many types of bundled performance data in addition to timekeeping. The range of information captured commonly includes a driver's fuel efficiency and idling time, speed, geolocation and geofencing (notifying a dispatcher if a truck has departed from a predetermined route or arrived at a terminal), lane departures and braking/acceleration patterns, cargo status (e.g., the temperature of a refrigerated trailer), and vehicle maintenance/diagnostic information." (Levy 2015: 164)
	• "The provision of additional contextual information via the electronic system equips the company dispatcher to manage his or her workforce and evaluate employee performance with less dependence on a driver's claims about conditions that the dispatcher cannot directly observe." (Levy 2015: 169)

- "Fleet management systems restructure organizational information flows by reconstituting truckers' embodied work as a set of divisible, rationalized data points, presented in an apparently neutral format. These data are divorced from the context of road conditions, the contingencies of weather and shippers' schedules, and other individuated circumstances." (Levy 2015: 169)

- "When monitoring systems are used, truckers are no longer the sole holders of relevant information, as monitoring systems distribute it to remote dispatchers. […] when fleet management systems are used to transmit information from trucks to dispatchers at an employer's home office, employers have much more information at their disposal – both aggregated data about drivers' performance, as described, and additional information that imputes to the dispatcher knowledge about the driver's internal and local conditions." (Levy 2015: 167)

- "the systems enable a temporal shift in information flows, as information is distributed in real time. […] Information about where a driver is, whether he is moving and how quickly, and how long he has been on the road or on a break is constantly updated. Using a 'breadcrumb' map view, dispatchers can watch all of a fleet's truck drivers move across the country in real time, and can see all drivers' to-the-minute drive time data in an orderly spreadsheet as it happens. The real-time nature of this information distribution means dispatchers can see violations as they happen, and can even anticipate violations before they occur." (Levy 2015: 168–169)

"Family man" identity

Panoptic electronic surveillance fosters self-control

- "Some of my trucker informants are self-described 'family men,' with strongly professed Christian values and traditional notions of gender roles, who proudly show me pictures of children and grandchildren they are helping to provide for through their labor." (Levy 2015: 162)

- "it is also likely that the fact that the data are being collected – the reality of which drivers are very much aware – prevents drivers from making claims that the data would not support: it is difficult for a driver to say he is out of driving hours in order to avoid an undesirable load assignment, because he knows that those data are readily accessible by dispatchers and trip planners." (Levy 2015: 168)

Professional identity/occupational pride

- "Drivers frequently share information among themselves on CB radios, on online forums, in informal conversations at truck stops, and in other venues. These exchanges build community and social solidarity among drivers, support their occupational identities, and encourage the formation of professional pride." (Levy 2015: 170)

- "Traditionally, truckers' value and a good deal of their occupational pride arises directly from their knowledge, often gleaned from years of experience, of the daily 'ins and outs' of driving a truck […]. For many drivers, then, professionalism and occupational pride are deeply entwined with knowledge of biophysical and local conditions, which have long been of primary value in the effective completion of their work tasks." (Levy 2015: 165–166)

Outcome control

Comparative performance assessment (scorecard)

- "the value of [drivers'] knowledge is displaced by fleet management systems that provide services such as automatic routing and geolocation, remote diagnostics, geofencing, hours-of-service monitoring, and tracking of other fine-grained indicators like fuel use and hard braking incidents. These modules accumulate and summarize information in order to create detailed performance metrics for drivers. Comparisons can be easily made for different periods of time, both within and across drivers, across groups of drivers (as defined by back-office managers on any basis: managers can compare customizable driver groups based on type of haul, driver experience level, or any other imaginable axis of variation), or between a company's fleets and industry averages. This aggregated information, summarized in quantifiable and easily comparable metrics, becomes a highly valued management tool." (Levy 2015: 166–167)

Table 6.5 (cont.)

Control element	Exemplary quote(s)
Gamified rewards via small incentives	• "Many firms go further by directly tying small financial incentives to the rankings produced by fleet management systems. These incentives often cost firms very little, but coupled with the pride (or embarrassment) of one's comparative ranking, were considered effective tools for aligning the goals of firms and employees." (Levy 2015: 170)
Sharing performance data with peers	• "organizations enact control by resocializing electronically derived information, strategically deploying it into employees' social lives – truckers' relationships with their coworkers [...] – in order to pressure employees into compliance with organizational aims." (Levy 2015: 160)
	• "fleet management systems enable information about truckers' activities to be shared without their direct agency or consent in order to create competition among workers. Many fleet managers post or distribute rankings based on drivers' 'scorecards,' which the systems make technically very easy to produce. Scorecards display driver safety records, hours of service, or other performance indicators that align with organizational goals; fuel efficiency is a very popular metric, given the high present price of fuel and its significant impact on trucking companies' financial bottom lines. The ability to easily aggregate, specify, parse, and compare these data across multiple drivers is one of the chief advantages of such systems, particularly for larger companies. By posting performance data where drivers can see them, companies create social pressure for comparatively underperforming drivers to improve and compete." (Levy 2015: 170)
Collective shaming of underperformers	• "This strategy, then, depends on drivers feeling interpersonally shamed by their coworkers ('the butt of the jokes') as a result of inefficient performance." (Levy 2015: 170)
Bonus checks sent directly to drivers' spouses	• "one firm sends small bonus checks for the highest performing drivers (as determined by driver scorecard data) to the drivers' wives, in the wives' names. The idea behind the program, as it was described to me, is that wives come to expect the checks periodically (as 'a profit-sharing arrangement,' in recognition of a wife's familial support of her trucker husband); wives are expected to create pressure for their husbands to continue meeting the company's organizational performance benchmarks. Recalling the strong 'family man' mentality many truckers exhibit, it is perhaps unsurprising that firms' control techniques capitalize on this normative orientation toward economic provision for one's family." (Levy 2015: 171)
Award ceremonies/ banquets for drivers' families	• "Firms' efforts to resocialize electronically derived data do not end within the company. Firms also invoke social pressures in drivers' own non-trucking communities as well, particularly among their families. Incentives like awards ceremonies and banquets, to which drivers' families are invited, are common strategies." (Levy 2015: 171)

of the job, with numerous exigencies and contingencies, such as weather, construction, and accidents, makes the traditional trucking industry a particularly challenging context for organizational control. Until recently, the job's inherent information asymmetry made it difficult, if not impossible, for managers to supervise truckers directly. Furthermore, the 13-day time lag before drivers were required to submit the government-mandated time logs offered ample opportunity for drivers to game or manipulate any attempts at oversight, which afforded truckers more autonomy than many of their blue-collar colleagues in more traditional work settings (Levy 2015).

Toward the end of the last century, following government mandates, the industry has gradually introduced electronic monitoring systems that can capture very granular, real-time data not only on drivers' behavior but also on context conditions, such as traffic and weather, that can be aggregated and analyzed by digital fleet management systems (Levy 2015). Access to such aggregated real-time information shifts information asymmetry from remote drivers back to managers and allows them to direct and intervene in real time. Dispatchers can watch truck drivers move across the country in real time and therefore see violations as they happen or even before they occur (Levy 2015).

It is further evident from Figure 6.1 that the three core themes of real-time data availability, quantification/aggregation, and resocialization, and many of their underlying control elements, complement each other. Specifically, in addition to monitoring drivers' behavior in real time, which stymies gaming and manipulation efforts, digitally aggregated driver scorecards also allow for effective outcome control, such as comparative performance evaluations and incentive pay. Resocializing aggregate driver data by publicly sharing scorecards and rankings among fellow drivers further creates a new form of peer control. Resocializing driver scorecards can even be used for pressure from third parties, such as drivers' families, especially when coupled with public recognition, awards, and incentives – as the not-so-subtle distribution of bonus checks to, and in the name of, drivers' spouses demonstrates (Levy 2015).

Despite these advantages for organizational control, the fundamental shift in information asymmetry caused by technological developments has also created a rift between trucking companies and their drivers, highlighting the existence of trade-offs and unintended consequences. In particular, much of the drivers' identities and professional pride rested on their exclusive and superior knowledge of the situation, combined with their autonomy to chart their own course, with each driver being the "captain of his ship" (Levy 2015: 167). Not surprisingly, many drivers consider comprehensive digital surveillance and dispatcher direction and interference a lack of trust and an unwarranted intrusion of their autonomy. As one of Levy's (2015: 170) interviewees put it: "You, as a professional, you know when your body is tired. You know when your mind is fatigued. You know when you need to stop and rest. That dispatcher doesn't know. And by God, that electronic device certainly does not know." The negative impact of increasingly coercive digital surveillance and control on drivers' identities and professional pride further increases the stress of a job already characterized by physical deprivation and loneliness and is likely to worsen the critical shortage of truck drivers in the United States (Goodman 2022).

In sum, advances in electronic surveillance offer trucking companies unprecedented opportunities to monitor and direct truckers in real time. At the same time, however, the coercive nature of contemporary fleet management systems has undermined truckers' identities, professional pride, and intrinsic motivation. This illustrates an inherent trade-off in trucking companies' control configurations between improving rational goal and process outcomes on the one hand, and having to accept a detrimental impact on human resource outcomes, such as job satisfaction and driver retention, on the other hand.

6.2.4   Case Study: GitLab

Our second case study complements and contrasts our discussion of the remote and relatively low-skilled work truckers perform with an analysis of a company employing a similarly remote but higher-skilled workforce. GitLab operates a digital platform for software development, security, and operations. It was formally established in 2014 to continue the development of an open-source, code-sharing platform initially created by Ukrainian developer Dmitriy Zaporozhets and Dutch developer and current CEO Sid Sijbrandij in 2011.[4] From the outset, GitLab encouraged remote work, or work from anywhere (WFA). Today, GitLab is recognized as one of the largest entirely remote companies in the world (Sijbrandij 2023). With an estimated 30 million registered users, including more than one million active licensed users, GitLab offers its platform on a freemium basis, with an open core that makes core tools available at no cost for individual contributors, and offering more advanced editions as a paid service.[5] As of 2023, the company employs over 2,000 people in sixty-five countries. In contrast to the blue-collar truckers who were the focus of our previous case study, most of GitLab's workers are software developers and programmers or information and communications technology (ICT) managers. According to the International Labor Organization classification, the associated ISCO Codes 2511 and 2512 require a skill level of four out of four, putting GitLab's workers in the highest tier with regards to job skills.[6] With a pre-IPO valuation of up to $6 billion (Wilhelm 2021),

---

[4] https://about.gitlab.com/company/
[5] https://about.gitlab.com/blog/2018/11/09/monetizing-and-being-open-source/
[6] https://ilostat.ilo.org/resources/concepts-and-definitions/classification-occupation/

GitLab Inc. was considered the first partially Ukrainian unicorn in 2018. It went public on October 14, 2021, and is listed on the Nasdaq Global Select Market (ticker symbol GTLB). Figure 6.2 illustrates GitLab's control configuration elements supporting four core themes, and Table 6.6 presents the associated heat map. Table 6.7 provides exemplary quotes for all control elements.

Discussion. It is important to understand that GitLab did not become a remote work organization during the COVID-19 lockdown. At first, it was a pragmatic decision. Since the founders were from different countries, no one wanted to move, and people felt more productive working from home. Three times in the company's history, it has tried to offer workers a more or less traditional office environment, but workers did not accept the offer to work in a corporate office, and the company saw no productivity gains from face-to-face collaboration.

The challenge for GitLab's control configuration is to keep its workers happy and satisfied while collaborating effectively in an all-remote setting across hierarchical ranks to succeed as an organization. GitLab's control configuration builds on the core themes of (1) full documentation of activities, (2) transparency in all standards and procedures, and (3) a high level of task modularity to deal with (4) WFA/asynchronous coordination. To attract, select, and retain qualified workers, in addition to a formal pre-employment background check, GitLab employs extensive socialization and onboarding, weekly check-in calls on Mondays, and an annual community event in person.

In addition, formal behavior control is critical. GitLab made the effort to document all activities and record them in the company handbook, which contained 2,722 pages at the beginning of 2023. The company handbook is openly accessible to all GitLab workers, and also to the public. If there are any questions, the "Handbook First" mandate applies, which means that workers should consult the handbook before proceeding. If they do not find an answer in the handbook, they should ask their manager or knowledgeable peers and document what they have found out in the handbook. The process is enabled by predefined collaboration tools and the lived values of open and direct feedback among peers.

GitLab further emphasizes self-control. The executive team gives workers central goals (objectives and key results or OKRs), but the workers have operational autonomy not only over when and where they work but also over how they complete their tasks. This underscores the importance placed on what GitLab's CEO Sijbrandij calls "One-Management": Workers should take care of managing themselves, because it is not the time investment that counts and is rewarded, but the result for the customer.

In sum, GitLab relies on complementary, reinforcing elements of input, behavior, and outcome control at the managerial level, among peers, and for

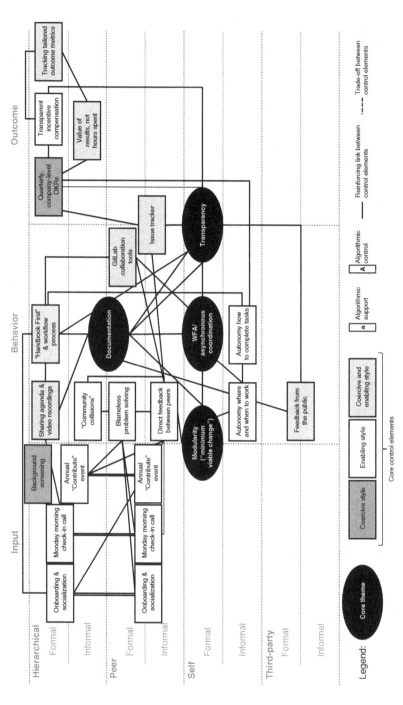

Figure 6.2 GitLab's control configuration

Table 6.6 *GitLab's control configuration heat map*

Control dimension	Target			Formality		Direction				Style		Controller	
Control element	I	B	O	F	I	H	P	S	T	C	E	H	A
Background screening	X			X		X				X		X	
Onboarding & socialization	X	X		X	X	X	X				X	X	
Monday morning check-in call	X	X		X	x	X	x				X	X	
Annual "Contribute" event	X			x	X	X	x				X	X	
Sharing agenda & video recordings		X		X		X				X	X	X	
"Handbook First" & workflow process		X		X		X				X	X	X	
"Community collisions"		X			X	X					X	X	
Blameless problem-solving		X		X		X	X				X	X	
GitLab collaboration tools		X		X			X			X	X	X	
Direct feedback between peers		X			X		X				X	X	
Issue tracker		X	X	X	x	x	X		x	X	X	X	
Autonomy where and when to work		X		x	X			X			X	X	
Autonomy how to complete tasks		X		x	X			X			X	X	
Feedback from the public		X		X					X		X	X	
Quarterly, company-level OKRs			X	X		X				X	X	X	
Transparent incentive compensation			X	X		X					X	X	
Tracking tailored outcome metrics			X	X		X				x	X	X	
Value of results, not hours spent			X		X	X				X	X	X	

Legend: Columns from left to right: target (I = input, B = behavior, O = outcome); formality (F = formal, I = informal); direction (H = hierarchical, P = peer, S = self, T = third-party); style (C = coercive, E = enabling); controller (H = human, A = algorithm); X = heavy focus on this control dimension; x = partial focus on this control dimension; empty cell = no focus on this control dimension.

Table 6.7 *Illustrative quotes for elements in GitLab's control configuration*

Control element	Exemplary quote(s)
Input control	
Background screening	• "GitLab will obtain and review background information of covered prospective, and, as applicable, current team members as allowed by local law." (GitLab 2023b)
Onboarding and socialization	• "The company's leaders note that employees accustomed to a culture of emails, phone calls, and meetings may struggle to change old habits; they solve that problem with training during onboarding and beyond." (Choudhury 2020: 64)
	• "they developed a system of onboarding 'buddies' where each new hire was paired with another GitLab employee, generally from another department and generally someone who had been working at the company for at least one year. Those buddies served as the new hires' point person for any questions about GitLab [...]. The veteran buddies were also tasked with checking in with the new hires regularly during their early months on the job, and acted as a sounding board for them. This provided opportunities for them to step in and correct any lingering 'bad habits,' as Darren [Murph, GitLab's Head of Remote] put it, whether that was an overreliance on email or Slack rather than working in the GitLab tool, or a tendency to take on too-large tasks rather than working iteratively." (Choudhury & Salomon 2023a: 2)
Monday morning check-in call	• "For years, GitLab had held a Monday morning company check-in call." (Choudhury & Salomon 2023a: 2)
Annual "Contribute" event	• "GitLab offsites also played a central role in creating this sense of community. Offsites were held annually, with the full GitLab team flying to places like New Orleans or Prague for a week of themed workshops and activities, focused on strategizing and team building rather than day-to-day company operations. As Marin [Jankovski, GitLab's Director of Engineering] explained, meeting your colleagues in person allowed you to build relationships that facilitated work throughout the year, whether because you better understood their communication style or simply credited them with having good intentions during a tense online exchange." (Choudhury & Salomon 2023a: 7)
	• "The only instance where all GitLab employees can be co-located is in the yearly 'Contribute' event, a mostly informal corporate get-together for GitLab team members to 'get face-time with one another, build community and reinforce cultural values.'" (Choudhury et al. 2020: 2)
Behavior control	
Sharing agenda and video recordings	• "to support the team members unable to attend a given call, [CEO Sid Sijbrandij] emphasized the need to document everything clearly. This included recording the meeting itself, but also publishing an agenda ahead of the call to give team members unable to attend a chance to ask questions in writing in advance. It also meant ensuring that any decisions made during the meeting were clearly communicated to all team members." (Choudhury & Salomon 2023b: 1)
	• "Ahead of meetings, organizers post agendas that link to the relevant [handbook] sections to allow invitees to read background information and post questions. Afterward recordings of the sessions are posted on GitLab's YouTube channel, agendas are edited, and the handbook is updated to reflect any decisions made." (Choudhury 2020: 64)

| "Handbook First" & workflow process | • "We have an amazing handbook that allows us to collaborate, onboard new people, and think collectively." (GitLab 2023b)
• "The handbook is a really great resource. Because so much is documented, you have this safety zone, where you can go look and find [an answer to] something, even if no one else is online." (Choudhury & Salomon 2023a: 6)
• "At GitLab all team members have access to a 'working handbook,' which some describe as the 'central repository for how we run the company.' [...] All employees are encouraged to add to it and taught how to create a new topic page, edit an existing one, embed video, and so forth." (Choudhury 2020: 64)
• "The handbook [...] provides a single source of truth accessible to anyone at any time. Our team members can't stop by a peer's office to ask for help, but they can consult an up-to-date, collectively edited resource to get the answers they need." (Sijbrandij 2023: 32)
• "The GitLab handbook both documents and reflects our culture. It is an evolving online encyclopedia that contains more than 2,000 web pages of information, including answers to basic questions such as 'How do I create a merge request?' and 'How do I file an expense report?' and a list of the 22 ways we reinforce our values, from promoting only those people who espouse them to having a corporate songbook full of adaptations such as 'You're the Iteration,' sung to the tune of Chicago's 'You're the Inspiration,' which we often belt out on team karaoke nights." (Sijbrandij 2023: 31–32)
• "Having a 'handbook first' mentality ensures there is no duplication; the handbook is always up to date, and others are better able to contribute." (GitLab 2023b)
• "If what they need to know isn't [in the handbook], the next step is to work with colleagues via Slack or Zoom to understand or decide on the right information or course of action and then add those insights to the handbook. It takes a bit of time and energy in the short term but creates great long-term benefits." (Sijbrandij 2023: 32)
• "The 'git' workflow process: it is a structured process any contribution to the code base and the handbook undergoes. There is no alternative way to edit the code or the handbook than following the 'git' workflow process. [...] In order to modify the page, the employee needs to [...] [m]odify it [...], [t]hen do a 'merge request' [...]. After an automated technical check to verify that there is no technical incompatibility in the way information was added, the maintainer, by looking at the changes, would decide whether to approve the request. This is the git process needed for every change made to the code base – the repository of code that comprises the GitLab product – and in fact also to the handbook. It represents a process that allows for distributed asynchronous work but also checks for potential coordination failures and clarity on decision rights." (Choudhury et al. 2020: 3) |
| "Community Collisions" | • "[CEO Sid Sijbrandij:] 'I know at Pixar they placed the restroom centrally so people would bump into each other – but why depend on randomness for that? Why not step it up a notch and actually organize the information communication?' These 'mixers' often include senior and C-suite executives. When I described them to my HBS colleague Christina Wallace, she gave them a nice name: community collisions." (Choudhury 2020: 66) |

Table 6.7 (cont.)

Control element	Exemplary quote(s)
Blameless problem-solving	• "[CEO Sid Sijbrandij: The handbook contains] instructions for arranging one-on-one time with me [the CEO], and a schedule of my regular office hours, during which I meet virtually with any and all team members to talk about how we can get better at incremental innovation and reducing the scope of each project so that we can ship sooner." (Sijbrandij 2023: 32) • "Investigate mistakes in a way that focuses on the situational aspects of a failure's mechanism and the decision-making process that led to the failure, rather than cast blame on a person or team. We hold blameless root cause analyses and retrospectives for stakeholders to speak up without fear of punishment or retribution." (GitLab 2023b)
GitLab collaboration tools	• "In order for this all-remote environment to work, for all of us to be effective, we all need to work within GitLab. Otherwise processes break down." (Choudhury & Salomon 2023a: 6)
Direct feedback between peers	• "To achieve results, team members must work together effectively. At GitLab, helping others is a priority, even when it is not immediately related to the goals that you are trying to achieve. Similarly, you can rely on others for help and advice – in fact, you're expected to do so. [...] We're all for accurate assessment, but we think it must be done in a kind way. Give as much positive feedback as you can, and do it in a public way. [...] Give negative feedback in the smallest setting possible. One-on-one video calls are preferred." (GitLab 2023b) • "Keep an eye out for others who may be struggling or stuck. If you see someone who needs help, reach out and assist, or connect them with someone else who can provide expertise or assistance. We succeed and shine together!" (GitLab 2023b)
Issue tracker	• "In the interest of transparency and accountability, all of these goals and tasks – as well as the progress of ongoing projects – were visible to the public via the GitLab *issue tracker*." (Choudhury & Salomon 2023a: 4, emphasis in original) • "Use issues to collaborate on ideas, solve problems, and plan work. Share and discuss proposals with your team and with outside collaborators." (GitLab 2023a)
Autonomy where and when to work	• "GitLab has employees across almost all time zones across the globe, and it has no predetermined working hours. GitLab employees are free to determine the time of the day they prefer to work." (Choudhury et al. 2020: 2) • "'one-management', that is, to be able to manage your time and schedule on your own as a remote worker." (HBR Idea Cast 2022)
Autonomy how to complete tasks	• "We trust team members to do the right thing instead of having rigid rules." (GitLab 2023b) • "how to meet those OKRs [objectives and key results] was left to the relevant teams. Teams set key performance indicators and assigned action items to specific individuals, leaving each worker to determine how best to complete those tasks." (Choudhury & Salomon 2023a: 4)

Feedback from the public	• "Anyone can chime in on any subject, including people who don't work at GitLab." (GitLab 2023b)
	• "The value of transparency extended throughout GitLab's online presence, and the company also made most meetings, documents, and even salary calculator (which adjusted based on position, experience, and geographic location) available to the public." (Choudhury & Salomon 2023a: 4–5)

Outcome control

Quarterly, company-level OKRs	• "I work with the executive team to set company-level objectives and key results (OKRs) for each quarter, but the relevant teams decide how they want to meet those goals." (Sijbrandij 2023: 31)
Transparent incentive compensation	• "GitLab publicly shares the compensation calculator it uses to determine employee salary. The calculator computes a salary according to the job role, the level of expertise within the specific job role and a location factor. Each salary is computed using the San Francisco job market as a reference point and adapted to the cost of living and market conditions of the city where the GitLab employee lives. Employees also take stock options – these are assigned to every member of GitLab and pre-determined according to job role, irrespective of location. Each job role has a pre-determined number of stock options (not value). Employees can also be awarded discretionary bonuses for instantiating company values." (Choudhury et al. 2020: 4)
Tracking tailored outcome metrics	• "Rather than tracking hours logged, we follow the metrics that matter most for each department. For salespeople, they are sales totals and client satisfaction; for customer support staffers, they're response and resolution time; for software engineers, speed of development and deployment." (Sijbrandij 2023: 31)
Value of results, not hours spent	• "Values are what the organization cares about. At GitLab the top two values are results and iteration." (Sijbrandij 2023: 31)
	• "Success isn't measured in input such as hours spent at an office. It's about output – what you achieve." (Sijbrandij 2023: 31)

each worker him- or herself to sustain its WFA organization. Onboarding and continuous socialization through weekly check-in calls and "community collisions" complement GitLab's control configuration. As even the founders admit, the centralized approach, with the handbook at the nexus, can become the Achilles heel of GitLab's control configuration if GitLab fails to consistently follow the handbook first rule (GitLab 2023b), or if the manual is not up-to-date, comprehensive, or clear enough to provide immediate answers and guidance to workers. If there are unresolved issues in the handbook, or only minor inconsistencies in the guidance provided that require clarification, the problem of GitLab's globally distributed workforce is exacerbated. This can be particularly problematic for projects that require concurrent team collaboration, as opposed to the prevailing sequential logic at GitLab, where one worker hands off a work package to another, and the modular logic of asynchronous communication works just fine. We briefly address this problem, which is exacerbated as GitLab grows in scope and global size, in Section 6.6.

6.2.5   Comparison of US Trucking Companies and GitLab

The two control configurations we just discussed (US trucking companies and GitLab) share a number of important features. To mitigate the information asymmetry stemming from workers not being co-located, both invest heavily in behavior control and incentive-based outcome control. In both cases, there are further strong complementary effects between control elements, both within and between control targets, directions, and degrees of formality. But there are also significant differences between the two cases. Whereas GitLab grants their workers broad autonomy, largely trusts them to manage themselves, and sees its own role as that of an enabler, trucking companies have implemented a much more coercive and intrusive electronic surveillance system and often resort to micro-managing their drivers, with predictable negative effects on drivers' identities and job satisfaction. In contrast to GitLab, the trucking companies even resocialize competitive driver performance data to enroll drivers' families as an additional source of outcome control.

The second major difference between the two cases' control configurations is task interdependence. In contrast to the "lone wolf" nature of trucking, GitLab's business model requires a much higher degree of collaboration among workers to complete their work. This task interdependence results in a much stronger focus on documentation, transparency, and modularity – as evident from GitLab's core themes as well as several control elements, such as "Handbook first" and the "issue tracker" – and makes comparative/competitive outcome control much more challenging.

Last, whereas truckers seem to be attracted to, and self-select into, the profession, and there are almost no input controls besides background checks and license requirements, the unique nature of GitLab's WFA model requires both a careful screening of applicants for a strong fit with the company and ongoing socialization efforts to correct any lingering "bad habits." In line with prior research (e.g., Valsecchi 2006), these two case studies show that, even with the support of electronic monitoring and (big) data analytics, organizational control of remote workers remains a complex endeavor, but also highlights that companies have to adapt their approach to the interdependence and complexity of, as well as the skill level required for, the performed tasks.

6.3   From Stable, Full-time Work to Alternative
Work Arrangements

In addition to a significant increase in remote and virtual work as illustrated in our last two case studies, we are also witnessing a proliferation of alternative work arrangements, such as temporary work, contingent work, and independent contractors or freelancers, which comprise up to a third of the working-age population in the Western world (McKinsey Global Institute 2016). These work arrangements are not under an organization's administrative control and contain no mutual expectations of continued employment (Ashford et al. 2007), which has important implications for shared identities, loyalties, and norms.

6.3.1   Challenges to Shared Identities, Loyalties, and Norms

According to a Gallup (2018) report, 88 percent of traditional workers have a manager, compared with 77 percent of temporary and contingent workers, and only 52 percent of independent contractors and freelancers. Moreover, contingent workers are often involved with multiple organizations at the same time (Ashford et al. 2018), and thus find themselves subject to the authority of more than one "employer" (Rubery et al. 2003). Hence, the traditional assumption of relatively stable, hierarchical, and dyadic control relationships between managers and workers is no longer valid for many alternative work arrangements (Wiener et al. 2019). As a consequence, alternative workers' psychological contracts with the organization differ from those of traditional workers (cf., McDonald & Makin 2000), with important implications for shared identities, loyalties, and norms.

Issues with organizational identification arise, for instance, when workers from temporary agencies identify less with their host organizations, or have to grapple with the question of which "master" to serve (Cappelli & Keller 2013).[7] Many organizations do not invest in their alternative workers' training, but shift that burden to the workers themselves (Wood et al. 2019), further reducing their shared identities and loyalties. On the flipside, alternative workers expect that their association with an organization will not last very long and, as a result, they are less concerned with impression management, or how others judge their behavior, and they tend to seek feedback less frequently (Ashford et al. 2007). This feature of alternative work arrangements further undermines the incentive and coordination functions of both behavior and peer control. Of course, peer control is also less effective because alternative workers have fewer relationships within their organizations: Only 73 percent of temporary and contingent workers, and only 58 percent of independent contractors are part of a team, compared with 81 percent of traditional workers (Gallup 2018).

Informal control appears similarly problematic for alternative work arrangements, which are not conducive to the creation of organizational norms and identities, and in which workers develop little loyalty toward their often multiple (simultaneous) "employers" (Barley et al. 2017). The fleeting nature of alternative workers' employment in any given organization and the resulting challenges for cultivating their work identities (Petriglieri et al. 2019) render any attempt of organizational control relying on a sense of community and socialization into the organization futile (Ashford et al. 2007).

Outcome control, in contrast, could become even more attractive. Along with the motivational effect of providing workers with higher perceived autonomy (Evans et al. 2007), outcome control can be implemented even more cost-effectively in alternative work arrangements, as organizations are able to quickly terminate a contract if results fall short of expectations (Ashford et al. 2007; Spreitzer et al. 2017). We would also expect input control to be effective in alternative work arrangements. A careful selection of workers to guarantee a good fit of workers' characteristics and values with the organization and with assigned tasks (Schafheitle et al. 2020) can help mitigate the challenges of such work arrangements to organizational identity and allow for better incentive alignment between workers and the organization. Given the lack of shared identities, loyalties, and norms, we would further expect workers to fall back on self-control, as it remains one of the few viable options to monitor and discipline their behavior. Last, while the lack of organizational identification and goal congruence undermines the effectiveness of enabling control (Adler & Borys 1996), we would expect coercive control to become the preferred choice in alternative work arrangements, given its greater focus on conformity, compliance, and avoiding any deviation from standard procedure.

---

[7] An interesting side effect is that a higher percentage of alternative workers also reduces regular workers' identification with their organization because of a decline in the perceived status of the workplace (Eldor & Cappelli 2020).

6.3.2   Case Study

As we have described earlier, the shift from stable, full-time work to alternative work arrangements poses its own challenges and calls into question common assumptions about shared identities, loyalties, and norms in organizations. However, since contemporary alternative work relationships are commonly found in platform-mediated gig work, we do not present a separate case study here. Instead, in Section 6.5, we present two case studies – Uber and Upwork – which are also representative of alternative work relationships.

6.4   From Human Managers to Algorithmic Control

As outlined in Section 5.3.4, algorithms can provide support to managers (with humans in the loop), but they can also remove human supervision from the work site. Many organizations have already started to take humans out of the loop by delegating tasks, such as scheduling, monitoring, and evaluating workers, to computer algorithms, with human intervention occurring only reactively, or when explicitly requested. As we will discuss later, algorithmic control can be more comprehensive, instantaneous, and interactive – but also more opaque – than human managers (Kellogg et al. 2020). This trend toward algorithmic control has two important implications for organizational control: Relaxing the traditional assumption of managers' bounded rationality and an (often intentional) shift of information asymmetry from workers – but also from managers – to algorithms.

6.4.1   Relaxing Managerial Bounded Rationality

Monitoring benefits. As we have discussed in Section 5.1.2, a growing body of evidence suggests that machine learning (ML) algorithms – although not without flaws – are actually less biased and more accurate than the humans they replace (e.g., Kleinberg et al. 2017). One of the reasons for their accuracy is that algorithms greatly expand previous control mechanisms in both scope and frequency (Kellogg et al. 2020). Algorithms can engage in much more comprehensive data collection, aggregation, and analysis than human managers. As we discussed in Section 5.3.1, algorithmic control is no longer restricted to observable work behaviors, but encompasses attitudinal, emotional, and physiological data on workers, as well as contextual data gathered from the ubiquitous computing devices that surround them. Algorithmic control also extends surveillance beyond the workplace and deep into workers' private lives.

Incentive and coordination benefits. Algorithms also have beneficial effects on the incentive and coordination functions of control. Algorithms can provide workers with instantaneous feedback. In contrast to traditional hierarchical control, which relies on annual or semi-annual performance reviews to reward or discipline workers, algorithmic control can provide real-time feedback to workers and managers (Cascio & Montealegre 2016; Kellogg et al. 2020). For example, some call centers already employ ML algorithms that transcribe and analyze calls in real-time to offer guidance to workers based on the questions customers ask (Deighton 2021). The guidance can entail pop-up script suggestions for things to say and reminders for agents to adapt their approach (e.g., "slow down" or "you're talking over the customer"). Other types of algorithms are incorporated into existing platforms, such as Slack or Gmail, and warn workers when the language they use in internal or external conversations does not comply with organizational policies, helping organizations curb litigation and reputational risks stemming from worker behavior (Carnevali 2021). Compared to traditional managers, such algorithmic behavior control can be both more timely and frequent, and it can be more easily scaled. Whereas managers in a call center may have listened in on two calls per agent per week, algorithms can be deployed to monitor and assist in every single call of every single agent at the same call center.

Leveraging algorithms' potential for instantaneous feedback, companies such as General Electric and IBM have either eliminated and replaced, or at least supplemented, their annual performance reviews by introducing feedback applications that allow managers to provide feedback – and workers to request feedback from managers, peers, and subordinates – at any time (Rivera et al. 2021). These algorithmic feedback applications can provide worker guidance as well as fulfill potential education and training needs in a much more timely and efficient way. As a result, algorithms are capable of more objective and precise predictions provided in real time, thereby mitigating the constraints of human bounded rationality (Adner et al. 2019), which can help improve the incentive and coordination functions of control.

The collection and analysis of extremely granular or "little" data encompassing even minute details of individual workers' behavior (Cukier & Mayer-Schoenberger 2013; Newell & Marabelli 2015) further allows algorithms to go beyond predicting overall trends and, instead, predict the behavior and performance outcomes of specific workers. As a result, in contrast to boundedly rational managers' reliance on one-size-fits-all approaches to reward or discipline workers, algorithms can customize behavior control efficiently and effectively, providing personalized feedback to individual workers (Kellogg et al. 2020). Some authors have even argued that algorithms are capable of actually addressing workers' fundamental psychological needs – autonomy, competence, and relatedness (cf., Deci et al. 2017) – and thereby cater to human nature much better than human managers (Quaquebeke & Gerpott 2023). With their ability to provide direction and feedback at a level of granularity, personalization, and immediacy that is impossible for human managers to match, algorithms can fulfill workers' need for autonomy, thereby enhancing their intrinsic motivation, and engage workers in real-time learning, thereby playing to their sense of competence. Algorithms' increasingly human-like features[8] are further designed to encourage workers to project human qualities and engage in bonding, thereby catering to workers' need for relatedness. Perhaps not surprisingly, experimental studies have shown that particularly lay people adhere more to advice when they think it comes from an algorithm than from a person, an effect researchers labeled "algorithm appreciation" (Logg et al. 2019).

In contrast to the overt nature of traditional behavior control, algorithmic behavior control can also be less obtrusive in terms of how it directs, evaluates, and disciplines workers. Behavioral economics defines *nudging* as using subtle differences in choice and information architecture to predictably alter people's behavior without forbidding any options or changing their economic incentives significantly (Thaler & Sunstein 2008), that is, without infringing on people's autonomy (Uzunca & Kas 2023). Algorithms can nudge workers to exhibit the desired behavior by displaying only certain information to workers, and restricting other information, or by presenting workers with choices and opportunities preselected by the algorithm (Newell & Marabelli 2015; Schafheitle et al. 2020).

Algorithms have additional advantages when it comes to outcome control. Algorithms are capable of differentiating and personalizing rewards and penalties to best meet individual workers' needs (Colbert et al. 2016), thereby further enhancing their incentive function. Algorithms also allow organizations to "gamify" the reward system for a more positive and fun experience (Colbert et al. 2016) and penalize underperformers in real time. Algorithms can do this by aggregating quantitative and qualitative feedback about worker performance from both internal and external sources on an ongoing basis, resulting in real-time ratings and relative rankings of workers (Kellogg et al. 2020). Organizations can then use these ratings and rankings to engender competition between workers, with the algorithm providing intermittent feedback on how workers perform at the game (Elliott & Long 2016; Ranganathan & Benson 2020; Stark & Pais 2020). Making workers' rewards, at least partially, dependent on the outcomes of such games helps create incentives and further align interests. Besides enabling social games, the quantification of work inherent in algorithms can also facilitate "auto-games" (i.e., games workers design and play by themselves), by offering clear personal objectives, the means to compete with oneself, and private, real-time feedback. Under those conditions, workers (often inadvertently) transform their tasks into independent, individual-level games (Ranganathan & Benson 2020) that represent an algorithm-supported

---

[8] Several natural language-processing algorithms have already passed the Turing test, which examines whether a machine can engage in a conversation with a human without being detected as a machine (Else 2023).

form of self-control. As is evident from the earlier description, algorithmic control not only prescribes tasks and directs workers but also simultaneously gathers data on task completion and rewards or penalizes workers, thereby blending bureaucratic and normative forms of organizational control effectively (Elliott & Long 2016).

In addition to their benefits for behavior and outcome control, the ability of algorithms to analyze unstructured data from outside the workplace and make predictions about future behavior based on that data allows organizations to expand or even automate input control (Schafheitle et al. 2020). As mentioned in Section 5.3.1, companies rely increasingly on social media profiling to predict job applicants' and workers' personalities, which can be used during hiring and promotion processes (Chamorro-Premuzic et al. 2017). Recruiters also use social media to screen and vet applicants (Berkelaar 2014), and 93 percent of recruiters will check an applicant's social profile before making a hiring decision (Jobvite 2019). Since they do not require people to complete an assessment, companies can save time and perform these screenings at a much larger scale than traditional psychological profiling, allowing companies to dramatically increase their candidate pools (Chamorro-Premuzic et al. 2017). Companies have also started to scrutinize their workers' use of social media to understand their emotions at work, with the stated goal of helping workers and managers access their emotions, relate their emotional patterns to moments of high and low productivity, and promote positive attitudes at work (De Choudhury & Counts 2013).

In sum, by continuously measuring workers' abilities, skills, and attitudes, and matching them to jobs, teams, or project demands, the timing of input control can be expanded from before a worker has signed a contract, to their entire tenure with the organization. Algorithms can also fire underperforming workers rapidly or automatically and replace them with substitute workers (Kellogg et al. 2020), thereby effectively automating input control.

By blending input, behavior, and outcome control algorithmically, organizations can design highly individualized work experiences that are tailored to individual engagement. However, the lack of connections to and interactions with peers can also lead to tasks becoming isolating, repetitive, and fatiguing. To address this issue, some organizations attempt to reconstitute a collective work experience and culture by leveraging algorithmic performance data to create a digital arena for competitive, albeit mostly online, interactions among peers. In one example of a big-box warehouse (Elliott & Long 2016), workers were ranked in real time by order fulfillment – and the rankings were displayed for everyone to see – with material consequences for individual workers, and with the entire shift being defined by collective goals that were set in advance. By sharing algorithmically derived behavior or performance data across workers, algorithmic control can therefore lead workers to change their behavior to match that of their peers. Even more strikingly, workers themselves used the performance data to construct an informal status hierarchy, in which workers ranked each other, competed, and derided those who failed to meet informal standards. As this example shows, algorithmic control can mimic both peer control and self-control (Kellogg et al. 2020).

Last, algorithmic control can be much more comprehensive in terms of how it evaluates, directs, and disciplines workers, thereby constraining workers in a much stricter way than under previous control regimes (Kellogg et al. 2020), with the potential to make control regimes much more coercive than ever before. Moreover, algorithms have the potential to render informal controls obsolete. Increasing datafication technologies permit the direct monitoring of attitudes, values, and emotions (Cram & Wiener 2020; Schafheitle et al. 2020). In addition, subtle forms of algorithmic control, such as nudging, can help influence, and even change, workers' habits and attitudes, thereby reducing the need for traditional informal controls.

Limitations. Besides its advantages for mitigating managerial bounded rationality, algorithmic control also has its limitations. For instance, contemporary algorithms are largely restricted to machine-readable data at the expense of additional contextual information. This restriction not only limits algorithms' ability to make accurate and fair managerial decisions (Newlands 2021) but also delegitimizes contextual information for organizational control. As Levy (2015: 161) has cautioned, "[b]y converting work practices into ostensibly objective, morally neutral records of human action, information technologies legitimate certain types of knowledge and experience, while rendering others invisible and nonactionable." Moreover, algorithms still lack reflexivity – they simply carry out their instructions, regardless of the situation. This makes them both reliable and unbiased in routine situations, but the lack of reflexivity becomes problematic in novel situations, such as inherently unpredictable and complex social settings (Rahman 2021). In those situations, which are not part of their training data, or only to a very limited extent, algorithms will still apply their encoded instructions, often with unintended (social) consequences.

Algorithms' capacity for nudging and gamification has also attracted criticism. Some authors consider even benevolent nudges as manipulative or as paternalism in disguise (e.g., Bovens 2009). Nudging can, of course, also be used with ill intent. Nudges that do not promote the nudged person's well-being, and nudges that are not transparent, not easy to opt out of, or that are misleading, constitute evil or dark nudges, sludges, or phishing (Akerlof & Shiller 2015; Thaler 2015). Other researchers have warned that both social games and auto-games, with their often opaque reward systems and rapid responsiveness of rewards, can be frustrating and stressful for workers. These games can also be quite addictive and could impair workers' capacity to set limits for their work – in a sense, gamification could entice workers to "binge work" (Kellogg et al. 2020; Ranganathan & Benson 2020).

6.4.2   Shifting Information Asymmetry from Workers and Managers to Algorithms

As we have outlined in Section 5.1.2, ML algorithms rely on complex webs of correlational inference, that are often opaque and inscrutable, even to their architects (Burrell 2016; Demetis & Lee 2018). The information asymmetries arising from this black-box problem of algorithms are, however, not random and are often deliberately created by designers and embraced by managers (Kellogg et al. 2020). The less workers understand about the inner workings of control algorithms, the less likely they will try and succeed in gaming the system (Faraj et al. 2018). Algorithms are further capable of adapting rapidly, which helps them remain opaque and avoid scrutiny (Orlikowski & Scott 2014). Even if workers manage to reverse-engineer an algorithm at a given point in time, the algorithm can update instantaneously, based on real-time data, which renders workers' current understanding obsolete (Rahman 2021). Moreover, their inability to understand or reverse-engineer the nature of the control algorithm makes workers believe that they are under constant surveillance, and thereby leads them to police their own behavior, that is, engage in effective self-control (Cram & Wiener 2020). Indeed, recent empirical work has found that workers tend to avoid algorithmic scrutiny and punishment by engaging in anticipatory compliance practices to "pacify the algorithm," or by effectively internalizing the algorithm's decision mechanisms, and thereby regulating themselves accordingly (Bucher et al. 2021a). Finally, algorithmic control, especially nudges, can be much more unobtrusive compared to traditional forms of control, which makes it less likely to be noticed by workers, even though it can have powerful effects (Kellogg et al. 2020).

Besides these positive effects for organizational control's incentive function, shifting information asymmetries to algorithms can also undermine control's coordination and incentive functions. Algorithmic control, by design, offers very limited insight into *why* rewards and punishments were applied, and algorithmic recommendations are often not comprehensible to workers (Kellogg et al. 2020). In a sense, algorithmic control creates a new, invisible iron cage, "whose bars are not readily graspable for bending – where rules are not readily understood or available for interpretation and scrutiny" (Faraj et al. 2018: 68; see also Rahman 2021). This is problematic, particularly for enabling and self-control, which require an understanding of cause-and-effect relationships to be effective. The inscrutability of algorithmic control also results in workers developing, at best, a superficial understanding of the controlled task, and thus they have very little opportunity to learn from mistakes

(Newell & Marabelli 2015). Furthermore, without managers, workers often have no one to help them understand a problem they are trying to solve, or to give them feedback on what worked and what did not work (Kellogg et al. 2020). This is particularly problematic for behavior control, which is effective precisely because it can foster a dialogue between workers and managers who are sharing up-to-date information that permits timely, corrective interventions into the monitored processes (Kirsch 1996). The absence of such feedback loops further undermines the coordination function of control.

The opacity of algorithms evaluating, directing, and disciplining workers also encroaches on procedural due process, which can frustrate workers, and thereby undermine the incentive function of control. Algorithmic control can further alienate workers by depriving them of autonomy over their own actions. As outlined earlier, algorithmic restrictions can limit workers' choices more extensively than before. The continuous nudging and rapid responsiveness of gamified rewards in algorithmic control regimes can compromise workers' autonomy to set moral and practical limits for their work, resulting in "technostress" and threatening workers' welfare (Kellogg et al. 2020). Moreover, with managers out of the picture, workers have only very limited recourse to find out why they received a negative evaluation or other penalty – a situation Gray and Suri (2019) labeled "algorithmic cruelty" – which further undermines workers' belief in the procedural fairness of the control system (Kellogg et al. 2020). This can lead to frustration, non-compliance, workarounds, manipulation, or outright sabotage (Cram & Wiener 2020; Veen et al. 2020), jeopardizing the effectiveness of algorithmic controls.

Addressing these downsides, recent work has found holistic combinations of algorithmic and managerial control to be effective. In their study of a digital marketing agency, Kessinger and Kellogg (2019) demonstrated how managers were able to soften the edges of algorithmic control by engaging in relational work with workers, which reduced workers' stress and encouraged learning. While humans in the loop help mitigate some of the downsides of algorithmic control, rendering algorithmic decisions more accountable (Raisch & Krakowski 2021), prior research also cautions that humans are not very effective at monitoring and overriding automation (Cram & Wiener 2020). Other experimental studies found that giving workers a small amount of control over the prediction of an algorithm can mitigate algorithm aversion (Dietvorst et al. 2016).

6.4.3   Case Study: Amazon Warehouses

An insightful illustration of an algorithmic(ally supported) organizational control configuration can be found within Amazon, which is a US-headquartered, multinational technology company whose business model revolves around e-commerce, cloud computing, online advertising, digital streaming, and AI.

The focus of our case study is on Amazon's warehouse workers, also known as fulfillment center associates, who work in approximately 800,000 square-foot fulfillment centers that employ up to 5,000 full-time workers each. Most of these workers are hired on a permanent basis as part of a traditional work arrangement, work face-to-face, and perform functions involving picking, packing, and shipping of books, toys, and household goods.

Despite most warehouse work being blue-collar, Amazon's warehouse workers come from diverse backgrounds and across all education levels (Vallas et al. 2022). Workers are scheduled in shifts, and shifts fluctuate throughout the year to reflect demand. Most of the year, workers work four 10-hour shifts, totaling a 40-hour workweek, but during peak time, this increases to six 10-hour day shifts or five 12-hour night shifts, for a total of 60 hours (Asher Hamilton & Cain 2019).

We exclude two groups of Amazon warehouse workers from our analysis: temporary or seasonal workers, who have few if any rights or benefits, and are commonly used by Amazon in its warehouses to address seasonal demands; and warehouse workers who perform indirect functions in quality control, training, or handling of non-conforming or oversized packages (Vallas et al. 2022). Figure 6.3 presents Amazon warehouses' control configuration, with its associated heat map presented in Table 6.8. Illustrative quotes for each control element are provided in Table 6.9.

Discussion. To achieve its guiding principles of efficiency and excellence[9] in its warehouses, Amazon relies predominantly on hierarchical, formal, mostly coercive, and mostly algorithmic(ally supported) control across all three control targets: from worker training (input control), via algorithmic scheduling, nudging through a patented wristband technology, and gamified behavior control (behavior control), to the gamification of rewards and algorithmic termination (outcome control). However, the control configuration also shows that Amazon does not solely rely on coercive mechanisms but also seeks to elicit workers' consent to managerial authority via identity control, in which the firm selects and rewards workers who invest in their identity as "diligent workers," often assigning them to positions that confer a "trusted worker" status on them (Vallas et al. 2022). In addition, the quantification of workers' outcomes relative to their peers – in real-time and often displayed for everyone to see – further entices workers to engage in self-control and auto-gamification.

Amazon's control configuration clearly benefits from positive reinforcement effects. Its extensive algorithmic surveillance of workers' real-time behaviors (on and off the task) and outcomes (via algorithmic performance measurement) feeds information to subtle (e.g., wristbands nudging workers for a more efficient task completion) and not-so-subtle behavior and outcome controls, such as games and competitions, variable incentive pay,

---

[9] www.aboutamazon.com/about-us

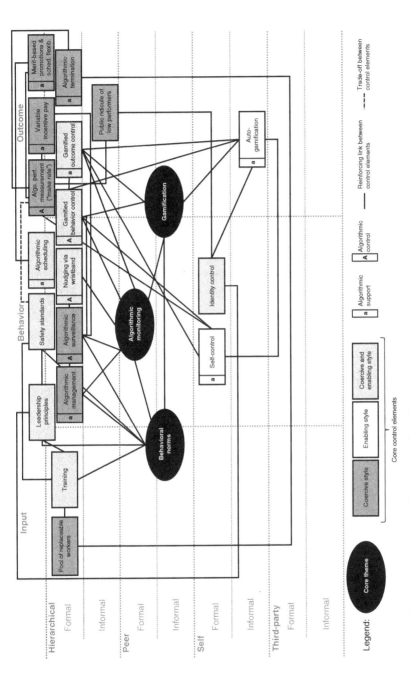

Figure 6.3 Amazon warehouses' control configuration

Table 6.8 *Amazon's control configuration heat map*

Control dimension	Target			Formality		Direction				Style		Controller	
Control element	I	B	O	F	I	H	P	S	T	C	E	H	A
Pool of replaceable workers	X			X		X				X		X	
Training	X			X		X				X	X	X	
Leadership principles	x	X		X		X				X	X	X	
Safety standards		X		X		X				X	X	X	
Algorithmic scheduling		X		X		X				X	X	X	x
Algorithmic management		X		X		X				X		X	x
Algorithmic surveillance		X		X		X				X		X	X
Nudging via wristband		X		X		X				X	X	X	X
Gamified behavior control		X	x	X		X				X	X	X	X
Self-control		X		X				X		X	X	X	
Identity control		X		X				X		X	X	X	
Algorithmic perf. measurement ("make rate")			X	X		X				X		X	X
Variable incentive pay			X	X		X				X		X	x
Merit-based promotions and scheduling flexibility			X	X		X				X	X	X	x
Gamified outcome control			X	X		X				X		X	x
Algorithmic termination			X	X		X				X		X	x
Public ridicule of low performers			X		X					X		X	x
Auto-gamification			X		X			X			X		x

Legend: Columns from left to right: target (I = input, B = behavior, O = outcome); formality (F = formal, I = informal); direction (H = hierarchical, P = peer, S = self, T = third-party); style (C = coercive, E = enabling); controller (H = human, A = algorithm); X = heavy focus on this control dimension; x = partial focus on this control dimension; empty cell = no focus on this control dimension.

Table 6.9 *Illustrative quotes for elements in Amazon warehouses' control configuration*

Control element	Exemplary quote(s)
Input control	
Pool of replaceable workers	• "Jake [a warehouse worker in Florida] estimated he was hired along with 75 people, but that he was the only one remaining when his back finally gave out, and most had been turned over twice. 'You're just a number, they can replace you with anybody off the street in two seconds,' he said. 'They don't need any skills. They don't need anything. All they have to do is work real fast.'" (Dzieza 2020)
Training	• "Amazon says retraining is part of the process to get workers up to standards and that it only changes rates when more than 75 percent of workers at a facility are meeting goals. The bottom 5 percent of workers are placed on a training plan, according to the company." (Lecher 2019)
Behavior control	
Leadership principles	• "[Amazon founder and former CEO Jeff] Bezos was determined almost from the moment he founded Amazon in 1994 to resist the forces he thought sapped businesses over time – bureaucracy, profligate spending, lack of rigor. As the company grew, he wanted to codify his ideas about the workplace, some of them proudly counterintuitive, into instructions simple enough for a new worker to understand, general enough to apply to the nearly limitless number of businesses he wanted to enter and stringent enough to stave off the mediocrity he feared. The result was the leadership principles, the articles of faith that describe the way Amazonians should act. In contrast to companies where declarations about their philosophy amount to vague platitudes, Amazon has rules that are part of its daily language and rituals, used in hiring, cited at meetings and quoted in food-truck lines at lunchtime." (Kantor & Streitfeld 2015)
Safety standards	• "The health, wellness, and safety of our workers is our number one priority. Everyone has the right to a safe and healthy workplace with appropriate rules and practices for reporting and preventing accidents, injuries, and unsafe conditions, procedures, or behaviors." (https://sustainability.aboutamazon.com/human-rights/principles)
Algorithmic scheduling	• "The company does instruct workers on the safe way to move their bodies and handle equipment." (Evans 2019) • "scheduling algorithms are now ubiquitous. At the facilities where Amazon sorts goods before delivery, for example, workers are given skeleton schedules and get pinged by an app when additional hours in the warehouse become available, sometimes as little as 30 minutes before they're needed." (Dzieza 2020)
Algorithmic management	• "When Jake [an Amazon worker] started working at a Florida warehouse, he was surprised by how few supervisors there were: just two or three managing a workforce of more than 300. 'Management was completely automated,' he said." (Dzieza 2020)
Algorithmic surveillance	• "In Amazon warehouses, employees are monitored by sophisticated electronic systems to ensure they are packing enough boxes every hour." (Kantor & Streitfeld 2015) • "Amazon is known to track how fast its warehouse workers can pick and package items from its shelves, imposing strictly timed breaks and targets. It issues warning points for those who don't meet its goals or who take extended breaks." (Ghosh 2018)

Table 6.9 (cont.)

Control element	Exemplary quote(s)
Nudging via wristband	• "What if your employer made you wear a wristband that tracked your every move, and that even nudged you via vibrations when it judged that you were doing something wrong? [...] Amazon's proposed technology would emit ultrasonic sound pulses and radio transmissions to track where an employee's hands were in relation to inventory bins, and provide 'haptic feedback' to steer the worker toward the correct bin. The aim, Amazon says in the patent, is to streamline 'time consuming' tasks, like responding to orders and packaging them for speedy delivery. With guidance from a wristband, workers could fill orders faster." (Yeginsu 2018)
	• "The wristbands, developed in the name of greater efficiency, track and guide workers' hands toward product locations by sending feedback to workers when their hand is in close proximity of the pick location. [...] The Amazon patent points to a device that is many steps beyond the current generation of hands-free RF [radio frequency] scanners. [...] The data are valuable to warehouse operators, since they monitor worker productivity as well as safety hazards. Yet the same technologies that are augmenting worker movements also are surveilling them." (Gutelius & Theodore 2019: 57)
Gamified behavior control	• "Inside several of Amazon's cavernous warehouses, hundreds of employees spend hours a day playing video games. Some compete by racing virtual dragons or sports cars around a track, while others collaborate to build castles piece by piece. [...] they're racing to fill customer orders, their progress reflected in a video game format that is part of an experiment by the e-commerce giant to help reduce the tedium of its physically demanding jobs. If it helps improve the efficiency of work like plucking items from or stowing products on shelves for 10 hours a day or more, all the better. The video games are optional for the thousands of 'pickers' and 'stowers' across a handful of the company's warehouses. [...] Developed by Amazon, the games are displayed on small screens at employees' workstations. As robots wheel giant shelves up to each workstation, lights or screens indicate which item the worker needs to put into a bin. The games can register the completion of the task, which is tracked by scanning devices, and can pit individuals, teams or entire floors in a race to pick or stow Lego sets, cellphone cases or dish soap, for instance. Game-playing employees are rewarded with points, virtual badges and other goodies throughout a shift. Think Tetris, but with real boxes. [...] With names like MissionRacer, PicksInSpace, Dragon Duel and CastleCrafter, the games have simple graphics akin to early Nintendo games like Super Mario Bros, workers say." (Bensinger 2019)
	• "The games are a response to worker complaints that Amazon's push for more automation has made laborers feel like cogs in a bigger machine, as they increasingly work alongside robots. By fostering workplace competition through games, Amazon is also slyly pushing workers to raise the stakes among themselves to pack more boxes." (Bensinger 2019)
	• "Workers [...] said the games have indeed helped ease the tedium of the job, adding variety to tasks that otherwise can be physically demanding and monotonous. One worker said she had at times picked nearly 500 items off the roving shelves in one hour, egged on by the game pitting her against other pickers to compel a racecar around a track. She said pickers and stowers compete with one another to complete video game tasks faster, meaning they are moving more real merchandise onto trucks that bring the items to customers' doorsteps." (Bensinger 2019)
	• "[Warehouse worker Jake] was encouraged to move even faster by a giant leaderboard, featuring a cartoon sprinting man, that showed the rates of the 10 fastest workers in real time. A manager would sometimes keep up a sports announcer patter over the intercom – 'In third place for the first half, we have Bob at 697 units per hour,' Jake recalled." (Dzieza 2020)

Self-control	"Chaz, [a warehouse worker] from New Jersey, explained that 'figuring out promotions and how to get ahead' requires being 'a self-learner, a self-starter, you got to be motivated to do it'." (Vallas et al. 2022: 441)
Identity control	"Amazon has made good use of the workers' pre-existing cultural repertoires, adopting practices aimed at rewarding and retaining workers who invest in the 'diligent worker' identity. Here we refer to the company's establishment of symbolic positions as learning ambassadors, problem solvers, quality control specialists, and other Tier One positions which confer greater autonomy and recognition (but no greater pay) than ordinary workers receive. The company also provides periodic announcements of its top performers, bestowing 'favored worker' status (along with Amazon branded e-swag and occasional scheduling privileges) on those who have posted the best UPH [units per hour] levels. Such practices capitalize on the cultural repertoires that many workers have inherited, providing sanctioned spaces for the performance of a company-aligned identity." (Vallas et al. 2022: 437)
	"Normative control represents the company's effort to establish job structures and rewards that encourage workers to invest in the diligent worker identity. By rewarding workers with job assignments that confer a modicum of recognition, the company manages to elicit active consent, encouraging a stratum of workers to align their identities with the company's goals." (Vallas et al. 2022: 439)
Outcome control	
Algorithmic performance measurement ("make rate")	"'We have performance expectations for every Amazon associate, and we measure actual performance against those expectations,' said spokeswoman Lindsay Campbell in a statement, noting that the company offers coaching to help those who are underperforming." (Bensinger 2019)
	"Digital Taylorism is well under way in some parts of the warehousing industry. Amazon has attracted significant attention for the productivity rates the company expects of order pickers, and recent media reports detail the difficulty some workers have as they attempt to 'make rate.' Careful tracking of productivity has led to termination when employees are not reaching the target rate, and workers report feeling anxiety about the possibility of being terminated." (Gutelius & Theodore 2019: 55)
	"[Eastvale, CA, warehouse worker Candice] Dixon's scan rate – more than 300 items an hour, thousands of individual products a day – was being tracked constantly, the data flowing to managers in real time, then crunched by a proprietary software system called ADAPT. She knew, like the thousands of other workers there, that if she didn't hit her target speed, she would be written up and, if she didn't improve, she eventually would be fired." (Evans 2019)
	"Crucially, when workers describe their fear of being fired, they almost always reference the company's sophisticated system of digital or algorithmic controls, which management uses to police each worker's productivity. This is most pronounced among workers performing direct functions, who use scanners to process each item they must handle. These input devices enable management not only to track the precise location of items in the system but also to generate a detailed, real-time record of individual workers' performance levels, which are automatically compared against the expected production rate and against other workers in the department. The system automatically flags workers with deficient performance records, who are then vulnerable to 'coaching,' as pro-company workers called it, followed by formal warnings, and eventually termination." (Vallas et al. 2022: 434–435)

Table 6.9 (cont.)

Control element	Exemplary quote(s)
	• "Every task in Amazon's fulfillment centers has a rate. Workers say the two most demanding jobs are 'stow' and 'pick.' When goods come into the fulfillment center, they're unboxed and sent to stowers, who scan and place the goods onto the shelves carried by the orange Roomba-like robots that roll along the floor. That item is now in stock. When an item is ordered, a robot rolls a shelf up to a 'picker,' who grabs it, scans it, and puts it on a conveyor belt to be packaged and sent out. Depending on their station, workers are shown a range of graphics displaying whether they're meeting their rate or falling behind. Some are shown the amount of time they've been working and the number of items they've scanned, along with a moving average, which drops if you take time to go to the bathroom or have a problem with your workstation. Others are shown a graph that rises and falls, and that turns green, yellow, or red depending on how fast they're working." (Dzieza 2019)
	• "Management uses two distinct measures of individual performance. The first – Units per Hour or UPH – measures the speed at which workers operate. Each worker's rate and percentile ranking are prominently displayed on monitors and hard copy print outs in many production areas, the better to foster a sense of accountability, discipline, and competition among workers. [...] The second performance metric, Time off Task (TOT), records the number of minutes during each shift when workers have shown no measurable productivity. The system normally allots workers a five-minute period during which inactivity is not flagged. Beyond this, the digital clock starts ticking, measuring the number of minutes each worker has failed to engage in productive activity. TOT levels amounting to an hour or more can be cause for summary termination, but smaller levels are also cause for discipline. [...] the mundane reality is that the TOT metric heightens workers' sense that they are digitally tethered to their jobs and must constantly keep working." (Vallas et al. 2022: 435)
	• "As ever-increasing production targets flow down from corporate, regional managers lean on warehouse directors, who put pressure on the supervisors who oversee all those water spiders [workers who bring boxes of merchandise to stowers], stowers, pickers and packers. And the key to advancement is great production numbers." (Evans 2019)
	• "The Amazon tenure of Parker Knight, a disabled veteran who worked at the Troutdale, Oregon, warehouse this year, shows the ruthless precision of Amazon's system. Knight had been allowed to work shorter shifts after he sustained back and ankle injuries at the warehouse, but ADAPT [Amazon's proprietary software system] didn't spare him. Knight was written up three times in May for missing his quota. The expectations were precise. He had to pick 385 small items or 350 medium items each hour. One week, he was hitting 98.45% of his expected rate, but that wasn't good enough. That 1.55% speed shortfall earned him his final written warning – the last one before termination. 'You are expected to meet 100% of the productivity performance expectation,' the warning reads. Days later, the company informed him he was being fired because of an earlier confrontation over workers' compensation paperwork." (Evans 2019)
Variable incentive pay	• "staff could earn bonuses in the form of 'variable compensation pay,' or VCP, based on attendance and productivity, which usually doubles during peak weeks." (Asher Hamilton & Cain 2019)

Merit-based promotions & scheduling flexibility	• "Marie [a worker in Staten Island, NY] told us that 'Amazon gives everyone a chance to prove themselves... You can work hard, you can take on more responsibility, and prove that you can move up.'" (Vallas et al. 2022: 441)
	• "workers often discussed [job mobility], attaching much importance to their hopes of transferring to less onerous jobs or facilities or of being promoted to a Tier 3 position as a PA [Process Assistant, who oversees Tier One workers]. Such workers tended to fasten on individual mobility and achievement as features of the company that they particularly liked. August, a young worker from Louisiana had long sought a promotion and had finally succeeded. 'I have this feeling that I could move up in a higher position and keep making my way up this company'" (Vallas et al. 2022: 441)
	• "Amazon has creatively adopted provisions that define variability in workers' schedules as a reward – and one that workers highly value since it enables them to escape the relentless demands of their jobs." (Vallas et al. 2022: 441)
	• "VTO [voluntary time off] opportunities are so highly valued by workers that management can distribute them via a lottery (as if they were prizes to covet) or else bestow them on workers who have shown the best UPH [units per hour] rates for that shift. In this way management has framed a profit driven imperative – its need for temporal flexibility – as a benefit that workers can choose to invoke." (Vallas et al. 2022: 442)
	• "Thus being eligible for transfers, promotions, and flexibility regarding one's schedule were highly valued parts of workers' everyday working lives. [...] Yet crucially, these job rewards were only available to workers who had maintained their status as 'workers in good standing' – i.e., records that were free of any performance issues, warnings, or disciplinary infractions." (Vallas et al. 2022: 442)
Gamified outcome control	• "The company also provides periodic announcements of its top performers, bestowing 'favored worker' status (along with Amazon branded e-swag and occasional scheduling privileges) on those who have posted the best UPH [units per hour] levels." (Vallas et al. 2022: 437)
	• "In addition to cash, Amazon workers can be rewarded with 'swag bucks,' a kind of company currency that can be spent only inside Amazon. The incentives are designed to further increase productivity and are popular with some employees. The physical description of swag bucks – also known as 'Amazon bucks' – varied wildly. Allen [a former warehouse worker in Texas] said that in her warehouse they looked like a Monopoly bill with [Amazon founder and former CEO Jeff] Bezos' face. [...] Using swag bucks, workers can buy items like T-shirts, lanyards, and water bottles from Amazon. The company currency is available all year round, but sources told Business Insider there's more up for grabs during peak, especially during what's known as 'power hours.'" (Asher Hamilton & Cain 2019)
	• "Power hours are when managers try to pump up warehouse workers to work even harder for 60 minutes, sometimes motivating them by saying workers in other departments have been talking smack or outperforming them. At the end of the hour, staff members can be rewarded with swag bucks or prizes." (Asher Hamilton & Cain 2019)

Table 6.9 (cont.)

Control element	Exemplary quote(s)
	• "'I've personally won a 50-inch television,' Keion Burgess [a warehouse worker in Edison, NJ] said during the interview organized by Amazon. 'It's been great. We can win power hours in teams, or we can win them individually. It's a really great thing for us as associates. We love it.' During that same interview, Angelina Tramontano [another warehouse worker in Edison, NJ] added: 'After you work eight hours and you're really, really tired, I use it as an incentive to push myself to challenge myself to see if I can do it.' Tramontano also described witnessing colleagues win TVs, Xboxes, gift cards, and extra breaks. She once won an Echo Dot, Amazon's best-selling product last year." (Asher Hamilton & Cain 2019)
	• "Hafsa Hassan, an Amazon employee in Minnesota, said workers could also receive scratch-off tickets for excelling in 'minicompetitions.' Prizes can include laptops, headphones, or even Chipotle gift cards. Hassan said one manager in her warehouse would list employees' hourly rate from slowest to fastest to get people 'fired up.'" (Asher Hamilton & Cain 2019)
Algorithmic termination	• "Every worker has a 'rate,' a certain number of items they have to process per hour, and if they fail to meet it, they can be automatically fired" (Dzieza 2020)
	• "documents also show a deeply automated tracking and termination process. 'Amazon's system tracks the rates of each individual associate's productivity, [...] and automatically generates any warnings or terminations regarding quality or productivity without input from supervisors.'" (Lecher 2019)
	• "The system goes so far as to track 'time off task,' which the company abbreviates as TOT. If workers break from scanning packages for too long, the system automatically generates warnings and, eventually, the employee can be fired." (Lecher 2019)
	• "If a worker falls behind, they receive a warning. Multiple workers in [the Amazon fulfillment center in] Shakopee said it was common for workers to be fired on their fourth warning, and that the process felt automatic, with managers deferring to the software." (Dzieza 2019)
	• "Amazon was firing more than 10 percent of its staff annually, solely for productivity reasons." (Lecher 2019)
Public ridicule of low performers	• "[Hafsa Hassan, a warehouse worker in Minnesota:] 'The part that sucks is when someone's not packing up to the standards of the manager or the rate that's been put up. I've seen the manager make fun of people.'" (Asher Hamilton & Cain 2019)
Auto-gamification	• "UPH [Units per Hour] functions as an overbearing reality for many workers, who must monitor their own numbers at their work stations to ensure they can 'make rate' by the end of their shifts." (Vallas et al. 2022: 435)
	• "Magda [an Amazon sorter in Indiana] explained that her favorite part of the job is the contest it provides, which she always tries to win. 'I like my job. And for me, it is competitive. Do you understand me? I try to be on top. It's my daily goal to always be on top. To be number 1, or 2. To always be there. The more I put [out], the more I get excited about it, and I love my job more' [..]. Magda watches her co-workers during the working day and checks her own UPH [units per hour] constantly, making sure she remains at or near the top." (Vallas et al. 2022: 439)

merit-based promotions, and scheduling flexibility, as well as algorithmic termination for not meeting Amazon's demanding standards. Similarly, as the quotes in Table 6.9 illustrate, the competitive nature of working in the warehouses – which is deliberately manufactured by Amazon with the creation of games, "power hours," and competitive pay, promotions, and scheduling flexibility – puts pressure on workers to play along, self-control, and auto-gamify their own tasks.

As a whole, Amazon's control configuration has been an undeniable commercial success. For instance, Amazon's fulfillment center in Eastvale, CA, where "Amazon's cutting-edge technology, unrelenting surveillance and constant disciplinary write-ups pushed the Eastvale workers so hard that in the last holiday season, they hit a coveted target: They got a million packages out the door in 24 hours. Amazon handed out T-shirts celebrating their induction into the 'Million Unit Club.'" (Evans 2019). Across all of its US warehouses, Amazon has been able to significantly boost worker productivity. In 2016, the Institute for Local Self-Reliance found that Amazon required about half the workers a traditional retailer needs per $10 million in sales (Dzieza 2019). The high-velocity stream of data on workers and tasks further allows Amazon to continue experimenting with new ways of improving efficiency and excellence in its warehouses (Bensinger 2019).[10]

However, Amazon warehouses' control configuration also entails trade-offs and unintended consequences. Prioritizing rational goal outcomes, such as efficiency and speed, came at the expense of HR outcomes, such as individual workers' satisfaction and health. Regarding job satisfaction, while some workers appreciated the competitive nature of working in Amazon's warehouse, as evident from their comments in Table 6.9, many others considered the working conditions in Amazon's warehouses depersonalized and inhumane. They describe the atmosphere as "what I imagine a prison feels like. You felt like you were walking on eggshells" (Ghosh 2018). Many workers felt that the company treated them as if they were machines, and to satisfy Amazon's algorithms, they were forced to become machines themselves (Dzieza 2020). Sara, a warehouse worker in South Carolina, said that she worked in a legacy facility that "doesn't have robots. So we *are* the robots" (Vallas et al. 2022: 432, emphasis in original). Given this sentiment among workers, it is not surprising that many experience burnout, stress, and physical exhaustion (Gutelius & Theodore 2019; Yeginsu 2018).

Some industry observers also cautioned that the digital scrutiny and fine-grained spatial information necessary to make technologies, such as Amazon's patented wristbands, work raises questions about privacy as well as the extent of control a company should be able to exert over its workers (Gutelius &

---

[10] In 2022, Amazon "scrutinized every process path in [its] fulfillment centers […] and redesigned scores of processes and mechanisms, resulting in steady productivity gains and costs reductions over the last few quarters" (Amazon 2022: 3).

Theodore 2019). Even workers who were generally tolerant toward the abstract threat of surveillance were troubled by the potential of Amazon's algorithms to increasingly curtail their autonomy:

An Amazon worker in the Midwest described a bleak vision of the future. "We could have algorithms connected to technology that's directly on our bodies controlling how we work," he said. "Right now, the algorithm is telling a manager to yell at us. In the future, the algorithm could be telling a shock collar –" I laughed, and he quickly said he was only partly joking. After all, Amazon has patented tracking wristbands that vibrate to direct workers. (Dzieza 2020)

In addition to threats to their autonomy, Amazon workers also expressed concerns about their social isolation at work. The noise and frenetic pace of their jobs, as well as the constant turnover of the workforce, left them with few and relatively shallow connections to their co-workers. One worker admitted that he no longer bothered to learn his co-workers' names, since so many of them would be gone in a week or two, and instead, he called them "Hey you, person" (Vallas et al. 2022). Moreover, Amazon seems to embrace such a segmented and fractured workforce as it provides little basis for coalitions workers would need to build if they were to challenge managerial imperatives. By pitting workers against each other in competitive games, and openly ridiculing low-performers, Amazon can rest assured that its workers remain "[d]ivided against one another, isolated and individualized by the very design of their jobs and by divergent experiences of management's controls," and therefore, "workers are thrown back on their own devices. They cooperate with one another as their jobs require (even, our data suggest, across racial boundaries) but they fail to challenge the intensity of the demands the company places on their working lives – and their bodies" (Vallas et al. 2022: 445).

Besides these negative effects in job satisfaction, Amazon's control configuration also has a detrimental impact on worker health and safety. This impact stems from a fundamental trade-off inherent in Amazon's control configuration. While the company publicly espouses its investments in worker safety and health, and while it instructs workers on safe ways to move their bodies and handle equipment, many former workers reported that they had to break the safety rules in order to keep up or make their rates (Evans 2019). There are numerous reports, for instance, that relentlessly tracking workers' TOT (i.e., time off task, which is one of two key metric that can result in disciplinary action or even termination) has caught workers between wanting to stay hydrated and trying to avoid long treks across a giant warehouse to the bathroom (Evans 2019). This dilemma reportedly led workers to either forgo hydration, with detrimental consequences for their health and well-being; delaying trip to the restroom, with equally detrimental outcomes, such as workers being treated for repeated urinary tract infections (Evans 2023); or opting for alternative ways to relieve themselves, leading to their co-workers encountering bottles of urine on warehouse shelves (Ghosh 2018). This trade-off is likely to become even more pronounced in the future, as sophisticated surveillance algorithms can detect inefficiencies that a human manager never would – "a moment's downtime between calls, a habit of lingering at the coffee machine after finishing a task, a new route that, if all goes perfectly, could get a few more packages delivered in a day" (Dzieza 2020). In the past, these inefficiencies often provided workers with opportunities for a brief rest and recovery. But these little breaks and minor freedoms get optimized out by relentlessly optimizing algorithms, and workers jobs are becoming more intense and stressful as a consequence. An Amazon worker on the West Coast reported encountering a new device "that shines a spotlight on the item he's supposed to pick, allowing Amazon to further accelerate the rate and get rid of what the worker described as 'micro rests' stolen in the moment it took to look for the next item on the shelf" (Dzieza 2020).

Because of repeated and strenuous manual labor under ever-increasing demands, Amazon is also struggling with high and increasing injury rates among its warehouse workers. According to reports, almost 10 percent of its full-time workers sustained serious injuries in 2018, more than twice the national average for similar work (Dzieza 2020). Amazon's internal data shows that injury rates have gone up in each of the 4 years between 2016 and 2019, as – according to five former Amazon safety managers – the company's aggressive production demands have overwhelmed its safety teams' efforts to protect workers (Evans 2019). In 2019, Amazon fulfillment centers recorded 14,000 serious injuries, which are injuries that required days off or job restrictions (Evans 2020). Stress injuries, such as backaches or knee pain, are common enough for Amazon to reportedly install painkiller vending machines in its warehouses (Dzieza 2020).

Unfortunately, the more recent introduction of robots – which bring shelves of merchandise to stationary workers, instead of workers walking to obtain merchandise from stationary shelves – did not bring the promised respite from stress-induced injuries for Amazon's workers. On the contrary, the robots proved too efficient: "They could bring items so quickly that the productivity expectations for workers more than doubled, according to a former senior operations manager who saw the transformation. And they kept climbing. At the most common kind of warehouse, workers called pickers – who previously had to grab and scan about 100 items an hour – were expected to hit rates of up to 400 an hour at robotic fulfillment centers" (Evans 2020). Touted as a relief for workers, who no longer have to walk miles a day to find customer orders, it turned out that standing for 10 hours a day doing repetitive motions proved to be much harder on workers' bodies. And no longer being able to greet colleagues when moving through the facility left workers more isolated than ever at their individual workstations (Evans 2020).

In response to these unintended consequences of Amazon's efficiency-oriented control configuration, workers are increasingly confronting Amazon directly with protests and walk-outs and publicly voice their concerns about working conditions at the companies' warehouses (Dzieza 2020). Moreover, working conditions have also resulted in a wave of court cases against Amazon, and several state and federal governments have introduced legislation addressing workers' concerns. In early 2023, the state of New York, for instance, started regulating warehouse work quotas as "warehouse workers can't be forced to hit work quotas that would prevent them from taking meal and rest breaks and using the bathroom" (Evans 2023), and similar bills have been introduced in California and Minnesota.

6.5   From Traditional Work to Platform-mediated Gig Work

The final, and perhaps most profound, shift away from traditional work arrangements can be found in platform-mediated gig work. As outlined in Section 5.3.5, gig workers are not employees but work remotely for themselves. They have control over work processes, are hired on a task basis, and may work for multiple clients (or even platforms) simultaneously. By its very nature, platform-mediated gig work thus combines characteristics of all four technology-enabled organizational trends – electronic surveillance, remote work, alternative work, and algorithmic control – as well as their associated challenges for shared identities, loyalties, and norms; relaxed bounded rationality; and shifts in information asymmetries.

6.5.1   Challenges to Shared Identities, Loyalties, and Norms

In line with other forms of remote and alternative work, gig work presents a challenge to shared identities, loyalties, and norms (Burbano & Chiles 2022; Lehdonvirta 2016). Platform workers are self-employed, they do not have a common physical worksite, and there are often no managers or peers who can help generate shared identities, loyalties, and norms to control the execution of work (Gerber & Krzywdzinski 2019). Digital platforms often cultivate gig workers' identification with the work and with clients instead of their identification with the organization, thereby encouraging workers to view themselves as independent entrepreneurs (Rosenblat & Stark 2016; Veen et al. 2020). Platform workers are mostly left to control by themselves when, where, on which of the requested tasks, and how much they work. In sum, gig work does not allow for many traditional hierarchical control approaches, and challenges to shared identities, loyalties, and norms – combined with the absence of peers – make informal and peer control problematic.

Some studies have shown that it is possible to instill shared values and norms among gig workers, which decreases the occurrence of misconduct (e.g., Burbano & Chiles 2022). However, this work has also found that the positive effect of such norms is negated when workers are aware that they are also being monitored, as workers perceive the (threat of) surveillance as a lack of trust, which suggests the existence of crowding-out and substitution effects between different types of control in a gig work environment.

6.5.2   Relaxing Bounded Rationality and Shifting Information Asymmetry to Algorithms

The remote nature of gig work also creates information asymmetries for managers. This is because workers are neither directly observable nor present at designated workplaces (Burbano & Chiles 2022). As a result, gig work faces the same monitoring and coordination challenges associated with other forms of remote work. However, gig work arrangements can mitigate these challenges in two ways. First, gig work relies on algorithmic control to a much larger extent than other work arrangements (Kellogg et al. 2020). As we discussed in Chapter 5, employing algorithmic control helps mitigate managers' bounded rationality constraints and shifts information asymmetry back to digital platforms, which allows algorithmic control to unfold its monitoring, incentive, and coordination advantages. Specifically, algorithmic control can be much more comprehensive, and it allows for continuous nudging. It can further provide gig workers with direction and feedback at very high levels of granularity, personalization, and immediacy. We would expect this to result in effective behavior control, which, in turn, helps improve both incentives and coordination among platform-based gig workers. It also permits the gamification of rewards, which can enhance the incentive function of self-control and outcome control for gig workers.

Second, digital platforms outsource the control of gig workers systematically to third parties, thereby granting customers unprecedented authority to direct, monitor, and evaluate workers (Kuhn & Maleki 2017; Maffie 2022; Wood et al. 2019). In their analysis of fifteen micro- and macro-task platforms, Gerber and Krzywdzinski (2019) found that, even with all the recent progress in ML, a purely algorithmic form of outcome control is only feasible for the simplest of micro-tasks. All other tasks must be checked either by platform staff or by specifically assigned, qualified gig workers. However, the sheer number of tasks performed on digital platforms makes such human control impracticable. For this reason, digital platforms relegate control over worker performance to a complex system of digital worker surveillance as well as reviews or ratings by crowds of clients, that is, elaborate systems of third-party controls. Regarding the former, some digital platforms, especially ride-hailing and delivery platforms, display real-time tracking of gig workers to clients, allowing them to monitor workers' behavior. Regarding the latter, algorithms interpret, aggregate, and often combine client reviews with other performance metrics, such as work history or activity, and then publicly display them, providing both the workers and the market with visible feedback (Curchod et al. 2019; Faraj et al. 2018; Kuhn & Maleki 2017). Digital platforms therefore create public reputations and rankings among gig workers. These reputations help platforms allocate workers by stratifying them based on their experience and past performance, algorithmically filtering more tasks toward the highest-ranked gig workers, and limiting low-performing workers' access to tasks – or even rapidly and automatically firing underperforming workers and replacing them with substitute workers – thereby serving as a form of algorithmic input control (Kellogg et al. 2020; Veen et al. 2020; Wood et al. 2019). Third-party ratings also signal which workers need to be monitored by platform staff and how often, allowing for more efficient managerial behavior control. Since platform workers' reputations and rankings can influence their ability to secure gigs, workers tend to internalize the evaluation criteria and change their behavior to conform to those standards (Rahman 2021), thereby engaging in self-control. Last, reputations and rankings serve as outcome controls (i.e., they reward performance), which further entice gig workers to self-discipline as they strive for high scores in a gamified environment (Gerber & Krzywdzinski 2019).

There are downsides to such third-party control, however. Client surveillance of real-time worker movement becomes problematic, for instance, when there are glitches in geo-location technologies or when gig workers are given multiple tasks to complete, which may appear as erratic or lazy behavior to unaware clients (Newlands 2021). Moreover, on many platforms, clients are largely ignorant of how their ratings affect gig workers' platform visibility and scores (Rahman 2021). This limited knowledge that clients have about their role in influencing gig workers' platform success stands in stark contrast to the central and knowledgeable role that managers have in evaluating workers in traditional organizations. As a result of the shift in control to clients, and to managers' monitoring of worker-client interactions, digital platform workers have to negotiate their performance informally with clients. To avoid being sanctioned or excluded from future jobs by the algorithm, workers engage in compensatory practices, such as staying under the radar, undervaluing their work, purposely curtailing client outreach, and keeping their emotions in check (Bucher et al. 2021a). Such a system can have detrimental effects on workers' motivation and may lead them to engage in active countermeasures, such as gaming strategies, limiting or censoring their participation, or using political resources to alter the basis for their evaluation (Faraj et al. 2018). Many digital platforms have seen their workers turn to such algorithmic activism (Bronowicka & Ivanova 2020), which is not restricted to individual workers exploiting technological vulnerabilities. Instead, it often leads to collective activism by workers jointly guessing the rules of the game and sharing new ways to break or suspend the algorithmic rule in online forums dedicated to digital platforms.

Digital platforms are further unable to control workers' gaming attempts through traditional (hierarchical) control, because digital platforms insist that they do not technically employ workers, but merely serve as brokers between clients and independent contractors or freelancers. Instead, digital platforms resort to opacity to exert influence over workers and prevent gaming attempts (Rahman 2021; Veen et al. 2020). However, platforms' attempts to reign in workers' inclinations to game the system by making rating algorithms intentionally opaque come with their own challenges. The complexity and opacity of reputation-based systems can lead to misperceptions – workers often know very little about how rankings are derived, limiting their ability to learn from any feedback – and make these systems appear unpredictable and arbitrary to workers (Rahman 2021). Such misperceptions, lack of constructive feedback, and negative attitudes toward digital rankings are likely to undermine the incentive and coordination functions of such third-party control systems, thereby jeopardizing their effectiveness.

In sum, digital platforms create a novel form of information and power asymmetry, in which "control is radically distributed, whilst power remains centralized" (Kornberger et al. 2017: 79). In effect, platforms form a coalition of interest with an invisible crowd of largely anonymous clients (Orlikowski & Scott 2015). Workers find themselves simultaneously accountable to platform algorithms, which have the power to impose conditions and sanctions, and to clients, who have the power to post negative reviews and comments online (Curchod et al. 2019). However, there is no guarantee that the goals of the algorithm and the goals of the platform's clients are congruent. In fact, clients on work-for-hire platforms, such as Freelancer, may be interested in establishing long-term relationships with high-performing workers, whereas some platforms may incentivize their workers to continuously acquire new clients to maintain their high ratings on the platform (Bucher et al. 2021a). These goal incongruencies pose additional challenges to the effectiveness of this new form of organizational control.

6.5.3   Case Study: Uber

Perhaps the best-known example of a large, platform-mediated gig workforce is Uber. Uber Technologies Inc.'s ride-hailing platform was founded in 2009. By the end of 2022, Uber had approximately 32,800 employees, operated in more than 10,500 cities and around 70 countries, and connected 131 million monthly active platform clients (i.e., riders) with more than five million drivers to complete 7.6 billion trips in that year (Uber 2022). In 2023, Uber commands almost three quarters of the US ride-hailing market, up from 62 percent in early 2020 (Rana 2023b). To keep its labor costs and obligations low, Uber refers to its drivers as "driver-partners," thereby deliberately disassociating the company from an employer–employee relationship (Rosenblat 2016). Instead of their driver-partners receiving a salary, Uber frames its business model as drivers paying a licensing fee or commission for the right to use Uber's proprietary digital platform that connects them with paying riders (Rosenblat & Stark 2016).

Our discussion of Uber's control configuration will focus on the five million Uber drivers. These are alternative workers (i.e., independent contractors) who complete gig work mediated by a digital platform, and who are managed almost exclusively via algorithms, with little to no contact with human managers or their fellow drivers (Manriquez 2019). Uber drivers tend to be diverse regarding education, background, and motivation for driving part-time or full-time for the company. In the United Kingdom, for instance, a study found that most drivers were male immigrants primarily drawn from the bottom half of the income distribution (Berger et al. 2018), whereas drivers in the United States are, in terms of age and education, more similar to the general workforce than to taxi drivers and chauffeurs (Hall & Krueger 2018). Some drivers continue to hold a professional job and drive for Uber out of curiosity or to supplement their income; others rely solely on the income they generate by driving for Uber; and yet others drive for Uber while in transition to another job (Lee et al. 2015; Manriquez 2019).

Algorithms mediate every step of Uber's service delivery. Once drivers switch on Uber's ridesharing app, a proprietary proximity-based algorithm automatically matches them with ride requests, and drivers have up to 15 seconds to accept a request. The request includes information about a potential rider's location, rating, picture, and name, but not the rider's destination. If the driver accepts the request, the rider receives a notification, and the driver heads to the rider's location to start the ride. Pricing is determined by a standard fare and fluctuates according to a dynamic pricing algorithm. At the end of the ride, both rider and driver rate each other using a five-star scale, which is algorithmically aggregated and analyzed (Lee et al. 2015). Taking humans out of the loop allows a few human managers in each city to oversee Uber's millions of drivers at a global scale (Lee et al. 2015). Figure 6.4 presents Uber's control configuration, with its associated illustrative quotes in Table 6.10, and its associated heat map in Table 6.11.

Discussion. Like the US Trucking Cos. case discussed earlier, Uber's control over its five million drivers is challenged by the remote nature of the job, which would have traditionally resulted in information asymmetries in drivers' favor. To address this challenge, Uber's control configuration is organized around five core themes: Comprehensive electronic surveillance,

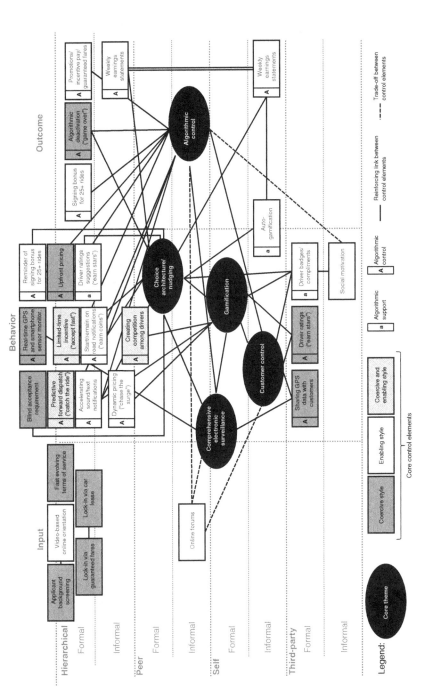

Figure 6.4 Uber's control configuration

Table 6.10 *Uber's control configuration heat map*

Control dimension	Target			Formality		Direction				Style		Controller	
Control element	I	B	O	F	I	H	P	S	T	C	E	H	A
Applicant background screening	X			X		X				X		X	
Video-based online orientation	X			X		X				X		X	
Fast evolving terms of service	X			X		X				X		X	
Lock-in via guaranteed fares	X			X	x	X				X		X	
Lock-in via car lease	X			X	x	X				X		X	
Online forums	X				X		X					X	
Blind acceptance requirement		X		X		X				X			X
Real-time GPS and smartphone sensor monitoring		X		X		X				X			X
Reminder of signing bonus for 25+ rides		X		X		X					X		X
Predictive forward dispatch ("catch the ride")		X		X		X					X		X
Limited-time incentive ("accept fast")		X		X		X					X		X
Upfront pricing		X		X		X							X
Accelerating sound/text notifications		X		X		X				X			X
Start/remain on road notifications ("earn coins")		X		X		X				X			X
Driver ratings suggestions ("earn stars")		X		x		X				X			x
Dynamic pricing ("chase the surge")		X			X			X			X		X
Creating competition among drivers		X			X		x			X			X
Auto-gamification		X	X						X	X		x	x
Sharing GPS data with customers		X	X	X		X			X			X	
Driver ratings ("earn stars")		X	X	X		X			X	X		X	
Driver badges/compliments		X	X	X		X			X	X		X	x
Social motivation		X	X		X			X			X		X
Signing bonus for 25+ rides		X	X	X		X					X		X
Algorithmic deactivation ("game over")			X	X		X				X			X
Promotions/incentive pay/guaranteed fares			X	X	X	X					X		X
Weekly earnings statements			X		X	X		X			X		X

Legend: Columns from left to right: target (I = input, B = behavior, O = outcome); formality (F = formal, I = informal); direction (H = hierarchical, P = peer, S = self, T = third-party); style (C = coercive, E = enabling); controller (H = human, A = algorithm); X = heavy focus on this control dimension; x = partial focus on this control dimension; empty cell = no focus on this control dimension

Table 6.11 *Illustrative quotes for elements in Uber's control configuration*

Control element	Exemplary quote(s)
Input control	
Applicant background screening	• "Anyone over 21 years of age with a valid drivers license and a personal vehicle in good condition can apply to be a driver. Companies screen applicants with a background check." (Lee et al. 2015: 1604)
Video-based online orientation	• "new drivers go through brief video-based online orientations." (Lee et al. 2015: 1604)
Fast-evolving terms of service	• "Drivers must perennially agree to new terms of service in order to log in to work – akin to signing a new employee manual every few days. [...] these forces leave drivers at a clear disadvantage. Drivers may not even have a record of the specific terms governing a particular period of time, let alone a clearly legible record of their transactions." (Calo & Rosenblat 2017: 1661)
	• "While Uber drivers use the system, they may be offered a plethora of temporary contracts around price and other factors, and they are perennially forced to agree to new terms of service such as new commission structures, when they log in to work. [...] Uber stands to profit from the inability of the driver to keep up with both the dizzying complexity of such documents and their high rate of change." (Calo & Rosenblat 2017: 1630)
Lock-in via guaranteed fares	• "guaranteed fare programs where drivers earn an hourly rate during set periods provided they meet objectives such as accepting a minimum proportion of ride requests, work for a minimum period, and complete a minimum number of trips [...] can hinder a driver's ability to accept jobs from competitors." (Cram & Wiener 2020: 4)
Lock-in via car lease	• "While Uber drivers own the vehicle and smartphones with the required GPS, in some instances Uber provides these phones and assists drivers in securing leases for vehicles." (Lobel 2016: 133)
	• "Uber has created a leasing program in an effort to accelerate its growth by more quickly adding drivers to the app. Uber has set up a subsidiary, Xchange Leasing, to lease cars directly to drivers." (Los Angeles Daily News 2015)
	• "Some of Uber's recent expansion has come from facilitating auto loans for drivers who will struggle to repay them. The payments are auto-deducted from the drivers' Uber earnings, a move that locks these drivers into their platform while further fostering a culture of control rather than community." (Sundararajan 2014)
Online forums	• "Unlike traditional taxi drivers, who seem to have more opportunities to socialize at designated taxi stations and talk directly to employees at their taxi dispatch firm, the Uber drivers we interviewed typically did not know any other Uber employees." (Möhlmann et al. 2021: 2012)

Table 6.11 (cont.)

Control element	Exemplary quote(s)
	• "Drivers have little direct contact with company representatives, but can interact with each other through online forums to gain social knowledge of the rideshare systems." (Lee et al. 2015: 1603)
	• "Although drivers stated that they cherish their self-identity as independent workers, they also consider it important to be part of a broader community of drivers. Many reported trying to compensate for the lack of membership of the Uber company through engagement in informal communities of Uber drivers in online forums [...] The algorithmic 'black box' seems to motivate drivers to join global online communities like UberPeople.net or social media groups to exchange thoughts and insights into how algorithms work and how to optimize behavior to get the most out of them." (Möhlmann et al. 2021: 2012)
	• "As drivers worked independently in distributed locations, online driver forums became a primary avenue for the driver socialization and system sensemaking. Drivers discussed the workings of the ridesharing systems' algorithmic management. One of the successful online sensemaking examples was about improving and maintaining driver performance in ratings and acceptance rate." (Lee et al. 2015: 1609)
Behavior control	
Blind acceptance requirement	• "Uber has a policy of blind ride acceptance, such that the driver does not know the destination of the passenger (and hence, the remunerative value of the trip) before she accepts it. This practice is touted as a means to ensure system efficiency and prohibit destination-based discrimination." (Calo & Rosenblat 2017: 1661)
Real-time GPS and smartphone sensor monitoring	• "Uber is to start tracking its drivers through the phones that they have in their car. The company will start watching the drivers through the sensors embedded in their phones to ensure that they are driving safely, it has said. The new system will use the gyrometers, GPS and accelerometers in drivers' phones to check in on what they are up to. It will then be able to know whether they are driving too fast or if they are given to braking too hard, for instance." (Griffin 2016)
	• "drivers in at least nine US cities including New York, Los Angeles and Chicago will be shown a summary of how smooth their driving was for each trip, including separate scores for acceleration and braking and a map highlighting the physical location of each incident. Any time drivers go over the speed limit, Uber will alert them within its app in real time. In different groups of test cities, Uber will also use the gyroscope inside drivers' phones to detect when they move or touch the device to, for example, compose a text while driving." (MacMillan 2016)
	• "When drivers log into the Uber app, every move is tracked, and detailed information is collected and analyzed in real time using the platform's learning algorithms." (Möhlmann et al. 2021: 2007)

Reminder of signing bonus for 25+ rides	• "Uber was increasingly concerned that many new drivers were leaving the platform before completing the 25 rides that would earn them a signing bonus. To stem that tide, Uber officials in some cities began experimenting with simple encouragement: You're almost halfway there, congratulations! While the experiment seemed warm and innocuous, it had in fact been exquisitely calibrated. The company's data scientists had previously discovered that once drivers reached the 25-ride threshold, their rate of attrition fell sharply." (Scheiber 2017)
Predictive forward dispatch ("catch the ride")	• "an algorithm called forward dispatch [...] dispatches a new ride to a driver before the current one ends. Forward dispatch shortens waiting times for passengers, who may no longer have to wait for a driver 10 minutes away when a second driver is dropping off a passenger two minutes away. Perhaps no less important, forward dispatch causes drivers to stay on the road substantially longer during busy periods – a key goal for [Uber]." (Scheiber 2017) • "an algorithm similar to a Netflix feature that automatically loads the next program, which many experts believe encourages binge-watching. In Uber's case, this means sending drivers their next fare opportunity before their current ride is even over. And most of this happens without giving off a whiff of coercion." (Scheiber 2017)
Limited-time incentive ("accept fast")	• "The driver has 30 seconds to accept or decline the ride in case of rejection, the ride is passed to another nearby driver. This limited-time incentive [...] prompted the drivers to click 'accept ride' fast enough as to secure the ride." (Manriquez 2019: 174)
Upfront pricing	• "the provision of information such as upfront pricing [...] encouraging drivers to take shorter routes." (Möhlmann et al. 2021: 2008)
Accelerating sound/ text notifications	• "Using various design techniques [such as] heat-wave maps of consumer demand, alluring visuals, and accelerating sound notifications, Uber replicates an individualized video-game experience" (Manriquez 2019: 173)
Start/remain on road notifications ("earn coins")	• "Uber also nudges offline drivers to work at certain times or in certain locations through various incentives and messaging. The result can be tantamount to shift work, although drivers are encouraged rather than scheduled to work at those times." (Rosenblat 2016) • "leveraging gamification strategies as a key mechanism to 'nudge' its drivers (e.g., 'Are you sure you want to go offline? Demand is very high in your area. Make more money, don't stop now')" (Cram & Wiener 2020: 4) • "Uber drivers become engrossed in the game of *earning coins*: that is in finding strategies to earn the most possible revenue when they logged-in into the application. [...] The absorbing game of *earning coins* – which was suggested by Uber and then further developed by the drivers – was successful in coupling the interest of Uber in maintaining a readily available labor supply with the interest of drivers in generating an adequate revenue in a non-fixed salary working arrangement." (Manriquez 2019: 173, 187; emphases in original) • "when drivers tried to log out, the app would frequently tell them they were only a certain amount away from making a seemingly arbitrary sum for the day, or from matching their earnings from that point one week earlier. The messages were intended to exploit another relatively widespread behavioral tic – people's preoccupation with goals – to nudge them into driving longer." (Scheiber 2017)

Table 6.11 (*cont.*)

Control element	Exemplary quote(s)
Driver ratings suggestions ("earn stars")	• "Uber also uses the ratings system to give drivers suggestions that are easily interpreted as requirements. For instance, one 'tips for how to improve' list from Uber notes, 'Riders give the best ratings to drivers who: Never ask for a 5-star review, but instead focus on providing an excellent experience; stay calm, patient, and polite with riders on the road; and go above and beyond to make the experience special, such as opening doors for riders when possible.'" (Kessler 2016)
Dynamic pricing ("chase the surge")	• "Uber's surge pricing model […] goes into effect when demand (passengers) outstrips supply (drivers) by a particular threshold. Visible to both riders and drivers, the creation of such surge pricing zones is billed as a means to ensure positive customer experience by enticing drivers to get on the road, although there is some evidence that it merely redistributes existing supply into high-demand areas. Drivers are alerted to surging zones through a heat map visualization, which shows where demand and fares will temporarily rise, by a magnitude that could range from 1.5x to 9.5x. Drivers are prompted by Uber's alerts to go online, or to keep driving (even as they click the 'log off' button) to get fares that are increased by the surge multiplier for a given region. Some drivers referred to surge as a 'herding tool' that ushered them into specific geofences. They receive emails and texts that predict high demand (which indicates 'surge will happen' to drivers) in advance." (Rosenblat 2016)
	• "Around 21% of UberX sessions in our dataset have some surge price exceeding 1.0x." (Cohen et al. 2016)
	• "Uber's surge pricing also operates to increase supply: more drivers turn on their Uber app when they see that the rates have increased. Uber reports that supply of drivers increases by seventy to eighty percent when surge pricing is introduced, and more importantly, it eliminates two-thirds of unfulfilled requests, which demonstrates the magic of the platform economy: supply, as well as demand, is highly elastic. This is a fundamentally responsive market-perfecting model." (Lobel 2016: 123)
	• "It was all day long, every day – texts, emails, pop-ups: 'Hey, the morning rush has started. Get to this area, that's where demand is biggest,' said Ed Frantzen, a veteran Uber driver in the Chicago area. 'It was always, constantly, trying to get you into a certain direction.' Some local managers who were men so far as to adopt a female persona for texting drivers, having found that the uptake was higher when they did. 'Laura' would tell drivers: 'Hey, the concert's about to let out. You should head over there,' said John P. Parker, a manager in Uber's Dallas office in 2014 and 2015, referring to one of the personas. 'We have an overwhelmingly male driver population.' Uber acknowledged that it had experimented with female personas to increase engagement with drivers." (Scheiber 2017)
	• "Sometimes Uber sends drivers notifications about where and when it predicts there will be high demand, such as, 'We also want to remind you that we predict New Year's Eve will be the busiest night of the year. With such high demand, it will be a great night to go out and drive!'" (Kessler 2016)
	• "this is effectively a way for Uber to schedule shifts." (Kessler 2016)
Creating competition among drivers	• "leveraging gamification strategies as a key mechanism […] to create competition among [drivers] (e.g., 'Unfortunately, your driver rating last week was below average.')." (Cram & Wiener 2020: 4)

Auto-gamification	"when workers can identify an objective to 'win' at the game, compare current performance to past performance, and access information on where they stand, they are likely to auto-gamify their work. [...] even in the absence of nudges and notifications that Uber and other digital platforms might send workers to encourage them to work faster, simply sharing quantitative performance data might lead workers to create individual auto-games that affect productivity and produce consent to work." (Ranganathan & Benson 2020: 600)
	"drivers developed strategies to mold their daily working routines in the application to minimize wasting time, and be able to accept rides at all possible moments." (Manriquez 2019: 174)
	"The digital platform and its underlying algorithms direct individual workers on which rides to take and what route to follow but does not provide much support on how to find purpose in the work beyond the task of driving. Instead, workers rely on interactions with touchpoints – in this context, the customer and the app – to derive their own meaning at work, either by building connections with customers (the relational game) or by earning as much as possible (the efficiency game)." (Cameron 2022: 246)
	"In the relational game, the primary goal of drivers was to create connections with customers and provide good customer service. To meet this goal, drivers managed customers by curating positive service encounters. What drivers classified as a 'win' in the relational game overlapped with [the company]'s goal of customer satisfaction, such that the digital platform supported the relational game. Ratings, compliments, and badges provided workers with feedback, confirming that their efforts were valued and that they were, indeed, 'winning.'" (Cameron 2022: 241)
	"In the efficiency game, the goal of drivers was to complete their rides as quickly as possible, ideally at the highest fare. To do so, drivers managed customers by depersonalizing the service encounter, minimizing conversation, and not offering additional services, such as carrying bags." (Cameron 2022: 244)
Sharing GPS data with customers	"In the efficiency game, [drivers] create their own tracking tools outside the app." (Cameron 2022: 231)
Driver ratings ("earn stars")	"Technology allows for a variety of real-time monitoring. Uber and Lyft allow users to see the GPS path and monitor the driver-chosen route. These types of systemic controls align incentives on both ends of the deal." (Lobel 2016: 153)
	"part of the surveillance component of the managerial structure is outsourced to consumers, which in addition serves to redirect concerns arising in the worksite to consumers, rather than to a management figure." (Manriquez 2019: 178)
	"[Customer] feedback generates instantaneous and recurrent performance evaluations that allow Uber to track worker performance and intervene with poor performers." (Rosenblat 2016)
	"passengers are empowered to act as middle managers over drivers, whose ratings directly impact their employment eligibility." (Rosenblat & Stark 2016: 3772).
Driver badges/ compliments	"Like players on video game platforms such as Xbox, PlayStation and Pogo, Uber drivers can earn badges for achievements like Above and Beyond (denoted on the app by a cartoon of a rocket blasting off), Excellent Service (marked by a picture of a sparkling diamond) and Entertaining Drive (a pair of Groucho Marx glasses with nose and eyebrows)." (Scheiber 2017)
	"Uber has experimented with [....] noncash rewards of little value that can prod drivers into working longer and harder – and sometimes at hours and locations that are less lucrative for them." (Scheiber 2017)

Social motivation	"many drivers we interviewed mentioned social motivations for rideshare driving. Several drivers, for example, weighed the fun of meeting and having conversations with new people and the desire to help out the community as greater than or equal to their motivation to earn extra income." (Lee et al. 2015: 1606)
	"several of our interviewees believe that driving for Uber and Lyft provides important public services. Given that much of this driving – especially in the college-student-heavy environment of Pittsburgh – takes place around bar time, these drivers take satisfaction from the fact that they are giving rides to people who might otherwise drive drunk." (Malin & Chandler 2017: 390)
Outcome control	
Signing bonus for 25+ rides	"[Uber] provides signing bonuses to new drivers that meet preliminary ride targets (e.g., complete 25 rides) (Scheiber 2017). The company introduced this intervention [...] in response to growing concerns about new drivers leaving the platform." (Cram & Wiener 2020: 4)
Algorithmic deactivation ("game over")	"Uber's three main performance metrics are the driver's rating, how many rides the driver accepts, and how many times they cancel a ride. Generally, Uber requires drivers to maintain a high ride acceptance rate, such as 80% or 90%, and a low cancellation rate, such as 5% in San Francisco (as of July 2015), or they risk deactivation (temporary suspension or permanent firing) from the platform." (Rosenblat 2016)
	"Drivers engaged in several strategies to ensure that they maintained an adequate star average in order to maintain *earning coins*, for if they fell in their average it was *game-over* for them." (Manriquez 2019: 176; emphases in original)
	"Drivers with a low average passenger rating and acceptance rate may be subject to review or even immediate deactivation on the ridesharing platform." (Lee et al. 2015: 1605)
Promotions/ incentive pay/ guaranteed fares	"Drivers are encouraged to keep a high ride acceptance rate through occasional promotions that offer a guaranteed hourly pay if the driver's acceptance rate is above a certain threshold." (Lee et al. 2015: 1605)
	"incentive pay offers drivers a premium to drive when and where demand is high and gives hourly guarantees that provide drivers an hourly rate, such as $22 or $40 per hour for a given shift, if they meet specific criteria during the guarantee period(s). Uber does not disclose the criteria by which select drivers are invited to participate in guarantees, which vary frequently." (Calo & Rosenblat 2017: 1664)
	"Uber also offers guaranteed fare programs where drivers earn an hourly rate during set periods provided they meet objectives such as accepting a minimum proportion of ride requests, work for a minimum period, and complete a minimum number of trips." (Cram & Wiener 2020: 4)
	"Long-standing drivers who maintain a high passenger rating and acceptance rate are occasionally promoted to become mentors or recruiters. In addition to driving for the service, mentors and recruiters recruit new drivers and oversee the application process, while earning extra income for these activities." (Lee et al. 2015: 1605)
Weekly earnings statements	"Uber also nudges drivers with information about their weekly earnings and costs." (Uzunca & Kas 2023: 674)

algorithmic control, choice architecture/nudging, customer control, and gamification. First, as soon as drivers log into the app, their every move is tracked via their phone's GPS, a host of other granular data is extracted from their phone's sensors (e.g., speed, acceleration, breaking, texting/calling while driving, etc.), aggregated across millions of drivers and billions of trips, and scrutinized in real time by big data analytics and ML algorithms. Such extensive electronic surveillance not only shifts information asymmetry back in favor of the company, but it also supplies the data underlying Uber's predictive analytics and ML. Second, many elements in Uber's control configuration are managed entirely by algorithms, with human managers largely out of the loop. Algorithmic control allows Uber to automatically enforce sanctions if drivers deviate from the algorithm's instructions or even ban drivers from the platform. Third, with the help of hundreds of social scientists and data scientists on its payroll (Scheiber 2017), Uber has created, and is constantly experimenting with and refining, a choice architecture, and keeps nudging drivers in real time toward the company's preferred outcomes. This often happens in a very subtle way, without drivers noticing that they are being manipulated to exhibit behaviors – such as working longer and harder, and sometimes accepting less lucrative rides and locations – that may not be in their own best interest. In sum, Uber managers are "using what they know about drivers, their control over the interface and the terms of transaction to channel the behavior of the driver in the direction they want it to go" (Scheiber 2017). Fourth, by holding drivers accountable to riders' evaluations, Uber further outsources part of its driver oversight to customers. And fifth, by combining complementary elements from these four core themes, Uber intentionally gamifies its driver experience.

It is evident from Figure 6.4 that Uber's control configuration is characterized by ample causal complexity, and complementary relationships between elements abound. At the core theme level, for instance, Uber's comprehensive electronic surveillance and customer ratings provide the data – both granular data on individual drivers and riders and big data aggregated across drivers and trips – that forms the backdrop for Uber's algorithmic control, choice architecture/nudging, and gamification. Many of the underlying elements also reinforce each other. For instance, elements such as predictive forward dispatch (nudging drivers to play "catch the ride"), limited-time incentives (nudging drivers to quickly accept new ride requests), dynamic pricing (nudging drivers to "chase the surge"), accelerating sound/text notifications (signaling increasing urgency to drivers), nudging drivers to start driving/remain on the road (to "earn coins") and to provide excellent customer experience (to "earn stars"), and creating competition among drivers are all designed to create a game-like atmosphere for drivers that keeps them engaged and nudges them in the direction favored by the platform. By selectively sharing comparative performance data with drivers, Uber also sets the stage for drivers engaging in auto-gamification by setting short- and mid-term goals for themselves.

While this control configuration has become the backbone of Uber's rapid growth and recent commercial success,[11] it also suffers from a number of inherent trade-offs and unintended consequences. In general, despite Uber's extensive investments in – and continuous recalibration of – its monitoring, incentives, and coordination functions, a fundamental conflict of interest remains that puts the platform and its drivers at odds with each other. While drivers generally focus their efforts on maximizing their earnings per hour, the platform's primary interest is in minimizing its customers' wait times (Scheiber 2017). The platform achieves this by incentivizing and nudging as many drivers as possible to get or stay on the road and head to areas of prospective demand, for instance, with predictive forward dispatches and surge pricing. However, drivers only get paid for rides that they complete, not for the time they spend looking for new rides, so having fewer fellow drivers on the road is better for them, as that means less idle time between rides (Singal 2017; Uzunca & Kas 2023). In other words, Uber expects its drivers to absorb the costs of being available and responsive to the platform without being guaranteed paid work (Rosenblat & Stark 2016). It comes as no surprise, then, that many drivers distrust Uber's attempts at nudging them and report feeling manipulated by the platform (Calo & Rosenblat 2017; Cram & Wiener 2020). Online forum posts by experienced drivers often advise other drivers to not chase the surge (Rosenblat 2016), and more than half of interviewed drivers reported that they were not influenced by what they perceived as fickle surge pricing information (Lee et al. 2015), undermining its effectiveness as a control.

Moreover, taking humans out of the loop in most of Uber's control elements has the advantages of greater reliability and scalability. On the flipside, however, it also creates the perception that the system runs itself, with many drivers referring to the algorithm as "the boss" (Möhlmann & Henfridsson 2019). With no human managers to support them, no human authority to appeal to in case of (perceived or real) unfair treatment by the algorithm, and no peers to commiserate in person, many drivers report feeling lonely, isolated, and dehumanized (Möhlmann & Henfridsson 2019; Rosenblat & Stark 2016). Comprehensive electronic surveillance and coercive algorithmic control further signal Uber's lack of trust in its own drivers, and the gamification of driver experience and outcome-based rewards and punishments tend to crowd out drivers' intrinsic and social motivations stemming from providing a public service (Lee et al. 2015; Malin & Chandler 2017).

---

[11] In the second quarter of 2023, Uber posted its first-ever operating profit since its 2009 founding (Rana 2023a).

Another trade-off inherent in Uber's control configuration stems from the deliberate opacity of many of Uber's controls. As is increasingly typical for algorithmic controls, the platform is intentionally creating new information asymmetries to stymie drivers' attempts at manipulating or gaming its algorithms (Chan & Humphreys 2018; Cram & Wiener 2020; Rosenblat & Stark 2016). If control algorithms are no longer transparent for drivers, however, they also lose part of their incentive and coordination function. An example that is particularly frustrating for drivers is Uber's reliance on customer ratings. In theory, the existence of such third-party ratings would incentivize drivers to create a good customer experience, thereby aligning customers' and drivers' goals. In practice, however, customer ratings remain unpredictable for drivers. It remains unclear what the cut-off point for drivers is before they are at risk of being dropped from the platform, and many circumstances, such as weather and traffic, are beyond drivers' control (Lee et al. 2015; Möhlmann et al. 2021). Customer ratings can unfairly penalize drivers for refusing customer demands that conflict with stated policies, such as customers demanding that drivers violate the speed limit (Riesman 2014), insisting on squeezing more people in the backseat of the car than legally permissible, or refusing to leave behind open alcohol containers (Raval & Dourish 2016). Also, passengers are generally unaware of the importance of receiving 5-star ratings for drivers to merely remain on the platform and often presume that four out of five stars is a good rating, but such a rating is actually a failing grade, resulting in drivers becoming at risk of being dropped from the platform (Rosenblat 2016; Rosenblat & Stark 2016; Uzunca & Kas 2023). Besides undermining its effectiveness as an incentive and coordination mechanism, the unpredictability of Uber's algorithmic controls, such as customer ratings, leads to driver frustration, distrust, and perceptions of unfairness,[12] and may ultimately result in frustrated drivers ignoring or manipulating[13] these controls, or even leaving the platform altogether. The

---

[12] Some researchers have argued that Uber's rating system allows customers to directly assert their preferences and biases in ways that companies are prohibited by law from doing. Such passenger-sourced discrimination may lead to lower ratings for drivers from protected classes, resulting in lower pay, and leaving them more vulnerable to termination by the platform (Calo & Rosenblat 2017).

[13] Common ways for drivers to manipulate the platform's algorithms – often promulgated by online forums – are to deactivate their GPS to avoid punishment for rejecting unprofitable rides (Bronowicka & Ivanova 2020; Möhlmann et al. 2021); only accepting rides that are close, as having to wait for a ride tends to negatively affect driver ratings, and declining riders with low customer ratings who are less likely to tip drivers (Chan & Humphreys 2018); arranging rides via phone, and then asking passengers to request a ride once they were in the driver's car to get matched (Lee et al. 2015); and parking in-between other ridesharing cars in order to not get any requests while taking a break, while leaving the driver app on to still benefit from an hourly payment promotion (Lee et al. 2015). More recently, drivers were reported to game Uber's system collectively by artificially causing surge pricing (Möhlmann & Henfridsson 2019).

question remains whether drivers will remain committed to an organization in which they feel constantly disadvantaged (Cameron 2022). According to Uber's own data, past retention rates were poor, with slightly more than half of drivers onboarded in 2013 remaining active on the platform a little over a year later (Hall & Krueger 2018). More recently, after the economy reopened in 2021, the platform was facing a debilitating driver shortage and had to make a number of changes that drivers had long been advocating for, in addition to offering substantial bonuses (Rana 2022, 2023b).

In sum, Uber's extensive attempts to control, nudge, and gamify tend to lose their effectiveness for incentivizing and coordinating their drivers over time, suggesting a temporal trade-off inherent in its algorithmic controls. But even when Uber's control attempts are working, many are inscrutable to drivers, offer no option for drivers to opt out, and often force or nudge them in a direction that is contrary to their own interests,[14] which qualifies these nudges as evil nudges (Uzunca & Kas 2023). By allowing few, if any, interactions between human managers and drivers, and by strategically restricting information accessible to drivers, Uber's control configuration is further symptomatic of the diminishing role of enabling control and the increasing reliance on coercive controls in digital platform businesses (Cram & Wiener 2020). As described in Section 4.1.5, this shift trades conformity and consistency for transparency, worker empowerment, and workers' motivation to perform their assigned tasks more efficiently and effectively (Adler & Borys 1996).

While Uber's control configuration suggests the platform's implicit acceptance of these trade-offs, studies of Uber's and other digital platform business models have suggested several ways to mitigate or even resolve at least some of these trade-offs and unintended consequences. First, researchers have argued that transparency could elicit greater motivation and cooperation with task assignments, especially undesirable ones. For instance, providing an explanation for – and allowing drivers to ask questions about – Uber's matching algorithm could improve drivers' trust in its recommendations and reduce their rejection of distant ride requests they commonly attribute to technical glitches (Lee et al. 2015). More recently, to stem a critical shortage of drivers after the US economy reopened after the COVID-19 pandemic, Uber started providing additional information for drivers, such as disclosing drop-off locations and expected earnings (Rana 2023b), or even allowing drivers to choose

---

[14] Reports have described drivers feeling overloaded by the daily flood of messages and notifications coming from the app (Cram & Wiener 2020), manipulated by the bait-and-switch nature of the surge pricing algorithm (Calo & Rosenblat 2017), and propelled into a similar emotional space as gambling by Uber's algorithms (Rosenblat & Stark 2016). Some drivers described feelings of addiction to clicking the "accept ride" button (Manriquez 2019) and spent over 100 hours per week on the app, influenced by the platform's nudging mechanisms (Scheiber 2017).

from a list of potential trips (Rana 2022). These transparency improvements allow drivers to make a more informed choice when accepting a trip, but they could also lead to drivers cherry-picking rides or avoiding certain neighborhoods, undermining Uber's goal of minimizing riders' wait times.

Second, Uber could take additional steps to increase the predictability and fairness of its control algorithms. For instance, they could protect their drivers from unfair customer ratings and complaints by providing an in-app timer to accurately measure the time drivers were supposed to wait for customers before being able to leave and collect their cancellation fee (Cutolo & Kenney 2021), or by adding video-recording features to its app as a safety measure, and to help adjudicating disputes between drivers and riders (Rana 2023b).

Third, the same data Uber is using to nudge drivers and gamify their experience could be harnessed for a more customized approach to control. For example, the real-time data Uber collects on braking, acceleration, and other driving patterns could be used to nudge a particular driver to take a needed break (Scheiber 2017). Uber's granular data on individual drivers could also be tapped to cater to a more diverse type of motivation, such as amplifying drivers' altruistic or social motivations by awarding them badges for being good conversationalists (Cameron 2022).

A fourth way to mitigate trade-offs and unintended consequences, and one often requested by interviewed drivers, would be to put human managers back in the loop. Contextually aware managers could help explain the rationale behind – and thereby rebuild trust in – Uber's algorithmic control system, solicit feedback from drivers to help further improve the system, help resolve disputes between drivers and riders, and, more generally, provide a human element and a social connection for drivers, making them feel less like they are being treated like machines (Möhlmann & Henfridsson 2019; Rosenblat & Stark 2016).

And last, Uber's control configuration could benefit from emulating elements of Airbnb's "platform culture" (Sundararajan 2014). In the past, Uber has created an intentional buffer between the platform and its drivers, thereby making the development of shared identities, loyalties, and norms all but impossible. The US-headquartered home-sharing platform Airbnb, in contrast, has invested heavily in creating community and a sense of partnership among hosts, by organizing conventions and meet-ups for hosts to exchange best practices, and by facilitating online host groups for knowledge exchanges. Such efforts helped Airbnb instill shared norms, values, and capabilities among hosts, much like in a traditional organizational culture. While industry differences may have facilitated Airbnb's platform culture, the platform culture of Uber's biggest competitor, Lyft, appears much closer to Airbnb's (Sundararajan 2014), providing proof of concept for the possibility of creating a platform culture in the ride-hailing industry.

6.5.4   Case Study: Upwork

In contrast to Uber's relatively low skill requirements, our next case study represents a digital platform for highly skilled workers. Upwork is a US-headquartered digital labor platform[15] that serves as an intermediary between freelance workers – such as programmers, graphic designers, or copywriters – and clients on a global scale (Waldkirch et al. 2021). Upwork was founded in 2014 through the merger of the two largest digital labor platforms – Elance.com and oDesk. com – and went public in 2018, with a market capitalization of roughly $2 billion. With a little over 1,600 employees worldwide (both full-time employees and freelancers sourced through the platform), over 800,000 clients, and over 18 million active freelancers in more than 180 countries, it has become the world's largest digital labor platform for skilled work.[16] As of August 2023, 73 percent of Upwork's freelance workers have a college degree (Upwork 2023) and perform discrete task-oriented projects, such as web design, app development, digital marketing, finance and accounting, strategic business consulting, and intellectual property law (Kinder et al. 2019). According to Upwork, their clients range in size from sole proprietors to Fortune 500 companies, and spend between a few hundred and tens of millions of dollars annually (Upwork 2021). Our case study focuses on Upwork's millions of freelancers, who are independent contractors working remotely on client projects.

Matches between clients and freelancers are made in three ways. First, prospective clients post jobs on the platform, which are supplemented by information about a client's business, its prior job postings, prior rates it had paid for jobs, and client ratings submitted by other freelancers (Minor & Yoffie 2018). Freelancers can then bid on jobs using a platform-specific currency, with free accounts being limited to about 30 bids per month, and paid accounts being limited to about 35 bids, with the option to pay for more (Kinder et al. 2019). Second, prospective clients have the option to proactively search the platform to find a freelancer of interest and then send them an invitation to submit a proposal for the job. And third, once a client has posted a job on the platform, Upwork's matching algorithms automatically suggest a number of freelancer profiles whose skills might be a good fit with the project (Minor & Yoffie 2018). Upwork jobs can be billed as hourly work or at a flat fee, and the platform collects fees through secured monetary transactions and an escrow service. For using the Upwork platform, freelancers are charged a service fee

---

[15] Digital labor platforms have also been referred to as "remote staffing marketplaces" (Kuhn 2016), "freelance contracting platforms" (Bucher et al. 2019), "crowdsourcing" (Cherry 2011; Huws 2016), and work in the "human cloud" (Moore et al. 2018).

[16] Competitors, such as Amazon Mechanical Turk and TaskRabbit, in contrast, focus on connecting clients with less skilled workers, such as identifying specific content in an image or video, writing product descriptions, or answering survey questions (Amazon Mechanical Turk), and furniture assembly, moving, delivery, or handyperson work (TaskRabbit).

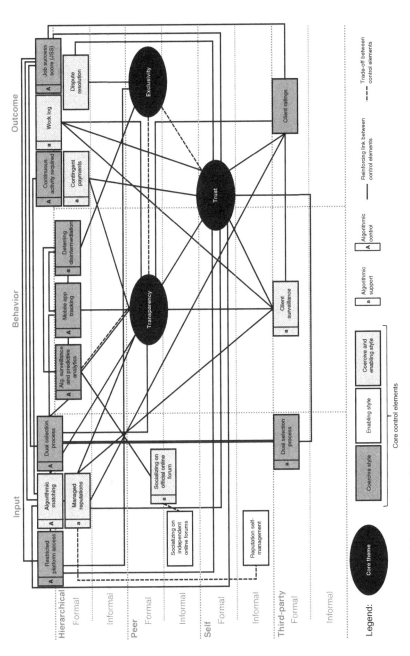

Figure 6.5 Upwork's control configuration

Table 6.12 *Upwork's control configuration heat map*

Control element	Target			Formality		Direction				Style		Controller	
	I	B	O	F	I	H	P	S	T	C	E	H	A
Restricted platform access	X			X		X				X			X
Algorithmic matching	X			X		X				X	X		X
Dual selection process	X			X		X			X	X		x	X
Managed reputations	X			X		X				X	X	X	x
Socializing on official online forum	X				X		X			X		X	
Socializing on independent online forums	X				X		X					X	
Reputation self-management	X				X			X				X	
Algorithmic surveillance and predictive analytics		X		X		X				X			X
Mobile app tracking		X		X		X				X			X
Deterring disintermediation		X		X		X				X		X	x
Client surveillance		X		X		X			X	X		X	x
Continuous activity required			X	X		X				X	X		X
Work log			X	X		X				X	X	X	x
Job success score (JSS)			X	X		X				X	X		X
Contingent payments			X	X		X				X	X	X	x
Dispute resolution			X	X		X				X	X	X	
Client ratings			X	X					X	X	X	X	

Legend: Columns from left to right: target (I = input, B = behavior, O = outcome); formality (F = formal, I = informal); direction (H = hierarchical, P = peer, S = self, T = third-party); style (C = coercive, E = enabling); controller (H = human, A = algorithm); X = heavy focus on this control dimension; x = partial focus on this control dimension; empty cell = no focus on this control dimension

Control element	Exemplary quote(s)
Input control	
Restricted platform access	• "online labor platforms such as [...] Upwork [...] automate HR-related decision making and execution in areas such as selection (e.g., an algorithm that grants or denies workers access to the Upwork platform)." (Meijerink et al. 2021: 2551)
	• "in order to be able to 'operate at scale', Upwork has digitalized several core processes including the acceptance and rejection of candidate profiles onto the platform: 'Upon registration, our machine learning algorithms assess a freelancer's potential to be successful on our platform based on the current supply and demand in addition to the skills in the freelancer's profile.'" (Upwork 2018: 6).
	• "Workers who pass this algorithmic review are granted access to the platform and will be able to bid on gigs and send out proposals." (Waldkirch et al. 2021: 7)
	• "In 2016, with several thousand new freelancers registering on Upwork each day, [former Upwork CEO Stephane] Kasriel believed that it had become increasingly important to the success of the community to balance freelancer skills with the availability of projects. Upwork began a program to 'curate' the marketplace to help ensure a better balance between supply and demand. When someone asked to register for Upwork, the company's systems reviewed their skills to determine whether there was demand in the marketplace. Furthermore, Upwork management wanted to maintain the quality of freelancers on its platform. For every 10,000 freelancers who signed up, approximately 200 would make it through the application process to become a part of the platform." (Minor & Yoffie 2018: 7)
Algorithmic matching	• "Matchmaking algorithms (which include ratings, evaluations, and feedback) connect freelancers and clients." (Kinder et al. 2019: 7)
	• "Using graph analysis and natural language processing, a method in which computers understand conversational speech and jargon, Elance-oDesk [now Upwork] is working to provide smart recommendations to its users. For example, if a business likes the profile of a freelancer, but that person is booked on another project, Elance and oDesk [which merged to create Upwork] serve up the profiles of other similar candidates." (Holzack 2014)
	• "After submitting the [job] post, the [client] business would immediately receive several profiles of freelancers who were potentially a good fit. The business could then choose to invite any of them to apply for the project. The business could also see a freelancer's past experience on the platform, including how many hours worked, number of jobs, kinds of jobs, earning rates, and ratings from past clients." (Minor & Yoffie 2018: 6)
	• "Upwork's automated system would continue to send the business additional applicants based on which freelancers the business interviewed. On the whole, data science was used to further help create successful matches." (Minor & Yoffie 2018: 6)
	• "Freelancers could also search for jobs when not invited to apply to a particular project. There could be thousands of possible projects. The freelancer would give a thumbs-up or -down to a particular posting. A machine learning algorithm would then highlight other relevant jobs." (Minor & Yoffie 2018: 6)

Table 6.13 (cont.)

Control element	Exemplary quote(s)
Dual selection process	• "workers are forced to continuously negotiate access to the platform. Here, they are subject to a 'dual selection' process: workers are both continuously selected by the algorithm with respect to platform access, and they are selected by clients for gigs. Only if workers manage to consistently and continuously pass both algorithmic and client selection will they be able to participate successfully on the platform." (Waldkirch et al. 2021: 20) • "The Employer interviewed each selected candidate via email, phone, or web-based video in order to finalize the hiring decision. If the Contractor was hired, a contract would be signed by both parties stipulating payment rate and other relevant details (fixed-price or time-based). The Employer then sent an email to the Contractor indicating that the assignment had begun." (Groysberg et al. 2011: 7) • "oDesk [now Upwork] collected information on the Contractor, including work experience, skills, and certifications. oDesk had developed a series of proprietary tests, which were available for Contractors to take, free of charge. The tests were administered by oDesk in conjunction with its partner Expert Rating. By 2010, there were 341 different technology tests, and new tests were constantly being developed based on feedback from the oDesk community and based on skills for which there was an increasing supply and/or demand. These tests provided Contractors with the opportunity to prove they had the skills they advertised, and Contractors were required to take these tests in order to receive ratings on a variety of skills. Employers were able to access this information, as well as comments provided by previous Employers." (Groysberg et al. 2011: 5)
Managed reputations	• "Freelancer profiles are constructed from numerous fields, which allow various levels of control. We have categorized freelancer profile components based on control limitations as follows: customizable information, Upwork generated information, and client-supplied information. Where customizable information spaces afford freelancers particular agency to present themselves to potential clients, client and Upwork generated information is more constrained through negotiations with clients as well as the platform's algorithms." (Kinder et al. 2019: 8) • "Freelancers have less power over Upwork-specific information, which is generated by the platform's algorithms. Many of these sets of information correspond with a visual demarcation, allowing clients to quickly sort through a freelancer pool without reviewing each freelancer's profile. These include skill test results, certifications, Top Rated status, and Job Success Score (JSS). JSS, reflected as a percentile out of 100, indicates freelancers' contract completion rate and client feedback, and requires workers to have been on the platform for a certain period of time. Consequently, newer users on the platform will not have a high JSS until they complete a set number of contracts that result in good reviews (platform newcomers can instead earn Rising Talent status)." (Kinder et al. 2019: 8) • "freelancers could earn a label of 'Rising Talent' that would appear on their profile. A new freelancer user earned this title when the system predicted that the individual had appropriate in-demand skills and experience. Since a new user did not have a history on the platform, Upwork would use data science analysis to predict the likelihood of a positive outcome based on the freelancer's skills, experience, and any tests taken." (Minor & Yoffie 2018: 7)

	• "Those [freelancers] within the 90th JSS percentile can attempt to achieve Top Rated status, which also requires further obligations from freelancers. These include prolonged and sustained activity on the platform, minimum earnings, profile completion, etc. Top Rated status is also visually reflected within the platform as a prominent badge on the freelancer's profile. These forms of information stand out on freelancers' profiles and strongly affect their ability to secure work." (Kinder et al. 2019: 8)
	• "High valued profile badges depend upon sustained freelancer engagement with specific aspects of the platform (ability tests, connects, proposals, etc.), which then earn them access to quality, legitimate clients." (Kinder et al. 2019: 16)
Socializing on official online forum	• "Upwork provides only one option for freelancers to connect with other freelancers (and clients with other clients) through the platform's Community Forum." (Kinder et al. 2019: 20)
	• "Upwork provides a public communication channel, the Community Forums, for users to gain platform literacies and connect with their global colleagues. As an extension of the platform's job searching/creating function, these forums are monitored by the platform and forum moderators frequently respond to posts from users. Since interactions are not anonymous (Community Forum activity requires an Upwork account), certain topics, particularly any that may imply violating Terms of Service, are not discussed." (Kinder et al. 2019: 10)
	• "the official Upwork forum restricts critical conversations between workers. According to Upwork's community guidelines, users of the official forum are not allowed to criticize the platform, to share warning letters or to talk about sanctioned or banned users." (Waldkirch et al. 2021: 8)
Socializing on independent online forums	• "a large online community of workers on Upwork (r/upwork on Reddit). The online community is independent of Upwork and largely functions as a digital social space where workers anonymously share stories, ask questions, and provide peer-feedback, tips, and guidance." (Waldkirch et al. 2021: 8)
	• "The conversation about training and development is an important mechanism in transferring knowledge and best-practices among workers and allowing individuals to 'learn the ropes'. Given frequent changes in platform design and rules, such crowd-coaching activities are vital for more tenured workers as well." (Waldkirch et al. 2021: 15)
	• "We observed that external forums had consistent exchanges regarding unclear JSS [Job Success Score] algorithms and topics that would violate Upwork's Community Forum Guidelines, such as discussing alternative payment methods. The Upwork subreddit has over 5,000 members and the comment threads on Upwork-focused YouTube videos demonstrate an active Upwork community that exists external from the platform itself." (Kinder et al. 2019: 10)
	• "Workers discuss how they can improve their self-presentation, and the crowd functions as a kind of sounding-board where workers can share their profiles and receive feedback and advice. For instance, the crowd discusses how to position a worker's person, skills, and experiences favorably to gain access to relevant gigs." (Waldkirch et al. 2021: 14, emphasis in original)

Table 6.13 (*cont.*)

Control element	Exemplary quote(s)
	• "this 'crowd-coaching' encompasses pricing strategies. Here, workers offer advice to peers with respect to dealing with demanding clients and avoiding exploitation or scams. In particular, the crowd often discusses how to arrive at an adequate hourly wage: setting the initial rate too high may prevent clients from hiring a worker; setting it too low may attract exploitative clients and devalue one's skill and work." (Waldkirch et al. 2021: 14, emphasis in original)
	• "the conversations also provide *coping and encouragement* as an important emotional outlet. Workers often come to vent and receive consolation and encouragement in the face of struggles and setbacks. Here, it is common to find threads about workers starting their *Tuesday vent time* because they were 'ghosted' by a client." (Waldkirch et al. 2021: 15, emphases in original)
Reputation self-management	• "customizable information spaces afford freelancers particular agency to present themselves to potential clients." (Kinder et al. 2019: 8)
	• "profiles allow workers to promote themselves through skill tests, certifications, and proficiencies." (Kinder et al. 2019: 7)
	• "[The platform] administers nearly 1,000 online skills tests so that freelancers can demonstrate their abilities in language translation, HTML coding or business math, among other competencies. The sites can also verify credentials that a freelancer claims to have, such as someone's score on the TOEFL exam for English language skills, or a certification as an Oracle database administrator. All of this information is included on a freelancer's profile, along with reviews from clients of the quality of their work." (Holzack 2014)
Behavior control	
Algorithmic surveillance and predictive analytics	• "Upwork relies on 'specific pattern-matching algorithms' to either detect unusual behavior or to predict future behavior [...] on the platform." (Waldkirch et al. 2021: 7)
	• "Analyzing community members' behavior allowed Upwork to detect suspicious activity and identify troublesome users." (Zhu et al. 2017: 10)
	• "The next frontier in data analytics was to predict freelancers' future performance before such behavior occurred. [Former Upwork CEO Stephane] Kasriel elaborated: If you've done a hundred jobs, we have a sufficient amount of data to be able to predict whether or not you're going to be successful. We try to identify who has a background that seems to be the best fit and highlight those people in search and various areas on the site." (Zhu et al. 2017: 10)
Mobile app tracking	• "We can use mobile to accelerate the time to hire and the time to results, because it's faster to find people and communicate back and forth. On mobile, we can simplify the overall user experience and make it very easy to learn. And we can give our community mobile technology to make it easier for them to work anywhere and have it all be tracked, monitored, and paid through the mobile device. So mobile can give us faster, better data, and expand the categories of work we can support." (Zhu et al. 2017: 10)
Deterring disintermediation	• "several programs were put in place to deter circumvention, such as removing last names from site postings to make it harder for freelancers and clients to connect on other platforms such as LinkedIn." (Yoffie & Ciechanover 2019: 2)
	• "Upwork employed data analytics to detect any suspicious activities and offered many features and services (e.g., help resolving disputes) to incentivize users to conduct all transactions on the platform. Moreover, it introduced a job success score for every freelancer, which was based on factors such as the number of repeat hires and long-term relationships with clients. This score, together with average client

Client surveillance	• "[Upwork] surveils chats and intervenes when transacting parties mention potential alliances with external platforms such as Skype or PayPal. Upwork also sustains platform-bound relationships between clients and freelancers through its Terms of Service, which aim to restrict the assemblage of a larger ecosystem through the threat of, for example, expulsion from the platform". (Kinder et al. 2019: 16) • "the platform utilizes a feature called 'work diary', which records keystrokes, takes regular snapshots of a worker's computer screen and can take pictures through the worker's webcam. Such elements of tracking and control – although technically optional – are becoming the norm, and workers feel increasingly obliged to adopt them." (Waldkirch et al. 2021: 16) • "employers essentially can look over workers' shoulders. 'The idea behind the screenshots is something similar to the physical office,' [former Upwork CEO Stephane] Kasriel said. 'You don't really know if the person is delivering quality work by screenshots. However, I can see from random screenshots that she seems to be working on the stuff I asked her to.'" (Holzack 2014) • "ODesk [now Upwork] Chief Executive Gary Swart says a client paying a freelancer likes knowing, 'You can't play Blackjack. You can't watch YouTube. Why? Because I'm watching you work.' When one oDesk client questioned an inflated bill from a freelancer, a check of the screen shots revealed he'd been watching a cricket game online. The freelancer reduced his bill." (Shellenbarger 2008) • "Clients can log into the system anytime and see whether contractors are working, what they're doing and how long it's taking them; clients' weekly bills are based largely on the data." (Shellenbarger 2008) • "The monitoring is not covert or unobtrusive, as the freelance workers are alerted by 'a small computer-screen icon [that] pops up at the bottom of their screen each time a screen shot has been taken.' [(Shellenbarger 2008)] They are regularly made aware that they are being observed." (Ajunwa et al. 2017: 746–747) • "Upwork Messages also provides an online messenger system allowing real-time discussion if desired." (Moore et al. 2018: 30)
Outcome control	
Continuous activity required	• "Not only must freelancers log onto the platform, but in order to avoid Upwork automatically rendering their profile invisible to clients, workers are required to earn money every 30 days. Rewards and badges, such as Top Rated and Rising Talent, also stipulate various on-platform activity levels (numbers of proposals submitted, work delivered, ratings averages) within specific time frames." (Kinder et al. 2019: 18)
Work log	• "Hours were automatically logged while the Contractor was signed into that account, thereby avoiding an inaccurate time log if the Contractor was working on multiple projects." (Groysberg et al. 2011: 7)

Table 6.13 (cont.)

Control element	Exemplary quote(s)
	• "Each week, the Contractor received a review log that detailed the work and associated time that had been logged [...]. After the Contractor reviewed and approved the log, it was sent to the Employer. Similarly, the Employer reviewed and approved the log if no changes needed to be made. Payment was then transferred from the Employer account to the Contractor account on a weekly basis, a week following the approval of the log." (Groysberg et al. 2011: 7)
Job success score (JSS)	• "Upwork's algorithms combine behavioral data (e.g., number of tasks completed) and customer evaluations to arrive at a so-called Job Success Score (JSS) that claims to capture a worker's job-related performance." (Meijerink et al. 2021: 2548)
	• "the algorithm also provides a numerical job success score (JSS) as a compound measure of worker performance." (Waldkirch et al. 2021: 7)
	• "A second program [Upwork instituted to explicitly help address the issue of trust on the online platform] was publishing job success scores. This was a score between zero and 100 based on feedback from clients upon the completion of a project. Finally, experienced freelancers could earn a 'Top Rated' title that appeared on their profile. This was earned based on their job success score, contingent upon using the platform for a minimum amount of billings and contracts. In addition to being able to show their title on their profile, Top Rated freelancers were provided several opportunities through seminars and resources to further their ability to advertise effectively in Upwork's marketplace." (Minor & Yoffie 2018: 7)
Contingent payments	• "In mid-2007, oDesk [now Upwork] introduced a new prong to its strategy, a modified version of the time-based contract, which incorporated the contingent payments associated with fixed-price contracts. These payments were contingent on Employer satisfaction." (Groysberg et al. 2011: 4)
	• "Freelancers produce work, clients select, hire, and pay workers, and the platform and its stockholders reap financial benefits from transaction fees. Upwork maintains this equilibrium of relationships through, as mentioned above, various levels of surveillance and threats of monetary loss. Payment is contingent upon screenshots observing hourly work." (Kinder et al. 2019: 17)
Dispute resolution	• "Upwork ensures clients their 'right to ownership of intellectual property' and will provide dispute assistance." (Moore et al. 2018: 30)
	• "If necessary, [Upwork] can handle on-platform mediation and dispute resolution between users." (Kinder et al. 2019: 7)
Client ratings	• "Both workers and clients rate each other once a job is completed, and the client's feedback is then processed through Upwork's algorithm to generate a JSS [Job Success Score] for freelancers. A worker's success in competing against many other freelancers is contingent upon maintaining a higher JSS, a system that Freelancer 3 described as 'five stars or fail.'" (Kinder et al. 2019: 13)

of 20 percent on the first $500, 10 percent between $500 and $10,000, and 5 percent beyond that (Kinder et al. 2019). Figure 6.5 presents Upwork's control configuration, Table 6.12 contains quotes that illustrate the control elements, and Table 6.13 presents the associated heat map.

Discussion. Upwork's control configuration revolves around three core themes: transparency, trust, and exclusivity. Upwork's business model is built on mediating the relatively inefficient market for skilled temporary or freelance work on a global scale. Both transparency and trust in its matching capabilities, and in the management of the subsequent task completion, are key to its commercial success. An important risk factor for Upwork's business model is that successfully matched clients and freelancers could take their collaboration outside the platform to save on the fees Upwork charges for its services, thereby disintermediating the platform as the exclusive connection between freelancers and clients, and depriving Upwork of vital revenue streams associated with the use of its platform. Given the critical importance of these themes, most of Upwork's control elements support one or more of the three core themes.

Much like Uber's, Upwork's control configuration relies heavily on algorithms, and ML algorithms are supporting or even replacing managerial control across all control targets. Moreover, strong complementarities between control elements characterize Upwork's control configuration. For instance, the work diary application that is part of Upwork's client surveillance can benefit both clients and freelancers. Clients can confirm logged work remotely, and freelancers can document the work they completed through Upwork's system, protecting them in case of a dispute (Kinder et al. 2019). The Job Success Score (JSS) not only serves as a crucial input for Upwork's matchmaking algorithm but also contains factors – such as average client ratings from past transactions, the number of repeat hires, and long-term client relationships – that make it a bulwark against freelancers' inclinations to take jobs and client relationships outside the platform (Zhu et al. 2017).[17]

Upwork's control configuration also includes a complete reinforcing feedback loop. Data obtained from hierarchical algorithmic surveillance (behavior control) and client ratings (outcome control) become constituent elements of a freelancer's JSS (outcome control), which, in turn, becomes a crucial ingredient for algorithmic matching, the dual selection process, and managed reputations (all input controls).

However, Upwork's control configuration also contains inherent trade-offs and unintended consequences at both the control element level and the core theme level. At the control element level, Upwork's hierarchical input

---

[17] Interestingly, Upwork also created barriers for clients to obtain freelancers' contacts and engage them outside the purview of Upwork's platform, such as not providing contact information and electronically monitoring freelancer-client interactions on the platform (Kinder et al. 2019).

control via managing freelancers' reputations affords freelancers limited discretion – information that freelancers can customize is complemented by information generated by Upwork's algorithms and information provided by clients (Kinder et al. 2019) – thereby limiting freelancers' agency to self-manage their reputations. There are also temporal trade-offs among control elements. For example, Upwork's reliance on JSS and hierarchically managed freelancer reputations in its algorithmic matching process leaves newer freelancers, who are unable to compete on these metrics, with few options other than to compete by undercutting going rates for jobs (Kinder et al. 2019). While the resulting bidding war for jobs may allow newer freelancers to build their Upwork profile, it may also drive more experienced freelancers with higher rates to leave the platform, thereby undermining clients' confidence in future matching processes and, ultimately, the platform's value proposition.

At the core theme level, the transparency and trust required for successful matches on Upwork's platform also increase the risk that clients connect directly with freelancers, thereby disintermediating the platform as the exclusive connection between freelancers and clients. A recent study provides empirical support for this trade-off, finding that while trust increases the likelihood of hiring high-quality freelancers, sufficiently high levels of trust also increase disintermediation, thereby offsetting the revenue gains from hiring high-quality freelancers (Gu & Zhu 2021).

Like Uber's drivers, freelancers frequently complained about Upwork's algorithmic control elements and sometimes even resisted, challenged, or gamed them. Many freelancers perceived Upwork's platform access algorithms as opaque and unpredictable, and it was not uncommon for prospective freelancers to have their profiles automatically rejected by the platform multiple times. As one freelancer put it on an unofficial online forum dedicated to Upwork: "I had submitted my profile probably over 50 times now, and they just kept rejecting me with their 'over 10'000 freelancers with my skill' email" (Waldkirch et al. 2021: 13). Moreover, the only way for freelancers to find new clients is to submit bids on the platform, yet many freelancers reported that there was little clarity about how many bids were allowed before the platform intervened. Suspended freelancers also received little information, and had few options for recourse, as the following forum post illustrates: "I got banned for applying to too many proposals. I made my account last week and decided to apply to proposals that i feel i can handle. The other day i logged in and my account was suspended. There was no reason, or email or anything about why it was suspended" (Waldkirch et al. 2021: 13). Such sudden, unannounced suspensions threatened the freelancers' livelihoods and left them frustrated and angry at the perceived arbitrariness and injustice.

Freelancers were equally frustrated with Upwork's matching and scoring algorithms. Regarding the former, it often remained unclear to them why the algorithm suggested certain jobs to some workers but not to others, despite similar skill sets (Waldkirch et al. 2021). Regarding the latter, freelancers' dissatisfaction with the JSS score stems from two issues: First, it focuses less on their actual performance, such as the quality of the work they delivered, or how satisfied the client was, and instead takes into account several other non-work-related factors, such as whether the client provided feedback at all, or how long a contract was kept open. Second, freelancers do not really know what they are being evaluated on. To make matters worse for freelancers, Upwork allows clients to provide feedback that remains invisible to freelancers, but visible to the algorithm, which allows unhappy clients to covertly punish freelancers (Waldkirch et al. 2021). A forum post highlighting freelancers' resignation in the face of such information asymmetry deadpans that "[t]here are three great mysteries in the world: 1] Stonehenge 2] Pyramids 3] JSS," and another complains that JSS "is like alchemy, nobody really has a clear formula on how it works except Upwork" (Waldkirch et al. 2021: 15 and 9, respectively).

As a consequence, unofficial online forms have become the preferred venues for collective sensemaking attempts, with freelancers trying to reverse-engineer the system to either work with it, or game it, in order to improve their scores, for instance, by offering clients a refund to avoid a negative score, despite having delivered quality work (Waldkirch et al. 2021). One interviewed freelancer admitted to gaming the platform by creating a separate client account to post jobs and get estimates on price points for different tasks (Kinder et al. 2019). Because of intentional information asymmetries, restrictions on direct communications between clients and freelancers to combat disintermediation, constant electronic surveillance of both the platform and the official online forum,[18] and the platform's lack of responsiveness to freelancer questions and concerns,[19] training and development (as a part of input control) at Upwork appear to be effectively outsourced to unofficial online forums. This not only further undermines freelancers' sense of community and attachment to the platform but also increases their motivation to bypass the platform for future jobs, which stands in direct conflict with Upwork's core theme of exclusivity.

---

[18] Forum posts are testaments to freelancers' almost paranoid fear of being caught in even innocuous infractions, such as complaining to the official platform support channels, using certain forbidden words in the chat feature, or logging into the platform while traveling abroad, which could result in automatic suspension from the platform (Waldkirch et al. 2021).

[19] One freelancer shared this frustrating experience with Upwork's human and nonalgorithmic freelancer support: "UpWork instantly suspends me [...] At this point I just want my hard earned money and my existing clients to get the work I already finished. I tried calling, emailing, live chat, twitter [...] Nobody on upwork cares at all" (Waldkirch et al. 2021: 18).

6.5.5   Comparison of Uber and Upwork

Both Uber and Upwork are representative of platform-mediated gig work, and therefore share many of the same organizational control elements, such as algorithmic matching processes, extensive algorithmic surveillance of workers (and often clients), and deputizing customers to become a critical (third) party to the companies' control configurations. Both configurations rely heavily on formal and algorithmic(ally supported) control, and both exhibit extensive complementarities between control elements. But both also contain trade-offs and unintended consequences, often related to workers' frustration with – from their perspective – opaque, unpredictable, and unfair algorithms, which leads to workers resisting, challenging, or gaming the controls.

Besides these similarities, there are also a few notable differences between the two platforms. Upwork's business model relies on more qualified and talented workers, and therefore puts a much greater emphasis on input controls, compared to Uber. Both platforms constitute remote work, but Uber's client interactions are face-to-face, whereas Upwork's are exclusively remote/digital, which requires more sophisticated control elements for clients to verify workers' efforts and outcomes, such as the work log and contingent payments. On the flipside, Uber relies heavily on the gamification of both behavior and outcome control, whereas such an approach is largely absent at Upwork, presumably because tasks completed on Upwork's platform are inherently more interesting, and its workers are therefore more intrinsically motivated, which reduces the need for gamification. Another key difference between the two platforms' control configurations is Upwork's preoccupation with workers' and clients' attempts to disintermediate their relationship, and thereby cut the platform off from its primary source of revenues – the usage fees it charges clients. In contrast to Uber's business model – where drivers and riders transacting outside the platform is not only much less likely but also makes much less economic sense for them – a significant number of control elements at Upwork (such as restricted platform access, algorithmic surveillance, and mobile app tracking) are therefore targeted at maintaining its status as the exclusive intermediary between freelancers and clients. Despite these differences, as well as numerous trade-offs and unintended consequences, both Uber and Upwork represent proof of concept for sophisticated organizational control configurations governing platform-mediated gig work.

6.6   Configurational Dynamics

Thus far, we have considered control configurations as something static, a snapshot in time. In the best case, a balanced approach with reinforcing elements across the control dimensions exerts a positive influence on intended outcomes. We have also discussed how trade-offs between control elements, between different levels (individual, team, organization), between outcome dimensions (adaptability, human relations, process, rational goal), and across time (short-term versus long-term) can undermine the effectiveness of control configurations. In the case studies we discussed in Sections 6.2 to 6.5, however, we also observed dynamic adaptations. These adaptations were triggered in part by internal or external pressures from stakeholders or technological innovations and partly had their root cause in trade-offs and conflicts between control elements. The case of US trucking companies (Section 6.2.3), for instance, already alludes to the fundamental change this industry experienced. Prior to the introduction of electronic monitoring systems in response to government safety mandates, the job's inherent information asymmetry made it difficult, if not impossible, for managers to supervise truckers directly. Once the industry adopted electronic monitoring systems capable of capturing granular, real-time data on both driver behavior and contextual conditions, as well as digital fleet management systems that aggregated and analyzed the data, a fundamental shift in information asymmetry occurred from drivers to trucking companies. This helped reshape US trucking companies' control configurations. These redesigned control configurations allowed for much more efficient and effective behavior and outcome control, as well as improved ways to resocialize performance data by sharing it with fellow drivers or even drivers' families, exposing truckers to new forms of peer and third-party control. However, real-time and pervasive electronic surveillance also clashed with truckers' identities and professional pride, exposing new frictions in trucking companies' control configurations.

In the case of GitLab (Section 6.2.4), the company's growing size and global scale prompted a change in the control configuration. More specifically, the original control configuration, with a heavy reliance on informal input control, such as the CEO's personal presence in Monday morning check-in calls and his attempts to speak personally with many of the call participants, was no longer feasible when significantly increased numbers of workers were spread across nearly every time zone. As a result, "[t]eam updates were down to a couple of sentences and personal updates were eliminated completely. This had made the call more efficient, but it was clearly no longer an effective way to engage employees and build a cohesive company community" (Choudhury & Salomon 2023a: 2). The handbook at the heart of GitLab's control configuration also began to reach its limits as the company grew, and there were more and more situations where the handbook was no longer up-to-date, or it became difficult to find relevant instructions for a given situation due to the sheer amount of information in the handbook, which had grown to over 2,722 pages in 2023. The growing pains GitLab experienced suggest that there might be a natural limit on the size and complexity of organizations that follow a "Work-From-Anywhere" control configuration.

Both Amazon warehouses' (Section 6.4.3) and Uber's (Section 6.5.3) highly efficient and effective control configurations were put to the test when media reports started highlighting their detrimental effects on worker satisfaction, health, and safety. Resulting worker protests, legal actions, and (pending) labor legislation forced both companies to make concessions to workers and legislators, which led to changes in their control configurations. After public scrutiny of its safety records, walk-outs, and support from prominent politicians, Amazon implemented changes to its policies and, among other things, no longer penalizes workers for missing work due to illness (Bloodworth 2018). At Uber, high turnover, a devastating labor shortage after the reopening of the post-pandemic economy, and increasing competition from Lyft led to significant concessions to Uber's drivers, such as displaying rider destinations for trip requests (Rana 2023b), allowing riders to tip drivers directly on the app (Hawkins 2017), and providing drivers with weekly summaries on how fares are divided, showing them how much Uber kept, and what went to taxes and other charges (Rana 2023b) – all of which constitute changes to Uber's control configuration.

A few researchers have explicitly studied changes in control configurations over time. In Sections 6.6.1 to 6.6.3, we will briefly review two published case studies in the organizational control literature – Blue Whale (Cardinal et al. 2004, 2018) and Commerzbank (Beese et al. 2023) – as well as a recent working paper that uses our control framework to study how the control configuration of a large multinational enterprise's sustainability program changed over time (Chochoiek et al. 2023).

6.6.1   Case Study: Blue Whale's Transformation

Cardinal and colleagues' (2004) research, which is listed in Table 6.1, combines control targets (input, behavior, outcome) and formality (formal, informal) to describe the four distinct control configurations they observed in the 10-year evolution of a short-haul moving company named Blue Whale. From the beginning, Blue Whale's founders – Brad Armstrong, an attorney and entrepreneur, and Blake Miller, a young mover himself – wanted to change the moving industry's standard way of doing business, which relied on spot-market labor, and was paying workers per move. The founders deemed this to be neither customer- nor worker-oriented, with the result that workers did not identify much with their employers. Even though the founders wanted to change standard industry practice, in the start-up phase of Blue Whale, they mimicked industry standards of market-based controls. To attract workers, however, they deviated from the standard and hired movers as permanent employees, and not as contractors. In addition, Miller supplemented their approach with informal behavior and informal outcome control by personally engaging workers with "close personal supervision, role modeling, and informal feedback" (p. 415) to produce desired behavior, attitudes, and outcomes. In the long run, the founders wanted to "create a culturally rich and rewarding corporate environment," that is "family-like" (p. 415) and helps foster sustainable client relationships. To realize this objective, the founders added informal controls, which were "driven by a sense of shared values for quality and service" (p. 415). Miller came to "personify Blue Whale culture" (p. 418), and his "idiosyncratic set of controls helped him personally motivate the movers" (p. 418), and "to focus the team on outcomes" (p. 418). Movers were hired based on their fit with this organizational culture. In this second phase, informal input, behavior, and outcome control were dominating. Over time, however, this control configuration had to be adapted to the needs of the growing organization, and to the founder's being less and less able to be present for everyone all the time. Miller reacted by installing a second hierarchical level. He "began to use the senior movers to impart the organization's culture to the less senior movers" (p. 419) and make sure workers "self-monitored [and were] peer-monitored" (p. 419). It became apparent, however, that the growing organization lacked sufficient financial controls and especially a formal, codified control system, and Miller suffered a burnout and took an extended sabbatical. Thus, while worker morale (a human relations outcome) was still very high at the end of this second phase, rational goal outcomes, such as costs and profitability, were suffering.

To address these challenges and the absence of his co-founder, Armstrong reacted with several radical changes. He eliminated all informal controls, which in his view fostered a "buddy-buddy atmosphere [that] could be both unprofessional and legally perilous" (p. 420). He also hired a professional operations manager, an accountant, and a consulting firm to become "a much more formalized 'business-like' company" (p. 420). In sum, he formalized all three control targets, resulting in "[i]ncreasingly legalistic controls" (p. 420) and a more bureaucratic organization. To prevent workers from circumventing the new formal controls by going directly to Miller as they used to, Armstrong relocated management offices. The professionalized accounting revealed, for the first time, the precarious financial situation of the company. This resulted in no bonus payments for workers for the first time in company history, which was communicated in writing, and not, as in the past, in personal conversations. The "[i]ncreased formalization, which they were now pursuing as a response to every problem, simply added fuel to the fires of resentment and distrust" (p. 422). The workers' resentment led to counterproductive work behavior that culminated in movers striking for a day, and office workers stealing from the firm. This imbalance between formal and informal controls therefore resulted not only in a trust crisis, unintended turnover, and the termination of office staff, but also in a financial crisis for the firm.

In phase 4, Miller and Armstrong took drastic action. They replaced themselves with two professional managers who reinstated centralized, close, and personal control over processes, mandated standardized customer relations training, and replaced the old manual with one that was easier to understand. They also reintroduced informal practices, such as an open-door policy and occasional small parties from earlier times when Miller was in charge. In contrast to the imbalance inherent in the previous control approach, the new managers used "a broad array of both formal and informal controls in a more balanced and integrative approach" (p. 424). As a result, performance improved, and workers were more satisfied.

In sum, the unique needs Blue Whale faced at different points during its evolution triggered changes to its control configuration. Moreover, Cardinal et al.'s (2004, 2018) study observed reinforcing effects among the control elements, but also the shortcomings of relying on only one control dimension, thereby highlighting the importance of balance among the elements in control configurations, as well as their fit with specific situational requirements. Blue Whale's initial resistance to, but later embrace of, bureaucratic controls is further reminiscent of the widely propagated, but largely refuted, image of these control approaches as rigid, conformist, and disenfranchising for workers (for details, see Monteiro & Adler 2022, as well as our discussion of bureaucracy in Section 3.1.4).

6.6.2   Case Study: Commerzbank's Transformation

Whereas Cardinal et al.'s case study discusses organizational control dynamics triggered by internal factors – that is, control requirements of different stages in the growth and evolution of a startup company – Beese and colleagues' (2023) study analyzes control configuration changes triggered by external pressures. Between 2008 and 2018, Commerzbank, the second-largest German bank, implemented four control configuration changes in response to external changes – including the 2008 financial crisis and the acquisition of a competitor – as well as internal changes, including several technology realignments and resulting cultural adjustments. As shown in our earlier overview of control configurations in the literature (Table 6.1), Beese and colleagues (2023) used a combination of the three targets (input, behavior, outcome), formality (formal, informal), and direction (hierarchical, self) for their control configurations. They distilled three control configurations with significant differences, including one that focused more on formal control elements in times of crisis and financial scarcity, and two that complemented formal with informal control elements to support innovative activities and corporate renewal. In the first configuration, Commerzbank had defined a clear goal for its organization to respond to the uncertain situation with simultaneously scarce resources and strong financial pressure, namely with *"focus, optimization, downsizing"* (p. 98, emphasis in original). Commerzbank supplemented this formal outcome control with a high degree of formal input and formal behavior control. It also emphasized input control by selecting staff with the appropriate qualifications and attributes for a new task force, with the mission to develop options for the future of the company. In the two subsequent configurations, informal self-control and clan control complemented the formal controls. For example, project teams were asking the central coordination unit proactively for support (self-control), engaged in more networking, and jointly discussed possible futures for the organization (clan control). Across the entire evolution of Commerzbank, Beese and colleagues (2023) stress the importance of configurations allowing for a balance between short-term and long-term goals, and between local project needs and global organizational targets. Such a balance was achieved by combining different formal control targets in the first configuration and complementing formal controls with informal controls in the latter two configurations. According to this study's findings, compared to formal controls, informal controls take longer to make an impact but are critical for gaining worker support by providing a "degree of safety and stability" (p. 101). Informal controls are also better equipped for handling uncertain or turbulent situations because they can be implemented even in the absence of clear targets and roadmaps. In conclusion, Beese and colleagues (2023) recommend that organizations engage in "ongoing re-evaluation of [control] structures and activities" as a "routinised practice" (p. 100).

6.6.3   Case Study: A Large Multinational Enterprise's Sustainability Transformation

Our last case study, discussed in Chochoiek and colleagues' (2023) working paper, represents the most comprehensive test of our control framework in the literature to date. This study incorporates the control dimensions of target, formality, direction, and style to describe the environmental sustainability efforts and the associated control configuration dynamics of MultiCon, a large multinational enterprise (MNE) headquartered in Germany. Over a 48-month period, the authors collected real-time observational data and showed how internal and external stakeholder demands resulted in changes to the control configuration.

Initially, responding to external pressures, such as coordinated actions and well-publicized protests by environmental activists, MultiCon's top executives opted for a classic top-down, coercive, formal, and outcome-oriented control configuration. However, when it became evident that internal stakeholders, such as workers and managers across corporate divisions and regions, had developed increasingly diverging perceptions of MultiCon's sustainability goals, the control configuration had to be adapted. Complementing the existing outcome controls, the company launched new behavior-oriented control measures, for example, by introducing new sustainability assessment approaches that were codified and shared via a new corporate directive. To balance these coercive controls, the MNE also introduced enabling input controls, such as carefully staffing newly established corporate sustainability committees and clearly communicating member roles and responsibilities.

Chochoiek and colleagues (2023) further find that, within a given control configuration, holistic approaches can incorporate not just different targets and degrees of formality but can also comprise different control directions and styles. A control configuration can, for example, include top-down, peer, self-, and third-party control, all at the same time. However, for both the initial implementation of sustainability and the final phase of this program, the authors find that MultiCon used a more classic control configuration, consisting of formal, outcome-oriented, top-down, and coercive control elements. Similar to the other control configuration dynamics cases, the key to any effective control configuration at MultiCon was obtaining a balance between control dimensions, in this case, particularly between coercive and enabling forms of control.

As these case studies have reminded us, organizations and their environments are in constant flux, and we need to consider time as an additional contextual variable. Core control themes, control elements, and their interactions can change over time, and the internal and external fit they exhibited at one point might be lost over time. To address these changes over time, "configurational approaches need to be sensitive to the dynamic, changing elements in organizations and society," and especially "the decline of existing organizational configurations and their replacement with new configurations is an important topic for research" (Hinings 2018: 506). This is in line with Miller (1996: 510), who also stressed the dynamic nature of configurations and maintained that "a good configuration is the possibility it allows for ultimate reassessment and reconfiguration."

7   New Directions for Organizational Control

Because of these linkages across problems, we also conjecture that it will be rare to find new forms of organizing that display novelty in the manner in which only one of the basic problems of organizing is solved. More typically, we may expect to see frequently occurring clusters of solutions across forms of organizing; in this sense, new forms of organizing may, in fact, be new bundles of old solutions. (Puranam et al. 2014: 174)

We started this journey with a deep dive into the long and multidisciplinary history of organizational control (Chapters 2 and 3). Over more than a century, starting with Taylor's (1911) work on scientific management, this literature has developed profound insights and produced empirical support for its key tenets (Chapter 3). It has influenced both multiple academic disciplines and generations of managers and business practice (Chapter 4). However, we are also witnessing profound changes in the very foundation this literature is built on (Chapter 5), raising the question of whether this theory can survive the contemporary economic and organizational landscape, or whether we need to rethink our control theories and management approaches. In Chapter 6, we therefore questioned key assumptions and proposed a configurational approach to address these challenges and reconceptualize organizational control for the twenty-first century.

In this concluding chapter, we outline the implications of our reconceptualization of organizational control and highlight new directions for theory and practice. In line with our introductory quote, we will discuss both newly emerging forms of control and novel combinations and configurations of established control elements that have the potential to address the changes we witness in organizations and their environments. We briefly outline additional challenges to fundamental assumptions of control research – from revisiting the assumptions of self-interest and goal conflict and why perceptions of control matter (often more than intentions) to moving beyond one-size-fits-all control approaches and embracing truly customized approaches. We conclude with a discussion of new forms of organizing that emerge in contemporary economies and that would benefit from future research.

7.1   New Forms of Control

In both our literature review and the case studies we presented in Chapter 6, we observed several new forms of organizational control that could provide the impetus for future research and practice. We will highlight the emerging role of algorithmic control before summarizing new forms of control along the dimensions we identified in our organizing framework.

7.1.1   Algorithmic Control

Advantages and challenges of algorithmic control. Our analysis of algorithmic control confirmed that this novel form of control represents not only a quantitative change in the intensity of control but also a qualitative change, or a "genetic variation [...] in terms of comprehensiveness and instantaneity of information collected and analysed" (Aloisi & De Stefano 2022). The case studies of Amazon, Uber, and Upwork in particular have demonstrated the potential of algorithmic(ally supported) control to make control more efficient and effective across all targets. In addition to assisting human controllers, algorithms have also replaced humans as controllers, thereby fully automating control. Algorithms took over input control at Upwork and decided on platform access and algorithmic matching of freelancers and clients on the platform; Uber's real-time GPS and smartphone sensor monitoring has at least partially automated the platform's control of driver behavior; and algorithmic outcome control is a deciding factor in Amazon warehouse workers' scheduling, promotions, and terminations. As we have seen in our case studies, algorithms are capable of more comprehensive data collection, aggregation, and analysis than human managers and extend control beyond observable behaviors and the confines of the workplace. They can provide instantaneous feedback, tailored to each individual worker's needs and preferences, at a level of granularity, personalization, and immediacy that is impossible for human managers to match. Algorithms can also differentiate and personalize rewards and penalties to best meet individual workers' needs, and they can aggregate and share behavior and performance data more widely with team members to engender competition among peers, gamify rewards, and facilitate peer control among competing workers. By nudging workers, algorithms can also control in a much more subtle way than traditional forms of control. In sum, our case studies confirmed the monitoring, incentive, and coordination advantages of algorithmic(ally supported) control over more traditional control forms, and we would expect these advantages to drive their continuing proliferation across tasks, organizations, and industries.

However, algorithmic control also has its challenges. Besides workers' mixed reactions to being controlled by an algorithm, which we discussed earlier, algorithmic control exacerbates the risk of what Muller (2018) has called "the tyranny of metrics." This line of research builds on the well-established insight that individuals focus their efforts on what is measured and rewarded or penalized. This can be especially problematic for algorithmic controls, as they require explicit, measurable, and codifiable behaviors or outcomes. However, what is measurable (and therefore measured and rewarded) may or may not be aligned with what is actually in the best interest of an organization, and an exclusive focus on these measures could actually undermine productivity (Aloisi & De Stefano 2022). When designing an algorithmic control system, it is therefore important to remember Muller's (2018: 18) warning that "not everything that is important is measurable, and much that is measurable is unimportant." Without a critical reflection on what algorithmic controls are focused on, they can turn control from a means to foster desired outcomes into an end by itself (Bromley & Powell 2012; Waldkirch et al. 2021) and become a burden rather than a motivational tool, with negative effects on worker relations (Bamberger et al. 2014).

To combat such an algorithmic tyranny of metrics and to address other worker concerns, a particularly promising approach for both research and practice is examining how human agency (i.e., workers and managers) and algorithmic agency interact in a dynamic way to influence outcomes (cf., Meijerink et al. 2021). Early research has suggested that human managers in the loop can provide the much-needed social element missing in algorithmic control and help mitigate other shortcomings of algorithmic control (e.g., Kessinger & Kellogg 2019). Moreover, despite the increasing adoption of algorithmic control, most organizations still underutilize its most promising features. More specifically, a recent survey of almost 9,000 business and HR leaders reveals that most of the responding organizations collect worker data for descriptive purposes regarding turnover (82 percent), salary costs (68 percent), and workforce composition (53 percent). In contrast, predictive and prescriptive algorithms are rarely used (Deloitte 2020). This oversight provides a promising avenue for both future research and management practice.

The emergence of generative artificial intelligence (AI). Whereas the traditional, discriminative AI models we observed in our case studies rely on categorically labeled training data to make predictions classifying new data inputs, November 2022 marked a new age for AI – the introduction of generative AI models to the wider public. OpenAI's ChatGPT reached 100 million users in just 2 months and has spawned a number of competitors, such as Google's Bard. The main difference between discriminative and generative AI models is that the latter can generate new content, often in unstructured forms, such as written text or images. Generative AI analyzes the underlying distribution of large amounts of unlabeled training data to understand how the data is generated. It then applies the learned probability distribution to generate similar but new data that closely mimics the training data – for example, to predict the next word in a sentence, the next pixel in an image, or the next chord in a piece of music. This is done iteratively to build an original essay, image, or song with strong probabilistic inferences to the original training data (Foster 2023).

Despite their advanced capabilities, the latest generation of generative AI suffers from many of the same problems as discriminative AI models, such as inaccuracies, biases, misspecifications, and opacity, even for their designers (see Sections 5.1.2 and 6.4 for details). In fact, one of the downsides of its versatility is that generative AI can provide less accurate results, is prone to "hallucinations," or answering questions with plausible but untrue assertions, and does not provide the underlying reasoning or sources, which poses additional challenges for AI risk management (McKinsey & Company 2023b).

Despite these challenges and risks, generative AI has tremendous potential to remake many organizational tasks, including organizational control. The appeal of generative AI is twofold: its ease of use and its versatility. Their intuitive user interface allows essentially anyone with access to a PC or mobile device and an internet connection to ask these generative AI models questions in natural language. Moreover, while previous generations of discriminative AI models had rather narrow applications and could often perform only one task, generative AI models can give rise to many applications. A recent McKinsey article provides the following illustration of generative AI-supported behavior control:

> Imagine a customer sales call, for example. A specially trained AI model could suggest upselling opportunities to a salesperson, but until now those were usually based only on static customer data obtained before the start of the call, such as demographics and purchasing patterns. A generative AI tool might suggest upselling opportunities to the salesperson in real time based on the actual content of the conversation, drawing from internal customer data, external market trends, and social media influencer data. At the same time, generative AI could offer a first draft of a sales pitch for the salesperson to adapt and personalize. (McKinsey & Company 2023b)

Another use case for generative AI-based organizational control that is supported by recent research is socializing new workers as part of input control. A recent study of over 5,000 customer support agents has found, for instance, that the introduction of a generative AI-based conversational assistant increased productivity, customer sentiment, and worker retention and decreased requests for managerial intervention, but predominantly for novice and low-skilled workers (Brynjolfsson et al. 2023). These results suggest that generative AI models can help disseminate the institutional knowledge of more experienced workers to help newer workers move down the experience curve, but also that the benefits are limited and may not apply to more experienced workers. Besides socializing new workers, all workers could query a generative AI feedback system, for instance, to visualize their career development and obtain personalized assessments of their strengths and weaknesses as well as recommendations for improvement and training (McKinsey & Company 2023a). Enabling such generative AI models are artificial neural networks that are inspired by the billions of neurons that make up our human brains. These networks are trained on extremely large quantities of unstructured, unlabeled data in a variety of formats, such as text, images, video, audio, and computer code, using deep (i.e., many-layered) machine learning (ML) processes. The versatility of neural network training data, combined with reduced labeling requirements compared to predictive AI, makes it easy for organizations to adopt generative processes without significantly overhauling their existing data. As a consequence, generative AI can be used to automate, augment, and accelerate a wider range of tasks across an organization's functions (McKinsey & Company 2023b), including organizational control.

7.1.2   Control Target

In addition to emphasizing the potential of such entirely new forms of (algorithmic) control, our reconceptualization also highlights the increasing scope of input, behavior, and outcome control, which may also reinforce data security and privacy concerns.

Expanding the scope of input control. The literature has traditionally conceptualized input control as an ex ante control. Selecting workers who are a good fit for the organization, socializing and training them, or staffing project teams all take place *before* workers join organizations or teams. However, assessing workers' qualifications and attitudes, and matching them to certain tasks, teams, or entire organizations is a continuous challenge, and input control should therefore be conceptualized and designed as a continuous control. Verifying workers' attributes to assess their work eligibility and fit is, in fact, monitoring worker qualifications – and from an organizational perspective, it would be ideal to monitor such qualifications on an ongoing basis, and not just once. In that manner, input control would no longer be restricted to the initial verification that an individual meets the requirements of an organization, job, or task, but can be expanded to workers' entire tenure with the organization (Schafheitle et al. 2020).

There are also novel forms of input control, such as translating the images of interviewees' verbal and non-verbal behaviors into psychological profiles that allow predictions, reducing biases of especially untrained interviewers, and further reducing costs; or assessing talent through ML algorithms that convert workers' digital records (e.g., their social media footprints) into psychological profiles that can be used to determine future performance, leadership potential, or the risk of counterproductive behaviors (Chamorro-Premuzic et al. 2017).

Another novel form of input control could help enhance worker socialization (McFarland & Ployhart 2015). No longer constrained by a particular physical location, organizations' social media presence could offer additional opportunities to socialize workers with consistent messages and experiences. The increased accessibility and interactive nature of social media can help workers identify with the organization by interacting with peers and customers, and at times when it is convenient for them. On the flipside, there are also risks. Especially when users remain anonymous, organizations may have to combat destructive behavior and content, such as disengaged workers spreading their discontent or even misinformation quickly and widely, and hence undermining engagement and a shared organizational identity much more than if workers were only socialized locally (McFarland & Ployhart 2015).

More recently, algorithms have fueled a proliferation of gamified candidate and worker assessments. People prefer video games in assessments, and significant similarities exist between online role-playing games and actual workplace situations – for example, the requirements of cooperation and coordination with others, team building, leadership, and decision-making. More importantly, research has found a considerable overlap between the mental processes needed to win at video games and those that comprise work-relevant cognitive abilities. This suggests game-based assessments as a novel avenue for measuring critical talent attributes, such as fluid intelligence, integrity, and curiosity (see, e.g., Chamorro-Premuzic et al. 2017, for a review).

Expanding the scope of monitoring to include private worker data. Ever since Henry Ford unleashed private investigators to monitor workers' private lives (Ajunwa et al. 2017), organizations have been busy expanding their collection of worker data beyond the confines of the workplace. Three key areas illustrate this collection of novel data, the resulting new potential for control, and the changing role of workers who often provide data on all aspects of their lives voluntarily: social media platforms, productivity and collaboration platforms, and corporate health and wellness programs. Monitoring these areas grants organizations data that was formerly out of reach or limited to informal control interactions, and they can exploit this data across all control targets.

With the advent of social media platforms, organizations no longer restrict themselves to logging keystrokes and tracking workers' locations via GPS on their work phones. They also track if and when workers use private online services like Gmail, Facebook, Instagram, or Twitter at work, and what they post there (Ajunwa et al. 2017). There are few legal limits on the collection of workers' social media data uploaded in their spare time. This voluntarily provided online content is permanently accessible and can be easily recorded, aggregated, and analyzed – not only by friends and followers on social media, but also by third parties and, of course, by managers to inform their employment, staffing, and promotion choices (i.e., their engagement in input control). Such background checks on social media activities may, however, entail that "personal information presented out of context or inaccurately may lead employers to judge candidates unfairly without their knowledge or without an opportunity for rebuttal. Worse yet, the surreptitious quality of the information search may be a backdoor to illegal discrimination" (Sánchez Abril et al. 2012: 87).

Workers' social media presence, especially among heavy users, such as the millennial generation, also allows organizations to harvest vast amounts of behavioral and attitudinal data (Chamorro-Premuzic et al. 2017), and companies have started scrutinizing workers' use of social media to understand their emotions at work (De Choudhury & Counts 2013). Social media profiling also enables the prediction of future behavior based on workers' personalities and sentiments, including "psychosocial traits such as introversion, social and personal frustrations, divided loyalty, entitlement/narcissism, and predisposition toward law enforcement, political beliefs and group dynamics" (Mitrou et al. 2014: 4). Furthermore, such social media-based personality predictions tend to be even more accurate than those of human observers (Youyou et al. 2015).

Moreover, workers embedded in ubiquitous computing environments and interacting with social media never know who reads or evaluates their data, and there are legitimate fears that private information is being (mis)used by others. In this way, workers become objects of constant and multilateral surveillance, and the perception of permanent visibility moves surveillance from a panopticon, in which the few watch the many, to an omniopticon, in which the many (including superiors, peers, and third parties) watch the many (Brivot & Gendron 2011; Mitrou et al. 2014). This constant and amorphous threat can cause workers to (re)act anxiously and in an inhibited manner (Fairweather 1999); to find themselves having to choose between overt communication and covert behavior (Gibbs et al. 2013); and to face new forms of workplace bullying (Hall & Joiner 2014). The ability to remain anonymous on social media further lowers the threshold for destructive peer behavior (McFarland & Ployhart 2015).

Although they represent the most widely used forum, social media platforms are not the only instance of workers unwittingly participating in their own surveillance. Real-time productivity and collaboration platforms like Yammer (Microsoft) and Chatter (Salesforce) can also be used for worker surveillance and control (Ajunwa et al. 2017). Gisbert Rühl, the former CEO of Klöckner, for example, deliberately used Yammer to communicate with the entire organization, which was otherwise organized into virtual groups, to solve problems and contribute ideas (Colbert et al. 2016). However, there are also downsides to this type of technology-mediated communication. Compared to face-to-face communication, technology-mediated communication makes it difficult to ask questions to which there are no easy answers, to develop closeness between managers and workers, and to convey the feeling of being known and understood (Colbert et al. 2016).

A third set of tools for companies to indirectly gather data on their workers are corporate health and wellness programs. These programs offer health risk assessment, weight reduction and smoking cessation programs for workers, and are often backed by governments. Organizations typically partner with third-party wellness companies that then collect and analyze worker data, such as data on physical activity, drug prescriptions, and so on. In the United States, nearly two thirds of all companies, and 99 percent of large companies (those with 200+ employees), provide some kind of wellness program (Ajunwa et al. 2017). Companies incentivize their workers to use these programs, for instance, by distributing free electronic fitness trackers like Fitbit or Jawbone, and then use data gathered by these wearable devices to reward positive lifestyle choices, such as exercise and sleep (O'Connor 2015). By acquiring wellness data that are mostly unregulated and unprotected, organizations can also circumvent potential legal constraints in collecting personally identifying information (Ajunwa et al. 2017).

As illustrated by social media platforms, productivity and collaboration tools, and corporate health and wellness programs, surveillance in the workplace has moved beyond a solely authoritarian regime that subjects workers to discreet and predictable surveillance at the hands of managers. Instead, surveillance has become ostensibly more participatory, with organizations expecting workers to support surveillance by participating in productivity applications and wellness programs that organizations promote as beneficial for workers (Ajunwa et al. 2017).

Data security and privacy concerns. Despite the opportunities such an (algorithmic) expansion of input, behavior, and outcome control offers for organizations, it also raises increasing concerns and, often, pushback from workers. In both their personal and professional lives, workers across all generations increasingly demand transparency about how their employer and other organizations collect, store, and use information about them. According to Deloitte's (2019) Global Millennial Survey, for instance, over 70 percent of millennials are apprehensive about the security of their personal data held by businesses and governments.

People generally use what is called the privacy calculus to weigh the positive and negative consequences of a particular disclosure of information (Cichy et al. 2021). Perceived benefits of information sharing include financial rewards or content tailored to the individual's own preferences. Perceived costs result from threats to the individual's privacy. In most cases, people do not seek absolute privacy but are willing to surrender it partially for certain benefits that come from sharing data (Dinev & Hart 2006). However, research also cautions that people generally underestimate the extent to which they are subject to electronic surveillance, overestimate the accuracy and reliability of information being gathered about them, and express a certain amount of fatalism toward the inevitability of ever more far-reaching electronic surveillance, which leads them to willingly, albeit naively, participate in their own surveillance (Best 2010).

There are also demographic differences when it comes to privacy expectations. Owing to their identity being a synthesis of real-life and online expressions of themselves, millennials are less reluctant to share information that some people might consider personal or sensitive (Anantatmula & Shrivastav 2012). However, millennials also feel that it is inappropriate for others to collect, aggregate, and then act on the information they share online – especially of their private lives – for hiring, evaluation, and promotion decisions. They therefore oppose a cross-contextual flow of information and, instead, expect privacy within the information's intended network and context (Sánchez Abril et al. 2012). On the flipside, the millennial generation may be more at risk of improper workplace practices and/or employer sanctions for their online activity, because they are such heavy users of social media sites (Hurrell et al. 2017). Overall, women and parents expressed the greatest concerns about data collection, and were most resolute in their desire for data protection and online security (Deloitte 2019). Going forward, organizations will need to carefully balance increasingly comprehensive technological surveillance opportunities, on the one hand, with workers' concerns for data security and privacy, on the other hand.

Growing privacy concerns and well-publicized data breaches have also resulted in a flurry of recent privacy regulations, and they continue to trigger often fierce public debates about privacy rights in the twenty-first-century workplace. On the one hand, technological advances allow for more comprehensive and intrusive surveillance of workers – both at and outside their workplace – which is no longer confined to observable behaviors but extends to attitudes, feelings, and even workers' physiological and medical characteristics. On the other hand, what is legally permissible varies greatly and depends on the legal jurisdiction, labor laws, data protection policies, and the existence of organized labor unions that might act as a counterweight to worker surveillance. However, with technologies advancing quickly, privacy regulation often lags behind and, in some cases, new advancements remain entirely unregulated, resulting in a patchwork of regulation with many legal loopholes.

In the United States, federal regulations do not specifically address workplace surveillance or provide restrictions on how intrusive it can be (Ajunwa et al. 2017). The same relatively lax rules apply to workers' electronic communications. All US laws around worker privacy place a high priority on employers' legitimate business interests. As a result, collecting, evaluating, and making decisions based on data from social media websites remains legal in the United States, and there is no obligation to disclose the methods used to obtain information. Only the exercise of coercion to gain access to this data is prohibited (Sánchez Abril et al. 2012). Unsurprisingly, US courts have mostly sided with employers who monitor their workers, arguing that on-the-job surveillance using company resources (e.g., the organization's computer network or email) is permissible (Cascio & Montealegre 2016).

There are also differences within the United States, with some states explicitly enshrining worker privacy, especially that of state workers, in their constitutions. While only a few states, including Delaware, Connecticut, and New York, currently require employers to inform their workers about electronic surveillance (Aloisi & De Stefano 2022; Gadinis & Miazad 2020), legislators in multiple states, including California and Colorado, are making efforts to address the issue of worker surveillance (Francis & Kletzien 2022; Ram et al. 2022).

European countries also differ regarding their privacy-related legal frameworks. In the United Kingdom, for instance, employers have broad rights to monitor workers' use of social networking sites and often discipline workers for alleged misuse (Hurrell et al. 2017). The European Union (EU), in contrast, has traditionally attached greater importance to data protection and safeguarding individuals' privacy than the United States and the United Kingdom. The EU's Data Directive empowers the European Data Protection Supervisor, individual National Data Protection Authorities (NDPAs), and various non-governmental organizations to investigate personal data breaches (Ajunwa et al. 2017). These powers to investigate general data breaches have been further increased in the recent, and even stricter, EU General Data Protection Regulation (GDPR).[1]

Within the EU, Germany stands out for its even stricter privacy regulations. According to the Federal Labor Court, Germany's highest court for labor disputes, German organizations are not allowed to monitor workers at the workplace without a concrete suspicion of a criminal offense or a serious breach of duty. This means that the monitoring of a worker's computer without a concrete suspicion is not permissible under German privacy law. For many years, German courts have also ruled against disproportionate video surveillance, especially in the workplace, and court cases must exclude evidence obtained in violation of German privacy law from their proceedings (Böhm & Ströbel 2017). Some companies, including Amazon and the German online retailer Zalando, have been sharply criticized for using top-down and lateral surveillance software, respectively, and court cases are pending. Zalando, for instance, was accused of using a software called Zonar that asks workers to monitor each other and report any presumed misbehavior to their managers (Hagelüken & Kläsgen 2019; Zeit Online 2019). German laws also govern the collection of worker information on social media, requiring that an organization has informed its workers of its intentions in advance (Hurrell et al. 2017).

---

[1] https://gdpr.eu/what-is-gdpr/

An additional complication for privacy regulation arises from the blurring boundaries between work-related and private activities, and with it comes the question of what behavior and activities may be monitored and evaluated. For instance, the mainstream media have featured numerous examples of businesses disciplining workers for their social media activities – that is, activities mostly classified as private (Conway 2008; Watt 2011) – with courts siding with both companies (e.g., Neuburger 2008) and workers (e.g., Armour 2011). Many organizations have set up guidelines for the use of personal blogs and social media. However, since these policies expand into workers' personal lives, these policies, unlike earlier monitoring measures, pose new challenges for businesses in the form of possible legal claims filed on behalf of workers (Alge & Hansen 2014).

In light of constraining legal frameworks, companies increasingly shift from collecting personally identifying (and therefore legally protected) information, such as health records, to acquiring unprotected and largely unregulated proxies and metadata, such as information on worker wellness, online search queries, social media activity, and outputs of predictive big data analytics (Ajunwa et al. 2017). While legally permissible, at least for now, these types of data have the potential to reveal equally sensitive aspects of workers' private lives, and therefore represent an equally problematic invasion of privacy by corporations.

In contrast to these legal requirements for privacy, a number of particularly sensitive processes and procedures in organizations are subject to legal *transparency* requirements. This is the case, for example, for hospital treatments[2] and for hiring decisions in public and some private organizations, such as universities and government agencies,[3] where transparency requirements are intended to combat discrimination. An example is the recently introduced pay transparency laws to help prevent pay discrimination and disparities. At least seven US states, such as California, Colorado, and Nevada, as well as cities, such as New York City and Cincinnati, have implemented legislation that requires organizations to publish salary ranges for job postings (Jackson 2022).

In sum, there are two conflicting trends regarding privacy. On the one hand, there are legitimate transparency needs by the public to ensure compliance and equity, and algorithmic surveillance and the resulting electronic data repositories might actually help organizations comply with those regulations. On the other hand, workers also have legitimate privacy expectations, and legislators across the globe are increasingly willing to protect these expectations, albeit with significant differences across geographies.

---

[2] www.cms.gov/hospital-price-transparency   [3] https://euraxess.ec.europa.eu/jobs/charter/code

7.1.3   Control Formality

As we discussed in Chapter 6, algorithms have the potential to make informal controls redundant. Subtle forms of algorithmic control, such as nudging, can directly influence and in some cases even change workers' habits
and attitudes, thereby reducing the need for traditional informal controls.
Furthermore, since all algorithmic controls, by definition, require the formal codification of inputs, behaviors, or outcomes, the technology experts
interviewed by Schafheitle and colleagues (2020: 473) classified algorithmic
control as inherently formal and judged the formal-informal distinction to be
"partly artificial and arbitrary."

Nevertheless, informal control remains important, especially with regard
to traditional (i.e., non-algorithmic) hierarchical and peer control. Informal
controls were part of all of our case studies' control configurations. At
GitLab in particular, informal controls play an important role in maintaining
effective work relationships in an all-remote environment. GitLab's informal
control comprises all three control targets and all four directions, starting
with onboarding and socialization in deliberately designed informal interaction spaces and a culture of direct communication among workers, to
informal tracking of outcome metrics. While informal control at GitLab is
predominantly enabling, in other cases, it can be both enabling and coercive
or only coercive (e.g., the public ridicule of low performance at Amazon
warehouses). In the three configuration dynamics case studies described in
Section 6.6, we have also observed how important a balance between formal
and informal controls is. We learned from the Commerzbank case study that
informal controls may take longer to become effective but may help obtain
worker support by providing a sense of stability, especially in times of crisis
and turbulence.

While we do not expect to find an effective control configuration that consists exclusively of informal controls, we expect that informal controls will
continue to be important as a complement to formal controls or as a counter-
balance to the unintended consequences of formal controls, particularly for
HR outcomes. We see great potential for research examining the mix of formal
and informal control in effective (and ineffective) configurations, exploring
the direction(s) (i.e., hierarchical, peer, self, or third-party) in which informal
control might be most effective, and ascertaining the style (i.e., coercive or
enabling) that effective informal control takes.

7.1.4   Control Singularity

Advances in algorithm-supported electronic surveillance – capturing not only
inputs, behaviors, and outcomes, but also attitudes and emotions – have largely

resolved the fundamental trade-off between control targets that the classic organizational control literature (e.g., Eisenhardt 1985) has assumed. As a result, the costs of measuring behaviors and their outcomes are less of a consideration, and the choice of singular control targets, contingent on whatever controls managers have accurate, complete, and affordable information on, is no longer necessary.

Our configurational theorizing approach presented in Chapter 6 is based on a strong holistic perspective, that is, the need to consider different control dimensions simultaneously to account for the causal complexity among control elements and the potential for complementarity and substitution. All of the presented case studies demonstrated a positive reinforcing effect among different control elements. Thus, at first glance, the dimension of control singularity seems to have lost its significance, as holistic approaches have become the norm in both research and practice and form the basis of a configurational approach to control.

However, we might observe strong holistic control configurations with regard to control targets (e.g., input, behavior, and outcome), but they might consist of only one control direction (e.g., hierarchical), which would make them singular in terms of the control direction. Extending control configurations from typical combinations of only two control dimensions – prior research most commonly combined target and formality – to include the additional dimensions of direction and style, as well as the question of whether a human is controlling, alone or algorithmically supported, or whether it is a pure algorithm without human involvement, raises promising new research questions.

7.1.5   Control Direction

By incorporating control direction into our control configuration logic, we broaden the view from the dominant top-down focus of control and show how critical peer, self, and third-party control can be to organizations' control configurations. For example, GitLab relies strongly on peer control to enable its "work from anywhere" (WFA) model. GitLab also relies heavily on its remote workers' engagement in self-control. Self-control also plays a role in the other case studies' control configurations, attesting to its increasing importance, partly as a response to the trend toward individual purpose (see Section 5.2.3), but also as a way for individual workers to thrive in organizational environments where traditional top-down control by managers is less present or possible (see the so-called unbossed organizations in Section 7.4.4). This is the case, for example, in remote work settings or in freelance work, where workers have less attachment and loyalty to their employer, and largely lack shared identities and norms. Self-control has the potential to fill this gap.

Most relevant (and most novel for the control literature) is the active role third parties play in controlling, particularly gig workers. Third parties' involvement can relax the monitoring requirements of managers and thereby become a very efficient form of control. However, it might not always be perceived as fair and thus have detrimental effects on HR outcomes. This is evident, for example, in driver ratings at Uber and client ratings at Upwork. We also found evidence for the relevance of control direction in our control dynamics case studies. At MultiCon, for instance, a balance of control directions was employed to smooth the transition from one development phase to the next.

Algorithmic control also has an impact on control direction, as it can be used to mimic peer control and facilitate self-control. When organizations make aggregated data on worker behavior and performance available to peers, it can lead to behavioral adjustment, as lower-performing workers attempt to emulate their higher-performing peers. Kellogg et al. (2020) even showed that workers themselves use such performance data to informally establish a status hierarchy to evaluate themselves and others, to compete, and to ridicule co-workers who do not meet these standards.

7.1.6   Control Style

Along with the traditional conceptualization of organizational control as coercive – that is, as a heavy-handed, bureaucratic, and authoritative attempt to secure worker effort and compliance through threats or force – contemporary research and practice increasingly recognize control as enabling. When control is used in an enabling style, it attempts to provide workers with guidance and clarification of their responsibilities, thereby increasing transparency and empowering workers to deal more effectively with their tasks. However, this enabling style often requires more frequent and intensive interaction between workers and managers.

We might expect coercive control to be more effective in alternative work arrangements, mostly because of its focus on conformity, compliance, and avoiding any deviation from standard procedure, which would enhance the monitoring function of control. At the same time, we would expect enabling control to be less effective when organizational identification and goal congruence are lower. However, in our two case studies representing alternative work arrangements, we observed a mix of coercive and enabling control elements at Uber, and a predominantly coercive style at Upwork, particularly of hierarchical and third-party controls. It is important to understand, however, that the same control elements were used in both coercive and enabling styles. Thus, in a blending of styles, the same control element might simultaneously attempt to prevent worker deviation from standardized processes *and* provide necessary information to the worker. Such a blending of styles deserves further research attention, as does the question of which style (coercive, enabling, or a blend of both) is more conducive to a particular control configuration, and under which conditions.

Last, algorithmic control paves the way for an ever more coercive style. By more comprehensively evaluating, directing, and disciplining workers, it has the potential to constrain workers in a much stricter way than under traditional, human-based control regimes. However, algorithmic control can also be used to communicate the rationale behind a control element, and also to share behavior and outcome data with workers. This would provide workers with the relevant information to adjust their behavior, thereby – via an enhanced incentive and coordination function – enabling them to act more effectively. That is, technology-enabled algorithmic control can be used in both coercive and enabling styles (cf., Aloisi & De Stefano 2022), and we have only started to see organizations tap into that potential.

7.2   New Combinations of Control

In addition to these new forms of control, our reconceptualization of organizational control also emphasizes new combinations of existing controls. Our prior discussion explicitly acknowledges the causal complexity inherent in the phenomenon, which expresses itself in both complementary (i.e., reinforcing) effects and substitution effects (i.e., trade-offs and goal conflicts), highlighting the value of a configurational approach.

7.2.1   Causal Complexity of Organizational Control

Classic organizational control research (e.g., Eisenhardt 1985; Ouchi 1977, 1979; Ouchi & Maguire 1975) and most of the more recent research, including our own, has subscribed to a contingency logic, with task and manager characteristics determining the choice between different dimensions of control (see Sections 3.4 and 4.1.3 for details). In contrast, both our meta-analytical review of the literature and the case studies we discussed in Chapter 6 provide ample evidence of complementary or reinforcing effects between controls, highlight important substitution effects between controls, and expose trade-offs between different controls and their impact on outcomes.

7.2.2   Reinforcing Effects among Controls

Most notable across all our case studies were the reinforcing effects of different control dimensions. In particular, advances in electronic surveillance of workers, both on and off the task, coupled with algorithmic(ally) supported) big data analytics, enable organizations to engage in much more comprehensive, real-time, and customized behavior control than ever before. In addition, the above-mentioned advances also enable organizations to nudge individual workers toward preferred behaviors in real time, which enhances behavior control's monitoring, incentive, and coordination benefits. The timely, granular, and wide-ranging data generated from such behavior control can further enhance outcome control by making it timelier, more nuanced, and customizable for each worker. Aggregating such behavior and outcome data across workers also allows for gamifying control, which improves both behavior and outcome control's monitoring, incentive, and coordination benefits. Sharing comparative performance data, such as worker scorecards and rankings, across teams or even across the entire organization, further enhances peer control's monitoring, incentive, and coordination functions. Similarly, sharing behavior and outcome data with customers allows for much more effective third-party control. Pitting workers against each other in a gamified competition, even if participation is not mandatory, reinforces certain behavior metrics and outcome metrics, which likely enhances both the likelihood and effectiveness of workers' engagement in self-control. Coming full circle, comprehensive behavior and outcome data should also improve the effectiveness of input control. This can be achieved by providing feedback on the most desirable and effective attitudes and behaviors that input control can reinforce, by selectively hiring workers with such attributes, and also by socializing and training workers accordingly.

The case studies we discussed, such as Cardinal et al.'s (2004, 2018) longitudinal analysis of control configuration dynamics in a moving company, further corroborate the existence of complementary effects between control dimensions, in this case by allowing formal controls to compensate for the shortcomings inherent in informal controls, and vice versa. Moreover, complementary effects between controls are not restricted to the target of control. For example, as we have seen in our comparison of US trucking companies' and GitLab's control configurations, as well as Uber's and Upwork's, enabling control approaches can amplify the effectiveness of peer control, clan control, and self-control by enhancing information exchanges between managers and workers to ensure workers comprehend the rationale for the control system and how their individual tasks fit into the broader organization.

7.2.3   Trade-offs among Controls and Unintended Consequences

We also found ample evidence of trade-offs and unintended consequences. At the level of control direction, as our Uber case study has demonstrated, hierarchical outcome-based rewards and punishments tend to crowd out workers' intrinsic and social motivation, thereby undermining the likelihood of self-control. At the level of control functions, as we have seen across many of the case studies we discussed, more intrusive digital surveillance of workers' behavior simultaneously supports this control's incentive function (in the form of more timely, frequent, personalized incentives) and undermines its incentive function (as decreased autonomy is demotivating, and as extrinsic motivation can crowd out intrinsic motivation). Coercive forms of control, such as algorithmic(ally supported) controls that are intentionally designed to remain opaque for workers, may support these controls' incentive function, as they are less likely to be gamed. At the same time, however, not having a clear understanding of the rationale for and logic behind these controls will undermine their coordination function. Furthermore, while the autonomy and freedom associated with outcome control are motivating for workers, behavior control, especially the enabling kind, allows for better coordination between managers and workers, and among workers themselves.

At the level of control outcomes, input control's ability to align interests via the creation of shared identities, loyalties, and norms might lead to better process, HR, and rational goal outcomes. However, it might also deprive a team of workers of the variability that is conducive to creativity and innovation, thereby affecting adaptability outcomes in a negative way. Similarly, rigid behavior controls may streamline processes and enhance rational goal outcomes but also suppress healthy creative deviations from standardized processes, thereby jeopardizing adaptability outcomes. Moreover, as we have witnessed in many of our case studies, such rigid behavior controls can deprive workers of their autonomy and self-determination, thereby undermining HR outcomes, such as job satisfaction. Similarly, the beneficial effects of outcome control on rational goal outcomes may be counterbalanced by outcome control's risk transfer from the company to the worker, which could make workers reluctant to engage in inherently risky creative or innovative behavior. As the Amazon and Uber case studies have demonstrated, prioritizing rational goal outcomes, such as efficiency and speed, can come at the expense of HR outcomes, such as worker satisfaction, health, and safety. Last, we have also seen evidence of temporal trade-offs in our case studies, such as the conflicting effects of controls on short-term versus long-term outcomes, especially in the Uber and Upwork case studies.

7.2.4   Goal Conflict

As we have outlined in Chapter 2, our conceptualization of organizational control is goal oriented, with control mechanisms directly tied to specific organizational goals (Cardinal et al. 2017; Sitkin et al. 2010b). However, we have just discussed how control configurations might entail trade-offs when it comes to different outcome dimensions. Moreover, two novel contexts of control can create an even more direct goal conflict. First, alternative work arrangements place workers under the authority of more than one "employer" at any given time, such as the agency that formally employs a temporary worker and the client organization the worker is embedded in; or a digital labor platform, such as Upwork, and a client whose project an Upwork freelancer is contracted to complete. It is conceivable that the goals of the temp agency or digital labor platform and the goals of the client (organization) diverge – as we have seen in the case of clients and freelancers colluding to eliminate Upwork from their relationship. The potential of such goal conflict further increases the causal complexity inherent in any control configuration covering alternative workers. Second, submitting workers to third-party controls, as we have seen especially in the Upwork and Uber case studies, may also create goal conflict. In the Uber case, riders' requests might directly conflict with Uber's corporate goals, putting drivers in the uncomfortable situation of having to choose between following Uber's guidelines and risking a negative customer rating, or complying with the rider's request and risking a penalty from Uber's control algorithm or facing a traffic violation.

7.2.5   The Value of a Configurational Approach to Organizational Control

Taken together, these findings highlight the causal complexity of the organizational control phenomenon, which the configurational approach we presented in Chapter 6 is ideally suited to address. Moreover, our co-citation analysis in Section 3.2 has demonstrated the multi-disciplinary nature of organizational control research, and recent trends, such as technological advances as well as demographic, socio-cultural, political, and legal changes, make it more important than ever to acknowledge multiple theoretical and disciplinary vantage points when theorizing about contemporary organizational control. Again, a configurational approach is uniquely suited to embrace and leverage insights and novel ideas from such a diverse set of perspectives. We hope that future research will harness this approach to step outside disciplinary boundaries and beyond analyzing (underspecified) models with limited sets of controls, to truly appreciate the multifaceted complexity of the phenomenon.

On the practitioner side, a configurational approach can help managers understand that the changes they make in one aspect of organizational control are likely to have ripple effects on the effectiveness of decisions made in other aspects (cf., Monteiro & Adler 2022). Managers are often overwhelmed by best practice recommendations, but the best practice concept without context can be misleading (cf., Brynjolfsson & Milgrom 2012). When managers implement these practices in their own organizations, they rarely have as much success as the exemplar they seek to imitate. By highlighting complementarities among controls, as well as important boundary conditions, a configurational approach can help solve this managerial conundrum. In sum, "[p]ortraying control in configurations offers the best opportunity for control research to reflect organizational reality and management practice and, thus, to influence new theories and approaches to studying organizational control" (Cardinal et al. 2018: 84).

7.3   New Challenges to Fundamental Assumptions

Chapters 5 and 6 have outlined how recent technological, demographic/sociocultural, and organizational developments challenge fundamental assumptions underlying organizational control theory, such as information asymmetry; shared identities, loyalties, and norms; bounded rationality; stable, hierarchical, dyadic relationships; and human controllers. There are reasons to critically examine other, and perhaps more implicit, assumptions, such as workers being solely driven by self-interest; the existence of inevitable goal conflict between workers and managers/organizations; that managerial control intentions closely match workers' perceptions of both the type and efficacy of the chosen control arrangement; and that one standardized set of controls will fit all workers. In this chapter, we will discuss these assumptions as well as the implications of relaxing them in the pursuit of our reconceptualization of organizational control.

7.3.1   Self-Interest and Goal Conflict

Scholars of organizational control, dating back to the ancient Sumerians and Chinese we discussed in Section 3.1.1, view workers as self-interested and assume an inevitable goal conflict between individuals and organizations. Self-interest and goal conflict are also fundamental tenets of both agency theory (Section 3.3.2) and transaction cost theory (Section 3.3.3), both of which assume that information asymmetries in their favor allow workers to become "selfish opportunists who, unless monitored effectively, will exploit owner-principles" (Miller & Sardais 2011: 6). As a consequence of such self-interest and goal conflict, "most people must be coerced, controlled, directed, or threatened with punishment to get them to put forth adequate effort toward the achievement of organizational objectives" (McGregor 1960: 34). However, as we have discussed in Section 5.4, conceptualizing organizational control as such a contested terrain – that is, treating workers as neither trustworthy nor cooperative – can have unintended consequences and might even lead to a vicious cycle between ever-increasing managerial control and worker resistance (Aloisi & De Stefano 2022; Ghoshal & Moran 1996).

Eisenhardt (1989a) was one of the first researchers to relax the assumption of self-interest. If workers would act in a selfless manner, they would behave in the best interest of the organization, regardless of whether managers monitor their behavior or incentivize certain outcomes. This could be the case, for instance, in an organization where workers exhibit high degrees of shared identities, loyalties, and norms, such as in highly socialized or clan-oriented organizations (Ouchi 1979). Contributing to this discussion, Cram, Wiener, and colleagues (2020, 2019) have proposed examining the purpose of control. Control purpose answers the question of *why* control is used and differentiates between value appropriation and value creation purposes (cf., Gulati & Singh 1998). When control purpose is about value appropriation, the underlying assumption is workers' self-interest. Control then serves to align workers' interests with organizational goals and to ensure that they do not act opportunistically (Wiener et al. 2019). In line with classic agency theory (see Section 3.3.2), control thus serves a monitoring and incentive function to reduce agency risks, such as a lack of effort. However, an exclusive focus on value appropriation falls short of accounting for situations in which organizational and worker interests might already be aligned and, consequently, little or no appropriation concerns exist. In this case, workers would act as stewards of the organization (Davis et al. 1997; Donaldson 1990), that is, they are intrinsically motivated and identify closely with their organization and its mission (Sundaramurthy & Lewis 2003). However, even in the absence of appropriation concerns, there is still a need for coordination (Gulati & Singh 1998). Organizational control's value creation purpose therefore focuses on coordinating and integrating all the relevant skills and knowledge of a diverse set of workers (Cram & Wiener 2020; Wiener et al. 2019). This coordination can be achieved, for instance, by facilitating interactions and cooperation via regular meetings to share best practices.

This distinction between value appropriation and value creation highlights the conflicting assumptions of worker self-interest, which is rooted in agency and transaction cost theories, and selflessness, which is rooted in stewardship theory (Davis et al. 1997; Donaldson 1990). Instead of simply assuming one extreme or the other, we encourage future research to consider both theoretical perspectives as complementary, and to examine varying degrees of worker self-interest and goal conflict, their individual and combined influence on teams and organizations, and the potential for adapting control configurations based on these contingencies.

7.3.2   Control Intentions versus Perceptions: Why Perceptions Matter

Another implicit assumption in the control literature that is sometimes questioned, but has rarely been examined systematically (see Sitkin et al. 2020 for a recent review of the literature), is that the intent behind a particular control is what drives the control's impact on outcomes. Given human managers' bounded rationality, as well as growing diversity in the backgrounds, experiences, and attitudes of today's workforce (Section 5.2), it may be more important than ever to distinguish between a manager's intentions for a particular control and how individual workers perceive this control and its effects.

In line with a small but growing literature, we expect workers' perceptions about controls to be important for their behavioral consequences and other outcomes, especially because workers' attitudes and behaviors are most closely associated with their perceptions of their situation (Beijer et al. 2021; Groen et al. 2018). In support of that argument, Speklé et al. (2017) found that HR outcomes, including workers' intrinsic motivation, depend on the perceived control style. Positive results only occurred with an enabling control style that workers perceived as empowering them, by providing valuable information and allowing them to make their own choices about their actions.

Despite these insights, Sitkin and colleagues (2020: 340) concluded their review by pointing out that "theorists have developed a relatively limited understanding regarding how individuals experience, attend to, comprehend, and address the potentially wide array of control elements they encounter." An early exception was Ouchi's (1978) study of the transmission of control through organizational hierarchy, which reported a control loss across the hierarchy. Building on this work, Wiener and colleagues (2016) defined *control congruence* as the degree of similarity between managers' and workers' perceptions of the existing controls. They further distinguished between two types of congruence. The first type, *communicational congruence*, is similar to Ouchi's control transmission consistency, and is defined as the degree of shared understanding between the manager and the worker regarding the deployed control. Examining this form of congruence, Wozniak (2023) found that the most negative reactions to a monitoring system come from workers who do not know if they are being monitored, for what reason, and how the monitoring is being conducted – which is when communicational congruence is low. The second type, *evaluational congruence*, is defined as the level of agreement between manager and worker regarding the appropriateness of the existing controls (Wiener et al. 2016). In contrast, most control research has focused on implemented controls, implicitly assuming no perceptual gap between managers' intentions and workers' perceptions (Long & Sitkin 2018). However, without considering deviating control perceptions, "current control theories may contain significant misspecifications and inaccuracies" (Sitkin et al. 2020: 356).

According to this line of research, any control element or configuration of control elements managers put in place might be misunderstood (i.e., suffer from communicational incongruence) or perceived as inappropriate (i.e., suffer from evaluational incongruence). Investigating these two perceptual incongruences between managers and workers could provide fruitful avenues for future research. On the flipside, misperceptions or misinterpretations of control might exacerbate the vicious cycle between managerial control and worker resistance (Aloisi & De Stefano 2022; Ghoshal & Moran 1996).

7.3.3   From One-Size-Fits-All to Customized Control

If it is indeed workers' perceptions of control that drive many of its effects, it stands to reason that organizations may want to account for these perceptions, and also for differences across workers' perceptions, in the design of their control regime. In Section 5.2, we summarized recent demographic and socio-cultural trends, including the increasing diversity of the workforce, and possible generational differences in attitudes and values about careers, work–life balance, retirement, and, more generally, the way people want to work and the type of organization they want to work for. We concluded that to manage these workers effectively, a traditional one-size-fits-all approach, often in the form of command–and–control, is no longer viable, and managers need to adapt their approaches to accommodate diverse backgrounds and expectations. Especially for the management of millennials, such a customized approach might change the role of managers to acting as personal coaches and career developers (Colbert et al. 2016; Gallup 2016).

In the past, such customization of control for individual workers would not have been feasible or cost-effective. However, with algorithmic support, this could soon become the reality in many organizations. By analyzing massive and rich data sets in real time, at marginal human and financial cost, algorithms have the potential to identify patterns that humans could not, and increase the accuracy of predictions (Baum & Haveman 2020). Algorithms therefore open the possibility of on-demand and personalized control across all three targets, with the potential to meet individual workers' – or generations of workers' – unique needs for autonomy, competence, and relatedness. Returning to our previous discussion of the perception of control, it also seems prudent to invest in worker-specific communication, clarification, and justification of a chosen control configuration to reduce the likelihood of perceptual gaps between managers and workers.

A customized control approach, however, also has to manage the inherent tension between the advantages associated with tailoring control to each workers' individual needs, and the implications of such an approach for the perceived fairness and equity among workers. Consider a situation where a manager (intentionally or unintentionally) treats remote workers differently than workers who come into the office. While this differential control approach might help address each group's needs in a much better way, it will likely increase tension between the two groups. Research examining this issue found that a more equitable approach to monitoring both types of work arrangements proved to be more productive (Lautsch & Kossek 2011).

Last, organizational and task characteristics might impose a natural limit on how much control can be customized in a given organization. As we saw in the GitLab case study, the degree of task interdependence may limit managers' discretion when it comes to granting workers flexibility in terms of the time and place they are allowed to work.

7.4   New Forms of Organizing

In addition to enabling new forms, and new combinations, of control, technological and organizational developments are also starting to change the very nature of work and organizations. As Barley and Kunda (2001: 82) remind us:

In preindustrial societies work was unremarkable: It was woven seamlessly into the fabric of everyday life [and] activities were governed by the cyclical rhythms of nature and the necessities of living: the passing of the seasons, alternations of day and night, pangs of hunger, the need to mend torn clothing, and so on. During the Industrial Revolution, however, people began to segregate work from other spheres of life. Segments of the day were set aside for work and separated from family, community, and leisure by the punching of a time clock or a blast of a factory whistle. Work was also segmented in space; people began to go routinely to a particular place in order to work and then returned from that place when work was done. This temporal and spatial localization of work stimulated a change in the meaning of "job" and gave rise to a larger lexicon for talking about work and the division of labor. [...] Organizations, rather than tasks, now gave jobs their warrant and integrity. From an individual's perspective, when strung together in meaningful sequences, jobs now comprised 'careers,' which often entailed advancement within an organization and a source of identity.

In our postindustrial society, however, the notion of people holding jobs may no longer be an adequate representation of the world of work. The digitization of tasks has enabled the disaggregation of work, both temporally and geographically, giving rise to remote, virtual, or hybrid work arrangements and blurring the boundaries between home and work. Moreover, lower transaction costs associated with contracting out work have allowed alternative work arrangements, such as temporary work, contingent work, and freelance work, to flourish; and a growing share of the post-industrial workforce is comprised of gig workers performing (micro-)tasks. In a sense, we start to see mounting evidence in favor of Barley and Kunda's (2001: 83) more than two decades-old prediction that "work life may be reacquiring some of its preindustrial parsing."

7.4.1   Gig Work

As we have seen in our discussion of digital platforms and the gig economy (Section 5.3.5), even formal organizations and their hierarchical division of labor are no longer inevitable. At least for some tasks, formal organizations may no longer be needed, or they may only be needed as intermediaries matching independent workers and tasks. Davis (2013), for instance, depicted the case of an entrepreneur building an application without the need to leave his/her couch (see Hinings et al. 2018, for a similar example). The entrepreneur creates a webpage on WordPress, hires coders on Upwork, and sells the application either on an app store, such as Apple's App Store or Google Play, or uses a payment system, such as Square. A decade ago, Davis (2013) concluded that Meyer and Rowan's (1977: 345) poetic description of the postindustrial organization has essentially come true: In a hyperrationalized postindustrial economy like the United States, "the building blocks for organizations come to be littered around the societal landscape; it takes only a little entrepreneurial energy to assemble them into a structure." However, as the Uber and Upwork case studies in Sections 6.5.3 and 6.5.4 illustrate, these new ways of organizing work also present new challenges for organizational control, especially when it comes to managing the trade-off between organizational flexibility and maintaining control over, and encouraging workers' commitment to, their work.

Moreover, despite its promise and increasing impact in many industries, such as transportation (Uber), lodging (Airbnb), freelance work (Upwork), and many others, an important legal dispute looms large over this novel form of work: the employment status and corresponding rights and benefits of alternative and gig workers, to whom the usual regulation governing the relationship between employers and workers does not apply. This is a controversial issue that has triggered heated debates in the general public, winding its way through the court systems in a number of countries, and resulted in several governments taking legislative actions (Meijerink & Keegan 2019; Rosenblat & Stark 2016). In May 2021, the Biden administration stopped a bill introduced by the prior (Trump) administration that would have made it easier in the United States for companies to classify gig workers as contractors instead of employees. Moreover, in October 2022, the US Department of Labor proposed a rule that would make it more difficult for companies to treat workers as independent contractors and would require workers to be considered employees when they are economically dependent on a company (Wiessner et al. 2022).

Similar legal debates about the status of gig workers take place in many countries, and depend on the local labor law and tax law. Some countries, such as the United Kingdom, are still considered attractive locations for gig workers, as the jurisdiction supports their status as self-employed, and taxes for self-employed workers only apply to their profits (and not to their total income). In France, a country with comparatively strict labor laws, the distinction between self-employed and freelance work is particularly important and is determined by the relationship with the service provider. Factors considered in making this decision are the integration into the (host) company, who provides the work equipment, and the degree of control exercised by the (host) organization (International Labour Organization 2013).

The fact that gig work is mediated by digital platforms further complicates issues related to legal employment status. On the one hand, independent contract work is characterized as a direct relationship involving just two parties – the workers and the client organizations they contract with – with the work process being controlled by the worker (Cappelli & Keller 2013). This means that an independent contractor's only employer is him- or herself. On the other hand, gig workers on digital labor platforms nominally contract as individuals with clients, but the platform is an important third party to the relationship. Some advocates have therefore suggested that a new "dependent contractor" classification be created in US law to provide on-demand platform workers with an intermediate status between independent contractors and dependent employees (Kuhn & Maleki 2017).

At the time of writing this book, discussions continue, and neither the affected employers, like Uber, nor – and this is more surprising – the people who are supposed to be protected by the new laws, which are the gig workers themselves, agree with the proposed legal changes. Some gig workers do not want to be classified as employees, because that would mean losing the very flexibility and autonomy that come with being a gig worker. There is also a noticeable reaction from employers to the new law, with some reducing their business and making it more difficult for gig workers to find work (Clark 2021). Ongoing uncertainty about the legal classification of workers, and especially legal differences between cities, states, and countries, has increased the likelihood of costly mistakes (Jacobson 2021) and continues to make gig work a complex challenge for organizations.

7.4.2   Blockchains and Smart Contracts

Another recent technological development with direct relevance for new forms of organizing is blockchains. Blockchains are defined as cryptography-based, decentralized chains of blocks of digital records that are shared within a peer-to-peer network (Lumineau et al. 2021). Blockchains eliminate the reliance on intermediaries and instead keep distributed ledgers of all transactions that are continuously verified and propagated to the rest of the system. Since individual participants are unable to falsify transaction records, all recorded information is immutable and trustworthy, eliminating the need for interpersonal trust in either other participants or a third party (Lumineau et al. 2021).

The popular press has hailed blockchains as a technological revolution (Tapscott & Tapscott 2016) that "could someday underlie everything from how we vote to who we connect with online to what we buy" (Mims 2018: B4). Even academic experts regard blockchains as one of the most disruptive technological innovations of our times and expect them to fundamentally change how collaborations are organized (e.g., Lumineau et al. 2021; Murray et al. 2021). Gartner Research estimates the business value-added of blockchains to grow to slightly more than $176 billion by 2025, and to exceed $3.1 trillion by 2030 (Lovelock et al. 2017). McKinsey expects around 10 percent of global GDP to be associated with blockchains by 2027, with its impact spreading across a variety of industries, such as pharmaceuticals, healthcare, and information and telecommunications (McKinsey & Company n.d.). Blockchains have progressed far beyond the widely popular cryptocurrencies and provide an infrastructure for organizing transactions in many fields and applications, such as payment processing, tracking songs in the music industry, securely transmitting medical records, and tracing bills of lading in the transportation industry (Catalini 2017; Friedlmaier et al. 2016). However, the implementation of blockchains has not been without challenges, and many of the early adopters, such as Maersk and IBM's shipping platform TradeLens, have discontinued projects built on blockchain technology (Bousquette 2022).

Most interesting for our discussion are the more complex, automated blockchain transactions called "smart contracts" (Murray et al. 2021). These smart contracts are algorithms that allow parties who do not know or trust each other to engage in a transaction, by automatically executing the transaction when pre-specified conditions in the protocols are satisfied. Instead of depending on human agents or third-party intermediaries, smart contracts rely on trusted data feeds called "oracles" to trigger the preprogrammed protocols stored on a blockchain to automatically execute the transaction. Examples of such "oraclized" data inputs can be anything from fully autonomous sensors (e.g., rain gauges, digital thermometers) and online inputs (e.g., website traffic, stock price changes, sporting outcomes) to real-world human decisions (e.g., court rulings, trade agreements) (Murray et al. 2021). A smart employment contract, for instance, would have to articulate all stipulations and possible contingencies upfront, such as the work to be performed, the expected quality of such work, and the compensation for it. Moreover, all conditions would need to be objective measures that can be codified and verified before a payment could be released. This codification requirement inherent in smart contracts explains why they are challenging to implement for more complex, higher-level tasks and jobs, and are therefore more suitable for governing the job requirements of entry-level workers.

In addition to fully automating the monitoring function of control, smart contracts also facilitate the incentive function (Lumineau et al. 2021). Since smart contracts automatically execute transactions, they drastically reduce the leeway the transacting parties have to engage in opportunistic behavior. Moreover, blockchain records are virtually impossible to tamper with and are easily traceable, which makes ex-post opportunistic behaviors more easily detectable.

Smart contracts can also enhance coordination between transacting parties. Blockchains not only support day-to-day communication and information exchange between parties, but they also facilitate the distribution of rights and responsibilities in a relationship, such as the division of labor, roles, and task descriptions (Lumineau et al. 2021). Given blockchains' role as written and traceable knowledge repositories, every authorized member can obtain information about the responsibilities for tasks, how it is ensured that tasks are performed in a preplanned manner, and how these tasks fit into the collective goal.

Together, their monitoring, incentive, and coordination advantages reduce or even eliminate the costs to enforce smart contracts. However, smart contracts may also come with higher costs to write them. This is especially true for transactions, such as R&D collaborations or building a power plant, that are characterized by high levels of uncertainty and will therefore likely have to adapt to unforeseen and unpredictable contingencies that are difficult, if not impossible, to specify and codify ex ante (Lumineau et al. 2021). For these types of tasks, perfect planning is virtually impossible, and the need to maintain flexibility is critical, making smart contracts a suboptimal control choice.

Smart contracts also increasingly incorporate AI and ML to automatically create protocols and execute them with little or no human oversight or intervention (Murray et al. 2021). Research and practice therefore need to critically examine the role of smart contracts as agents, and clarify the role of managers as principals/owners in determining the initial protocols and contingencies when designing smart contracts. For this reason, researchers stress the continued need for human managers, even in the context of smart contracts: "When rare events occur that are not (or cannot be) anticipated in the contingencies of an organization's preprogrammed smart contracts, we hold that humans are still necessary to orchestrate a pathway forward. This suggests that without a certain degree of human intervention, smart contracts alone may be ill-equipped to deal with reality as it unfolds in real time" (Murray et al. 2021: 636).

7.4.3 Decentralized Autonomous Organizations (DAOs)

A new organizational form that harnesses blockchain technology is decentralized autonomous organizations (DAOs), such as the blockchain-based Bitcoin and Ethereum cryptocurrencies. DAOs are *decentralized*, as they are governed by a group of peer owners that own governance tokens, with none of the peer owners having the ability to dominate the others. DAOs also are *autonomous*, as they operate through algorithms, with all the relevant rules that guide the organization's operations programmed into smart contracts (De Man et al. 2019; Lumineau et al. 2021). Since there is no need to trust any individual person or firm, DAOs have been referred to as being trustless (Machart 2020). Instead, participants trust in the system as a whole, similar to trusting that a legal contract is enforceable in court. Trust in DAOs emerges from the system and from any governance decisions being "on-chain" (which means they are open to the public to verify), decentralized (with many actors keeping each other in check), using cryptocurrency proofs (i.e., relying on mathematical assurances), and using economic/game-theoretic assurances (the cost to acquire a majority of the tokens that allows any individual to validate transactions unilaterally) (Machart 2020). Cryptographic verification also eliminates the need for, and therefore the cost of, an internal or external controller or auditor. All DAOs' members can participate in decision-making processes and have access to information about the organization's activities and finances. DAOs also provide the advantages of lower entry barriers and simple global access through anonymous operations.

DAOs have many use cases,[4] including proposal execution (e.g., automated market makers), funding for decentralized projects (e.g., MetaCartel Ventures), crowdfunding (e.g., ConstitutionDAO that was formed to purchase an original copy of the US constitution, or BlockbusterDAO that has been formed to purchase the Blockbuster brand with the goal to turn it into a decentralized movie platform), decentralized application governance (e.g., DAOs with dApps), non-fungible token (NFT)-based investing (e.g., HeadDAO, in which members have collective ownership of blue-chip NFTs), metaverse decentralization (e.g., Decentralized DAO) (Howell 2022), and impact DAOs (e.g., Klima DAO) (Jirásek in press). Despite their promise, the inflexible nature of DAOs – which requires easily traceable and automatically verifiable activities as well as all possible contingencies being encoded ex ante – currently restricts them to the execution of mostly routine tasks with low complexity. More important for our purposes, there are limits to blockchains' abilities when it comes to tracking and automatically verifying workers' activities, which might require subjective assessments (Machart 2020). Despite their current limitation to relatively routine tasks, DAOs' ability to avoid some of the problems of human-based organizations, like opaque decision-making and opportunistic behavior, will likely generate more interest in, and more applications for, these novel organizational forms in the near future, which could give rise to an entirely new form of organizational control.

7.4.4   Self-organization, Holacracies, and "Unbossing"

In direct contrast to the unprecedented technological opportunities for algorithmic(ally supported) hierarchical surveillance and control – which, in some organizations, such as Amazon and Uber, have already become reality – the topic of self-organization has also gained importance across many

---

[4] For an overview of DAO use cases, see: https://deepdao.io/organizations

types of organizations. The basic idea is to replace the organizational hierarchy that has evolved in a more stable world, in which less skilled workers benefit from a classic command-and-control approach. According to its proponents, by tapping into the ideas and creative potential of all organizational members, self-managed organizations can adapt more quickly and flexibly, and are therefore better suited to deal with today's complex, rapidly changing environment and knowledge-based or creative work. Self-organization can assume different forms (Lee & Edmondson 2017) ranging from small units of an organization being converted into self-organized teams (Manz 1992; Stewart & Manz 1995) to fundamental changes in the design of the organization at large, such as the creation of a holacracy (Robertson 2015).

In traditional managerial hierarchies, managers are responsible for the allocation, management, and monitoring of work and, in some cases, for the execution of the work itself. Workers typically lack formal decision-making authority in all areas except work execution.[5] Self-organization, in contrast, is characterized by a radical decentralization of authority and the elimination of the traditional manager–subordinate relationship as the key mechanism of control (Lee & Edmondson 2017). Decision-making responsibility is delegated to lower management levels, and hierarchical coordination by managers is reduced in favor of horizontal coordination, allowing organizations to become more innovative by utilizing the analytical and creative potential of all members. Self-organization further empowers workers with more decentralized and democratic decision processes and facilitates their personal development, resilience, and fulfillment (Foss & Klein 2019). To accomplish work, self-organization requires teams to collectively define and assign roles to individual team members. Decision power is conferred on roles rather than individuals, and roles are not bound to individuals, but are defined around the work (Bernstein et al. 2016; Schell & Bischof 2022). An example of such self-organization can be found in the music-streaming company Spotify. Spotify organizes their so-called "squad" teams around the principles of autonomy, alignment, and collective ownership. Each squad is small, with eight or fewer team members, and is empowered to make decisions about what initiative to pursue, how to implement it, and how to collaborate without requiring formal managerial approval (Albanese 2018).

There are three main advantages of self-organization. First, by having to negotiate with one another, team members allocate roles to those best equipped to carry them out, thereby matching individual capabilities with organizational goals (Lee & Edmondson 2017). This negotiated matching process allows individuals to select roles that play to their strengths and interests

---

[5] However, managers reserve the right to overrule workers and direct how they should do their jobs – and they often do – which explains the ubiquity of the term "micromanagement."

while simultaneously serving as a safety check against matches that might be useful to one person but detrimental to the team. Furthermore, since team members are responsible for the process and have a choice regarding role assignments, they have a greater sense of ownership and control, which has long been associated with creative problem solving, motivation, engagement, and organizational commitment (Bailyn 1985; Cordery et al. 1991; Paolillo & Brown 1978). Second, in traditional hierarchies, managers have the authority to prescribe what must be done – and how – because of their job title, and not because they have any particular insight. Self-organization, in contrast, allows for decisions to be made closer to – and be responsive to the requirements of – the actual work (Bernstein et al. 2016). Third, self-organization allows for a faster response to emerging market needs. Instead of running ideas up the flagpole and waiting for decisions to come back down, team members can go directly to the people holding the affected roles and thereby avoid the red tape and obligatory signoffs that tend to delay decision-making in traditional hierarchies. Without the intricate webs of job titles, job descriptions, and reporting relationships, communication becomes more efficient and is less likely to be watered down or misinterpreted through management layers (Bernstein et al. 2016). However, self-managing teams can also bear unwanted side effects, such as excessive peer pressure, which can hurt the team's balance and performance (Khanagha et al. 2022). Furthermore, in truly self-managed teams, there is no managerial authority to counter these destructive effects of excessive peer pressure.

A contemporary type of self-managing organization is a *holacracy* (Robertson 2015). Holacracies are typically guided by a purpose and embrace a set of detailed organizational design prescriptions that are outlined in the "holacracy constitution"[6] – a living document signed by top executives, which is accessible to every member of the organization (Robertson 2015; Schell & Bischof 2022). The structure of a holacratic organization consists of a hierarchy of fluid teams or "circles." New circles can emerge and old ones can disappear, based on changes in the organization's needs and objectives. Circles are nested by vertical double linking, with each higher-level circle electing a member to represent the circle at a lower-level circle and vice versa, thereby establishing communication channels between circles (Robertson 2015). While circles design and govern themselves, the constitution specifies the rules by which circles are created, revised, and removed and establishes broad guidelines for how circles should identify and assign roles, what boundaries these roles should have, and how circles should interact (Bernstein et al. 2016). As in other forms of self-organization, decision-making authority is distributed not among individuals, but among circles and individuals' roles within circles

---

[6] www.holacracy.org/constitution/5

(Lee & Edmondson 2017). Individuals usually hold multiple roles in various circles,[7] and if an individual is not a good fit for a specific role, then the role can be reassigned to someone else (Bernstein et al. 2016; Schell & Bischof 2022). However, roles are also flexible, and they can be revised and adapted in regular "governance meetings."

Holacracies grant individuals broad autonomy over how they execute their roles. Instead of trying to attain consensus before deciding, which can take time, holacracies rely on decision-making by consent, which implies that if no one has a serious objection, a decision can be made. As a result, each member, regardless of his or her hierarchical position, can make quick decisions within the confines of their roles. At times, a decision overlaps with another person's role, creating potential tension. Then, a learning process unfolds, and subsequent decision-making processes are adjusted to include the affected members (Robertson 2015).

Despite their promise as an organization-wide form of self-managing teams, holacracies also face several challenges. The organizational complexity resulting from a proliferation of roles, and an increasingly fragmented organization, can complicate both individuals' efforts to actually do their work and executives' efforts to design and implement compensation and reward systems – and it can make it difficult to hire individuals into the organization and into specific roles (Lee & Edmondson 2017). Moreover, to capitalize on the benefits of self-organization we discussed earlier, all members must exercise their power and voice, which does not always happen. Even in self-managed organizations, leadership remains indispensable:

You might assume that the three goals of self-management structures – designing roles that match individual capabilities with organizational goals, making decisions closer to the work, and responding to emerging market needs – would make leaders less relevant. Yet one of the greatest challenges of implementing the goals at scale is insufficient leadership. When leadership is a shared responsibility, everyone must understand and practice it. You end up with *more* formal team leaders as the number of modules increases. Since adopting holacracy, Zappos has gone from 150 team leaders to 300 lead links, who are responsible for its 500 circles. (Bernstein et al. 2016: 48, emphasis in original)

Even if individuals want to step up, it can be difficult for them to find their way amidst the plethora of circle and role descriptions, which can make a holacracy appear "almost as onerous as the Byzantine hierarchy it replaced" (Bernstein et al. 2016: 46). It is therefore a myth that holacratic organizations have no formal structure. In fact, as is evident from the double-linked hierarchy of circles, holacracies often have *more* structure than traditional hierarchies

---

[7] Case in point, 2 years after online retailer Zappos adopted holacracy, the average number of roles per employee grew from one to more than seven (Bernstein et al. 2016).

(Bernstein et al. 2016). Furthermore, holacracies do not eliminate hierarchies entirely. At Zappos, for instance, roles are still arranged in a formal hierarchy, with some circles holding responsibilities that encompass the responsibilities of smaller circles (Lee & Edmondson 2017). Moreover, their detailed constitution as well as the detailed circle and role descriptions suggest that holacracies are not necessarily less formal than traditional hierarchies.

In terms of our organizational control framework, holacracies are characterized by a holistic approach comprising all three control targets. They rely heavily on clearly defined roles and decision processes (i.e., formal behavior control) as well as stated objectives to realize set targets (i.e., formal outcome control). Holacracies also rely on intensive onboarding processes (i.e., formal and informal input control) to ensure that new members understand their role(s), the interrelationship with other roles, the boundary conditions set by the holacracy constitution, and the purpose of the organization and the specific circles they are part of. Holacracies thus rely heavily on formal controls complemented by informal controls. However, holacracies rely much less on top-down control compared to hierarchies, and more on self-control and peer control, with all members of self-managing circles holding each other accountable (Ackermann et al. 2021). Last, holacracies are designed as an enabling form of control, which is evident, among others, from team members' involvement in the design and government of circles and roles, matching capabilities with roles, information sharing across double-linked circles, as well as tensions across circles being framed as learning and adaptation opportunities.

Despite some management consultants advocating holacracy as a replacement for top-down design, hierarchy, and managerial authority, holacracies have mainly been adopted by small and medium-sized organizations, with Zappos being the best-known exception of a larger firm following holacratic principles (Bernstein et al. 2016). In line with contingency theoretic logic (Section 3.3.4), their ability to quickly adapt to changing requirements would further suggest that holacracies are best suited for fast-changing environments in which their advantages for making fast decisions outweigh their challenges – which is exactly the situation most start-up companies are in (Bernstein et al. 2016).

Although holacracies are a fairly recent development, observers' reactions have been divided into three opposing camps (Bernstein et al. 2016). The first camp celebrates these "boss-less" and "flat" organizations as catalysts for flexibility, engagement, and creativity, while the second denounces holacracies as naïve social experiments that ignore how work is done in organizations. The third camp dismisses holacracies as yet another management consulting fad that consists largely of old wine in new bottles. Monteiro and Adler (2022: 451) provide an apt but acerbic summary of this camp's view, including its limitation to rapidly changing environments:

Often presented as an unprecedented novelty in organization design, [holacracy] is, we suggest, more plausibly understood as an updated, IT-enabled version of the workflow bureaucracy documented by the Aston group. Its extensive formalization and the idea of differentiating roles from the people who fill them will look familiar to anyone who has read Weber. Holacracy's commitment to the idea that work units should govern their internal work processes in a collegial manner was never excluded from Weber's ideal-type, and it was a key part of Blau's "dynamic" variety of bureaucracy (Blau 1963). The novelty here is in how holacracies – in the pursuit of adaptability over reliability – forego strategic synergy and economies of scale and scope for market responsiveness and rapid incremental adaptation. Classic contingency theory suggests there are limits to how far such an organizational form can diffuse across the variegated economic landscape.

All three camps' blanket arguments, however, tend to overlook an important point. While organization-wide approaches to self-organization, such as holacracies, are, at best, challenging, elements of self-organization can become valuable tools for organizations of all kinds, and even large organizations could adopt certain aspects of this approach (Bernstein et al. 2016). A project-level approach to self-organization is *Agile*.[8] Originally conceived by a group of software developers in reaction to what they perceived as micro-management of many software-development projects, Agile aims at integrating the principles of modern teamwork with project management. Agile emphasizes cooperation among self-organizing, cross-functional teams in which individuals have fixed roles and accountability. These teams then use fixed meetings and processes – often with colorful names, such as "sprints," "scrums," "burn-down charts," and "poker planning"[9] – in support of making iterative progress toward well-defined goals (De Man et al. 2019). In contrast to full-fledged holacracies, which are mostly smaller organizations, Agile has been implemented by large, multinational companies, such as Barclays, Ericsson, Microsoft, Google, and Spotify (Foss & Klein 2019).

Another trend following the idea of self-organization is "unbossing." Partly inspired by Gary Hamel's (2011) "no-manager movement" and its accompanying battle cry, "bureaucracy must die" (Hamel 2014), established organizations have started initiatives to shift away from hierarchical management structures. In 2018, for instance, Novartis's CEO Vasant Narasimhan initiated the "Unbossed Leadership Experience," with the goal to empower organizational members to take ownership of their own development and to help managers become servant leaders who act as role models by setting their teams' success above their own.[10] While such calls for unbossing and extremely flat organizational settings without any hierarchy or authority are

---

[8] https://agilemanifesto.org/
[9] For more information on these Agile methods, see Rigby et al. (2016) and De Man et al. (2019).
[10] www.novartis.com/about/strategy/people-and-culture/we-create-unbossed-environment

fashionable, they have not been without criticism. Foss and Klein (2019, emphasis in original), for instance, concluded their discussion of the boss-less company as follows:

[S]ome individuals or groups need to bear the final responsibility, and be held accountable for the firm's actions – the buck has to stop *somewhere*. […] You don't need a boss to tell you what to do throughout the day or how to interact with other people. But you do need an entrepreneur to launch a venture or establish a sharing platform, an owner or owners to advance the capital and take responsibility for the overall aims of the project, and managers to establish and enforce the rules of the game. That's what modern management is all about – designing the system in which empowered, knowledge-based workers can thrive. But the basic system with workers and managers is the same.

In line with our discussion of holacracies, the takeaway from the idea of unbossing is actually more nuanced than the often heated debate about its merits would suggest. The question is not whether today's organizations should no longer have hierarchies or managerial authority, but what characteristics such authority should have. The kernel of truth in calls for boss-less organizations is that, for many routine tasks, workers no longer require a manager to direct and monitor them, and we have seen that such tight supervision can actually backfire. However, for defining and implementing the organization's overall purpose, and for setting at least some guardrails for workers' behaviors, managerial authority is still necessary. Far from making them obsolete, the current business environment, with its exciting developments in information technology and new forms of organizing, therefore appears to make good managers more important than ever (Foss & Klein 2019).

7.5   Conclusion

Throughout our book, we have maintained that organizational control is fundamental to all forms of organizing, and the topic has attracted sustained research interest for over a century, resulting in a rich and multi-disciplinary literature. However, we have also seen recent technological and organizational changes challenge the very foundation that our theories and managerial implications are built on, raising the question of how the field can move forward and contribute to our understanding of managing workers in today's economy. Acknowledging the field's multi-disciplinary nature, as well as the causal complexity of the phenomenon, the configurational approach we proposed allows us not only to describe archetypes of control configurations found in a diverse set of organizations, but also to outline recommendations for how organizations can mitigate inherent trade-offs and unintended consequences that undermine the fit and effectiveness of such archetypes. Our discussion of novel forms and combinations of control, as well as new forms of organizing, is intended as a catalyst for future research in this area and as an inspiration for managers and other practitioners thinking about how to manage workers in the twenty-first century.

In conclusion, it is worth remembering Ashford and colleagues' (2018: 24) warning from the beginning of our book that "the new world of work is on our doorstep, and organizational studies seem woefully unprepared." With our book, we intend to open the door, highlight the most important new and emerging trends, and take a first step toward the reconceptualization of organizational control for contemporary organizational realities.

References

Abdi M. & Aulakh P. S. (2012). Do country-level institutional frameworks and inter-firm governance arrangements substitute or complement in international business relationships? *Journal of International Business Studies*, 43(5), 477–97.

Abernethy M. A. & Stoelwinder J. U. (1995). The role of professional control in the management of complex organizations. *Accounting, Organizations and Society*, 20(1), 1–17.

Achor S., Reece A., Kellerman G. R., & Robichaux A. (2018). 9 out of 10 people are willing to earn less money to do more-meaningful work. *Harvard Business Review*, November 6, https://hbr.org/2018/11/9-out-of-10-people-are-willing-to-earn-less-money-to-do-more-meaningful-work.

Achrol R. S. & Gundlach G. T. (1999). Legal and social safeguards against opportunism in exchange. *Journal of Retailing*, 75(1), 107–24.

Ackermann M., Schell S., & Kopp S. (2021). How Mercedes-Benz addresses digital transformation using holacracy. *Journal of Organizational Change Management*, 34(7), 1285–99.

Adler P. S. (1999). Building better bureaucracies. *Academy of Management Perspectives*, 13(4), 36–47.

Adler P. S. & Borys B. (1996). Two types of bureaucracy: Enabling and coercive. *Administrative Science Quarterly*, 41(1), 61–89.

Adler P. S. & Chen C. X. (2011). Combining creativity and control: Understanding individual motivation in large-scale collaborative creativity. *Accounting, Organizations and Society*, 36(2), 63–85.

Adner R., Puranam P., & Zhu F. (2019). What is different about digital strategy? From quantitative to qualitative change. *Strategy Science*, 4(4), 253–61.

Aguinis H., Dalton D. R., Bosco F. A., Pierce C. A., & Dalton C. M. (2011). Meta-analytic choices and judgment calls: Implications for theory building and testing, obtained effect sizes, and scholarly impact. *Journal of Management*, 37(1), 5–38.

Aguinis H., Gottfredson R. K., & Wright T. A. (2011). Best-practice recommendations for estimating interaction effects using meta-analysis. *Journal of Organizational Behavior*, 32(8), 1033–43.

Aguinis H., Pierce C. A., Bosco F. A., Dalton D. R., & Dalton C. M. (2011). Debunking myths and urban legends about meta-analysis. *Organizational Research Methods*, 14(2), 306–31.

Ahrens T. & Chapman C. S. (2002). The structuration of legitimate performance measures and management: Day-to-day contests of accountability in a U.K. restaurant chain. *Management Accounting Research*, 13(2), 151–71.

Ahrens T. & Chapman C. S. (2004). Accounting for flexibility and efficiency: A field study of management control systems in a restaurant chain. *Contemporary Accounting Research*, 21(2), 271–301.

Ahrens T. & Chapman C. S. (2007). Management accounting as practice. *Accounting, Organizations and Society*, 32(1), 1–27.

Ahrens T. & Mollona M. (2007). Organisational control as cultural practice: A shop floor ethnography of a Sheffield steel mill. *Accounting, Organizations and Society*, 32(4), 305–31.

Aiello J. R. & Svec C. M. (1993). Computer monitoring of work performance: Extending the social facilitation framework to electronic presence. *Journal of Applied Social Psychology*, 23(7), 537–48.

Aiken L. S. & West S. G. (1991). *Multiple regression: Testing and interpreting interactions*. Thousand Oaks, CA: SAGE.

Ajunwa I., Crawford K., & Schultz J. (2017). Limitless worker surveillance. *California Law Review*, 105(3), 735–76.

Akerlof G. A. & Shiller R. J. (2015). *Phishing for phools: The economics of manipulation and deception*. Princeton, NJ: Princeton University Press.

Akkermans H., Van Oppen W., Wynstra F., & Voss C. (2019). Contracting outsourced services with collaborative key performance indicators. *Journal of Operations Management*, 65(1), 22–47.

Albanese J. (2018). Four ways millennials are transforming leadership. *Inc.com*, November 14, www.inc.com/jason-albanese/four-ways-millennials-are-transforming-leadership.html.

Albertini E. (2019). The contribution of management control systems to environmental capabilities. *Journal of Business Ethics*, 159(4), 1163–80.

Alchian A. A. & Demsetz H. (1972). Production, information costs, and economic organization. *American Economic Review*, 62(5), 777–95.

Alexander A., De Smet A., Langstaff M., & Ravid D. (2021). What employees are saying about the future of remote work. April 1, www.mckinsey.com/capabilities/people-and-organizational-performance/our-insights/what-employees-are-saying-about-the-future-of-remote-work.

Alexander A., De Smet A., & Mysore M. (2020). Reimagining the postpandemic workforce. *McKinsey Quarterly*, July 7, www.mckinsey.com/capabilities/people-and-organizational-performance/our-insights/reimagining-the-postpandemic-workforce.

Alge B. J. & Hansen S. D. (2014). Workplace monitoring and surveillance research since "1984": A review and agenda. In Coovert MD, & Thompson LF (eds), *The psychology of workplace technology*. New York: Routledge, 207–37.

Alharthi A., Krotov V., & Bowman M. (2017). Addressing barriers to big data. *Business Horizons*, 60(3), 285–92.

Allen T. D., Golden T. D., & Shockley K. M. (2015). How effective is telecommuting? Assessing the status of our scientific findings. *Psychological Science in the Public Interest*, 16(2), 40–68.

Aloisi A. & De Stefano V. (2022). Essential jobs, remote work and digital surveillance: Addressing the COVID⊠19 pandemic panopticon. *International Labour Review*, 161(2), 289–314.

Alvesson M. & Kärreman D. (2004). Interfaces of control. Technocratic and socio-ideological control in a global management consultancy firm. *Accounting, Organizations and Society*, 29(3–4), 423–44.

Alvesson M. & Kärreman D. (2007). Unraveling HRM: Identity, ceremony, and control in a management consulting firm. *Organization Science*, 18(4), 711–23.

Alvesson M. & Willmott H. (2002). Identity regulation as organizational control: Producing the appropriate individual. *Journal of Management Studies*, 39(5), 619–44.

Alwin D. F. & Hauser R. M. (1975). The decomposition of effects in path analysis. *American Sociological Review*, 40(1), 37–47.

Amabile T. M., Conti R., Coon H., Lazenby J., & Herron M. (1996). Assessing the work environment for creativity. *Academy of Management Journal*, 39(5), 1154–84.

Amazon (2022). Annual report. https://s2.q4cdn.com/299287126/files/doc_financials/2023/ar/Amazon-2022-Annual-Report.pdf.

Amodei, D., Olah, C., Steinhardt, J., Christiano, P., Schulman, J., & Mané, D. (2016). Concrete problems in AI safety. arXiv preprint arXiv:1606.06565.

Anantatmula V. S. & Shrivastav B. (2012). Evolution of project teams for Generation Y workforce. *International Journal of Managing Projects in Business*, 5(1), 9–26.

Anderson E. (1985). The salesperson as outside agent or employee: A transaction cost analysis. *Marketing Science*, 4(3), 234–54.

Anderson E. & Oliver R. L. (1987). Perspectives on behavior-based versus outcome-based salesforce control systems. *Journal of Marketing*, 51(4), 76–88.

Anderson E. & Weitz B. (1992). The use of pledges to build and sustain commitment in distribution channels. *Journal of Marketing Research*, 29(1), 18–34.

Anderson J. C. & Narus J. A. (1984). A model of the distributor's perspective of distributor-manufacturer working relationships. *Journal of Marketing*, 48(4), 62–74.

Andrews K. R. (1980). *The concept of corporate strategy*. Homewood, IL: R. D. Irwin.

Angwin J., Larson J., Mattu S., & Kirchner L. (2016). Machine bias: There's software used across the country to predict future criminals. And it's biased against blacks. *ProPublica*, May 23, www.propublica.org/article/machine-bias-risk-assessments-in-criminal-sentencing.

Anteby M. (2008). Identity incentives as an engaging form of control: Revisiting leniencies in an aeronautic plant. *Organization Science*, 19(2), 202–20.

Anteby M. & Chan C. K. (2018). A self-fulfilling cycle of coercive surveillance: Workers' invisibility practices and managerial justification. *Organization Science*, 29(2), 247–63.

Anthony C. (2021). When knowledge work and analytical technologies collide: The practices and consequences of black boxing algorithmic technologies. *Administrative Science Quarterly*, 66(4), 1173–212.

Anthony R. N. (1965). *Planning and control systems: A framework for analysis: Studies in management control*. Boston, MA: Division of Research, Graduate School of Business Administration, Harvard University.

Anthony R. N. & Govindarajan V. (2001). *Management control systems*, 10th ed. Boston, MA: McGraw-Hill Irwin.

Argyris C. (1952). *The impact of budgets on people*. New York: Controllership Foundation.

Armour S. (2011). American Medical settles case in Facebook dismissal. *Bloomberg*, February 7, www.bloomberg.com/news/articles/2011-02-07/american-medical-settles-u-s-case-in-dismissal-tied-to-facebook.

Arrow K. J. (1974). *The limits of organization*. New York: W. W. Norton.

Arrow K. J. (1985). The economics of agency. In Pratt JW, & Zeckhauser RJ (eds), *Principals and agents: The structure of business*. Cambridge, MA: Harvard University Press, 37–51.

Arthur J. B. (1994). Effects of human resource systems on manufacturing performance and turnover. *Academy of Management Journal*, 37(3), 670–87.

Arya A., Glover J. C., & Sivaramakrishnan K. (1997). The interaction between decision and control problems and the value of Information. *Accounting Review*, 72(4), 561–74.

Asher Hamilton I. & Cain Á. (2019). Amazon warehouse employees speak out about the "brutal" reality of working during the holidays, when 60-hour weeks are mandatory and ambulance calls are common. *Business Insider*, February 19, www.businessinsider.com/amazon-employees-describe-peak-2019-2.

Ashford S. J., Caza B. B., & Reid E. M. (2018). From surviving to thriving in the gig economy: A research agenda for individuals in the new world of work. *Research in Organizational Behavior*, 38(4), 23–41.

Ashford S. J., George E., & Blatt R. (2007). Old assumptions, new work: The opportunities and challenges of research on nonstandard employment. *Academy of Management Annals*, 1(1), 65–117.

Ashton K. (2009). That 'internet of things' thing. *RFID Journal*, 22(7), 97–114.

Bailey C., Lips-Wiersma M., Madden A., Yeoman R., Thompson M., & Chalofsky N. (2019). The five paradoxes of meaningful work: Introduction to the special Issue 'Meaningful work: Prospects for the 21st century'. *Journal of Management Studies*, 56(3), 481–99.

Bailyn L. (1985). Autonomy in the industrial R&D lab. *Human Resource Management*, 24(2), 129–46.

Baiman S. (1982). Agency research in managerial accounting: A survey. *Journal of Accounting Literature*, 1(Spring), 154–213.

Baiman S. (1990). Agency research in managerial accounting: A second look. *Accounting, Organizations and Society*, 15(4), 341–71.

Balakrishnan S. & Koza M. P. (1993). Information asymmetry, adverse selection and joint ventures: Theory and evidence. *Journal of Economic Behavior and Organization*, 20(1), 99–117.

Balasubramanian N., Ye Y., & Xu M. (2022). Substituting human decision-making with machine learning: Implications for organizational learning. *Academy of Management Review*, 47(3), 448–65.

Baliga B. R. & Jaeger A. M. (1984). Multinational corporations: Control systems and delegation issues. *Journal of International Business Studies*, 15(2), 25–40.

Bamberger P. A., Biron M., & Meshoulam I. (2014). *Human resource strategy: Formulation, implementation, and impact*, 2nd ed. New York: Routledge.

Bamberger P. A. & Fiegenbaum A. (1996). The role of strategic reference points in explaining the nature and consequences of human resource strategy. *Academy of Management Review*, 21(4), 926–58.

Banker R. D., Lee S.-Y., Potter G., & Srinivasan D. (1996). Contextual analysis of performance impacts of outcome-based incentive compensation. *Academy of Management Journal*, 39(4), 920–48.

Banker R. D., Potter G., & Srinivasan D. (2000). An empirical investigation of an incentive plan that includes nonfinancial performance measures. *The Accounting Review*, 75(1), 65–92.

Barker J. R. (1993). Tightening the iron cage: Concertive control in self-managed teams. *Administrative Science Quarterly*, 38(3), 408–37.

Barley S. & Kunda G. (2001). Bringing work back in. *Organization Science*, 12(1), 76–95.

Barley S. R. (1986). Technology as an occasion for structuring: Evidence from observations of CT scanners and the social order of radiology departments. *Administrative Science Quarterly*, 31(1), 78–108.

Barley S. R. (1996). Technicians in the workplace: Ethnographic evidence for bringing work into organization studies. *Administrative Science Quarterly*, 41(3), 404–41.

Barley S. R., Bechky B. A., & Milliken F. J. (2017). The changing nature of work: Careers, identities, and work lives in the 21st century. *Academy of Management Discoveries*, 3(2), 111–15.

Barley S. R. & Kunda G. (1992). Design and devotion: Surges of rational and normative ideologies of control in managerial discourse. *Administrative Science Quarterly*, 37(3), 363–99.

Barnard C. I. (1938). *The functions of the executive*. Cambridge, MA: Harvard University Press.

Barnard C. I. (1968). *The functions of the executive*. Cambridge, MA: Harvard University Press.

Barocas S. & Selbst A. D. (2016). Big data's disparate impact. *California Law Review*, 104(3), 671–732.

Barrero J. M., Bloom N., & Davis S. J. (2021). Why working from home will stick. *National Bureau of Economic Research Working Paper Series*, No. 28731, https://doi.org/10.3386/w28731.

Bartel C. A., Wrzesniewski A., & Wiesenfeld B. M. (2012). Knowing where you stand: Physical isolation, perceived respect, and organizational identification among virtual employees. *Organization Science*, 23(3), 743–57.

Baum J. A. C. & Haveman H. A. (2020). The future of organizational theory. *Academy of Management Review*, 45(2), 268–72.

Baumeister R. F., Bratslavsky E., Muraven M., & Tice D. M. (1998). Ego depletion: Is the active self a limited resource? *Journal of Personality and Social Psychology*, 74(5), 1252–65.

Baysinger B. & Hoskisson R. E. (1990). The composition of board of directors and strategic control: Effects on corporate strategy. *Academy of Management Review*, 15(1), 72–87.

Bazerman M. H., Tenbrunsel A. E., & Wade-Benzoni K. (1998). Negotiating with yourself and losing: Making decisions with competing internal preferences. *Academy of Management Review*, 23(2), 225–41.

BBC (2020). Facebook and Google extend working from home to end of year. May 8, www.bbc.com/news/business-52570714.

Beatty R. P. & Zajac E. J. (1994). Managerial incentives, monitoring, and risk bearing: A study of executive compensation, ownership, and board structure in initial public offerings. *Administrative Science Quarterly*, 39(2), 313–35.

Bedford D. S. (2015). Management control systems across different modes of innovation: Implications for firm performance. *Management Accounting Research*, 28(3), 12–30.

Bedford D. S. (2020). Conceptual and empirical issues in understanding management control combinations. *Accounting, Organizations and Society*, 86(4), 101187.

Bedford D. S. & Malmi T. (2015). Configurations of control: An exploratory analysis. *Management Accounting Research*, 27, 2–26.

Bedford D. S., Malmi T., & Sandelin M. (2016). Management control effectiveness and strategy: An empirical analysis of packages and systems. *Accounting, Organizations and Society*, 51, 12–28.

Beese J., Haki K., Schilling R., Kraus M., Aier S., & Winter R. (2023). Strategic alignment of enterprise architecture management–How portfolios of control mechanisms track a decade of enterprise transformation at Commerzbank. *European Journal of Information Systems*, 32(1), 92–105.

Beijer S., Peccei R., Van Veldhoven M., & Paauwe J. (2021). The turn to employees in the measurement of human resource practices: A critical review and proposed way forward. *Human Resource Management Journal*, 31(1), 1–17.

Bélanger F., Watson-Manheim M. B., & Swan B. R. (2013). A multi-level socio-technical systems telecommuting framework. *Behaviour and Information Technology*, 32(12), 1257–79.

Bello D. C. & Gilliland D. I. (1997). The effect of output controls, process controls, and flexibility on export channel performance. *Journal of Marketing*, 61(1), 22–38.

Benbasat I. & Taylor R. N. (1978). The impact of cognitive styles on information system design. *MIS Quarterly*, 2(2), 43–54.

Bensinger G. (2019). "MissionRacer": How Amazon turned the tedium of warehouse work into a game. *Washington Post*, May 21, www.washingtonpost.com/technology/2019/05/21/missionracer-how-amazon-turned-tedium-warehouse-work-into-game/.

Bergen M., Dutta S., & Walker O. C. (1992). Agency relationships in marketing: A review of the implications and applications of agency and related theories. *Journal of Marketing*, 56(3), 1–24.

Berger C. (2022). Yelp's CEO thinks hybrid work is "hell." His solution: Take the company fully remote. June 23, https://fortune.com/2022/06/23/yelp-ceo-jeremy-stoppelman-slams-hybrid-work-closes-offices/.

Berger T., Frey C. B., Levin G., & Danda S. R. (2018). Uber happy? Work and well-being in the "gig economy." Working paper presented at the 68th Panel Meeting of Economic Policy, www.oxfordmartin.ox.ac.uk/publications/uber-happy-work-and-wellbeing-in-the-gig-economy/.

Bergh D. D., Aguinis H., Heavey C., Ketchen D. J., Boyd B. K., Su P., Lau C. L. L., & Joo H. (2016). Using meta-analytic structural equation modeling to advance strategic management research: Guidelines and an empirical illustration via the strategic leadership-performance relationship. *Strategic Management Journal*, 37(3), 477–97.

Berkelaar B. L. (2014). Cybervetting, online information, and personnel selection: New transparency expectations and the emergence of a digital social contract. *Management Communication Quarterly*, 28(4), 479–506.

Berle A. A. & Means G. C. (1932). *The modern corporation and private property*. New York: MacMillan.

Bernstein E., Bunch J., Canner N., & Lee M. (2016). Beyond the holacracy hype. *Harvard Business Review*, 94(7–8), 38–49.

Bersin J. (2017). Catch the wave: The 21st-century career. *Deloitte Review*, 21, 62–79.

Best K. (2010). Living in the control society: Surveillance, users and digital screen technologies. *International Journal of Cultural Studies*, 13(1), 5–24.

Bettis R. A. & Hu S. (2018). Bounded rationality, heuristics, computational complexity, and artificial intelligence. In Augier M, Fang C, Rindova VP (eds), *Behavioral strategy in perspective*. Bingley, UK: Emerald Publishing Limited, 139–50.

Bhimani A. (1999). Mapping methodological frontiers in cross-national management control research. *Accounting, Organizations and Society*, 24(5), 413–40.

Bigley G. A. & Roberts K. H. (2001). The incident command system: High-reliability organizing for complex and volatile task environments. *Academy of Management Journal*, 44(6), 1281–99.

Bijlsma-Frankema K. & Costa A. C. (2005). Understanding the trust-control nexus. *International Sociology*, 20(3), 259–82.

Birkinshaw J., Manktelow J., D'Amato V., Tosca E., & Macchi F. (2019). Older and wiser? How management style varies with age. *MIT Sloan Management Review*, 60(4), 75–81.

Bisbe J., Batista-Foguet J.-M., & Chenhall R. (2007). Defining management accounting constructs: A methodological note on the risks of conceptual misspecification. *Accounting, Organizations and Society*, 32(7), 789–820.

Bisbe J. & Otley D. (2004). The effects of the interactive use of management control systems on product innovation. *Accounting, Organizations and Society*, 29(8), 709–37.

Blau P. M. (1963). *The dynamics of bureaucracy: A study of interpersonal relations in two government agencies*. Chicago, IL: University of Chicago Press.

Blau P. M. & Scott W. R. (1962). *Formal organizations: A comparative approach*. San Francisco, CA: Chandler Pub. Company.

Bloodworth J. (2018). *Hired: Six months undercover in low-wage Britain*. London, UK: Atlantic Books.

Bloom N., Liang J., Roberts J., & Ying Z. J. (2015). Does working from home work? Evidence from a Chinese experiment. *Quarterly Journal of Economics*, 130(1), 165–218.

Bodie M. T., Cherry M. A., McCormick M. L., & Jintong T. (2017). The law and policy of people analytics. *University of Colorado Law Review*, 88(4), 961–1042.

Böhm W.-T. & Ströbel L. (2017). New case law on restrictions for employee monitoring in the workplace in Germany. August 18, www.hldataprotection.com/2017/08/articles/international-eu-privacy/new-case-law-on-restrictions-for-employee-monitoring-in-the-workplace-in-germany/.

Bonacich P. (1987). Power and centrality: A family of measures. *American Journal of Sociology*, 92(5), 1170–82.

Bonner J. M., Ruekert R. W., & Walker O. C. (2002). Upper management control of new product development projects and project performance. *Journal of Product Innovation Management*, 19(3), 233–45.

Bonner S. E. & Sprinkle G. B. (2002). The effects of monetary incentives on effort and task performance: Theories, evidence, and a framework for research. *Accounting, Organizations and Society*, 27(4), 303–45.

Borgatti S. P., Everett M. G., & Freeman L. C. (2002). *Ucinet for Windows: Software for social network analysis*. Boston, MA: Analytic Technologies.

Bourgeois L. J. (1985). Strategic goals, perceived uncertainty, and economic performance in volatile environments. *Academy of Management Journal*, 28(3), 548–73.

Bousquette I. (2022). Blockchain fizzles in shipping. *Wall Street Journal*, December 16, B4.

Bovens L. (2009). The ethics of nudge. In Grüne-Yanoff T, & Hansson SO (eds), *Preference change: Approaches from philosophy, economics and psychology*. Dordrecht, Netherlands: Springer, 207–19.

Bower J. L. (1970). *Managing the resource allocation process*. Boston, MA: Harvard Business School Press.

Bower J. L. & Doz Y. (1979). Strategy formulation: A social and political process. In Schendel D, & Hofer CW (eds), *Strategic management: A new view of business policy and planning*. Boston, MA: Little, Brown, 152–66.

Boyer K. K. & Lewis M. W. (2002). Competitive priorities: Investigating the need for trade-offs in operations strategy. *Production and Operations Management*, 11(1), 9–20.

Brahm T. & Kunze F. (2012). The role of trust climate in virtual teams. *Journal of Managerial Psychology*, 27(6), 595–614.

Braumann E. C., Grabner I., & Posch A. (2020). Tone from the top in risk management: A complementarity perspective on how control systems influence risk awareness. *Accounting, Organizations and Society*, 84(3), 101128.

Braverman H. (1974). *Labor and monopoly capital: The degradation of work in the twentieth century*. New York: Monthly Review Press.

Braverman H. (1998). *Labor and monopoly capital: The degradation of work in the twentieth century*, 25th anniversary edition ed. New York: Monthly Review Press.

Brayne S. & Christin A. (2021). Technologies of crime prediction: The reception of algorithms in policing and criminal courts. *Social Problems*, 68(3), 608–24.

Brech E. F. L. (1965). *Organisation: The framework of management*, 2nd ed. London, UK: Longmans.

Brehm J. W. (1966). *A theory of psychological reactance*. Oxford, UK: Academic Press.

Brice J., Nelson M., & Gunby N. W. (2011). The governance of telecommuters: An agency and transaction cost analysis. *Academy of Strategic Management Journal*, 10(1), 1–17.

Briers M. & Chua W. F. (2001). The role of actor-networks and boundary objects in management accounting change: A field study of an implementation of activity-based costing. *Accounting, Organizations and Society*, 26(3), 237–69.

Brivot M. & Gendron Y. (2011). Beyond panopticism: On the ramifications of surveillance in a contemporary professional setting. *Accounting, Organizations and Society*, 36(3), 135–55.

Brocklehurst M. (2001). Power, identity and new technology homework: Implications for "new forms" of organizing. *Organization Studies*, 22(3), 445–66.

Bromley P. & Powell W. W. (2012). From smoke and mirrors to walking the talk: Decoupling in the contemporary world. *Academy of Management Annals*, 6(1), 483–530.

Bronowicka J. & Ivanova M. (2020). Resisting the algorithmic boss: Guessing, gaming, reframing and contesting rules in app-based management. *SSRN Working Paper*, https://ssrn.com/abstract=3624087.

Brucks M. S. & Levav J. (2022). Virtual communication curbs creative idea generation. *Nature*, 605(7908), 108–12.

Bruns W. J. & Waterhouse J. H. (1975). Budgetary control and organization structure. *Journal of Accounting Research*, 13(2), 177–203.

Brynjolfsson E., Li D., & Raymond L. R. (2023). Generative AI at work. *National Bureau of Economic Research Working Paper Series*, 31161.

Brynjolfsson E. & Milgrom P. (2012). Complementarity in organizations. In Gibbons R, & Roberts J (eds), *The handbook of organizational economics*. Princeton, NJ: Princeton University Press, 11–55.

Bucher E. L., Fieseler C., & Lutz C. (2019). Mattering in digital labor. *Journal of Managerial Psychology*, 34(4), 307–24.

Bucher E. L., Schou P. K., & Waldkirch M. (2021a). Pacifying the algorithm–Anticipatory compliance in the face of algorithmic management in the gig economy. *Organization*, 28(1), 44–67.

Bucher E. L., Schou P. K., & Waldkirch M. (2021b). Vox populi et vox regni: Investigating digital voice channels in the gig economy. *Academy of Management Proceedings*, https://doi.org/10.5465/AMBPP.2021.13192abstract.

Buffa E. S. (1984). *Meeting the competitive challenge: Manufacturing strategy for U.S. companies*. Homewood, IL: Dow Jones-Irwin.

Burbano V. C. & Chiles B. (2022). Mitigating gig and remote worker misconduct: Evidence from a real effort experiment. *Organization Science*, 33(4), 1273–99.

Burchell S., Clubb C., Hopwood A., Hughes J., & Nahapiet J. (1980). The roles of accounting in organizations and society. *Accounting, Organizations and Society*, 5(1), 5–27.

Burgelman R. A. (1983). A model of the interaction of strategic behavior, corporate context, and the concept of strategy. *Academy of Management Review*, 8(1), 61–70.

Burns T. & Stalker G. M. (1961). *The management of innovation*. London, UK: Tavistock Publications.

Burrell J. (2016). How the machine "thinks": Understanding opacity in machine learning algorithms. *Big Data & Society*, 3(1), 205395171562251.

Bursztynsky J. (2022). Elon Musk tells Tesla workers to return to the office full time or resign. *CNBC*, June 1, www.cnbc.com/2022/06/01/elon-musk-reportedly-tells-tesla-workers-to-be-in-office-full-time-or-resign.html.

Burton A. & Confino P. (2022). Elon Musk says only "exceptional" Twitter employees can work from home. Here's how he defines this type of worker. *Fortune*, November 14, https://fortune.com/2022/11/14/elon-musk-only-exceptional-twitter-employees-work-from-home/.

Bushman R. M. & Smith A. J. (2001). Financial accounting information and corporate governance. *Journal of Accounting and Economics*, 32(1), 237–333.

Caglio A. & Ditillo A. (2008). A review and discussion of management control in inter-firm relationships: Achievements and future directions. *Accounting, Organizations and Society*, 33(7–8), 865–98.

Calo R. & Rosenblat A. (2017). The taking economy: Uber, information, and power. *Columbia Law Review*, 117(6), 1623–90.

Cameron J. & Pierce W. D. (1994). Reinforcement, reward, and intrinsic motivation: A meta-analysis. *Review of Educational Research*, 64(3), 363–423.

Cameron K. S. & Caza A. (2004). Introduction: Contributions to the discipline of positive organizational scholarship. *American Behavioral Scientist*, 47(6), 731–9.

Cameron K. S. & Spreitzer G. M. (eds) (2012). *The Oxford handbook of positive organizational scholarship*. Oxford, UK: Oxford University Press.

Cameron L. D. (2021). (Relative) freedom in algorithms: How digital platforms repurpose workplace consent. *Academy of Management Proceedings*, https://journals.aom.org/doi/10.5465/AMBPP.2021.238.

Cameron L. D. (2022). "Making out" while driving: Relational and efficiency games in the gig economy. *Organization Science*, 33(1), 231–52.

Cameron L. D. & Rahman H. (2022). Expanding the locus of resistance: Understanding the co-constitution of control and resistance in the gig economy. *Organization Science*, 33(1), 38–58.

Cammann C. (1976). Effects of the use of control systems. *Accounting, Organizations and Society*, 1(4), 301–13.

Cao Z. & Lumineau F. (2015). Revisiting the interplay between contractual and relational governance: A qualitative and meta-analytic investigation. *Journal of Operations Management*, 33–34(1), 15–42.

Cappelli P. & Keller J. R. (2013). Classifying work in the new economy. *Academy of Management Review*, 38(4), 575–96.

Cardinal L. B. (2001). Technological innovation in the pharmaceutical industry: The use of organizational control in managing research and development. *Organization Science*, 12(1), 19–36.

Cardinal L. B., Kreutzer M., & Miller C. C. (2017). An aspirational view of organizational control research: Re-invigorating empirical work to better meet the challenges of 21st century organizations. *Academy of Management Annals*, 11(2), 559–92.

Cardinal L. B., Sitkin S. B., & Long C. P. (2004). Balancing and rebalancing in the creation and evolution of organizational control. *Organization Science*, 15(4), 411–31.

Cardinal L. B., Sitkin S. B., & Long C. P. (2010). A configurational theory of control. In Sitkin SB, Cardinal LB, & Bijlsma-Frankema KM (eds), *Organizational control*. Cambridge, UK: Cambridge University Press, 51–79.

Cardinal L. B., Sitkin S. B., Long C. P., & Miller C. C. (2018). The genesis of control configurations during organizational founding. In Joseph J, Baumann O, Srikanth K, & Burton RM (eds), *Advances in strategic management: Organization design*. Bingley, UK: Emerald Publishing, 83–114.

Carnevali D. (2021). LitLingo draws investors for AI-driven communications checker. *Wall Street Journal*, July 7, www.wsj.com/articles/litlingo-draws-investors-for-ai-driven-communications-checker-11625659201.

Cascio W. F. & Montealegre R. (2016). How technology is changing work and organizations. *Annual Review of Organizational Psychology and Organizational Behavior*, 3(1), 349–75.

Catalini C. (2017). How blockchain applications will move beyond finance. *Harvard Business Review*, March 2, https://hbr.org/2017/03/how-blockchain-applications-will-move-beyond-finance.

Celly K. S. & Frazier G. L. (1996). Outcome-based and behavior-based coordination efforts in channel relationships. *Journal of Marketing Research*, 33(2), 200–10.

Challagalla G. N. & Shervani T. A. (1996). Dimensions and types of supervisory control: Effects on salesperson performance and satisfaction. *Journal of Marketing*, 60(1), 89–105.

Chalos P. & O'Connor N. G. (2004). Determinants of the use of various control mechanisms in US–Chinese joint ventures. *Accounting, Organizations and Society*, 29(7), 591–608.

Chamorro-Premuzic T., Akhtar R., Winsborough D., & Sherman R. A. (2017). The datafication of talent: How technology is advancing the science of human potential at work. *Current Opinion in Behavioral Sciences*, 18, 13–16.

Chan N. K. & Humphreys L. (2018). Mediatization of social space and the case of Uber drivers. *Media and Communication*, 6(2), 29–38.

Chandler A. D. (1962). *Strategy and structure: Chapters in the history of the American industrial enterprise*. Cambridge, MA: MIT Press.

Chatman J. A. (1991). Matching people and organizations: Selection and socialization in public accounting firms. *Administrative Science Quarterly*, 36(3), 459–84.

Chatterjee S., Sarker S., & Valacich J. S. (2015). The behavioral roots of information systems security: Exploring key factors related to unethical IT use. *Journal of Management Information Systems*, 31(4), 49–87.

Chen C. (2004). Searching for intellectual turning points: Progressive knowledge domain visualization. *Proceedings of the National Academy of Sciences*, 101, 5303–10.

Chen C. (2006). CiteSpace II: Detecting and visualizing emerging trends and transient patterns in scientific literature. *Journal of the American Society for Information Science and Technology*, 57(3), 359–77.

Chen C. (2017). Science mapping: A systematic review of the literature. *Journal of Data and Information Science*, 2(2), 1–40.

Chen C., Ibekwe-SanJuan F., & Hou J. (2010). The structure and dynamics of cocitation clusters: A multiple-perspective cocitation analysis. *Journal of the American Society for Information Science and Technology*, 61(7), 1386–409.

Chen C. & Morris S. (2003). Visualizing evolving networks: Minimum spanning trees versus pathfinder networks. *Proceedings of the IEEE Symposium on Information Visualization*, Seattle, WA.

Chen L., Zaharia M., & Zou J. (2023). How is ChatGPT's behavior changing over time? *Working Paper*, https://arxiv.org/abs/2307.09009.

Chen W., Huang Chua C. E., Young R., & Xu X. (2022). Explaining reverse outcome tight control: A case study of mindless/mindful governance. *Project Management Journal*, 53(3), 309–24.

Chen Y., Ramamurthy K., & Wen K.-W. (2012). Organizations' information security policy compliance: Stick or carrot approach? *Journal of Management Information Systems*, 29(3), 157–88.

Cheng J. L. C. & McKinley W. (1983). Toward an integration of organization research and practice: A contingency study of bureaucratic control and performance in scientific settings. *Administrative Science Quarterly*, 28(1), 85–100.

Cheng M. M. & Hackett R. D. (2021). A critical review of algorithms in HRM: Definition, theory, and practice. *Human Resource Management Review*, 31(1), 100698.

Chenhall R. H. (2003). Management control systems design within its organizational context: Findings from contingency-based research and directions for the future. *Accounting, Organizations and Society*, 28(2), 127–68.

Chenhall R. H. & Moers F. (2015). The role of innovation in the evolution of management accounting and its integration into management control. *Accounting, Organizations and Society*, 47(3), 1–13.

Cherry M. A. (2011). A taxonomy of virtual work. *Georgia Law Review*, 45(4), 951–1013.

Chiapello E. (1996). Les typologies des modes de contrôle et leurs facteurs de contingence: Un essai d'organisation de la littérature. *Comptabilité Contrôle Audit*, 2(2), 51–74.

Child J. & McGrath R. G. (2001). Organizations unfettered: Organizational form in an information-intensive economy. *Academy of Management Journal*, 44(6), 1135–48.

Chochoiek C., Kortus L., Kreutzer M., & Gutmann T. (2023). Walk the talk in a VUCA world: Rebalancing control configurations to implement sustainability strategies. *Strategic Management Society 43rd Annual Conference*, Toronto, Canada.

Choi T. Y., Dooley K. J., & Rungtusanatham M. (2001). Supply networks and complex adaptive systems: Control versus emergence. *Journal of Operations Management*, 19(3), 351–66.

Choudhury P. (2020). Our work-from-anywhere future. *Harvard Business Review*, 98(6), 58–67.

Choudhury P., Crowston K., Dahlander L., Minervini M. S., & Raghuram S. (2020). GitLab: Work where you want, when you want. *Journal of Organization Design*, 9(1), 1–17.

Choudhury P., Foroughi C., & Larson B. (2019). Work from anywhere or co-locate? Autonomy versus learning effects at the United States Patent Office. *Harvard Business School Working Paper*, 19–054.

Choudhury P. & Salomon E. (2023a). GitLab and the future of all-remote work (A). *Harvard Business School Case Study #9-620-066*, 1–19 [permission obtained from Harvard Business Publishing].

Choudhury P. & Salomon E. (2023b). GitLab and the future of all-remote work (B). *Harvard Business School Case Study #9-620-117*, 1–4 [permission obtained from Harvard Business Publishing].

Choudhury P., Starr E., & Agarwal R. (2020). Machine learning and human capital complementarities: Experimental evidence on bias mitigation. *Strategic Management Journal*, 41(8), 1381–411.

Choudhury V. & Sabherwal R. (2003). Portfolios of control in outsourced software development projects. *Information Systems Research*, 14(3), 291–314.

Chow C. W., Kato Y., & Shields M. D. (1994). National culture and the preference for management controls: An exploratory study of the firm-labor market interface. *Accounting, Organizations and Society*, 19(4), 381–400.

Chow C. W., Shields M. D., & Wu A. (1999). The importance of national culture in the design of and preference for management controls for multi-national operations. *Accounting, Organizations and Society*, 24(5), 441–61.

Chown J. (2021). The unfolding of control mechanisms inside organizations: Pathways of customization and transmutation. *Administrative Science Quarterly*, 66(3), 711–52.

Christie A. A. & Zimmerman J. L. (1994). Efficient and opportunistic choices of accounting procedures: Corporate control contests. *Accounting Review*, 69(4), 539–66.

Chua W. F. & Mahama H. (2007). The effect of network ties on accounting controls in a supply alliance: Field study evidence. *Contemporary Accounting Research*, 24(1), 47–86.

Cichy P., Salge T. O., & Kohli R. (2021). Privacy concerns and data sharing in the Internet of Things: Mixed methods evidence from connected cars. *MIS Quarterly*, 45(4), 1863–91.

Cilluffo A. & Cohn D. V. (2019). 6 demographic trends shaping the U.S. and the world in 2019. *Pew Research Center Fact Tank Report*, April 11, https://pewrsr.ch/2Gaolyp.

Cisco (2013). Embracing the internet of everything to capture your share of $14.4 trillion. *Cisco White Paper*, www.cisco.com/c/dam/en_us/about/ac79/docs/innov/IoE_Economy.pdf.

Clark T. (2021). The gig is up: An analysis of the gig-economy and an outdated worker classification system in need of reform. *Seattle Journal for Social Justice*, 19(3), 769–808.

Coase R. H. (1937). The nature of the firm. *Economica*, 4(November), 386–405.

Cobb A. T., Stephens C., & Watson G. (2001). Beyond structure: The role of social accounts in implementing ideal control. *Human Relations*, 54(9), 1123–53.

Cohen A. (2021). How to quit your job in the great post-pandemic resignation boom. *Bloomberg*, May 10, www.bloomberg.com/news/articles/2021-05-10/quit-your-job-how-to-resign-after-covid-pandemic.

Cohen J. (1960). A coefficient of agreement for nominal scales. *Educational and Psychological Measurement*, 20(1), 37–46.

Cohen P., Hahn R., Hall J., Levitt S., & Metcalfe R. (2016). Using big data to estimate consumer surplus: The case of Uber. *National Bureau of Economic Research*, September, www.nber.org/papers/w22627.

Colbert A., Yee N., & George G. (2016). The digital workforce and the workplace of the future. *Academy of Management Journal*, 59(3), 731–9.

Coleman J. S. (1990). *Foundations of social theory*. Cambridge, MA: Belknap Press.

Coletti A. L., Sedatole K. L., & Towry K. L. (2005). The effect of control systems on trust and cooperation in collaborative environments. *The Accounting Review*, 80(2), 477–500.

Collins F. (1982). Managerial accounting systems and organizational control: A role perspective. *Accounting, Organizations and Society*, 7(2), 107–22.

Constantinides P., Henfridsson O., & Parker G. G. (2018). Introduction: Platforms and infrastructures in the digital age. *Information Systems Research*, 29(2), 381–400.

Conway L. (2008). Virgin Atlantic sacks 13 staff for calling its flyers "chavs." *Independent*, November 1, www.independent.co.uk/news/uk/home-news/virgin-atlantic-sacks-13-staff-for-calling-its-flyers-chavs-982192.html.

Cooper C. D. (2015). Entrepreneurs of the self: The development of management control since 1976. *Accounting, Organizations and Society*, 47, 14–24.

Cooper C. D. & Kurland N. B. (2002). Telecommuting, professional isolation, and employee development in public and private organizations. *Journal of Organizational Behavior*, 23(4), 511–32.

Cordery J. L., Mueller W. S., & Smith L. M. (1991). Attitudinal and behavioral effects of autonomous group working: A longitudinal field study. *Academy of Management Journal*, 34(2), 464–76.

Costanza D. P., Badger J. M., Fraser R. L., Severt J. B., & Gade P. A. (2012). Generational differences in work-related attitudes: A meta-analysis. *Journal of Business and Psychology*, 27(4), 375–94.

Courtright S. H., McCormick B. W., Mistry S., & Wang J. (2017). Quality charters or quality members? A control theory perspective on team charters and team performance. *Journal of Applied Psychology*, 102(10), 1462–70.

Cousins P. D. & Menguc B. (2006). The implications of socialization and integration in supply chain management. *Journal of Operations Management*, 24(5), 604–20.

Cram W. A. & Wiener M. (2020). Technology-mediated control: Case examples and research directions for the future of organizational control. *Communications of the Association for Information Systems*, 46(4), 70–91.

Crosno J. L. & Brown J. R. (2015). A meta-analytic review of the effects of organizational control in marketing exchange relationships. *Journal of the Academy of Marketing Science*, 43(3), 297–314.

Crozier M. (1964). *The bureaucratic phenomenon*. Chicago, IL: University of Chicago Press.

Cukier K. & Mayer-Schoenberger V. (2013). The rise of big data: How it's changing the way we think about the world. *Foreign Affairs*, 92(3), 28–40.

Curchod C., Patriotta G., Cohen L., & Neysen N. (2019). Working for an algorithm: Power asymmetries and agency in online work settings. *Administrative Science Quarterly*, 65(3), 644–76.

Cutolo D. & Kenney M. (2021). Platform-dependent entrepreneurs: Power asymmetries, risks, and strategies in the platform economy. *Academy of Management Perspectives*, 35(4), 584–605.

Cutter C. & Dill K. (2021). Remote work is the new signing bonus. *Wall Street Journal*, June 26–27, B1.

Cyert R. M. & March J. G. (1963). *A behavioral theory of the firm*. Englewood Cliffs, NJ: Prentice-Hall.

D'Arcy J., Hovav A., & Galletta D. (2009). User awareness of security countermeasures and its impact on information systems misuse: A deterrence approach. *Information Systems Research*, 20(1), 79–98.

Daft R. L. & Macintosh N. B. (1984). The nature and use of formal control systems for management control and strategy implementation. *Journal of Management*, 10(1), 43–66.

Dahlstrom R. & Nygaard A. (1999). An empirical investigation of ex post transaction costs in franchised distribution channels. *Journal of Marketing Research*, 36(2), 160–70.

Dalton D. R., Aguinis H., Dalton C. M., Bosco F. A., & Pierce C. A. (2012). Revisiting the file drawer problem in meta-analysis: An assessment of published and nonpublished correlation matrices. *Personnel Psychology*, 65(2), 221–49.

Daniel S. J. & Reitsperger W. D. (1991a). Linking quality strategy with management control systems: Empirical evidence from Japanese industry. *Accounting, Organizations and Society*, 16(7), 601–18.

Daniel S. J. & Reitsperger W. D. (1991b). Management control systems for J.I.T.: An empirical comparison of Japan and the U.S. *Journal of International Business Studies*, 22(4), 603–17.

Das T. K. & Teng B.-S. (1998). Between trust and control: Developing confidence in partner cooperation in alliances. *Academy of Management Review*, 23(3), 491–512.

Das T. K. & Teng B.-S. (2001). Trust, control, and risk in strategic alliances: An integrated framework. *Organization Studies*, 22(2), 251–83.

Davis G. F. (2013). After the corporation. *Politics and Society*, 41(2), 283–308.

Davis G. F. (2015). Editorial essay: What is organizational research for? *Administrative Science Quarterly*, 60(2), 179–88.

Davis J. H., Schoorman F. D., & Donaldson L. (1997). Toward a stewardship theory of management. *Academy of Management Review*, 22(1), 20–47.

De Choudhury M. & Counts S. (2013). Understanding affect in the workplace via social media. *Proceedings of the 2013 Conference on Computer Supported Cooperative Work*, San Antonio, TX.

De Jong B., Bijlsma-Frankema K. M., & Cardinal L. B. (2014). Stronger than the sum of its parts? The performance implications of peer control combinations in teams. *Organization Science*, 25(6), 1703–21.

De Man A.-P., Koene P., & Ars M. (2019). *How to survive the organizational revolution: A guide to agile contemporary operating models, platforms and ecosystems.* Amsterdam, Netherlands: BIS Publishers.

De Smet A., Dowling B., Hancock B., & Schaninger B. (2022). The Great Attrition is making hiring harder: Are you searching the right talent pools? *McKinsey Quarterly*, 58(4), 1–13.

De Smet A., Dowling B., Mysore M., & Reich A. (2021). It's time for leaders to get real about hybrid. *McKinsey Quarterly*, 57(3), 1–10.

De Smet A., Mugayar-Baldocchi M., Reich A., & Schaninger B. (2023). Gen what? Debunking age-based myths about worker preferences. *McKinsey Insights on People and Organizational Performance*, April 20, www.mckinsey.com/capabilities/people-and-organizational-performance/our-insights/gen-what-debunking-age-based-myths-about-worker-preferences.

Deal J. J., Altman D. G., & Rogelberg S. G. (2010). Millennials at work: What we know and what we need to do (if anything). *Journal of Business and Psychology*, 25(2), 191–9.

Deci E. L. (1971). Effects of externally mediated rewards on intrinsic motivation. *Journal of Personality and Social Psychology*, 18(1), 105–15.

Deci E. L., Koestner R., & Ryan R. M. (1999). A meta-analytic review of experiments examining the effects of extrinsic rewards on intrinsic motivation. *Psychological Bulletin*, 125(6), 627–68.

Deci E. L., Olafsen A. H., & Ryan R. M. (2017). Self-determination theory in work organizations: The state of a science. *Annual Review of Organizational Psychology and Organizational Behavior*, 4(1), 19–43.

DeCoster D. T. & Fertakis J. P. (1968). Budget-induced pressure and its relationship to supervisory behavior. *Journal of Accounting Research*, 6(2), 237–46.

Deighton K. (2021). Your call may be recorded (and analyzed by a bot). *Wall Street Journal*, May 6, www.wsj.com/articles/your-call-may-be-recorded-and-analyzed-by-a-bot-11620320134.

Dekker H. C. (2004). Control of inter-organizational relationships: Evidence on appropriation concerns and coordination requirements. *Accounting, Organizations and Society*, 29(1), 27–49.

Dekker H. C. (2008). Partner selection and governance design in interfirm relationships. *Accounting, Organizations and Society*, 33(7–8), 915–41.

Delbridge R. (2010). Critical perspectives on organizational control: Reflections and prospects. In Bijlsma-Frankema KM, Cardinal LB, & Sitkin SB (eds), *Organizational control*. Cambridge, UK: Cambridge University Press, 80–108.

Deloitte (2015). Get out of your own way: Unleashing productivity. March 26, www2.deloitte.com/content/dam/Deloitte/au/Documents/Building%20Lucky%Country/deloitte-au-btlc-get-out-your-own-way-230217.pdf.

Deloitte (2019). The Deloitte Global Millennial Survey 2019. Optimism, trust reach troubling low levels. www2.deloitte.com/content/dam/Deloitte/global/Documents/About-Deloitte/deloitte-2019-millennial-survey.pdf.

Deloitte (2020). The social enterprise at work: Paradox as a path forward. *Deloitte Insights*, May 15, www2.deloitte.com/us/en/insights/focus/human-capital-trends/2020/technology-and-the-social-enterprise.html.

Demetis D. S. & Lee A. S. (2018). When humans using the IT artifact becomes IT using the human artifact. *Journal of the Association for Information Systems*, 19(10), 929–52.

Denison E. F. (1978). *Effects of selected changes in the institutional and human environment upon output per unit of input*. Brookings General Series Reprint #335. Washington, DC: Brookings.

Dermer J. D. (1974). Interactive effects of uncertainty and self-control on the acceptance of responsibility for, and satisfaction with, performance. *Human Relations*, 27(9), 911–24.

Devaraj S., Hollingworth D. G., & Schroeder R. G. (2004). Generic manufacturing strategies and plant performance. *Journal of Operations Management*, 22(3), 313–33.

Di Tullio D. & Staples D. S. (2013). The governance and control of open source software projects. *Journal of Management Information Systems*, 30(3), 49–80.

Diamandis P. H. & Kotler S. (2020). *The future is faster than you think. How converging technologies are transforming business, industries, and our lives*. New York: Simon & Schuster.

Dietvorst B. J., Simmons J. P., & Massey C. (2016). Overcoming algorithm aversion: People will use imperfect algorithms if they can (even slightly) modify them. *Management Science*, 64(3), 1155–70.

Dill K. (2022). This could have been an email and other ways to have better meetings. *Wall Street Journal*, January 6, www.wsj.com/articles/this-could-have-been-an-email-and-other-ways-to-have-better-meetings-11641474003.

Dinev T. & Hart P. (2006). An extended privacy calculus model for e-commerce transactions. *Information Systems Research*, 17(1), 61–80.

Donaldson L. (1990). The ethereal hand: Organizational economics and management theory. *Academy of Management Review*, 15(3), 369–81.

Doty D. H. & Glick W. H. (1994). Typologies as a unique form of theory building: Toward improved understanding and modeling. *Academy of Management Review*, 19(2), 230–51.

Doty D. H., Glick W. H., & Huber G. P. (1993). Fit, equifinality, and organizational effectiveness: A test. *Academy of Management Journal*, 36(6), 1196–250.

Drazin R. & Van de Ven A. H. (1985). Alternative forms of fit in contingency theory. *Administrative Science Quarterly*, 30(4), 514–39.

Drucker P. F. (1999). Knowledge-worker productivity: The biggest challenge. *California Management Review*, 41(2), 79–94.

Duggan J., Sherman U., Carbery R., & McDonnell A. (2020). Algorithmic management and app-work in the gig economy: A research agenda for employment relations and HRM. *Human Resource Management Journal*, 30(1), 114–32.

Dunbar R. L. M. & Statler M. (2010). A historical perspective on organizational control. In Bijlsma-Frankema KM, Cardinal LB, & Sitkin SB (eds), *Organizational control*. Cambridge, UK: Cambridge University Press, 16–48.

Durand R., Hawn O., & Ioannou I. (2017). Willing and able: A general model of organizational responses to normative pressures. *Academy of Management Review*, 44(2), 299–320.

Dutton J. E., Glynn M. A., & Spreitzer G. M. (2006). Positive organizational scholarship. In Greenhaus JH, & Callanan G (eds), *Encyclopedia of career development*. Thousand Oaks, CA: SAGE, 641–4.

Dutton J. E. & Wrzesniewski A. (2020). What job crafting looks like. *Harvard Business Review*, March 12, https://hbr.org/2020/03/what-job-crafting-looks-like.

Duxbury L., Higgins C., & Neufeld D. (1998). Telework and the balance between work and family: Is telework part of the problem or part of the solution? In Igbaria M, & Tan M (eds), *The virtual workplace*. Hershey, PA: Idea Group, 218–55.

Dyer J. H. & Singh H. (1998). The relational view: Cooperative strategy and sources of interorganizational competitive advantage. *Academy of Management Review*, 23(4), 660–79.

Dzieza J. (2019). "Beat the machine": Amazon warehouse workers strike to protest inhumane conditions. *The Verge*, July 16, www.theverge.com/2019/7/16/20696154/amazon-prime-day-2019-strike-warehouse-workers-inhumane-conditions-the-rate-productivity.

Dzieza J. (2020). How hard will the robots make us work? *The Verge*, February 27, www.theverge.com/2020/2/27/21155254/automation-robots-unemployment-jobs-vs-human-google-amazon.

Economist (2019). Free exchange: Ageing is a drag. 430(9136), 78, www.economist.com/finance-and-economics/2019/03/28/slower-growth-in-ageing-economies-is-not-inevitable.

Economist (2021). Bartleby: Creatures of habit. 438(9228), 60, www.economist.com/business/2021/01/13/the-lockdown-has-caused-changes-of-routine.

Edwards R. (1979). *Contested terrain: The transformation of the workplace in the twentieth century*. London, UK: Heinemann.

Eisenberger R. & Cameron J. (1996). Detrimental effects of reward: Reality or myth? *American Psychologist*, 51(11), 1153–66.

Eisenhardt K. M. (1985). Control: Organizational and economic approaches. *Management Science*, 31(2), 134–49.

Eisenhardt K. M. (1989a). Agency theory: An assessment and review. *Academy of Management Review*, 14(1), 57–74.

Eisenhardt K. M. (1989b). Building theories from case study research. *Academy of Management Review*, 14(4), 532–50.

El-Ansary A. I. & Stern L. W. (1972). Power measurement in the distribution channel. *Journal of Marketing Research*, 9(1), 47–52.

Eldor L. & Cappelli P. (2020). The use of agency workers hurts business performance: An integrated indirect model. *Academy of Management Journal*, 64(3), 824–50.

Elias S. M. (2009). Restrictive versus promotive control and employee work outcomes: The moderating role of locus of control. *Journal of Management*, 35(2), 369–92.

Elliott C. S. & Long G. (2016). Manufacturing rate busters: Computer control and social relations in the labour process. *Work, Employment and Society*, 30(1), 135–51.

Ellis L. & Yang A. (2022). If your co-workers are 'quiet quitting,' here's what that means. *Wall Street Journal*, August 12, www.wsj.com/articles/if-your-gen-z-co-workers-are-quiet-quitting-heres-what-that-means-11660260608.

Else H. (2023). Abstracts written by ChatGPT fool scientists. *Nature*, 613(7944), 423.

Emirbayer M. & Mische A. (1998). What is agency? *American Journal of Sociology*, 103(4), 962–1023.

Empson L. (2021). Researching the post-pandemic professional service firm: Challenging our assumptions. *Journal of Management Studies*, 58(5), 1383–8.

Endenich C. & Trapp R. (2020). Ethical implications of management accounting and control: A systematic review of the contributions from the Journal of Business Ethics. *Journal of Business Ethics*, 163(2), 309–28.

Enzle M. E. & Anderson S. C. (1993). Surveillant intentions and intrinsic motivation. *Journal of Personality and Social Psychology*, 64(2), 257–66.

Errichiello L. & Pianese T. (2016). Organizational control in the context of remote work arrangements: A conceptual framework. In Epstein MJ, Verbeeten F, Widener SK (eds), *Performance measurement and management control: Contemporary issues*. Bingley, UK: Emerald Group Publishing Limited, Vol. 31, 273–305.

Eseryel U. Y., Crowston K., & Heckman R. (2021). Functional and visionary leadership in self-managing virtual teams. *Group & Organization Management*, 46(2), 424–60.

Etgar M. (1976). Channel domination and countervailing power in distributive channels. *Journal of Marketing Research*, 13(3), 254–62.

Etzioni A. (1961). *A comparative analysis of complex organizations: On power, involvement, and their correlates*. New York: Free Press of Glencoe.

Etzioni A. (1965). Organizational control structure. In March JG (ed), *Handbook of organizations*. Chicago, IL: Rand McNally, 650–77.

Evans D. S. & Schmalensee R. (2007). Industrial organization of markets with two-sided platforms. *Competition Policy International*, 3(1), 151–79.

Evans K. R., Landry T. D., Li P.-C., & Zou S. (2007). How sales controls affect job-related outcomes: The role of organizational sales-related psychological climate perceptions. *Journal of the Academy of Marketing Science*, 35(3), 445–59.

Evans L. & Kitchin R. (2018). A smart place to work? Big data systems, labour, control and modern retail stores. *New Technology, Work, and Employment*, 33(1), 44–57.

Evans W. (2019). Behind the smiles. *Reveal*, November 25, https://revealnews.org/article/behind-the-smiles/.

Evans W. (2020). How Amazon hid its safety crisis. *Reveal*, September 29, https://revealnews.org/article/how-amazon-hid-its-safety-crisis/.

Evans W. (2023). New York passes law to protect Amazon warehouse workers. *Reveal*, January 12, https://revealnews.org/article/new-york-passes-law-to-protect-amazon-warehouse-workers/.

Ezzamel M. & Willmott H. (1998). Accounting for teamwork: A critical study of group-based systems of organizational control. *Administrative Science Quarterly*, 43(2), 353–96.

Faems D., Janssens M., Madhok A., & Van Looy B. (2008). Toward a perspective on alliance governance: Connecting contract design, trust dynamics, and contract application. *Academy of Management Journal*, 51(6), 1053–78.

Fairweather N. B. (1999). Surveillance in employment: The case of teleworking. *Journal of Business Ethics*, 22(1), 39–49.

Fama E. F. (1980). Agency problems and the theory of the firm. *Journal of Political Economy*, 88(2), 288–307.

Fama E. F. & Jensen M. C. (1983). Separation of ownership and control. *Journal of Law and Economics*, 26(2), 301–25.

Faraj S., Pachidi S., & Sayegh K. (2018). Working and organizing in the age of the learning algorithm. *Information and Organization*, 28(1), 62–70.

Farr J. L., Fairchild J., & Cassidy S. E. (2014). Technology and performance appraisal. In Coovert MD, & Thompson LF (eds), *The psychology of workplace technology*, New York: Routledge, 76–98.

Fayol H. (1949). *General and industrial management*. London, UK: Pitman.

Feintzeig R. (2021). The pain of the never-ending work check-in. *Wall Street Journal*, July 19, www.wsj.com/articles/the-pain-of-the-never-ending-work-check-in-11626667260.

Felstead A., Jewson N., & Walters S. (2003). Managerial control of employees working at home. *British Journal of Industrial Relations*, 41(2), 241–64.

Fiss P. C. (2007). A set-theoretic approach to organizational configurations. *Academy of Management Review*, 32(4), 1180–98.

Flamholtz E. G. (1983). Accounting, budgeting and control systems in their organizational context: Theoretical and empirical perspectives. *Accounting, Organizations and Society*, 8(2), 153–69.

Flamholtz E. G., Das T. K., & Tsui A. S. (1985). Toward an integrative framework of organizational control. *Accounting, Organizations and Society*, 10(1), 35–50.

Fleming P. & Spicer A. (2003). Working at a cynical distance: Implications for power, subjectivity and resistance. *Organization*, 10(1), 157–79.

Flexjobs (2016). Survey: Parents rank work flexibility ahead of salary. www.flexjobs.com/blog/post/survey-parents-rank-work-flexibility-ahead-salary/.

Foss N. J. (2021). The impact of the COVID-19 pandemic on firms' organizational designs. *Journal of Management Studies*, 58(1), 270–4.

Foss N. J. & Klein P. G. (2019). No boss? No thanks. *Aeon*, January 14, https://aeon.co/essays/no-boss-no-thanks-why-managers-are-more-important-than-ever.

Foster D. (2023). *Generative deep learning: Teaching machines to paint, write, compose, and play*, 2nd ed. Sebastopol, CA: O'Reilly.

Francis M. H. & Kletzien S. L. (2022). New York law requires notice of employees' electronic monitoring effective May 7, 2022. *Holland & Knight Alert*, May 3, www.hklaw.com/en/insights/publications/2022/05/new-york-law-requires-notice-of-employees-electronic-monitoring.

Frazier G. L. (1983). Interorganizational exchange behavior in marketing channels: A broadened perspective. *Journal of Marketing*, 47(4), 68–78.

Free C. (2007). Supply-chain accounting practices in the UK retail sector: Enabling or coercing collaboration? *Contemporary Accounting Research*, 24(3), 897–933.

Freeman J. (2021). A war for talent. *Wall Street Journal*, October 7, www.wsj.com/articles/a-war-for-talent-11633623631.

Freeman L. C. (1977). A set of measures of centrality based on betweenness. *Sociometry*, 40(1), 35–41.

Frenkel S., Korczynski M., Donoghue L., & Shire K. (1995). Re-constituting work: Trends towards knowledge work and info-normative control. *Work, Employment and Society*, 9(4), 773–96.

Friedlmaier M., Tumasjan A., & Welpe I. M. (2018). Disrupting industries with block-chain: The industry, venture capital funding, and regional distribution of block-chain ventures. *Proceedings of the 51st Annual Hawaii International Conference on System Sciences (HICSS)*, (January). Hilton Waikoloa Village, Hawaii.

Fryxell G. E., Dooley R. S., & Vryza M. (2002). After the ink dries: The interaction of trust and control in US-based international joint ventures. *Journal of Management Studies*, 39(6), 865–86.

Fuller D., Logan B., & Valkova A. (2022). The great attrition in frontline retail – And what retailers can do about it, *McKinsey Podcast*, July 29, www.mckinsey.com/industries/retail/our-insights/the-great-attrition-in-frontline-retail-and-what-retailers-can-do-about-it.

Fuller L. & Smith V. (1991). Consumers' reports: Management by customers in a changing economy *Work, Employment and Society*, 5(1), 1–16.

Fullerton R. R., Kennedy F. A., & Widener S. K. (2013). Management accounting and control practices in a lean manufacturing environment. *Accounting, Organizations and Society*, 38(1), 50–71.

Furnari S., Crilly D., Misangyi V. F., Greckhamer T., Fiss P. C., & Aguilera R. (2021). Capturing causal complexity: Heuristics for configurational theorizing. *Academy of Management Review*, 46(4), 778–99.

Gadinis S. & Miazad A. (2020). Corporate law and social risk. *Vanderbilt Law Review*, 73(5), 1401–77.

Gajendran R. S. & Harrison D. A. (2007). The good, the bad, and the unknown about telecommuting: Meta-analysis of psychological mediators and individual consequences. *Journal of Applied Psychology*, 92(6), 1524–41.

Galbraith J. R. (1973). *Designing complex organizations*. Reading, MA: Addison-Wesley.

Galbraith J. R. (1977). *Organization design*. Reading, MA: Addison-Wesley.

Galletta D. F. & Polak P. (2003). An empirical investigation of antecedents of internet abuse in the workplace. *Proceedings of the Second Annual Workshop on HCI Research in MIS*, Seattle, WA.

Galliers R. D., Newell S., Shanks G., & Topi H. (2015). Call for papers: JSIS special issue on "The challenges and opportunities of 'datification' Strategic impacts of 'big' (and 'small') and real time data – For society and for organizational decision makers." *Journal of Strategic Information Systems*, 24(2), II–III.

Galliers R. D., Newell S., Shanks G., & Topi H. (2017). Datification and its human, organizational and societal effects: The strategic opportunities and challenges of algorithmic decision-making. *Journal of Strategic Information Systems*, 26(3), 185–90.

Gallup (2016). How millennials want to work and live. www.gallup.com/workplace/238073/millennials-work-live.aspx.

Gallup (2017). State of the American workplace. www.gallup.com/workplace/238085/state-american-workplace-report-2017.aspx.

Gallup (2018). Gallup's perspective on the gig economy and alternative work arrangements. www.gallup.com/workplace/240878/gig-economy-paper-2018.aspx.

Gallup (2023). Hybrid work. www.gallup.com/401384/indicator-hybrid-work.aspx.

Garcia-Arroyo J. & Osca A. (2021). Big data contributions to human resource management: A systematic review. *International Journal of Human Resource Management*, 32(20), 4337–62.

Gartner (2020). Future of work trends post COVID-19. www.gartner.com/smarterwithgartner/9-future-of-work-trends-post-covid-19.

Gartner (2022). HR Leaders Monthly: The importance of culture in hybrid work. www.gartner.com/en/human-resources/trends/hr-leaders-magazine-july-2022.

Gaski J. F. (1984). The theory of power and conflict in channels of distribution. *Journal of Marketing*, 48(3), 9–29.

Gavetti G., Levinthal D., & Ocasio W. (2007). Neo-Carnegie: The Carnegie School's past, present, and reconstructing for the future. *Organization Science*, 18(3), 523–36.

Gavin M. B., Green S. G., & Fairhurst G. T. (1995). Managerial control strategies for poor performance over time and the impact on subordinate reactions. *Organizational Behavior and Human Decision Processes*, 63(2), 207–21.

George G., Haas M. R., & Pentland A. (2014). Big data and management. *Academy of Management Journal*, 57(2), 321–6.

Gerber C. & Krzywdzinski M. (2019). Brave new digital work? New forms of performance control in crowdwork. In Steve PV, & Anne K (eds), *Work and Labor in the Digital Age*. Bingley, UK: Emerald Publishing Limited, Vol. 33, 121–43.

Gerdin J., Johansson T., & Wennblom G. (2019). The contingent nature of complementarity between results and value-based controls for managing company-level profitability: A situational strength perspective. *Accounting, Organizations and Society*, 79, 101058.

Geringer J. M. & Hebert L. (1989). Control and performance in international joint ventures. *Journal of International Business Studies*, 20(2), 235–54.

Germain R., Claycomb C., & Dröge C. (2008). Supply chain variability, organizational structure, and performance: The moderating effect of demand unpredictability. *Journal of Operations Management*, 26(5), 557–70.

Ghosh S. (2018). Undercover author finds Amazon warehouse workers in UK 'peed in bottles' over fears of being punished for taking a break. *Business Insider*, April 16, www.businessinsider.com/amazon-warehouse-workers-have-to-pee-into-bottles-2018-4.

Ghoshal S. & Moran P. (1996). Bad for practice: A critique of the transaction cost theory. *Academy of Management Review*, 21(1), 13–47.

Gibbons R. (1998). Incentives in organizations. *Journal of Economic Perspectives*, 12(4), 115–32.

Gibbs J. L., Rozaidi N. A., & Eisenberg J. (2013). Overcoming the "ideology of openness": Probing the affordances of social media for organizational knowledge sharing. *Journal of Computer-Mediated Communication*, 19(1), 102–20.

Gibson C. B., Huang L., Kirkman B. L., & Shapiro D. L. (2014). Where global and virtual meet: The value of examining the intersection of these elements in twenty-first-century teams. *Annual Review of Organizational Psychology and Organizational Behavior*, 1(1), 217–44.

Giddens A. (1984). *The constitution of society: Outline of the theory of structuration.* Berkeley, CA: University of California Press.

Giglioni G. B. & Bedeian A. G. (1974). A conspectus of management control theory: 1900-1972. *Academy of Management Journal*, 17(2), 292–305.

Gilson L. L., Mathieu J. E., Shalley C. E., & Ruddy T. M. (2005). Creativity and standardization: Complementary or conflicting drivers of team effectiveness? *Academy of Management Journal*, 48(3), 521–31.

GitLab (2023a). GitLab docs. https://docs.gitlab.com/ee/user/project/issues/.

GitLab (2023b). Handbook. https://about.gitlab.com/handbook/.

Gómez-Mejía L. R., Tosi H., & Hinkin T. (1987). Managerial control, performance, and executive compensation. *Academy of Management Journal*, 30(1), 51–70.

Gómez-Mejía L. R. & Wiseman R. M. (1997). Reframing executive compensation: An assessment and outlook. *Journal of Management*, 23(3), 291–374.

Gonedes N. J. (1970). Accounting for managerial control: An application of chance-constrained programming. *Journal of Accounting Research*, 8(1), 1–20.

Gonzalez-Mulé E. & Aguinis H. (2018). Advancing theory by assessing boundary conditions with metaregression: A critical review and best-practice recommendations. *Journal of Management*, 44(6), 2246–73.

Goo J., Kishore R., Rao H. R., & Nam K. (2009). The role of service level agreements in relational management of information technology outsourcing: An empirical study. *MIS Quarterly*, 33(1), 119–45.

Goodale J. C., Kuratko D. F., Hornsby J. S., & Covin J. G. (2011). Operations management and corporate entrepreneurship: The moderating effect of operations control on the antecedents of corporate entrepreneurial activity in relation to innovation performance. *Journal of Operations Management*, 29(1), 116–27.

Goodman P. S. (2022). The real reason America doesn't have enough truck drivers. *New York Times*, February 9, www.nytimes.com/2022/02/09/business/truck-driver-shortage.html.

Goold M. (1991). Strategic control in the decentralized firm. *MIT Sloan Management Review*, 32(2), 69–81.

Goold M. & Quinn J. J. (1990). The paradox of strategic controls. *Strategic Management Journal*, 11(1), 43–57.

Gorman P., Nelson T., & Glassman A. (2004). The millennial generation: A strategic opportunity. *Organizational Analysis*, 12(3), 255–70.

Govindarajan V. (1988). A contingency approach to strategy implementation at the business-unit level: Integrating administrative mechanisms with strategy. *Academy of Management Journal*, 31(4), 828–53.

Govindarajan V. & Gupta A. K. (1985). Linking control systems to business unit strategy: Impact on performance. *Accounting, Organizations and Society*, 10(1), 51–66.

Grabner I. (2014). Incentive system design in creativity-dependent firms. *The Accounting Review*, 89(5), 1729–50.

Grabner I., Klein A., & Speckbacher G. (2022). Managing the trade-off between autonomy and task interdependence in creative teams: The role of organizational-level cultural control. *Accounting, Organizations and Society*, 101(3), 101347.

Grabner I. & Moers F. (2013). Management control as a system or a package? Conceptual and empirical issues. *Accounting, Organizations and Society*, 38(6), 407–19.

Grafton J., Lillis A. M., & Widener S. K. (2010). The role of performance measurement and evaluation in building organizational capabilities and performance. *Accounting, Organizations and Society*, 35(7), 689–706.

Grant A. M. & Parker S. K. (2009). Redesigning work design theories: The rise of relational and proactive perspectives. *Academy of Management Annals*, 3(1), 317–75.

Grant Thornton (2019). Women in business: Building a blueprint for action. www .grantthornton.global/globalassets/global-insights---do-not-edit/2019/women-in-business/gtil-wib-report_grant-thornton-spreads-low-res.pdf.

Gray B. (1990). The enactment of management control systems: A critique of Simons. *Accounting, Organizations and Society*, 15(1), 145–8.

Gray M. L. & Suri S. (2019). *Ghost work: How to stop Silicon Valley from building a new global underclass*. San Francisco, CA: HMH Books.

Greenberger D. B. & Strasser S. (1986). Development and application of a model of personal control in organizations. *Academy of Management Review*, 11(1), 164–77.

Gregory R. W., Beck R., & Keil M. (2013). Control balancing in information systems development offshoring projects. *MIS Quarterly*, 37(4), 1211–32.

Grewal R., Kumar A., Mallapragada G., & Saini A. (2013). Marketing channels in foreign markets: Control mechanisms and the moderating role of multinational corporation headquarters-subsidiary relationship. *Journal of Marketing Research*, 50(3), 378–98.

Griffin A. (2016). Uber to start monitoring drivers through their phones to see whether they drive safely. *The Independent*, January 26, www.independent.co.uk/tech/uber-to-start-monitoring-drivers-through-their-phones-to-see-whether-they-drive-safely-a6834551.html.

Groen B. A. C., Van Triest S. P., Coers M., & Wtenweerde N. (2018). Managing flexible work arrangements: Teleworking and output controls. *European Management Journal*, 36(6), 727–35.

Groysberg B., Thomas D. A., & Tydlaska J. M. (2011). oDesk: Changing how the world works. *Harvard Business School Case Study #9-411-078*, 1–26 [permission obtained from Harvard Business Publishing].

Gruber M., de Leon N., George G., & Thompson P. (2015). Managing by design. *Academy of Management Journal*, 58(1), 1–7.

Gu G. & Zhu F. (2021). Trust and disintermediation: Evidence from an online freelance marketplace. *Management Science*, 67(2), 794–807.

Guajardo J. A., Cohen M. A., Kim S.-H., & Netessine S. (2012). Impact of performance-based contracting on product reliability: An empirical analysis. *Management Science*, 58(5), 961–79.

Guardian (2020). Twitter announces employees will be allowed to work from home "forever." May 12, www.theguardian.com/technology/2020/may/12/twitter-coronavirus-covid19-work-from-home.

Gulati R. (1995). Does familiarity breed trust? The implications of repeated ties for contractual choices in alliances. *Academy of Management Journal*, 38(1), 85–112.

Gulati R. & Singh H. (1998). The architecture of cooperation: Managing coordination costs and appropriation concerns in strategic alliances. *Administrative Science Quarterly*, 43(4), 781–814.

Gulati R. & Westphal J. D. (1999). Cooperative or controlling? The effects of CEO-board relations and the content of interlocks on the formation of joint ventures. *Administrative Science Quarterly*, 44(3), 473–506.

Gundlach G. T. & Cannon J. P. (2010). "Trust but verify"? The performance implications of verification strategies in trusting relationships. *Journal of the Academy of Marketing Science*, 38(4), 399–417.

Günther W. A., Mehrizi M. H. R., Huysman M., & Feldberg F. (2017). Debating big data: A literature review on realizing value from big data. *Journal of Strategic Information Systems*, 26(3), 191–209.

Gupta A. K. & Govindarajan V. (1991). Knowledge flows and the structure of control within multinational corporations. *Academy of Management Review*, 16(4), 768–92.

Gusenbauer M. & Haddaway N. R. (2020). Which academic search systems are suitable for systematic reviews or meta-analyses? Evaluating retrieval qualities of Google Scholar, PubMed, and 26 other resources. *Research Synthesis Methods*, 11(2), 181–217.

Gutelius B. & Theodore N. (2019). The future of warehouse work: Technological change in the U.S. logistics industry. *UC Berkeley Center for Labor Research and Education and Working Partnerships USA*, http://laborcenter.berkeley.edu/future-of-warehouse-work/.

Hadfield-Menell D. & Hadfield G. (2019). Incomplete contracting and AI alignment. *Proceedings of the 2019 AAAI/ACM Conference on AI, Ethics, and Society*, 417–22. Honolulu, HI.

Hafermalz E. (2021). Out of the panopticon and into exile: Visibility and control in distributed new culture organizations. *Organization Studies*, 42(5), 697–717.

Hagelüken A. & Kläsgen M. (2019). So überwacht Zalando seine Mitarbeiter. *Süddeutsche Zeitung*, November 19, www.sueddeutsche.de/wirtschaft/zalando-ueberwachung-zonar-1.4688431.

Hall J. V. & Krueger A. B. (2018). An analysis of the labor market for Uber's driver-partners in the United States. *Industrial and Labor Relations Review*, 71(3), 705–32.

Hall R. & Joiner S. (2014). Managing workplace bullying and social media policy: Implications for employee engagement. *Academy of Business Research Journal*, 1, 128–38.

Hamel G. (2011). First, let's fire all the managers. *Harvard Business Review*, 89(12), 48–60.

Hamel G. (2014). Why bureaucracy must die. *Fortune*, March 26, https://fortune.com/2014/03/26/why-bureaucracy-must-die/.

Handley S. M. & Angst C. M. (2015). The impact of culture on the relationship between governance and opportunism in outsourcing relationships. *Strategic Management Journal*, 36(9), 1412–34.

Handley S. M. & Benton W. C. (2013). The influence of task- and location-specific complexity on the control and coordination costs in global outsourcing relationships. *Journal of Operations Management*, 31(3), 109–28.

Handley S. M. & Gray J. V. (2013). Inter-organizational quality management: The use of contractual incentives and monitoring mechanisms with outsourced manufacturing. *Production & Operations Management*, 22(6), 1540–56.

Harrison G. L. & McKinnon J. L. (1999). Cross-cultural research in management control systems design: A review of the current state. *Accounting, Organizations and Society*, 24(5), 483–506.

Harrison J. R. & Carroll G. R. (1991). Keeping the faith: A model of cultural transmission in formal organizations. *Administrative Science Quarterly*, 36(4), 552–82.

Harter J. (2022). Is quiet quitting real? *Gallup Workplace*, September 6, www.gallup.com/workplace/398306/quiet-quitting-real.aspx.

Harter J. (2023). Are remote workers and their organizations drifting apart? *Gallup Workplace*, August 24, www.gallup.com/workplace/509759/remote-workers-organizations-drifting-apart.aspx.

Hartline M. D. & Ferrell O. C. (1996). The management of customer-contact service employees: An empirical investigation. *Journal of Marketing*, 60(4), 52–70.

Hartline M. D., Maxham J. G., & McKee D. O. (2000). Corridors of influence in the dissemination of customer-oriented strategy to customer contact service employees. *Journal of Marketing*, 64(2), 35–50.

Harvard Business Review Press (2016). Leading virtual teams. https://store.hbr.org/product/leading-virtual-teams-hbr-20-minute-manager-series/10005.

Haveman H. A. & Wetts R. (2019). Organizational theory: From classical sociology to the 1970s. *Sociology Compass*, 13(3), 1–14.

Hawkins A. J. (2017). Uber finally caves and adds a tipping option to its app. *The Verge*, June 20, www.theverge.com/2017/6/20/15840818/uber-tipping-option-app-seattle-minneapolis-houston.

Hayes R. H. & Abernathy W. J. (1980). Managing our way to economic decline. *Harvard Business Review*, 58(4), 67–77.

HBR Idea Cast (2022). Advice from the CEO of an all-remote company. GitLab's Sid Sijbrandij on building a company with no offices and employees spread around the world. Episode 877. https://hbr.org/podcast/2022/09/advice-from-the-ceo-of-an-all-remote-company.

Healy P. M. (1985). The effect of bonus schemes on accounting decisions. *Journal of Accounting and Economics*, 7(1), 85–107.

Heaphy E. D., Byron K., Ballinger G. A., Gittell J. H., Leana C., & Sluss D. M. (2018). The changing nature of work relationships. *Academy of Management Review*, 43(4), 558–69.

Heide J. B. & John G. (1988). The role of dependence balancing in safeguarding transaction-specific assets in conventional channels. *Journal of Marketing*, 52(1), 20–35.

Heide J. B. & John G. (1992). Do norms matter in marketing relationships? *Journal of Marketing*, 56(2), 32–44.

Heide J. B., Wathne K. H., & Rokkan A. I. (2007). Interfirm monitoring, social contracts, and relationship outcomes. *Journal of Marketing Research*, 44(3), 425–33.

Henderson J. C. & Lee S. (1992). Managing I/S design teams: A control theories perspective. *Management Science*, 38(6), 757–77.

Henri J.-F. (2006a). Management control systems and strategy: A resource-based perspective. *Accounting, Organizations and Society*, 31(6), 529–58.

Henri J.-F. (2006b). Organizational culture and performance measurement systems. *Accounting, Organizations and Society*, 31(1), 77–103.

Henri J.-F. (2008). Taxonomy of performance measurement systems. *Advances in Management Accounting*, 17, 247–88.

Hershatter A. & Epstein M. (2010). Millennials and the world of work: An organization and management perspective. *Journal of Business and Psychology*, 25(2), 211–23.

Hertel G., Geister S., & Konradt U. (2005). Managing virtual teams: A review of current empirical research. *Human Resource Management Review*, 15(1), 69–95.

Higgins J. P. T. & Thompson S. G. (2002). Quantifying heterogeneity in a meta-analysis. *Statistics in Medicine*, 21(11), 1539–58.

Hilbert M. & Lopez P. (2011). The world's technological capacity to store, communicate, and compute information. *Science*, 332(6025), 60–5.

Hill C. W. L. & Hoskisson R. E. (1987). Strategy and structure in the multiproduct firm. *Academy of Management Review*, 12(2), 331–41.

Hillier F. S. (1967). *Introduction to operations research*. San Francisco, CA: Holden-Day.

Hinds P. J. & Bailey D. E. (2003). Out of sight, out of sync: Understanding conflict in distributed teams. *Organization Science*, 14(6), 615–32.

Hinings B., Gegenhuber T., & Greenwood R. (2018). Digital innovation and transformation: An institutional perspective. *Information and Organization*, 28(1), 52–61.

Hinings C. R. (2018). Why should we bother? What are configurations for? *Strategic Organization*, 16(4), 499–509.

Hirst G., Van Knippenberg D., Chen C.-H., & Sacramento C. A. (2011). How does bureaucracy impact individual creativity? A cross-level investigation of team contextual influences on goal orientation-creativity relationships. *Academy of Management Journal*, 54(3), 624–41.

Hirst M. K. (1983). Reliance on accounting performance measures, task uncertainty, and dysfunctional behavior: Some extensions. *Journal of Accounting Research*, 21(2), 596–605.

Hitt M. A., Hoskisson R. E., Johnson R. A., & Moesel D. D. (1996). The market for corporate control and firm innovation. *Academy of Management Journal*, 39(5), 1084–119.

Hoch J. E. & Kozlowski S. W. J. (2014). Leading virtual teams: Hierarchical leadership, structural supports, and shared team leadership. *Journal of Applied Psychology*, 99(3), 390–403.

Hodgson D. E. (2004). Project work: The legacy of bureaucratic control in the postbureaucratic organization. *Organization*, 11(1), 81–100.

Hodson R. (1995). Worker resistance: An underdeveloped concept in the sociology of work. *Economic and Industrial Democracy*, 16(1), 79–110.

Hofstede G. H. (1981). Management control of public and not-for-profit activities. *Accounting, Organizations and Society*, 6(3), 193–211.

Hofstede G. H. (1980). *Culture's consequences: International differences in work-related values*. Beverly Hills, CA: SAGE.

Holmstrom B. (1979). Moral hazard and observability. *The Bell Journal of Economics*, 10(1), 74–91.

Holmstrom B. & Milgrom P. (1991). Multitask principal-agent analyses: Incentive contracts, asset ownership, and job design. *Journal of Law, Economics, and Organization*, 7(Special Issue), 24–52.

Holzack S. (2014). Elance-oDesk flings open the doors to a massive digital workforce. *Washington Post*, June 13, www.washingtonpost.com/business/freelancers-from-around-the-world-offer-software-developing-skills-remotely/2014/06/13/f5088c54-efe7-11e3-bf76-447a5df6411f_story.html.

Homburg C., Vomberg A., & Muehlhaeuser S. (2020). Design and governance of multichannel sales systems: Financial performance consequences in business-to-business markets. *Journal of Marketing Research*, 57(6), 1113–34.

Hoogeveen S. (2004). Using clan control to manage teleworkers. 1st Twente student conference on IT, June 14, Enschede, Netherlands, http://citeseerx.ist.psu.edu/viewdoc/download?doi=10.1.1.59.857&rep=rep1&type=pdf.

Hoskisson R. E. & Hitt M. A. (1988). Strategic control systems and relative R&D investment in large multiproduct firms. *Strategic Management Journal*, 9(6), 605–21.

Hoskisson R. E., Hitt M. A., & Hill C. W. L. (1993). Managerial incentives and investment in research and development in large multiproduct firms. *Organization Science*, 4(2), 325–41.

Howell J. (2022). Top decentralized autonomous organization (DAO): Use cases & examples. April 28, https://101blockchains.com/top-dao-use-cases-and-examples/.

Hsu J. S.-C., Shih S.-P., Hung Y. W., & Lowry P. B. (2015). The role of extra-role behaviors and social controls in information security policy effectiveness. *Information Systems Research*, 26(2), 282–300.

Hu Q., West R., & Smarandescu L. (2015). The role of self-control in information security violations: Insights from a cognitive neuroscience perspective. *Journal of Management Information Systems*, 31(4), 6–48.

Huber G. & Brown A. D. (2017). Identity work, humour and disciplinary power. *Organization Studies*, 38(8), 1107–26.

Huber T. L., Fischer T. A., Dibbern J., & Hirschheim R. (2013). A process model of complementarity and substitution of contractual and relational governance in IS outsourcing. *Journal of Management Information Systems*, 30(3), 81–114.

Huedo-Medina T. B., Sánchez-Meca J., Marín-Martínez F., & Botella J. (2006). Assessing heterogeneity in meta-analysis: Q statistic or I2 index? *Psychological Methods*, 11(2), 193–206.

Hughes D. E. & Ahearne M. (2010). Energizing the reseller's sales force: The power of brand identification. *Journal of Marketing*, 74(4), 81–96.

Hunter J. E. & Schmidt F. L. (2015). *Methods of meta-analysis: Correcting error and bias in research findings*, 3rd ed. Thousand Oaks, CA: SAGE.

Hunton J. E. & Norman C. S. (2010). The impact of alternative telework arrangements on organizational commitment: Insights from a longitudinal field experiment. *Journal of Information Systems*, 24(1), 67–90.

Hurrell S. A., Scholarios D., & Richards J. (2017). 'The kids are alert': Generation Y responses to employer use and monitoring of social networking sites. *New Technology, Work and Employment*, 32(1), 64–83.

Huws U. (2016). A review on the future of work: Online labour exchanges or crowdsourcing. *European Agency for Safety and Health at Work Discussion Paper*, https://osha.europa.eu/en/oshwiki/review-future-work-online-labour-exchanges-or-crowdsourcing.

IBM Institute for Business Value (2020). COVID-19 is significantly altering U.S. consumer behavior and plans post-crisis. May 1, https://newsroom.ibm.com/2020-05-01-IBM-Study-COVID-19-Is-Significantly-Altering-U-S-Consumer-Behavior-and-Plans-Post-Crisis.

Igbaria M. & Guimaraes T. (1999). Exploring differences in employee turnover intentions and its determinants among telecommuters and non-telecommuters. *Journal of Management Information Systems*, 16(1), 147–64.

Illegems V. & Verbeke A. (2004). Telework: What does it mean for management? *Long Range Planning*, 37(4), 319–34.

International Labour Organization (2013). Regulating the employment relationship in Europe: A guide to Recommendation No. 198. www.ilo.org/wcmsp5/groups/public/@ed_dialogue/@dialogue/documents/publication/wcms_209280.pdf.

International Labour Organization (2019). World employment social outlook: Trends 2019. www.ilo.org/global/research/global-reports/weso/2019/WCMS_670542/lang--en/index.htm.

International Labour Organization (2020). Working from home: Estimating the worldwide potential. www.ilo.org/global/topics/non-standard-employment/publications/WCMS_743447/lang--en/index.htm.

Ittner C. D. & Larcker D. F. (2001). Assessing empirical research in managerial accounting: A value-based management perspective. *Journal of Accounting & Economics*, 32(1), 349–410.

Ittner C. D., Larcker D. F., & Rajan M. V. (1997). The choice of performance measures in annual bonus contracts. *The Accounting Review*, 72(2), 231–55.

Jackson S. (2022). A pay transparency law recently went into effect in New York City. Here are the other cities and states with similar legislation, and what workers there should know. *Business Insider India*, November 8, www.businessinsider.in/careers/news/a-pay-transparency-law-recently-went-into-effect-in-new-york-city-here-are-the-other-cities-and-states-with-similar-legislation-and-what-workers-there-should-know-/slidelist/95381768.cms.

Jacobson A. (2021). Risks to employers in the growing gig economy. *Risk Management*, 68(5), 4–7.

Jaeger A. M. & Baliga B. R. (1985). Control systems and strategic adaptation: Lessons from the Japanese experience. *Strategic Management Journal*, 6(2), 115–34.

Jap S. D. & Ganesan S. (2000). Control mechanisms and the relationship life cycle: Implications for safeguarding specific investments and developing commitment. *Journal of Marketing Research*, 37(2), 227–45.

Jaworski B. J. (1988). Toward a theory of marketing control: Environmental context, control types, and consequences. *Journal of Marketing*, 52(3), 23–39.

Jaworski B. J. & MacInnis D. J. (1989). Marketing jobs and management controls: Toward a framework. *Journal of Marketing Research*, 26(4), 409–19.

Jaworski B. J., Stathakopoulos V., & Krishnan H. S. (1993). Control combinations in marketing: Conceptual framework and empirical evidence. *Journal of Marketing*, 57(1), 57–69.

Jayaraman V., Narayanan S., Luo Y., & Swaminathan J. M. (2013). Offshoring business process services and governance control mechanisms: An examination of service providers from India. *Production and Operations Management*, 22(2), 314–34.

Jensen M. C. & Meckling W. H. (1976). Theory of the firm: Managerial behavior, agency costs and ownership structure. *Journal of Financial Economics*, 3(4), 305–60.

Jermier J. M. (1998). Critical perspectives on organizational control. *Administrative Science Quarterly*, 43(2), 235–56.

Jerzy N. (2022). So erkennen Sie, ob Ihr Chef Sie überwacht. *Wirtschaftswoche*, Juni 30, www.wiwo.de/erfolg/beruf/kontrollen-im-buero-so-erkennen-sie-ob-ihr-chef-sie-ueberwacht/26221382.html.

Jirásek M. (in press). Klima DAO: A crypto answer to carbon markets. *Journal of Organization Design*, 12(2), 271–83.

Jobvite (2019). Social recruiting survey. www.jobvite.com.

Jordan M. I. & Mitchell T. M. (2015). Machine learning: Trends, perspectives, and prospects. *Science*, 349(6245), 255.

Joseph J., Baumann O., Burton R., & Srikanth K. (2019). Reviewing, revisiting, and renewing the foundations of organization design. *Advances in Strategic Management*, 40, 1–23.

Joseph J. & Gaba V. (2020). Organizational structure, information processing, and decision-making: A retrospective and road map for research. *Academy of Management Annals*, 14(1), 267–302.

Kantor J. & Streitfeld D. (2015). Inside Amazon: Wrestling big ideas in a bruising workplace. *New York Times*, August 15, www.nytimes.com/2015/08/16/technology/inside-amazon-wrestling-big-ideas-in-a-bruising-workplace.html.

Kaplan E. (2015). The spy who fired me: The human costs of workplace monitoring. *Harper's Magazine*, March, 31–40.

Kaplan R. S. & Norton D. P. (1992). The balanced scorecard: Measures that drive performance. *Harvard Business Review*, 70(1), 71–9.

Kaplan R. S. & Norton D. P. (1996). *The balanced scorecard: Translating strategy into action*. Boston, MA: Harvard Business Review Press.

Katsikeas C. S., Auh S., Spyropoulou S., & Menguc B. (2018). Unpacking the relationship between sales control and salesperson performance: A regulatory fit perspective. *Journal of Marketing*, 82(3), 45–69.

Katz L. F. & Krueger A. B. (2019). The rise and nature of alternative work arrangements in the United States, 1995-2015. *ILR Review*, 72(2), 382–416.

Kellogg K. C., Valentine M. A., & Christin A. (2020). Algorithms at work: The new contested terrain of control. *Academy of Management Annals*, 14(1), 366–410.

Kessinger R. & Kellogg K. (2019). Softening the edges of algorithmic evaluation: Relational work to mitigate negative worker outcomes associated with algorithmic evaluation. *Paper presented at the MIT Economic Sociology Working Group Seminar*, Cambridge, MA.

Kessler S. (2016). How Uber manages drivers without technically managing drivers. *Fast Company*, August 9, www.fastcompany.com/3062622/how-ubers-app-manages-drivers-without-technically-managing-drivers.

Khanagha S., Volberda H. W., Alexiou A., & Annosi M. C. (2022). Mitigating the dark side of agile teams: Peer pressure, leaders' control, and the innovative output of agile teams. *Journal of Product Innovation Management*, 39(3), 334–50.

Khandwalla P. N. (1974). Mass output orientation of operations technology and organizational structure. *Administrative Science Quarterly*, 19(1), 74–97.

Khansa L., Kuem J., Siponen M., & Kim S. S. (2017). To cyberloaf or not to cyberloaf: The impact of the announcement of formal organizational controls. *Journal of Management Information Systems*, 34(1), 141–76.

Kidwell R. E. (2005). Noncompliance at Dow Chemical. In Kidwell RE, & Martin CL (eds), *Managing organizational deviance*. Thousand Oaks, CA: SAGE, 151–5.

Kidwell R. E. & Sprague R. (2009). Electronic surveillance in the global workplace: Laws, ethics, research and practice. *New Technology, Work and Employment*, 24(2), 194–208.

Kim S. K. & Tiwana A. (2016). Chicken or egg? Sequential complementarity among salesforce control mechanisms. *Journal of the Academy of Marketing Science*, 44(3), 316–33.

Kinder E., Jarrahi M., & Sutherland W. (2019). Gig platforms, tensions, alliances and ecosystems: An actor-network perspective. *Proceedings of the ACM on Human-Computer Interaction*, 3(CSCW), 1–26.

King E., Finkelstein L., Thomas C., & Corrington A. (2019). Generational differences at work are small. Thinking they're big affects our behavior. *Harvard Business Review*, August 1, https://hbr.org/2019/08/generational-differences-at-work-are-small-thinking-theyre-big-affects-our-behavior.

Kipnis D. & Schmidt S. M. (1988). Upward-influence styles: Relationship with performance evaluations, salary, and stress. *Administrative Science Quarterly*, 33(4), 528–42.

Kirsch L. J. (1996). The management of complex tasks in organizations: Controlling the systems development process. *Organization Science*, 7(1), 1–21.

Kirsch L. J. (1997). Portfolios of control modes and IS project management. *Information Systems Research*, 8(3), 215–39.

Kirsch L. J. (2004). Deploying common systems globally: The dynamics of control. *Information Systems Research*, 15(4), 374–95.

Kirsch L. J. & Choudhury V. (2010). Toward a theory of relational control: How relationship structure influences the choice of control. In Sitkin SB, Cardinal LB, & Bijlsma-Frankema K (eds), *Organizational control*. Cambridge, UK: Cambridge University Press, 301–23.

Kirsch L. J., Ko D.-G., & Haney M. H. (2010). Investigating the antecedents of team-based clan control: Adding social capital as a predictor. *Organization Science*, 21(2), 469–89.

Kirsch L. J., Sambamurthy V., Ko D.-G., & Purvis R. L. (2002). Controlling information systems development projects: The view from the client. *Management Science*, 48(4), 484–98.

Klein B., Crawford R. G., & Alchian A. A. (1978). Vertical integration, appropriable rents, and the competitive contracting process. *Journal of Law and Economics*, 21(2), 297–326.

Klein K. J., Ziegert J. C., Knight A. P., & Xiao Y. (2006). Dynamic delegation: Shared, hierarchical, and deindividualized leadership in extreme action teams. *Administrative Science Quarterly*, 51(4), 590–621.

Kleinberg J., Lakkaraju H., Leskovec J., Ludwig J., & Mullainathan S. (2017). Human decisions and machine predictions. *Quarterly Journal of Economics*, 133(1), 237–93.

Kochhar R. & David P. (1996). Institutional investors and firm innovation: A test of competing hypotheses. *Strategic Management Journal*, 17(1), 73–84.

Kohli A. K., Shervani T. A., & Challagalla G. N. (1998). Learning and performance orientation of salespeople: The role of supervisors. *Journal of Marketing Research*, 35(2), 263–74.

Kolmar C. (2022). 23 essential gig economy statistics (2022): Definitions, facts, and trends on gig work. February 2, www.zippia.com/advice/gig-economy-statistics/.

Kornberger M., Pflueger D., & Mouritsen J. (2017). Evaluative infrastructures: Accounting for platform organization. *Accounting, Organizations and Society*, 60, 79–95.

Koufteros X., Verghese A., & Lucianetti L. (2014). The effect of performance measurement systems on firm performance: A cross-sectional and a longitudinal study. *Journal of Operations Management*, 32(6), 313–36.

Kownatzki M., Walter J., Floyd S. W., & Lechner C. (2013). Corporate control and the speed of SBU-level decision making. *Academy of Management Journal*, 56(5), 1295–324.

Kowske B. J., Rasch R., & Wiley J. (2010). Millennials' (lack of) attitude problem: An empirical examination of generational effects on work attitudes. *Journal of Business and Psychology*, 25(2), 265–79.

Krafft M. (1999). An empirical investigation of the antecedents of sales force control systems. *Journal of Marketing*, 63(3), 120–34.

Krahn H. J. & Galambos N. L. (2014). Work values and beliefs of 'Generation X' and 'Generation Y'. *Journal of Youth Studies*, 17(1), 92–112.

Krajewski L. J., Ritzman L. P., & Malhotra M. K. (2010). *Operations management: Processes and supply chains*, 9th ed. Upper Saddle River, NJ: Prentice Hall.

Kreutzer M., Cardinal L. B., Walter J., & Lechner C. (2016). Formal and informal controls as complements or substitutes? The role of the task environment. *Strategy Science*, 1(4), 235–55.

Kreutzer M. & Lechner C. (2010). Control configurations and strategic initiatives. In Sitkin SB, Cardinal LB, & Bijlsma-Frankema KM (eds), *Organizational control*. Cambridge, UK: Cambridge University Press, 463–503.

Kreutzer M., Walter J., & Cardinal L. B. (2015). Organizational control as antidote to politics in the pursuit of strategic initiatives. *Strategic Management Journal*, 36(9), 1317–37.

Kuhn K. M. (2016). The rise of the "gig economy" and implications for understanding work and workers. *Industrial and Organizational Psychology*, 9(1), 157–62.

Kuhn K. M. & Maleki A. (2017). Micro-entrepreneurs, dependent contractors, and instaserfs: Understanding online labor platform workforces. *Academy of Management Perspectives*, 31(3), 183–200.

Kunda G. (1992). *Engineering culture: Control and commitment in a high-tech corporation*. Philadelphia, PA: Temple University Press.

Kurland N. B. & Cooper C. D. (2002). Manager control and employee isolation in telecommuting environments. *Journal of High Technology Management Research*, 13(1), 107–26.

Kurland N. B. & Egan T. D. (1999). Telecommuting: Justice and control in the virtual organization. *Organization Science*, 10(4), 500–13.

Lake C. J., Highhouse S., & Shrift A. G. (2017). Validation of the job-hopping motives scale. *Journal of Career Assessment*, 26(3), 531–48.

Landis R. S. (2013). Successfully combining meta-analysis and structural equation modeling: Recommendations and strategies. *Journal of Business and Psychology*, 28(3), 251–61.

Langfield-Smith K. (1997). Management control systems and strategy: A critical review. *Accounting, Organizations and Society*, 22(2), 207–32.

Lassar W. M. & Kerr J. L. (1996). Strategy and control in supplier-distributor relationships: An agency perspective. *Strategic Management Journal*, 17(8), 613–32.

Lautsch B. A. & Kossek E. E. (2011). Managing a blended workforce: Telecommuters and non-telecommuters. *Organizational Dynamics*, 40(1), 10–17.

Lautsch B. A., Kossek E. E., & Eaton S. C. (2009). Supervisory approaches and paradoxes in managing telecommuting implementation. *Human Relations*, 62(6), 795–827.

Lawrence P. R. & Lorsch J. W. (1967). *Organization and environment: Managing differentiation and integration*. Boston, MA: Harvard University Publishing.

Lawrence P. R. & Lorsch J. W. (1969). *Organization and environment: Managing differentiation and integration*. Homewood, IL: Irwin.

Lecher C. (2019). How Amazon automatically tracks and fires warehouse workers for "productivity." *The Verge*, April 25, www.theverge.com/2019/4/25/18516004/amazon-warehouse-fulfillment-centers-productivity-firing-terminations.

Lechner C. & Kreutzer M. (2010). Coordinating growth initiatives in multi-unit firms. *Long Range Planning*, 43(1), 6–32.

Lee J.-N. & Kim Y.-G. (1999). Effect of partnership quality on IS outsourcing success: Conceptual framework and empirical validation. *Journal of Management Information Systems*, 15(4), 29–61.

Lee M. K., Kusbit D., Evan M., & Dabbish L. (2015). Working with machines: The impact of algorithmic and data-driven management on human workers. *Proceedings of the 33rd Annual ACM Conference on Human Factors in Computing Systems*, Seoul, Republic of Korea.

Lee M. Y. & Edmondson A. C. (2017). Self-managing organizations: Exploring the limits of less-hierarchical organizing. *Research in Organizational Behavior*, 37(1), 35–58.

Lehdonvirta V. (2016). Algorithms that divide and unite: Delocalisation, identity and collective action in 'microwork'. In Flecker J (ed), *Space, place and global digital work*. London, UK: Palgrave Macmillan, 53–80.

Leifer R. & Mills P. K. (1996). An information processing approach for deciding upon control strategies and reducing control loss in emerging organizations. *Journal of Management*, 22(1), 113–37.

Lemoine G. J., Parsons C. K., & Kansara S. (2015). Above and beyond, again and again: Self-regulation in the aftermath of organizational citizenship behaviors. *Journal of Applied Psychology*, 100(1), 40–55.

Levanon G. (2020). Remote work: The biggest legacy of COVID-19. *Forbes*, November 23, www.forbes.com/sites/gadlevanon/2020/11/23/remote-work-the-biggest-legacy-of-covid-19/?sh=a590d4c7f590.

Levine E. L. (1973). Problems of organizational control in microcosm: Group performance and group member satisfaction as a function of differences in control structure. *Journal of Applied Psychology*, 58(2), 186–96.

Levinthal D. A. (1988). A survey of agency models of organizations. *Journal of Economic Behavior and Organization*, 9(2), 153–85.

Levy K. & Barocas S. (2018). Refractive surveillance: Monitoring customers to manage workers. *International Journal of Communication*, 12, 1166–88.

Levy K. E. C. (2015). The contexts of control: Information, power, and truck-driving work. *The Information Society*, 31(2), 160–74.

Li J. J., Poppo L., & Zhou K. Z. (2010). Relational mechanisms, formal contracts, and local knowledge acquisition by international subsidiaries. *Strategic Management Journal*, 31(4), 349–70.

Li Y., Liu Y., Li M., & Wu H. (2008). Transformational offshore outsourcing: Empirical evidence from alliances in China. *Journal of Operations Management*, 26(2), 257–74.

Li Y., Xie E., Teo H.-H., & Peng M. W. (2010). Formal control and social control in domestic and international buyer-supplier relationships. *Journal of Operations Management*, 28(4), 333–44.

Liang H., Xue Y., & Wu L. (2013). Ensuring employees' IT compliance: Carrot or stick? *Information Systems Research*, 24(2), 279–94.

Likert R. (1961). *New patterns of management*. New York: McGraw-Hill.

Lindebaum D., Vesa M., & den Hond F. (2020). Insights from "The Machine Stops" to better understand rational assumptions in algorithmic decision making and its implications for organizations. *Academy of Management Review*, 45(1), 247–63.

LinkedIn (2022). 2022 global talent trends: The reinvention of company culture. www.linkedin.com/business/talent/blog/talent-strategy/global-talent-trends-report.

Lipsey M. W. & Wilson D. B. (2001). *Practical meta-analysis*. Thousand Oaks, CA: SAGE.

Lisi I. E. (2018). Determinants and performance effects of social performance measurement systems. *Journal of Business Ethics*, 152(1), 225–51.

Liu S. (2015). Effects of control on the performance of information systems projects: The moderating role of complexity risk. *Journal of Operations Management*, 36(1), 46–62.

Liu S. & Wang L. (2014). User liaisons' perspective on behavior and outcome control in IT projects. *Management Decision*, 52(6), 1148–73.

Liu Y., Luo Y., & Liu T. (2009). Governing buyer–supplier relationships through transactional and relational mechanisms: Evidence from China. *Journal of Operations Management*, 27(4), 294–309.

Lobel O. (2016). The law of the platform. *Minnesota Law Review*, 101(1), 87–166.

Logg J. M., Minson J. A., & Moore D. A. (2019). Algorithm appreciation: People prefer algorithmic to human judgment. *Organizational Behavior and Human Decision Processes*, 151(10), 90–103.

Long C. P. (2018). To control and build trust: How managers use organizational controls and trust-building activities to motivate subordinate cooperation. *Accounting, Organizations and Society*, 70(2), 69–91.

Long C. P. & Sitkin S. B. (2018). Control-trust dynamics in organizations: Identifying shared perspectives and charting conceptual fault lines. *Academy of Management Annals*, 12(2), 725–51.

Long C. P., Sitkin S. B., Cardinal L. B., & Burton R. (2015). How controls influence organizational information processing: Insights from a computational modeling investigation. *Computational and Mathematical Organization Theory*, 21(4), 406–36.

Lorange P. (1974). A framework for management control systems. *MIT Sloan Management Review*, 16(1), 41–56.

Lorange P., Scott Morton M. S., & Ghoshal S. (1986). *Strategic control systems*. St. Paul, MN: West Pub. Co.

Los Angeles Daily News (2015). California Public Utilities Commission probes Uber's car-leasing program. August 12, www.dailynews.com/2015/08/12/california-public-utilities-commission-probes-ubers-car-leasing-program/.

Loughry M. L. (2010). Peer control in organizations. In Sitkin SB, Cardinal LB, & Bijlsma-Frankema KM (eds), *Organizational control*. Cambridge, UK: Cambridge University Press, 324–61.

Loughry M. L. & Tosi H. L. (2008). Performance implications of peer monitoring. *Organization Science*, 19(6), 876–90.

Lovelock J.-D., Reynolds M., Granetto B., & Kandaswamy R. (2017). Forecast: Blockchain Business Value, Worldwide, 2017–2030. March 2, www.gartner.com/en/documents/3627117.

Lowe E. A. (1971). On the idea of a management control system: Integrating accounting and management control. *Journal of Management Studies*, 8(1), 1–12.

Luft J. & Shields M. D. (2003). Mapping management accounting: Graphics and guidelines for theory-consistent empirical research. *Accounting, Organizations and Society*, 28(2), 169–249.

Lui S. S. & Ngo H.-y. (2004). The role of trust and contractual safeguards on cooperation in non-equity alliances. *Journal of Management*, 30(4), 471–85.

Lumineau F., Wang W., & Schilke O. (2021). Blockchain governance: A new way of organizing collaborations? *Organization Science*, 32(2), 257–525.

Luo Y., Shenkar O., & Gurnani H. (2008). Control-cooperation interfaces in global strategic alliances: A situational typology and strategic responses. *Journal of International Business Studies*, 39(3), 428–53.

Lyons S. & Kuron L. (2014). Generational differences in the workplace: A review of the evidence and directions for future research. *Journal of Organizational Behavior*, 35, S139–S57.

MacCormack A. & Mishra A. (2015). Managing the performance trade-offs from partner integration: Implications of contract choice in R&D projects. *Production & Operations Management*, 24(10), 1552–69.

Machart F. (2020). The state of blockchain governance: Governance by and of blockchains. August 13, https://medium.com/greenfield-one/the-state-of-blockchain-governance-governance-by-and-of-blockchains-f6418c46077.

MacMillan D. (2016). Uber's app will soon begin tracking driving behavior. *Wall Street Journal*, June 29, www.wsj.com/articles/ubers-app-will-soon-begin-tracking-driving-behavior-1467194404.

Maffie M. D. (2022). The perils of laundering control through customers: A study of control and resistance in the ride-hail industry. *ILR Review*, 75(2), 348–72.

Makhija M. V. & Ganesh U. (1997). The relationship between control and partner learning-related joint ventures. *Organization Science*, 8(5), 508–27.

Malhotra A. & Majchrzak A. (2005). Virtual workspace technologies. *MIT Sloan Management Review*, 46(2), 11–14.

Malhotra A., Majchrzak A., & Rosen B. (2007). Leading virtual teams. *Academy of Management Perspectives*, 21(1), 60–70.

Malhotra D. & Murnighan J. K. (2002). The effects of contracts on interpersonal trust. *Administrative Science Quarterly*, 47(3), 534–59.

Malin B. J. & Chandler C. (2017). Free to work anxiously: Splintering precarity among drivers for Uber and Lyft. *Communication, Culture and Critique*, 10(2), 382–400.

Malmi T. & Brown D. A. (2008). Management control systems as a package: Opportunities, challenges and research directions. *Management Accounting Research*, 19(4), 287–300.

Mankins M., Brahm C., & Caimi G. (2014). Your scarcest resource. *Harvard Business Review*, 92(5), 74–80.

Manriquez M. (2019). Work-games in the gig-economy: A case study of Uber drivers in the city of Monterrey, Mexico. In Steve PV, & Anne K (eds), *Work and labor in the digital age*. Bingley, UK: Emerald Publishing Limited, 165–88.

Manz C. C. (1992). Self-leading work teams: Moving beyond self-management myths. *Human Relations*, 45(11), 1119–40.

March J. G. & Simon H. A. (1958). *Organizations*. New York: Wiley.

March J. G. & Simon H. A. (1993). *Organizations*, 2nd ed. Cambridge, MA: Blackwell.

Marginson D. E. W. (2002). Management control systems and their effects on strategy formation at middle-management levels: Evidence from a U.K. organization. *Strategic Management Journal*, 23(11), 1019–31.

Markham W. T., Bonjean C. M., & Corder J. (1984). Measuring organizational control: The reliability and validity of the control graph approach. *Human Relations*, 37(4), 263–93.

Markus M. L. (2017). Datification, organizational strategy, and IS research: What's the score? *Journal of Strategic Information Systems*, 26(3), 233–41.

Maruping L. M., Venkatesh V., & Agarwal R. (2009). A control theory perspective on agile methodology use and changing user requirements. *Information Systems Research*, 20(3), 377–99.

Mas A. & Moretti E. (2009). Peers at work. *American Economic Review*, 99(1), 112–45.

Massa F. G. & O'Mahony S. (2021). Order from chaos: How networked activists self-organize by creating a participation architecture. *Administrative Science Quarterly*, 66(4), 1037–83.

Mayo E. (1945). *The social problems of an industrial civilization*. Boston, MA: Division of Research, Graduate School of Business Administration, Harvard University.

McAfee A. & Brynjolfsson E. (2012). Big data: The management revolution. *Harvard Business Review*, 90(10), 60–8.

McDonald D. J. & Makin P. J. (2000). The psychological contract, organisational commitment and job satisfaction of temporary staff. *Leadership and Organization Development Journal*, 21(2), 84–91.

McFarland L. A. & Ployhart R. E. (2015). Social media: A contextual framework to guide research and practice. *Journal of Applied Psychology*, 100(6), 1653–77.

McGonigal J. (2011). *Reality is broken: Why games make us better and how they can change the world*. New York: Penguin Press.

McGrath R. G. (2014). Management's three eras: A brief history. *Harvard Business Review Blog*, July 30, https://hbr.org/2014/07/managements-three-eras-a-brief-history.

McGregor D. (1960). *The human side of enterprise*. New York: McGraw-Hill.

McKinsey & Company (2023a). Generative AI and the future of HR. June 5, www.mckinsey.com/capabilities/people-and-organizational-performance/our-insights/generative-ai-and-the-future-of-hr.

McKinsey & Company (2023b). What every CEO should know about generative AI. May 12, www.mckinsey.com/capabilities/mckinsey-digital/our-insights/what-every-ceo-should-know-about-generative-ai.

McKinsey & Company (n.d.). The top trends in tech. www.mckinsey.com/business-functions/mckinsey-digital/our-insights/the-top-trends-in-tech.

McKinsey Global Institute (2016). Independent work: Choices, necessity, and the gig economy. www.mckinsey.com/featured-insights/employment-and-growth/independent-work-choice-necessity-and-the-gig-economy.

McKinsey Global Institute (2020). What 800 executives envision for the postpandemic workforce. www.mckinsey.com/featured-insights/future-of-work/what-800-executives-envision-for-the-postpandemic-workforce.

McMahon J. T. & Perritt G. W. (1973). Toward a contingency theory of organizational control. *Academy of Management Journal*, 16(4), 624–35.

Meijerink J., Boons M., Keegan A., & Marler J. (2021). Algorithmic human resource management: Synthesizing developments and cross-disciplinary insights on digital HRM. *International Journal of Human Resource Management*, 32(12), 2545–62.

Meijerink J. & Keegan A. (2019). Conceptualizing human resource management in the gig economy: Toward a platform ecosystem perspective. *Journal of Managerial Psychology*, 34(4), 214–32.

Mercer (2020). Win with empathy: 2020 global talent trends study. www.mercer.com/our-thinking/career/global-talent-hr-trends.html.

Merchant K. A. (1981). The design of the corporate budgeting system: Influences on managerial behavior and performance. *Accounting Review*, 56(4), 813–29.

Merchant K. A. (1982). The control function of management. *Sloan Management Review*, 23(4), 43–55.

Merchant K. A. (1985). *Control in business organizations*. Marshfield, MA: Pitman.

Merchant K. A. (1988). Progressing toward a theory of marketing control: A comment. *Journal of Marketing*, 52(3), 40–4.

Merchant K. A. & Otley D. T. (2006). A review of the literature on control and accountability. In Chapman CS, Hopwood AG, & Shields MD (eds), *Handbooks of management accounting research*. Oxford, UK: Elsevier, 785–802.

Merchant K. A. & Van der Stede W. A. (2007). *Management control systems: Performance measurement, evaluation and incentives*, 2nd ed. Harlow, UK: Prentice Hall.

Merchant K. A. & Van der Stede W. A. (2012). *Management control systems: Performance measurement, evaluation and incentives*. Englewood Cliffs, NJ: Prentice Hall.

Merchant K. A., Van der Stede W. A., & Zheng L. (2003). Disciplinary constraints on the advancement of knowledge: The case of organizational incentive systems. *Accounting, Organizations and Society*, 28(2), 251–86.

Merton R. K. (1940). Bureaucratic structure and personality. *Social Forces*, 18(4), 560–8.

Meyer A. D., Tsui A. S., & Hinings C. R. (1993). Configurational approaches to organizational analysis. *Academy of Management Journal*, 36(6), 1175–95.

Meyer J. W. & Rowan B. (1977). Institutionalized organizations: Formal structure as myth and ceremony. *American Journal of Sociology*, 83(2), 340–63.

Miao C. F. & Evans K. R. (2012). The interactive effects of sales control systems on salesperson performance: A job demands-resources perspective. *Journal of the Academy of Marketing Science*, 41(1), 73–90.

Microsoft (2020). Quarterly earnings report. April 30, www.microsoft.com/en-us/microsoft-365/blog/2020/04/30/2-years-digital-transformation-2-months/.

Microsoft (2022). Work trend index: Annual report. March 16, www.microsoft.com/en-us/worklab/work-trend-index/great-expectations-making-hybrid-work-work/.

Midha V. & Bhattacherjee A. (2012). Governance practices and software maintenance: A study of open source projects. *Decision Support Systems*, 54(1), 23–32.

Miles R. & Snow C. (1978). *Organizational strategy, structure, and process*. New York: McGraw-Hill.

Milkman R., Elliott-Negri L., Griesbach K., & Reich A. (2021). Gender, class, and the gig economy: The case of platform-based food delivery. *Critical Sociology*, 47(3), 357–72.

Miller A. P. (2018). Want less-biased decisions? Use algorithms. *Harvard Business Review Online*, July 26, https://hbr.org/2018/07/want-less-biased-decisions-use-algorithms.

Miller D. (1986). Configurations of strategy and structure: Towards a synthesis. *Strategic Management Journal*, 7(3), 233–49.

Miller D. (1987). The genesis of configuration. *Academy of Management Review*, 12(4), 686–701.

Miller D. (1996). Configurations revisited. *Strategic Management Journal*, 17(7), 505–12.

Miller D. (2018). Challenging trends in configuration research: Where are the configurations? *Strategic Organization*, 16(4), 453–69.

Miller D. & Friesen P. H. (1982). Structural change and performance: Quantum versus piecemeal-incremental approaches. *Academy of Management Journal*, 25(4), 867–92.

Miller D., Friesen P. H., & Mintzberg H. (1984). *Organizations: A quantum view*. Englewood Cliffs, NJ: Prentice-Hall.

Miller D. & Sardais C. (2011). Angel agents: Agency theory reconsidered. *Academy of Management Perspectives*, 25(2), 6–13.

Mims C. (2018). Blockchain has power to transform. *Wall Street Journal*, March 12, B4.

Mims C. (2022). More bosses are spying: It could backfire. *Wall Street Journal*, September 17, B4.

Minor D. & Yoffie D. B. (2018). Upwork: Creating the human cloud. *Harvard Business School Case Study #9-718-402*, 1–25 [permission obtained from Harvard Business Publishing].

Mintzberg H. (1979). *The structuring of organizations*. Englewood Cliffs, NJ: Prentice-Hall.

Mintzberg H. (1980). Structure in 5's: A synthesis of the research on organization design. *Management Science*, 26(3), 322–41.

Mintzberg H. (1981). Organization design: Fashion or fit? *Harvard Business Review*, 59(1), 103–16.

Mintzberg H. (1989). *Mintzberg on management*. New York: Free Press.

Mintzberg H., Raisinghani D., & Théorêt A. (1976). The structure of "unstructured" decision processes. *Administrative Science Quarterly*, 21(2), 246–75.

Mintzberg H. & Waters J. A. (1985). Of strategies, deliberate and emergent. *Strategic Management Journal*, 6(3), 257–72.

Misangyi V. F. & Acharya A. G. (2014). Substitutes or complements? A configurational examination of corporate governance mechanisms. *Academy of Management Journal*, 57(6), 1681–705.

Misangyi V. F., Greckhamer T., Furnari S., Fiss P. C., Crilly D., & Aguilera R. (2017). Embracing causal complexity: The emergence of a neo-configurational perspective. *Journal of Management*, 43(1), 255–82.

Mitchell R. & Meacheam D. (2011). Knowledge worker control: Understanding via principal and agency theory. *The Learning Organization*, 18(2), 149–60.

Mitrou L., Kandias M., Stavrou V., & Gritzalis D. (2014). Social media profiling: A panopticon or omniopticon tool? *Proceedings of the 6th Conference of the Surveillance Studies Network*. Barcelona, Spain.

Mogg K. (2023). The "lazy-girl job" is in right now. Here's why. *Wall Street Journal*, July 25, www.wsj.com/articles/the-career-goal-of-the-moment-is-a-lazy-girl-job-f5075c4e.

Möhlmann M. & Henfridsson O. (2019). What people hate about being managed by algorithms, according to a study of Uber drivers. *Harvard Business Review*, August 30, https://hbr.org/2019/08/what-people-hate-about-being-managed-by-algorithms-according-to-a-study-of-uber-drivers.

Möhlmann M., Zalmanson L., Henfridsson O., & Gregory R. W. (2021). Algorithmic management of work on online labor platforms: When matching meets control. *MIS Quarterly*, 45(4), 1999–2022.

Mohr J. J., Fisher R. J., & Nevin J. R. (1996). Collaborative communication in interfirm relationships: Moderating effects of integration and control. *Journal of Marketing*, 60(3), 103–15.

Moise I. (2018). What's on your mind? Bosses are using artificial intelligence to find out. *Wall Street Journal*, March 28, www.wsj.com/articles/whats-on-your-mind-bosses-are-using-artificial-intelligence-to-find-out-1522251302.

Monteiro P. & Adler P. S. (2022). Bureaucracy for the 21st century: Clarifying and expanding our view of bureaucratic organization. *Academy of Management Annals*, 16(2), 427–75.

Moore P. V., Upchurch M., & Whittaker X. (eds) (2018). *Humans and machines at work: Monitoring, surveillance and automation in contemporary capitalism*. Cham, Switzerland: Springer.

Morath E. & Ip G. (2021). Tight labor market returns the upper hand to American workers. *Wall Street Journal*, June 20, www.wsj.com/articles/tight-labor-market-returns-the-upper-hand-to-american-workers-11624210501.

Müller-Stevens B., Widener S. K., Möller K., & Steinmann J.-C. (2020). The role of diagnostic and interactive control uses in innovation. *Accounting, Organizations and Society*, 80(3), 101078.

Muller J. Z. (2018). *The tyranny of metrics*. Princeton, NJ: Princeton University Press.

Mundy J. (2010). Creating dynamic tensions through a balanced use of management control systems. *Accounting, Organizations and Society*, 35(5), 499–523.

Murray A., Kuban S., Josefy M., & Anderson J. (2021). Contracting in the smart era: The implications of blockchain and decentralized autonomous organizations for contracting and corporate governance. *Academy of Management Perspectives*, 35(4), 622–41.

Neimark M. & Tinker T. (1986). The social construction of management control systems. *Accounting, Organizations and Society*, 11(4), 369–95.

Netland T. H., Schloetzer J. D., & Ferdows K. (2015). Implementing corporate lean programs: The effect of management control practices. *Journal of Operations Management*, 36(1), 90–102.

Neuburger J. D. (2008). Teacher fired for inappropriate behavior on MySpace page. *Mediashift*, October 15, https://mediashift.org/2008/10/teacher-fired-for-inappropriate-behavior-on-myspace-page289/.

Newell S. & Marabelli M. (2015). Strategic opportunities (and challenges) of algorithmic decision-making: A call for action on the long-term societal effects of "datification." *Journal of Strategic Information Systems*, 24(1), 3–14.

Newlands G. (2021). Algorithmic surveillance in the gig economy: The organization of work through Lefebvrian conceived space. *Organization Studies*, 42(5), 719–37.

Ng E. S. W., Schweitzer L., & Lyons S. T. (2010). New generation, great expectations: A field study of the millennial generation. *Journal of Business and Psychology*, 25(2), 281–92.

Nguyen B. (2022). Yelp's CEO says the company will go fully remote, closing offices in NYC, DC, and Chicago. *Business Insider*, June 23, www.businessinsider.com/yelp-ceo-fully-remote-work-policy-best-for-employees-business-2022-6.

Nidumolu S. R. & Subramani M. R. (2003). The matrix of control: Combining process and structure approaches to managing software development. *Journal of Management Information Systems*, 20(3), 159–96.

Novacek G., Lee J., & Krentz M. (2022). *Reinventing gender diversity programs for a post-pandemic world*. Boston Consulting Group. February 4, www.bcg.com/publications/2022/reinventing-gender-diversity-programs.

Nunnally J. C. (1978). *Psychometric theory*, 2nd ed. New York: McGraw-Hill.

O'Connell V. & O'Sullivan D. (2014). The influence of lead indicator strength on the use of nonfinancial measures in performance management: Evidence from CEO compensation schemes. *Strategic Management Journal*, 35(6), 826–44.

O'Connor S. (2015). Wearables at work: The new frontier of employee surveillance. *Financial Times*, June 8, www.ft.com/content/d7eee768-0b65-11e5-994d-00144feabdc0.

O'Leary M. B. & Mortensen M. (2010). Go (con)figure: Subgroups, imbalance, and isolates in geographically dispersed teams. *Organization Science*, 21(1), 115–31.

O'Reilly C. A. & Chatman J. A. (1996). Culture as social control: Corporations, cults, and commitment. *Research in Organizational Behavior*, 18, 157–200.

Ocasio W. (1997). Towards an attention-based view of the firm. *Strategic Management Journal*, 18(S1), 187–206.

Ocasio W. & Wohlgezogen F. (2010). Attention and control. In Sitkin SB, Cardinal LB, & Bijlsma-Frankema KM (eds), *Organizational control*. Cambridge, UK: Cambridge University Press, 191–221.

Okhuysen G. A., Lepak D., Ashcraft K. L., Labianca G., Smith V., & Steensma H. K. (2013). Theories of work and working today. *Academy of Management Review*, 38(4), 491–502.

Oldham G. R. & Hackman J. R. (2010). Not what it was and not what it will be: The future of job design research. *Journal of Organizational Behavior*, 31(2–3), 463–79.

Oliver C. (1991). Strategic responses to institutional processes. *Academy of Management Review*, 16(1), 145–79.

Oliver R. L. & Anderson E. (1994). An empirical test of the consequences of behavior- and outcome-based sales control systems *Journal of Marketing*, 58(4), 53–67.

Orlikowski W. J. (1991). Integrated information environment or matrix of control? The contradictory implications of information technology. *Accounting, Management and Information Technologies*, 1(1), 9–42.

Orlikowski W. J. & Scott S. V. (2014). What happens when evaluation goes online? Exploring apparatuses of valuation in the travel sector. *Organization Science*, 25(3), 868–91.

Orlikowski W. J. & Scott S. V. (2015). The algorithm and the crowd: Considering the materiality of service innovation. *MIS Quarterly*, 39(1), 201–16.

Otley D., Broadbent J., & Berry A. (1995). Research in management control: An overview of its development. *British Journal of Management*, 6(S1), S31–S44.

Otley D. T. (1978). Budget use and managerial performance. *Journal of Accounting Research*, 16(1), 122–49.

Otley D. T. (1980). The contingency theory of management accounting: Achievement and prognosis. *Accounting, Organizations and Society*, 5(4), 413–28.

Otley D. T. (1999). Performance management: A framework for management control systems research. *Management Accounting Research*, 10(4), 363–82.

Otley D. T. & Berry A. J. (1980). Control, organisation and accounting. *Accounting, Organizations and Society*, 5(2), 231–44.

Otley D. T. & Berry A. J. (1994). Case study research in management accounting and control. *Management Accounting Research*, 5(1), 45–65.

Ouchi W. G. (1977). The relationship between organizational structure and organizational control. *Administrative Science Quarterly*, 22(1), 95–113.

Ouchi W. G. (1978). The transmission of control through organizational hierarchy. *Academy of Management Journal*, 21(2), 173–92.

Ouchi W. G. (1979). A conceptual framework for the design of organizational control mechanisms. *Management Science*, 25(9), 833–48.

Ouchi W. G. (1980). Markets, bureaucracies, and clans. *Administrative Science Quarterly*, 25(1), 129–41.

Ouchi W. G. & Maguire M. A. (1975). Organizational control: Two functions. *Administrative Science Quarterly*, 20(4), 559–69.

Paolillo J. G. & Brown W. B. (1978). How organizational factors affect R&D innovation. *Research Management*, 21(2), 12–15.

Paresh D. (2023). Self-driving cars are being put on a data diet. *Wired*, May 11, www.wired.com/story/self-driving-cars-are-being-put-on-a-data-diet/.

Park Y., Fiss P. C., & El Sawy O. A. (2020). Theorizing the multiplicity of digital phenomena: The ecology of configurations, causal recipes, and guidelines for applying QCA. *MIS Quarterly*, 44(4), 1493–520.

Perrow C. (1972). *Complex organizations: A critical essay*. Glenview, IL: Scott, Foresman.

Petre J. (2018). Big Brother is watching loo: Fears over 'smart' lavatory that can test users for drugs, pregnancy and urine problems. *Daily Mail*, June 30, www .dailymail.co.uk/news/article-5905047/Fears-smart-lavatory-test-users-drugs-pregnancy-urine-problems.html.

Petriglieri G., Ashford S. J., & Wrzesniewski A. (2019). Agony and ecstasy in the gig economy: Cultivating holding environments for precarious and personalized work identities. *Administrative Science Quarterly*, 64(1), 124–70.

Pfeffer J. (1992). *Managing with power: Politics and influence in organizations*. Boston, MA: Harvard Business School Press.

Pfeffer J. & Salancik G. R. (1974). Organizational decision making as a political process: The case of a university budget. *Administrative Science Quarterly*, 19(2), 135–51.

Pfeffer J. & Salancik G. R. (1978). *The external control of organizations*. New York: Harper & Row.

Pfeffer V. (2023). Managing virtual work: Empirical investigations on the management of virtual teams, virtual employees and virtual onboarding. Unpublished dissertation: EBS Universität für Wirtschaft und Recht.

Pianese T., Errichiello L., & da Cunha J. V. (2023). Organizational control in the context of remote working: A synthesis of empirical findings and a research agenda. *European Management Review*, 20(2), 326–45.

Piccoli G. & Ives B. (2003). Trust and the unintended effects of behavior control in virtual teams. *MIS Quarterly*, 27(3), 365–95.

Pierce J. L. & Delbecq A. L. (1977). Organization structure, individual attitudes, and innovation. *Academy of Management Review*, 2(1), 27–37.

Pisano G. P. (1989). Using equity participation to support exchange: Evidence from the biotechnology industry. *Journal of Law, Economics, and Organization*, 5(1), 109–26.

Pisano G. P., Russo M. V., & Teece D. J. (1988). Joint ventures and collaborative arrangements in the telecommunications equipment industry. In Mowery D (ed), *International collaborative ventures in U.S. manufacturing*. Cambridge, MA: Ballinger, 23–70.

Podsakoff P. M., MacKenzie S. B., Lee J.-Y., & Podsakoff N. P. (2003). Common method biases in behavioral research: A critical review of the literature and recommended remedies. *Journal of Applied Psychology*, 88(5), 879–903.

Podsakoff P. M. & Organ D. W. (1986). Self-reports in organizational research: Problems and prospects. *Journal of Management*, 12(4), 531–44.

Pope D. G. (2009). Reacting to rankings: Evidence from "America's Best Hospitals." *Journal of Health Economics*, 28(6), 1154–65.

Poppo L. & Zenger T. R. (2002). Do formal contracts and relational governance function as substitutes or complements? *Strategic Management Journal*, 23(8), 707–26.

Poppo L., Zhou K. Z., & Zenger T. R. (2008). Examining the conditional limits of relational governance: Specialized assets, performance ambiguity, and long-standing ties. *Journal of Management Studies*, 45(7), 1195–216.

Porter M. E. (1996). What is strategy? *Harvard Business Review* (11–12), 61–78.

Posch A. (2020). Integrating risk into control system design: The complementarity between risk-focused results controls and risk-focused information sharing. *Accounting, Organizations and Society*, 86(2), 101126.

Pratt J. W. & Zeckhauser R. J. (1985). Principals and agents: An overview. In Pratt JW, & Zeckhauser RJ (eds), *Principals and agents: The structure of business*. Cambridge, MA: Harvard Business School Press, 1–35.

Prensky M. (2001). Digital natives, digital immigrants. *On the Horizon*, 9(5), 1–6.

Price D. J. (1965). Networks of scientific papers. *Science*, 149(3683), 510–15.

Puranam P., Alexy O., & Reitzig M. (2014). What's "new" about new forms of organizing? *Academy of Management Review*, 39(2), 162–80.

PwC (2022). Women in Work 2022: Building an inclusive workplace in a net zero world. www.pwc.co.uk/services/economics/insights/women-in-work-index.html.

Quaquebeke N. V. & Gerpott F. H. (2023). The now, new, and next of digital leadership: How artificial intelligence (AI) will take over and change leadership as we know it. *Journal of Leadership and Organizational Studies*, 30(3), 265–75.

Quattrone P. & Hopper T. (2005). A 'time–space odyssey': Management control systems in two multinational organisations. *Accounting, Organizations and Society*, 30(7), 735–64.

Quinn R. E. & Rohrbaugh J. (1983). A spatial model of effectiveness criteria: Towards a competing values approach to organizational analysis. *Management Science*, 29(3), 363–77.

Raghuram S., Hill N. S., Gibbs J. L., & Maruping L. M. (2019). Virtual work: Bridging research clusters. *Academy of Management Annals*, 13(1), 308–41.

Raghuram S. & Wiesenfeld B. (2004). Work⊠nonwork conflict and job stress among virtual workers. *Human Resource Management*, 43(2/3), 259–77.

Rahman H. A. (2021). The invisible cage: Workers' reactivity to opaque algorithmic evaluations. *Administrative Science Quarterly*, 66(4), 945–88.

Rahman H. A. & Valentine M. A. (2021). How managers maintain control through collaborative repair: Evidence from platform-mediated "gigs." *Organization Science*, 32(5), 1300–26.

Raisch S. & Krakowski S. (2021). Artificial intelligence and management: The automation-augmentation paradox. *Academy of Management Review*, 46(1), 192–210.

Ram N., Gray D., & Hu M. (2022). Mass surveillance in the age of COVID-19. In Hu M (ed), *Pandemic surveillance: Privacy, security, and data ethics*. Cheltenham, UK: Edward Elgar Publishing, 6–26.

Rana P. (2022). Uber introduces new app features to sweeten gig for drivers. *Wall Street Journal*, July 29, www.wsj.com/articles/uber-introduces-new-app-features-to-sweeten-gig-for-drivers-11659096300.

Rana P. (2023a). Uber's business is finally making money after years of losses. *Wall Street Journal*, August 1, www.wsj.com/articles/uber-q2-earnings-report-2023-453c335a.

Rana P. (2023b). What happened when Uber's CEO started driving for Uber. *Wall Street Journal*, April 7, www.wsj.com/articles/uber-ceo-started-driving-for-uber-5bef5023.

Ranganathan A. & Benson A. (2020). A numbers game: Quantification of work, autogamification, and worker productivity. *American Sociological Review*, 85(4), 573–609.

Raval N. & Dourish P. (2016). Standing out from the crowd: Emotional labor, body labor, and temporal labor in ridesharing. *Proceedings of the 19th ACM Conference on Computer-Supported Cooperative Work & Social Computing*, San Francisco, CA, USA.

Ravid D. M., Tomczak D. L., White J. C., & Behrend T. S. (2020). EPM 20/20: A review, framework, and research agenda for electronic performance monitoring. *Journal of Management*, 46(1), 100–26.

Reeves T. K. & Woodward J. (1970). The study of managerial control. In Woodward J (ed), *Industrial organization: Behaviour and control*. Oxford, UK: Oxford University Press, 37–56.

Rennstam J. & Kärreman D. (2020). Understanding control in communities of practice: Constructive disobedience in a high-tech firm. *Human Relations*, 73(6), 864–90.

Richardson J. & McKenna S. (2014). Reordering spatial and social relations: A case study of professional and managerial flexworkers. *British Journal of Management*, 25(4), 724–36.

Richter V., Janjic R., Klapper H., Keck S., & Reitzig M. (2023). Managing exploration in organizations: The effect of superior monitoring on subordinate search behavior. *Strategic Management Journal*, 44(9), 2226–54.

Riesman A. J. (2014). We asked 10 black-car drivers if they prefer working for Lyft or Uber: Here's why Lyft won by a landslide. *New York Magazine*, December 7, https://nymag.com/intelligencer/2014/12/lyft-uber-drivers.html.

Rigby D. K., Sutherland J., & Takeuchi H. (2016). Embracing agile. *Harvard Business Review*, 94(5), 40–50.

Rindova V. P. & Starbuck W. H. (1997). Ancient Chinese theories of control. *Journal of Management Inquiry*, 6(2), 144–59.

Ring P. S. & Van de Ven A. H. (1994). Developmental processes of cooperative inter-organizational relationships. *Academy of Management Review*, 19(1), 90–118.

Rivera M., Qiu L., Kumar S., & Petrucci T. (2021). Are traditional performance reviews outdated? An Empirical analysis on continuous, real-time feedback in the workplace. *Information Systems Research*, 32(2), 517–40.

Robertson B. J. (2015). *Holacracy: The new management system for a rapidly changing world*. New York: Henry Holt and Company.

Roethlisberger F. J. & Dickson W. J. (1939). *Management and the worker*. Cambridge, MA: Harvard University Press.

Rosenblat A. (2016). The truth about how Uber's app manages drivers. *Harvard Business Review*, April 6, https://hbr.org/2016/04/the-truth-about-how-ubers-app-manages-drivers.

Rosenblat A., Kneese T., & Boyd D. (2014). Workplace surveillance. *Data & Society Working Paper*. www.datasociety.net/pubs/fow/WorkplaceSurveillance.pdf.

Rosenblat A. & Stark L. (2016). Algorithmic labor and information asymmetries: A case study of Uber's drivers. *International Journal of Communication*, 10, 3758–84.

Rosenthal R. (1979). The "file drawer problem" and tolerance for null results. *Psychological Bulletin*, 86(3), 638–41.

Rotter J. B. (1954). *Social learning and clinical psychology*. Englewood Cliffs, NJ: Prentice-Hall.

Rotter J. B. (1966). Generalized expectancies for internal versus external control of reinforcement. *Psychological Monographs*, 80(1), 1–28.

Rousseau D. M., Ho V. T., & Greenberg J. (2006). I-deals: Idiosyncratic terms in employment relationships. *Academy of Management Review*, 31(4), 977–94.

Rubery J., Cooke F. L., Earnshaw J., & Marchington M. (2003). Inter-organizational relations and employment in a multi-employer environment. *British Journal of Industrial Relations*, 41(2), 265–89.

Rudolph C. W., Rauvola R. S., Costanza D. P., & Zacher H. (2021). Generations and generational differences: Debunking myths in organizational science and practice and paving new paths forward. *Journal of Business and Psychology*, 36(6), 945–67.

Rumelt R. P. (1974). *Strategy, structure, and economic performance*. Boston, MA: Harvard University Press.

Rummel A. & Feinberg R. (1988). Cognitive evaluation theory: A meta-analytic review of the literature. *Social Behavior and Personality*, 16(2), 147–64.

Rustagi S., King W. R., & Kirsch L. J. (2008). Predictors of formal control usage in IT outsourcing partnerships. *Information Systems Research*, 19(2), 126–43.

Ryall M. D. & Sampson R. C. (2009). Formal contracts in the presence of relational enforcement mechanisms: Evidence from technology development projects. *Management Science*, 55(6), 906–25.

Sachdev H. J., Bello D. C., & Pilling B. K. (1995). Control mechanisms within export channels of distribution. *Journal of Global Marketing*, 8(2), 31–50.

Saha G. C. & Theingi (2009). Service quality, satisfaction, and behavioural intentions. *Managing Service Quality: An International Journal*, 19(3), 350–72.

Sánchez Abril P., Levin A., & Del Riego A. (2012). Blurred boundaries: Social media privacy and the twenty⊠first⊠century employee. *American Business Law Journal*, 49(1), 63–124.

Sandelin M. (2008). Operation of management control practices as a package: A case study on control system variety in a growth firm context. *Management Accounting Research*, 19(4), 324–43.

Schafheitle S. D., Weibel A., Ebert I. L., Kasper G., Schank C., & Leicht-Deobald U. (2020). No stone left unturned: Towards a framework for the impact of datafication technologies on organizational control. *Academy of Management Discoveries*, 6(3), 455–87.

Scheiber N. (2015). A middle ground between contract worker and employee. *New York Times*, December 10, www.nytimes.com/2015/12/11/business/a-middle-ground-between-contract-worker-and-employee.html.

Scheiber N. (2017). How Uber uses psychological tricks to push its drivers' buttons. *New York Times*, April 2, www.nytimes.com/interactive/2017/04/02/technology/uber-drivers-psychological-tricks.html.

Schell S. & Bischof N. (2022). Change the way of working. Ways into self-organization with the use of holacracy: An empirical investigation. *European Management Review*, 19(1), 123–37.

Schendel D. E. & Hofer C. W. (1979). Introduction. In Schendel DE, & Hofer CW (eds), *Strategic management*. Boston, MA: Little, Brown, 1–22.

Schepers J., Falk T., de Ruyter K., de Jong A., & Hammerschmidt M. (2012). Principles and principals: Do customer stewardship and agency control compete or complement when shaping frontline employee behavior? *Journal of Marketing*, 76(6), 1–20.

Scholl W. (1999). Restrictive control and information pathologies in organizations. *Journal of Social Issues*, 55(1), 101–18.

Schott R. L. (2000). The origins of bureaucracy: An anthropological perspective. *International Journal of Public Administration*, 23(1), 53–78.

Schreyögg G. & Steinmann H. (1987). Strategic control: A new perspective. *Academy of Management Review*, 12(1), 91–103.

Scott W. R. (1992). *Organizations: Rational, natural, and open systems*, 3rd ed. Englewood Cliffs, NJ: Prentice-Hall.

Selviaridis K. & Wynstra F. (2015). Performance-based contracting: A literature review and future research directions. *International Journal of Production Research*, 53(12), 3505–40.

Sewell G. (1998). The discipline of teams: The control of team-based industrial work through electronic and peer surveillance. *Administrative Science Quarterly*, 43(2), 397–428.

Sewell G. (2012). Organizations, employees and surveillance. In Ball K, Haggerty K, & Lyon D (eds), *The handbook of surveillance studies*. London, UK: Routledge, 303–12.

Sewell G. & Taskin L. (2015). Out of sight, out of mind in a new world of work? Autonomy, control, and spatiotemporal scaling in telework. *Organization Studies*, 36(11), 1507–29.

Shah R. H. & Swaminathan V. (2008). Factors influencing partner selection in strategic alliances: The moderating role of alliance context. *Strategic Management Journal*, 29(5), 471–94.

Shalley C. E., Gilson L. L., & Blum T. C. (2000). Matching creativity requirements and the work environment: Effects on satisfaction and intentions to leave. *Academy of Management Journal*, 43(2), 215–23.

Shalley C. E., Zhou J., & Oldham G. R. (2004). The effects of personal and contextual characteristics on creativity: Where should we go from here? *Journal of Management*, 30(6), 933–58.

Sharma A. (1997). Professional as agent: Knowledge asymmetry in agency exchange. *Academy of Management Review*, 22(3), 758–98.

Shellenbarger S. (2008). Work at home? Your employer may be watching. *Wall Street Journal*, July 30, www.wsj.com/articles/SB121737022605394845.

Shi W. E. I., Connelly B. L., & Hoskisson R. E. (2017). External corporate governance and financial fraud: Cognitive evaluation theory insights on agency theory prescriptions. *Strategic Management Journal*, 38(6), 1268–86.

Short J. C., Payne G. T., & Ketchen D. J. (2008). Research on organizational configurations: Past accomplishments and future challenges. *Journal of Management*, 34(6), 1053–79.

Siggelkow N. (2001). Change in the presence of fit: The rise, the fall, and the renaissance of Liz Claiborne. *Academy of Management Journal*, 44(4), 838–57.

Siggelkow N. (2011). Firms as systems of interdependent choices. *Journal of Management Studies*, 48(5), 1126–40.

Sihag V. & Rijsdijk S. A. (2019). Organizational controls and performance outcomes: A meta-analytic assessment and extension. *Journal of Management Studies*, 56(1), 91–133.

Sijbrandij S. (2023). GitLab's CEO on building one of the world's largest all-remote companies. *Harvard Business Review*, (3–4), 30–3.

Simon H. A. (1947). *Administrative behavior: A study of decision-making processes in administrative organizations*. New York: Macmillan.

Simon H. A. (1957). *Administrative behavior: A study of decision-making processes in administrative organization*, 2nd ed. New York: MacMillan.

Simon H. A. (1996). *The sciences of the artificial*, 3rd ed. Cambridge, MA: MIT Press.

Simons R. (1987). Accounting control systems and business strategy: An empirical analysis. *Accounting, Organizations and Society*, 12(4), 357–74.

Simons R. (1990). The role of management control systems in creating competitive advantage: New perspectives. *Accounting, Organizations and Society*, 15(1), 127–43.

Simons R. (1991). Strategic orientation and top management attention to control systems. *Strategic Management Journal*, 12(1), 49–62.

Simons R. (1994). How new top managers use control systems as levers of strategic renewal. *Strategic Management Journal*, 15(3), 169–89.

Simons R. (1995a). Control in an age of empowerment. *Harvard Business Review*, (3–4), 80–8.

Simons R. (1995b). *Levers of control: How managers use innovative control systems to drive strategic renewal*. Boston, MA: Harvard Business School Press.

Simons R. (2000). *Performance measurement and control systems for implementing strategy*. Upper Saddle River, NJ: Prentice-Hall.

Singal J. (2017). Just how creepy are Uber's driver-nudges? *The Cut*, April 3, www.thecut.com/2017/04/just-how-creepy-are-ubers-driver-nudges.html.

Sitkin S. B., Cardinal L. B., & Bijlsma-Frankema K. M. (2010a). Control is fundamental. In Sitkin SB, Cardinal LB, & Bijlsma-Frankema KM (eds), *Organizational control*. Cambridge, UK: Cambridge University Press, 3–15.

Sitkin S. B., Cardinal L. B., & Bijlsma-Frankema K. M. (eds) (2010b). *Organizational control*. New York: Cambridge University Press.

Sitkin S. B., Long C. P., & Cardinal L. B. (2020). Assessing the control literature: Looking back and looking forward. *Annual Review of Organizational Psychology and Organizational Behavior*, 7(1), 339–68.

Sivadas E. & Dwyer F. R. (2000). An examination of organizational factors influencing new product success in internal and alliance-based processes. *Journal of Marketing*, 64(1), 31–49.

Skinner S. J. & Guiltinan J. P. (1985). Perceptions of channel control. *Journal of Retailing*, 61(4), 65–88.

Small G. & Vorgan G. (2008). *iBrain: Surviving the technological alteration of the modern mind*. New York: Harper Collins.

Small H. (1973). Co-citation in the scientific literature: A new measure of the relationship between two documents. *Journal of the American Society for Information Science*, 24(4), 265–9.

Smith C. G. & Tannenbaum A. S. (1963). Organizational control structure: A comparative analysis. *Human Relations*, 16(4), 299–316.

Smith T. J. & Nichols T. (2015). Understanding the Millennial generation. *Journal of Business Diversity*, 15(1), 39–47.

Snell S. A. (1992). Control theory in strategic human resource management: The mediating effect of administrative information. *Academy of Management Journal*, 35(2), 292–327.

Snell S. A. & Youndt M. A. (1995). Human resource management and firm performance: Testing a contingency model of executive controls. *Journal of Management*, 21(4), 711–37.

Soper S. (2020). Amazon drivers are hanging smartphones in trees to get more work. *Bloomberg Online*, September 1, www.bloomberg.com/news/articles/2020-09-01/amazon-drivers-are-hanging-smartphones-in-trees-to-get-more-work.

Speckbacher G. & Wabnegg M. (2020). Incentivizing innovation: The role of knowledge exchange and distal search behavior. *Accounting, Organizations and Society*, 86, 101142.

Spector P. E. (1982). Behavior in organizations as a function of employee's locus of control. *Psychological Bulletin*, 91(3), 482–97.

Speklé R. F. (2001). Explaining management control structure variety: A transaction cost economics perspective. *Accounting, Organizations and Society*, 26(4), 419–41.

Speklé R. F., Van Elten H. J., & Widener S. K. (2017). Creativity and control: A paradox – Evidence from the levers of control framework. *Behavioral Research in Accounting*, 29(2), 73–96.

Spreitzer G. M., Cameron L., & Garrett L. (2017). Alternative work arrangements: Two images of the new world of work. *Annual Review of Organizational Psychology and Organizational Behavior*, 4(1), 473–99.

Srivastava S. C. & Teo T. S. H. (2012). Contract performance in offshore systems development: Role of control mechanisms. *Journal of Management Information Systems*, 29(1), 115–58.

Standen P., Daniels K., & Lamond D. (1999). The home as a workplace: Work-family interaction and psychological well-being in telework. *Journal of Occupational Health Psychology*, 4(4), 368–81.

Stanko T. L. & Beckman C. M. (2015). Watching you watching me: Boundary control and capturing attention in the context of ubiquitous technology use. *Academy of Management Journal*, 58(3), 712–38.

Stanley T. D. & Jarrell S. B. (2005). Meta-regression analysis: A quantitative method of literature surveys. *Journal of Economic Surveys*, 19(3), 299–308.

Staples D. S. & Zhao L. (2006). The effects of cultural diversity in virtual teams versus face-to-face teams. *Group Decision and Negotiation*, 15(4), 389–406.

Stark D. & Pais I. (2020). Algorithmic management in the platform economy. *Sociologica*, 14(3), 47–72.

Statista (2016). Employment worldwide by 2020, by generation. December 31, www.statista.com/statistics/829705/global-employment-by-generation/.

Statista (2022). Employment rate of women in the U.S. 1990–2021. February 10, www.statista.com/statistics/192396/employment-rate-of-women-in-the-us-since-1990/.

Statista (2023). Share of old age population (65 years and older) in the total U.S. population from 1950 to 2050. October 10, www.statista.com/statistics/457822/share-of-old-age-population-in-the-total-us-population/.

Steel P. D., Beugelsdijk S., & Aguinis H. (2021). The anatomy of an award-winning meta-analysis: Recommendations for authors, reviewers, and readers of meta-analytic reviews. *Journal of International Business Studies*, 52(1), 23–44.

Steel P. D. & Kammeyer-Mueller J. D. (2002). Comparing meta-analytic moderator estimation techniques under realistic conditions. *Journal of Applied Psychology*, 87(1), 96–111.

Stendahl E., Schriber S., & Tippmann E. (2021). Control changes in multinational corporations: Adjusting control approaches in practice. *Journal of International Business Studies*, 52(3), 409–31.

Stewart A. & Stanford J. (2017). Regulating work in the gig economy: What are the options? *Economic and Labour Relations Review*, 28(3), 420–37.

Stewart G. L. & Manz C. C. (1995). Leadership for self-managing work teams: A typology and integrative model. *Human Relations*, 48(7), 747–70.

Stewart K. J. & Gosain S. (2006). The impact of ideology on effectiveness in open source software development teams. *MIS Quarterly*, 30(2), 291–314.

Stockton H., Filipova M., & Monahan K. (2018). The evolution of work. *Deloitte Insights*, January 30, www2.deloitte.com/us/en/insights/focus/technology-and-the-future-of-work/evolution-of-work-seven-new-realities.html.

Stouthuysen K., Slabbinck H., & Roodhooft F. (2012). Controls, service type and perceived supplier performance in interfirm service exchanges. *Journal of Operations Management*, 30(5), 423–35.

Strickland L. H. (1958). Surveillance and trust. *Journal of Personality*, 26(2), 200–15.

Stryker S. & Burke P. J. (2000). The past, present, and future of an identity theory. *Social Psychology Quarterly*, 63(4), 284–97.

Stump R. L. & Heide J. B. (1996). Controlling supplier opportunism in industrial relationships. *Journal of Marketing Research*, 33(4), 431–41.

Sundaramurthy C. & Lewis M. (2003). Control and collaboration: Paradoxes of governance. *Academy of Management Review*, 28(3), 397–415.

Sundararajan A. (2014). What Airbnb gets about culture that Uber doesn't. *Harvard Business Review*, November 27, https://hbr.org/2014/11/what-airbnb-gets-about-culture-that-uber-doesnt.

Sydow J. & Windeler A. (2003). Knowledge, trust, and control: Managing tensions and contradictions in a regional network of service firms. *International Studies of Management and Organization*, 33(2), 69–100.

Tang S.-H. & Hall V. C. (1995). The overjustification effect: A meta-analysis. *Applied cognitive psychology*, 9(5), 365–404.

Tannenbaum A. S. (1962). Control in organizations: Individual adjustment and organizational performance. *Administrative Science Quarterly*, 7(2), 236–57.

Tannenbaum A. S. (1968). *Control in organizations*. New York: McGraw-Hill.

Tapscott D. (2009). *Grown up digital: How the net generation is changing your world*. New York: McGraw-Hill.

Tapscott D. & Tapscott A. (2016). *Blockchain revolution: How the technology behind Bitcoin and other cryptocurrencies is changing the world*. New York: Portfolio/Penguin.

Taylor F. W. (1911). *The principles of scientific work*. New York: Harper & Row.

Thaler R. H. (2015). *Misbehaving: The making of behavioral economics*. New York: W. W. Norton.

Thaler R. H. & Sunstein C. R. (2008). *Nudge: Improving decisions about health, wealth, and happiness*. New York: Penguin Books.

Thompson J. D. (1967). *Organizations in action*. New York: McGraw-Hill.

Tichy N. M., Fombrun C. J., & Devanna M. A. (1982). Strategic human resource management. *Sloan Management Review*, 23(2), 47–61.

Tilford C. (2018). The Millennial moment – In charts. A quarter of the world's population are Millennials. What does data tell us? *Financial Times*, June 6, www.ft.com/content/f81ac17a-68ae-11e8-b6eb-4acfcfb08c11.

Tiwana A. (2010). Systems development ambidexterity: Explaining the complementary and substitutive roles of formal and informal controls. *Journal of Management Information Systems*, 27(2), 87–126.

Tiwana A. (2013). *Platform ecosystems: Aligning architecture, governance, and strategy*. San Francisco, CA: Morgan Kaufmann.

Tiwana A. (2015). Evolutionary competition in platform ecosystems. *Information Systems Research*, 26(2), 266–81.

Tiwana A. & Keil M. (2009). Control in internal and outsourced software projects. *Journal of Management Information Systems*, 26(3), 9–44.

Turco C. J. (2016). *The conversational firm: Rethinking bureaucracy in the age of social media*. New York: Columbia University Press.

Turner K. L. & Makhija M. V. (2006). The role of organizational controls in managing knowledge. *Academy of Management Review*, 31(1), 197–217.

Tushman M. L. & Nadler D. A. (1978). Information processing as an integrated concept in organizational design. *Academy of Management Review*, 3(3), 613–24.

Twenge J. M. (2006). *Generation me: Why today's young Americans are more confident, assertive, entitled-and more miserable than ever before.* New York: Free Press.

Tyler T. R. & Blader S. L. (2005). Can businesses effectively regulate employee conduct? The antecedents of rule following in work settings. *Academy of Management Journal*, 48(6), 1143–58.

U.S. Bureau of Labor Statistics Employment Projections program (2021). Accessed: 7/18/2022. www.bls.gov/emp/tables/median-age-labor-force.htm.

Uber (2022). Annual report. www.sec.gov/Archives/edgar/data/1543151/00015527 8123000195/e23076_uber-ars.pdf.

Upwork (2018). Upwork annual report 2018. https://investors.upwork.com/static-files/8d67d7b3-1e42-8c0-92db-e839a6d323f2.

Upwork (2021). Upwork investor day 2021 presentation. https://investors.upwork.com/static-files/11fe6ce1-8c50-40e5-9f4e-2710de4e27c8.

Upwork (2023). Upwork Q2 2023 investor presentation. https://investors.upwork.com/static-files/cf4ef777-2f78-49fb-8e85-3d60c54643c.

Uzunca B. & Kas J. (2023). Automated governance mechanisms in digital labour platforms: How Uber nudges and sludges its drivers. *Industry and Innovation*, 30(6), 664–93.

Vallas S. P., Johnston H., & Mommadova Y. (2022). Prime suspect: Mechanisms of labor control at Amazon's warehouses. *Work and Occupations*, 49(4), 421–56.

Vallas S. P. & Schor J. B. (2020). What do platforms do? Understanding the gig economy. *Annual Review of Sociology*, 46(1), 273–94.

Valsecchi R. (2006). Visible moves and invisible bodies: The case of teleworking in an Italian call centre. *New Technology, Work, and Employment*, 21(2), 123–38.

Van de Ven A. H. & Drazin R. (1985). The concept of fit in contingency theory. In Cummings LL, & Staw BM (eds), *Research in organizational behavior*. Greenwich, CT: JAI Press, 333–65.

Van de Ven A. H., Ganco M., & Hinings C. R. (2013). Returning to the frontier of contingency theory of organizational and institutional designs. *Academy of Management Annals*, 7(1), 393–440.

Van Hout M. (2009). Philips Design and ABN AMRO team up to create: An emotion mirroring system for online traders. October 13, www.design-emotion.com/2009/10/13/philips-design-and-abn-amro-team-up-to-create-an-emotion-mirroring-system-for-online-traders/.

Van Knippenberg D., Dahlander L., Haas M. R., & George G. (2015). Information, attention, and decision making. *Academy of Management Journal*, 58(3), 649–57.

Van Knippenberg D. & Van Schie E. C. M. (2000). Foci and correlates of organizational identification. *Journal of Occupational and Organizational Psychology*, 73(2), 137–47.

Van Maanen J. & Barley S. R. (1984). Occupational communities: Culture and control in organizations. *Research in Organizational Behavior*, 6, 287–365.

Veen A., Barratt T., & Goods C. (2020). Platform-capital's "app-etite" for control: A labour process analysis of food-delivery work in Australia. *Work, Employment and Society*, 34(3), 388–406.

Vélez M. L., Sánchez J. M., & Álvarez-Dardet C. (2008). Management control systems as inter-organizational trust builders in evolving relationships: Evidence from a longitudinal case study. *Accounting, Organizations and Society*, 33(7), 968–94.

Venkatraman N. & Ramanujam V. (1986). Measurement of business performance in strategy research: A comparison of approaches. *Academy of Management Review*, 11(4), 801–14.

Villiger J., Schweiger S. A., & Baldauf A. (2022). Making the invisible visible: Guidelines for the coding process in meta-analyses. *Organizational Research Methods*, 25(4), 716–40.

Viswesvaran C. & Ones D. S. (1995). Theory testing: Combining psychometric meta-analysis and structural equations modeling. *Personnel Psychology*, 48(4), 865–85.

Vosselman E. G. J. (2002). Towards horizontal archetypes of management control: A transaction cost economics perspective. *Management Accounting Research*, 13(1), 131–48.

Waldkirch M., Bucher E., Schou P. K., & Grünwald E. (2021). Controlled by the algorithm, coached by the crowd – How HRM activities take shape on digital work platforms in the gig economy. *International Journal of Human Resource Management*, 32(12), 2643–82.

Walsh J. P., Meyer A. D., & Schoonhoven C. B. (2006). A future for organization theory: Living in and living with changing organizations. *Organization Science*, 17(5), 657–71.

Walsh J. P. & Seward J. K. (1990). On the efficiency of internal and external corporate control mechanisms. *Academy of Management Review*, 15(3), 421–58.

Walter J., Kreutzer M., & Kreutzer K. (2021). Setting the tone for the team: A multi-level analysis of managerial control, peer control, and their consequences for job satisfaction and team performance. *Journal of Management Studies*, 58(3), 849–78.

Walton E. J. (2005). The persistence of bureaucracy: A meta-analysis of Weber's model of bureaucratic control. *Organization Studies*, 26(4), 569–600.

Walton R. E. (1985). From control to commitment in the workplace. *Harvard Business Review*, 63(2), 77–84.

Wang A. X. & MacLellan L. (2018). Herman Miller's new Aeron chair is an office spy, collecting data on your every move. *Quartz at Work*, March 14, https://qz.com/work/1218346/herman-millers-new-aeron-chair-is-an-office-spy-collecting-data-on-your-every-move.

Watt H. (2011). Naked civil servant who mocked Eric Pickles is stripped of job. *Telegraph*, July 4, www.telegraph.co.uk/news/politics/8614026/Naked-civil-servant-who-mocked-Eric-Pickles-is-stripped-of-job.html.

Weber M. (1946). *Essays in sociology*. New York: Oxford University Press.

Weber M. (1947). *The theory of social and economic organizations*. New York: Oxford University Press.

Weber M. (1978). *Economy and society: An outline of interpretive sociology*. Berkeley, CA: University of California Press.

Weitz B. A. (1981). Effectiveness in sales interactions: A contingency framework. *Journal of Marketing*, 45(1), 85–103.

Welbourne T. M. & Ferrante C. J. (2008). To monitor or not to monitor: A study of individual outcomes from monitoring one's peers under gainsharing and merit pay. *Group & Organization Management*, 33(2), 139–162.

Whelan E., McDuff D., Gleasure R., & Vom Brocke J. (2018). How emotion-sensing technology can reshape the workplace. *MIT Sloan Management Review*, 59(3), 7–10.

White H. D. & Griffith B. C. (1981). Author cocitation: A literature measure of intellectual structure. *Journal of the American Society for Information Science*, 32(3), 163–71.

Whitener E. M. (1990). Confusion of confidence intervals and credibility intervals in meta-analysis. *Journal of Applied Psychology*, 75(3), 315–21.

Widener S. K. (2007). An empirical analysis of the levers of control framework. *Accounting, Organizations and Society*, 32(7), 757–88.

Wiener M., Mähring M., Remus U., & Saunders C. (2016). Control configuration and control enactment in information systems projects: Review and expanded theoretical framework. *MIS Quarterly*, 40(3), 741–74.

Wiener M., Mähring M., Remus U., Saunders C., & Cram W. A. (2019). Moving IS project control research into the digital era: The "why" of control and the concept of control purpose. *Information Systems Research*, 30(4), 1387–401.

Wiersma U. J. (1992). The effects of extrinsic rewards in intrinsic motivation: A meta-analysis. *Journal of Occupational and Organizational Psychology*, 65(2), 101–14.

Wiessner D., Bose N., & Shepardson D. (2022). Biden labor proposal shakes up gig economy that relies on contractors. *Reuters*, October 11, www.reuters.com/world/us/new-biden-labor-rule-would-make-contractors-into-employees-2022-10-11/.

Wijethilake C., Munir R., & Appuhami R. (2018). Environmental innovation strategy and organizational performance: Enabling and controlling uses of management control systems. *Journal of Business Ethics*, 151(4), 1139–60.

Wilhelm A. (2021). Inside GitLab's IPO filing. *TechCrunch*, September 17, https://techcrunch.com/2021/09/17/inside-gitlabs-ipo-filing/.

Williamson O. E. (1975). *Markets and hierarchies: Analysis and antitrust implications.* New York: Free Press.

Williamson O. E. (1979). Transaction-cost economics: The governance of contractual relations. *Journal of Law and Economics*, 22(2), 233–61.

Williamson O. E. (1981). The economics of organization: The transaction cost approach. *American Journal of Sociology*, 87(3), 548–77.

Williamson O. E. (1985). *The economic institutions of capitalism: Firms, markets, relational contracting.* New York: Free Press.

Williamson O. E. (1991). Comparative economic organization: The analysis of discreet structural alternatives. *Administrative Science Quarterly*, 36(2), 269–96.

Wilner A., Christopoulos T., & Alves M. (2017). The online unmanaged organization: Control and resistance in a space with blurred boundaries. *Journal of Business Ethics*, 141(4), 677–91.

Wong M. (2020). Stanford research provides a snapshot of a new working-from-home economy. *Stanford News*, June 29, https://news.stanford.edu/2020/06/29/snapshot-new-working-home-economy/.

Wood A. J., Graham M., Lehdonvirta V., & Hjorth I. (2019). Good gig, bad gig: Autonomy and algorithmic control in the global gig economy. *Work, Employment and Society*, 33(1), 56–75.

Wood J. (2007). Methodology for dealing with duplicate study effects in a meta-analysis. *Organizational Research Methods*, 11(1), 79–95.

Woodcock J. & Johnson M. R. (2018). Gamification: What it is, and how to fight it. *Sociological Review*, 66(3), 542–58.

Wooldridge A. (2015). The Icarus syndrome meets the wearable revolution. *Korn/Ferry Briefings*, 6, 27–33.

Workman J. P., Homburg C., & Gruner K. (1998). Marketing organization: An integrative framework of dimensions and determinants. *Journal of Marketing*, 62(3), 21–41.

World Economic Forum (2016). The future of jobs: Employment, skill and workforce strategy for the fourth industrial revolution. January, www3.weforum.org/docs/WEF_Future_of_Jobs.pdf.

World Health Organization (2020). WHO Director-General's opening remarks at the media briefing on COVID-19. March 11, www.who.int/director-general/speeches/detail/who-director-general-s-opening-remarks-at-the-media-briefing-on-covid-19---11-march-2020.

Wozniak J. (2023). *Workplace monitoring and technology*. New York: Routledge.

Xie J. L., Schaubroeck J., & Lam S. S. K. (2008). Theories of job stress and the role of traditional values: A longitudinal study in China. *Journal of Applied Psychology*, 93(4), 831–48.

Yeginsu C. (2018). If workers slack off, the wristband will know (and Amazon has a patent for it). *New York Times*, February 1, www.nytimes.com/2018/02/01/technology/amazon-wristband-tracking-privacy.html.

Yoffie D. B. & Ciechanover A. M. (2019). Upwork in 2019. *Harvard Business School Case Study #9-719-509*, 1–4 [permission obtained from Harvard Business Publishing].

Youyou W., Kosinski M., & Stillwell D. (2015). Computer-based personality judgments are more accurate than those made by humans. *Proceedings of the National Academy of Sciences*, 112(4), 1036–40.

Zannetos Z. S. (1964). Some thoughts on internal control systems of the firm. *Accounting Review*, 39(4), 860–8.

Zeit Online (2019). Zalando soll Tausende Mitarbeiter systematisch kontrolliert haben. *Zeit Online*, November 19, www.zeit.de/arbeit/2019-11/ueberwachung-arbeitsplatz-zalando-zonar-mitarbeiter.

Zemke R., Raines C., & Filipczak B. (2000). *Generations at work: Managing the clash of veterans, Boomers, Xers, and Nexters in your workplace*. New York: Amacom.

Zeng W., Lillis A. M., Grafton J., & Dekker H. C. (2021). The influence of institutional differences on control mechanisms in alliances. *The Accounting Review*, 97(3), 415–41.

Zhong B., Makhija M. V., & Morris S. (2022). Abstract versus concrete: How managers' construal influences organizational control systems and problem solving. *Organization Science*, 33(6), 2322–45.

Zhou J. & George J. M. (2003). Awakening employee creativity: The role of leader emotional intelligence. *Leadership Quarterly*, 14(4), 545–68.

Zhou K. Z. & Poppo L. (2010). Exchange hazards, relational reliability, and contracts in China: The contingent role of legal enforceability. *Journal of International Business Studies*, 41(5), 861–81.

Zhou K. Z. & Xu D. (2012). How foreign firms curtail local supplier opportunism in China: Detailed contracts, centralized control, and relational governance. *Journal of International Business Studies*, 43(7), 677–92.

Zhu F., McDonald R., Iansiti M., & Smith A. (2017). Upwork: Reimagining the future of work. *Harvard Business School Case Study #9-616-027*, 1–22 [permission obtained from Harvard Business Publishing].

Zumbrun J. (2023). Why ChatGPT is getting dumber at basic math. *Wall Street Journal*, August 4, www.wsj.com/articles/chatgpt-openai-math-artificial-intelligence-8aba83f0.

Zupic I. & Čater T. (2015). Bibliometric methods in management and organization. *Organizational Research Methods*, 18(3), 429–72.

Index

Printed in the United States
by Baker & Taylor Publisher Services